Counting the Poor

International Policy Exchange Series

Published in collaboration with the
Center for International Policy Exchanges
University of Maryland

Series Editors

Douglas J. Besharov
Neil Gilbert

SCHOOL *of*
PUBLIC POLICY

Counting the Poor

*New Thinking about European
Poverty Measures and Lessons
for the United States*

EDITED BY

DOUGLAS J. BESHAROV

KENNETH A. COUCH

OXFORD
UNIVERSITY PRESS

MT

OXFORD
UNIVERSITY PRESS

Oxford University Press, Inc., publishes works that further
Oxford University's objective of excellence
in research, scholarship, and education.

Oxford New York
Auckland   Cape Town   Dar es Salaam   Hong Kong   Karachi
Kuala Lumpur   Madrid   Melbourne   Mexico City   Nairobi
New Delhi   Shanghai   Taipei   Toronto

With offices in
Argentina   Austria   Brazil   Chile   Czech Republic   France   Greece
Guatemala   Hungary   Italy   Japan   Poland   Portugal   Singapore
South Korea   Switzerland   Thailand   Turkey   Ukraine   Vietnam

Copyright © 2012 by Oxford University Press, Inc.

Published by Oxford University Press, Inc.
198 Madison Avenue, New York, New York 10016
www.oup.com

Oxford is a registered trademark of Oxford University Press

Library of Congress Cataloging-in-Publication Data

Counting the poor : new thinking about European poverty measures and lessons
for the United States / edited by Douglas J. Besharov, Kenneth A. Couch.
    p. cm. — (International policy exchange series)
  Includes bibliographical references and index.
  ISBN 978-0-19-986058-6 (hardcover: alk. paper) 1. Poverty—European Union countries.
2. Poverty—United States. I. Besharov, Douglas J. II. Couch, Kenneth A. (Kenneth Alan)
  HC240.9.P6C68 2012
  339.4'6094—dc23   2011040204

9 8 7 6 5 4 3 2 1

Printed in the United States of America
on acid-free paper

4/8/13

CONTENTS

IN MEMORIAM: JOACHIM R. FRICK (1962–2011)

During production of this volume, our friend and colleague Joachim R. Frick passed away in Berlin on December 16, 2011, after a valiant fight with cancer. We pause here to acknowledge our respect for him and we dedicate this volume to his memory. He was 49 years old.

With Joachim's death, the Socio-Economic Panel (SOEP) at DIW Berlin has lost one of its most brilliant minds—a valued, dedicated, and extremely productive colleague; and an internationally recognized pioneer of comparative panel analysis. It was in large part his hard work and tireless dedication that made the SOEP the internationally networked research infrastructure that it is today. His numerous publications made a major contribution to applied economic research, particularly in the field of distributional analysis. His unflagging commitment to the training of new generations of SOEP users will bear fruit for decades to come.

Joachim was born in Trier on August 13, 1962. He studied economics, business, and sociology at the University of Trier and received an MA in Economics (Diplom-Volkswirt) in 1988. On a scholarship from the German Academic Exchange Service (DAAD), he attended graduate studies at Clark University in Worcester, MA (USA), where he gathered international experience that would play an extraordinarily significant role in his subsequent research and his work developing the SOEP study. In 1996, he received a PhD in Social Science (Dr. rer. soc.) from the Faculty of Social Sciences at the Ruhr University Bochum with a dissertation entitled "Determinants of Regional Mobility." In 2006, he was awarded his habilitation (venia legendi) qualification in empirical economic research at the Berlin University of Technology (TU Berlin), where he served as Acting Professor of Empirical Economics in the Faculty of Economics and Management in 2008–2009. Joachim began his work at DIW Berlin in January 1989. In 2004, he became Deputy Director of the SOEP and Head of the SOEP Research Data Center (SOEP-RDC), where his responsibilities included coordinating the integration of SOEP data into international comparative panel databases (e.g., CNEF, ECHP, CHER, LIS, and LWS).

In the fall of 2010, Joachim was offered a full professorship (W3-Professur) at his alma mater and hometown university in Trier. He came very close to accepting the appointment, but after wrestling with the decision at length, he declined the offer and chose instead to remain in Berlin. This decision was based on DIW Berlin's offer to create a joint professorship (S-Professur) for him that would allow him to continue in his position at the SOEP while holding a full professorship at the Berlin University of Technology (TU Berlin). The TU Berlin Faculty Council had already set the official appointment procedure in motion when Joachim's cancer was discovered and his treatment began. It is tragic that his illness prevented him from attaining this ultimate tribute to his outstanding achievements in research and teaching.

During the past ten years Joachim has coordinated numerous externally funded projects, including many EU-financed research and infrastructural studies such as the European Panel Users Network (EPUNet), European Panel Analysis Group (EPAG), and the Consortium of Household Panels for European Socio-Economic Research (CHER). He was Co-PI of a large-scale comparative analysis of social inequalities that was funded by the Russell Sage Foundation. His last major project, "Life Courses and Retirement Provisions in Transition," which was funded by the Volkswagen Foundation, again broke new methodological ground in the statistical matching of SOEP data and administrative data.

Joachim's research interests centered on questions of social and welfare policy, and his work was consistently based on applied empirical analysis (focusing on issues of immigration, income distribution, housing costs, spatial mobility, and subjective well-being). Joachim also earned international recognition for his outstanding methodological work on the measurement of income in panel surveys (item nonresponse, imputation, and nonmonetary income components).

He had a passion for working in collaboration with other researchers around the world, for sharing and discussing ideas and interests in the context of comparative research. Joachim made research visits not only to many countries in Europe but also to the United States and Australia, making numerous friends wherever he went. His international orientation was also reflected in the many international conferences he attended, where his contribution as an internationally recognized scholar was always appreciated.

Joachim was a member of numerous scientific committees, including the Executive Council of the Luxembourg Income Study (LIS); the Scientific Board of the Swiss Household Panel (SHP); the International User Selection Panel of the European Centre for Analysis in the Social Sciences (ECASS) at the University of Essex, UK; and the International User Selection Panel of the Integrated Research Infrastructure in the Socio-Economic Sciences (IRISS) at CEPS/INSTEAD, Luxemburg.

We are all devastated by his death. Many of us have unforgettable memories of Joachim—his kindness, warmth, enthusiasm, and wonderful sense of humor. We mourn his loss and will carry his memory with us. We extend our deepest condolences to his family—to his wife Kristine, to his two daughters Anna and Katharina, to his parents, brother, and sister, and to many close friends. He will be greatly missed.

Selected Publications in Refereed Journals

Bird, E. J., J. R. Frick, and G. G. Wagner: "The Income of Socialist Upper Classes during the Transition to Capitalism—Evidence from Longitudinal East German Data," *Journal of Comparative Economics*, 26, 211–225, 1998.

Büchel, F., and J. R. Frick: "Immigrants in the UK and in West Germany—Relative Income Positions, Income Portfolio, and Redistribution Effects," *Journal of Population Economics*, 17, 553–581, 2004.

Büchel, F., and J. R. Frick: "Immigrant's Economic Performance across Europe—Does Immigration Policy Matter," *Population Research and Policy Review*, 24, 175–212, 2005.

Burkhauser, R. V., J. R. Frick, and J. Schwarze: "A Comparison of Alternative Measures of Economic Well-Being for Germany and the United States," *Review of Income and Wealth*, 43, 153–171, 1997.

D'Ambrosio, C., and J. R. Frick: "Income Satisfaction and Relative Deprivation: An Empirical Link," *Social Indicators Research*, 81, 497–519, 2007.

D'Ambrosio, C., and J. R. Frick: "Individual Well-Being in a Dynamic Perspective," *Economica*, doi:10.1111/j.1468-0335.2011.00896.x, forthcoming.

Frick, J. R., M. M. Grabka, and O. Groh-Samberg: "Economic Gains from Educational Transfers in Kind in Germany," *Journal of Income Distribution*, 19, 17–40, 2010.

Frick, J. R., and J. Goebel: "Regional Income Stratification in Unified Germany Using a Gini Decomposition Approach," *Regional Studies*, 42, 555–577, 2008.

Frick, J. R., J. Goebel, E. Schechtman, G. G. Wagner, and S. Yitzhaki: "Using Analysis of Gini (ANoGi) for Detecting Whether Two Sub-samples Represent the Same Universe: The German Socio-Economic Panel Study (SOEP) Experience," *Sociological Methods and Research*, 34, 427–468, 2006.

Frick, J. R., and M. M. Grabka: "Imputed Rent and Income Inequality: A Decomposition Analysis for the U.K., West Germany, and the USA," *Review of Income and Wealth*, 49, 513–537, 2003.

Frick, J. R., and M. M. Grabka: "Zur Entwicklung der Vermögensungleichheit in Deutschland," *Berliner Journal für Soziologie*, 19, 577–600, 2009.

Frick, J. R., M. M. Grabka, T. M. Smeeding, and P. Tsakloglou: "Distributional Effects of Imputed Rents in Five European Countries," *Journal of Housing Economics*, 19, 167–179, 2010.

Frick, J. R., S. P. Jenkins, D. R. Lillard, O. Lipps, and M. Wooden: "The Cross-National Equivalent File (CNEF) and Its Member Country Household Panel Studies," *Schmollers Jahrbuch—Journal of Applied Social Science Studies*, 127: 627–654, 2007.

Hauser, R., J. R. Frick, K. Mueller, and G. G. Wagner: "Inequality in Income: A Comparison of East and West Germans before Reunification and during Transition," *Journal of European Social Policy*, 4, 277–295, 1994.

Sierminska, E. M., J. R. Frick, and M. M. Grabka: "Examining the Gender Wealth Gap," *Oxford Economic Papers*, 62, 669–690, 2010.

Zaidi, A., J. R. Frick, and F. Büchel: "Income Mobility in Old Age in Britain and Germany," *Ageing and Society*, 25, 543–565, 2005.

CONTRIBUTORS

Richard Bavier
Retired
Vienna, Virginia

Douglas J. Besharov
Brody Professor of Public Policy
University of Maryland
College Park, Maryland

Andrea Brandolini
Bank of Italy and
Luxembourg Wealth Study
Rome, Italy

Richard V. Burkhauser
Cornell University
Ithaca, New York

Bea Cantillon
University of Antwerp
Antwerp, Belgium

Kenneth A. Couch
University of Connecticut
Storrs, Connecticut

Carlo del Ninno
The World Bank
Washington, District of Columbia

Michael F. Förster
Organization for Economic
   Co-operation and Development
Paris, France

Joachim R. Frick[†]
DIW Berlin
Berlin, Germany

Neil Gilbert
Chernin Professor of Social Welfare
University of California, Berkeley
Berkeley, California

Markus M. Grabka
DIW Berlin
Berlin, Germany

Margaret Grosh
The World Bank
Washington, District of Columbia

Bruce Headey
Melbourne Institute of Applied
   Economic and Social Research
Melbourne, Australia

Herwig Immervoll
OECD
Paris, France

David S. Johnson
U.S. Census Bureau
Washington, District of Columbia

Peter Krause
DIW Berlin
Berlin, Germany

[†] Dr. Joachim R. Frick unfortunately passed on December 16, 2011 before the book went to press.

Peter Lanjouw
The World Bank
Washington, District of Columbia

Silvia Magri
Bank of Italy
Rome, Italy

Isabelle Maquet
Social Protection Committee
European Commission
Brussels, Belgium

Eric Marlier
CEPS/INSTEAD Research Institute
Esch-sur-Alzette, Luxembourg

Marco Mira d'Ercole
Organization for Economic
    Co-operation and Development
Paris, France

Brian Nolan
University College Dublin
Dublin, Ireland

Timothy M. Smeeding
Institute for Research on Poverty,
    University of Wisconsin–Madison and
Luxembourg Wealth Study
Madison, Wisconsin

David Stanton
Social Protection Committee
European Commission
Richmond, United Kingdom

Holly Sutherland
Institute for Social and Economic
    Research (ISER), University of Essex
Colchester, United Kingdom

Emil Tesliuc
The World Bank
Washington, District of Columbia

Panos Tsakloglou
Athens University of Economics and
    Business
Athens, Greece

Karel Van den Bosch
University of Antwerp
Antwerp, Belgium

Tim Van Rie
University of Antwerp
Antwerp, Belgium

Gert G. Wagner
DIW Berlin
Berlin, Germany

Christopher T. Whelan
University College Dublin
Dublin, Ireland

Counting the Poor

Introduction

DOUGLAS J. BESHAROV AND KENNETH A. COUCH ∎

As this volume is going to press, the US government has begun a multiyear effort to change how it defines *poverty* and, thus, how it counts the number of poor Americans. Besides being a major technical challenge, defining poverty is a subjective and value-laden endeavor, further complicated by its political and budgetary implications. The *poverty rate* is one of the most visible ways in which nations measure the economic well-being of their low-income citizens and, either directly or indirectly, is a key element in deciding who should receive means-tested government benefits.

Many European countries, as well, are reconsidering how they measure poverty and material need. In sharp contrast to the current US approach, which primarily focuses on income relative to a basket of needs linked (even if indirectly) to a measure of expenditures, are various European approaches that seek to operationalize and measure the concept of *social exclusion,* defined by the European Commission (2004, 8) as the:

> process whereby certain individuals are pushed to the edge of society and prevented from participating fully by virtue of their poverty, or lack of basic competencies and lifelong learning opportunities, or as a result of discrimination. This distances them from job, income and education opportunities as well as social and community networks and activities.

Among the approaches for measuring social exclusion that are being considered are *minimum income standards* (that is, the minimum amount needed to participate in society determined by budgets varying by household type) (Bradshaw et al. 2008), multidimensional instruments that seek to measure both monetary and nonmonetary deprivation (Nolan and Whelan 2010), and nonincome, financial measures of consumption and wealth (Headey, Krause, and Wagner 2012, Chapter 17).

The most visible element of an income-based poverty measure is its income threshold, that is, the amount of income below which an individual, family, or household is to be considered *poor* or *at risk of poverty* (the Organization for Economic Co-operation and Development's [OECD] and European Union's [EU] terms, respectively). Broadly, there are two approaches to setting thresholds: *absolute* and *relative*.

Absolute poverty measures use as their income threshold a specific amount of income determined (accurately or not) as the amount needed to meet people's physical needs. But all absolute measures are, to an extent, relative; that is, they are based on the country's income distribution. Thus, reflecting the very low living standards in some countries, the World Bank measures poverty using an absolute measure (at 2005 international purchasing power parity) of about $1.25 in consumption per person per day (about $456 annually) for low-income, developing countries and about $2.50 (about $912 annually) for middle-income, developing countries (Chen and Ravallion 2008).

The US poverty measure is widely considered an absolute one, but, when it was first established, it also embodied an essential element of any relative measure because it was based on a 1960s Economy Food Plan—not a subsistence diet—multiplied by three (to reflect food's place in the overall household budget of average Americans) (Besharov and Germanis 2004). Hence, the US official poverty measure could be considered an *anchored relative measure,* because it was originally set, not at subsistence, but rather at the level of consumption of low-income Americans. The US Bureau of the Budget (now Office of Management and Budget) adopted this threshold as the official measure of poverty in the United States in 1968. Except for minor changes and annual adjustments for inflation, it has remained unchanged since then.[1]

Many observers believe that the US official poverty measure, essentially unchanged for more than 40 years, should be updated. An extensive literature documents its weaknesses and recommends changes (Besharov and Germanis 2004; Blank 2008; Citro and Michael 1995) aimed at both the poverty threshold as well as the measure of resources used to determine if a particular household is poor.

First, the threshold was originally a reflection of the place of food in a family's budget, but since it was set, food as a proportion of family budgets has declined from one-third to one-eighth, and thus does not reflect additional expenses in a family's budget that did not exist in 1963. (The cost of food has also declined.) In addition, the income thresholds do not adequately account for inflation, geographic differences in the cost of living, nor the number of adults and children residing together.

Second, the current US measure does not accurately count all the financial resources available to meet needs. The current measure does not count government tax credits (such as the Earned Income Tax Credit), nor in-kind, near-cash government transfers (such as Food Stamps; Women, Infants, and Children program; housing subsidies; and subsidized school meals). Despite the rapid growth in means-tested public spending, "our poverty statistics failed us," Rebecca Blank (2008, 239), then of the University of Michigan, lamented, "and made it easy to claim that public spending on the poor had little effect." Moreover, the current measure does not subtract state and local taxes or additional expenses (such as work expenses including transportation and child care and out-of-pocket medical care).

The Obama administration has proposed a major revision of the US official poverty measure, a description of which is beyond the purposes of this volume. Suffice it to say that, while the Obama administration's measure seeks to address many of the conceptual and practical issues raised under both absolute and relative measures, it would raise the level of the threshold and alter the way it is calculated, increasing the number of Americans counted as *poor.* One similarity worth noting between this new measure and the current one is that the poverty threshold would continue to be set relative to expenditures of a household at what is ultimately an arbitrary level of the distribution.

Purely relative poverty measures use as a threshold the income of a selected percentile of the society (which rises or falls depending on changes in the distribution of income in the particular country). European poverty thresholds, for example, are usually set at either 50 or 60 percent of median disposable household income (and sometimes at 40 or 70 percent). (As we will see, however, European countries also use absolute income thresholds to determine eligibility for social assistance and other forms of means-tested assistance.)

Prior to 2000, Eurostat calculated European poverty rates based on 50 percent of *mean* equivalized disposable household income (Hiilamo, Sallila, and Sund 2004, 5).[2] In that year, however, Eurostat changed the basis of its poverty measure to *median* equivalized disposable household income and raised the threshold to 60 percent (based on the recommendations of the 1998 Eurostat Task Force on Poverty and Social Exclusion).[3] In 2001, the EU adopted this definition as its *at-risk-of-poverty rate* (Atkinson, Marlier, and Nolan 2004; Nolan 2003). (The OECD [2008] commonly uses 50 percent of median income for its poverty definition.)

Some prefer such relative thresholds because they are said to reflect the amount of income needed to provide "decent living conditions" and to prevent the exclusion of people "from the goods and services that are customary in any given society" (Förster and Mira d'Ercole 2005). But, as Jonathan Bradshaw, a professor at York University, explains (2001, 5), "there never has been any scientific justification for the 60 per cent of median equivalent income threshold (or indeed the other relative income thresholds based on the mean or median)." Finnish researchers, Seppo Sallila, Heikki Hiilamo, and Reijo Sund (2006, 109) write:

> The scientific justification for the use of 60 percent of the median equivalent income threshold, or any other relative threshold based on the mean or median, is not very convincing (Bradshaw 2001). However, a fraction of incomes is nothing more than an agreement on the level of resources which guarantee the least amount of income for "normal life." A synthesis for different poverty-line definitions is given in Hagernaars and Van Praag (1985). However, in practice the most popular choices for poverty lines are given in terms of certain percentages of mean or median incomes of the population. The pragmatic question is whether median or mean income is more effective in capturing the middle class's changing perception of basic necessities.

Given the nature of these thresholds, relative poverty (whether based on 50 or 60 percent of median income) can also be seen as a measure of income or economic "inequality." Timothy Smeeding, of the University of Wisconsin and former director of the Luxembourg Income Study (LIS), explains (2005, 9): "Relative poverty rates are often taken as a proxy for inequality, since a more spread-out income distribution will tend to have a larger share of the population that has less than half of median income."

Absolute and relative thresholds do not have to result in different poverty rates; after all, they could both be set at the same income level. By way of comparison, in 2000, the US official poverty threshold for a family of four was about $22,000. However, if the US threshold were calculated using a relative measure of 60 percent of median income, then, for a family of four, it would be about $35,000 (Dalaker 2001). The result is a sharp difference in poverty rates. Under the official definition, the US poverty rate in 2000 was 11.3 percent. Using 60 percent of median income, the poverty rate was 24 percent (Besharov and Call 2009, 603). (All amounts are in 2009 dollars, unless otherwise specified.)

A very different picture emerges, however, when the US income threshold is used to calculate European poverty rates. Smeeding, for example, used the OECD's purchasing power parity exchange rates to convert the 2000 US absolute poverty threshold (adjusted for household size)[4] into the currency of other OECD countries and then calculated what would be their poverty rates under the American regime. The difference narrowed considerably, and all but disappeared when the US Earned Income Tax Credit and noncash benefits (such as Food Stamps and housing) were taken into account (especially at 125 percent of the poverty line).

Largely because of the differences in how poverty thresholds are set, and the very different poverty rates that result, many people think that the European experience has little to offer the United States, and vice versa. But, as the chapters in this collection amply demonstrate, beyond income thresholds, many common issues underlie both absolute and relative poverty measures—and scholars and policy makers on both sides of the Atlantic are grappling with them as they seek to measure and understand contemporary poverty.

At base, the construction of any poverty definition (relative or absolute) requires the selection of financial and other resources that will be counted as being available to the individual or household. That, in turn, requires a large number of judgments and analytical decisions that make it difficult to maintain the validity and reliability of the statistics. The overarching determination concerns which elements of income and wealth should be included and whether this should be augmented by assigning some monetary value to other resources that may be available, such as in-kind government benefits or private assets such as owner-occupied housing.

Thus, US and European researchers and policy makers face similar issues as they seek to improve their measurement of income, poverty, and material well-being. To learn more about European efforts, the University of Maryland School of Public Policy and the OECD convened more than 100 scholars and government officials from 24 countries in Paris, France, in March 2009. At the conference, 18 papers were presented in five broad topics together with commentaries by US scholars on each area. The invited authors and discussants are among the most prominent international analysts in the field of poverty and inequality measurement, and although some of the papers focus on specific countries or regions, their purpose is to provide applied demonstrations of overarching concepts.

A selection of 12 of those 18 original papers that focus more narrowly on poverty measurement along with the American commentaries are contained in this volume. The broad topical areas follow.

1. "European Measures of Income, Poverty, and Inequality" explores the relative poverty measures used by the OECD and the EU and what they reveal about poverty and income dispersion within and across member states.
2. "Broadening Measures of Income and Other Financial Resources" explores the ways in which the financial resources currently counted in the OECD and EU poverty measures might be expanded to include more forms of disposable income, such as (1) the value of in-kind, noncash housing, medical, and education benefits; (2) the imputed income from the rental value of housing and capital income from investments; and (3) the value of the benefits provided by employers to employees.

3. "Income Levels for Social Assistance and Their Behavioral Effects" explores the absolute thresholds for income eligibility for various types of income support programs, in both developed and developing countries, as well as their adequacy and behavioral consequences. (The programs include unemployment assistance, housing benefits, family benefits, special aid for lone-parent households, employment conditional benefits, and other forms of means-tested social assistance.)
4. "Nonincome Measures" explores household consumption, assets, wealth, and well-being as alternate or complementary poverty measures.
5. "Multidimensional Measures" explores the development and implementation of measures of social exclusion and deprivation and how they can supplement and illuminate income-based measures.

I. EUROPEAN MEASURES OF INCOME, POVERTY, AND INEQUALITY

The first section of this volume explores the statistical approaches used by the OECD and the EU. The OECD's methods are detailed in the second chapter of the volume, "The OECD Approach to Measuring Income Distribution and Poverty," by Michael F. Förster and Marco Mira d'Ercole.

As Förster and Mira d'Ercole describe, the OECD's primary approach for measuring poverty across its 30 member countries is relative, supplemented with information on median income and inequality in its member countries. The authors begin by briefly recounting the history of the OECD's measurement of poverty and inequality. Beginning in 1976, that work, though groundbreaking, was based on statistics computed by individual countries that were not directly comparable. Differences in statistics across countries in the report led to controversy regarding what lessons might be learned from it. Since then, the OECD has emphasized the construction and use of comparable data both across countries and over time. Having common measures across countries establishes a foundation of credibility for cross-national comparisons. Today, the OECD contracts with individual organizations in each member country to assemble comparable data for its published statistics.

Within the OECD approach to measuring poverty, the underlying income concept for measuring available resources is equivalized disposable household income. As Förster and Mira d'Ercole discuss in detail, this includes income from wages and salaries, self-employment, property, pensions, and cash transfers and adjusts those inflows for income, social security, and wealth taxes. The primary poverty threshold used within OECD statistical calculations is *50 percent of median equivalized household disposable income. Equivalized income* is defined as the household's total disposable income divided by its "equivalent size," to take account of the size and composition of the household, and is attributed to each household member.

To address the criticism that relative measures of poverty do not reveal how much material progress (loss) comes from economic growth (decline) over time, they also calculate anchored measures that gauge movements relative to a base period. A range of supplementary measures are also constructed (varying factors such as the method of equivalizing incomes and the relative poverty threshold).

A single summary statistic such as the relative poverty rate does not reveal what is happening throughout the distribution of income. For this reason, the OECD also produces comparable estimates for its member countries of different income concepts (e.g., mean, median) along with measures of inequality such as the Gini coefficient. Förster and Mira d'Ercole demonstrate the usefulness of this information in comparing median incomes, poverty rates, and Gini coefficients across member countries. What emerges from this analysis is a clear sense that for some relatively well-off countries whose economic fortunes in the period examined were positive and characterized by rising median income, relative poverty was on the increase because of widening inequality. Förster and Mira d'Ercole also demonstrate that, in virtually every member country, the net impact of government activities reduces measured income inequality.

In the third chapter, "Income Indicators for the EU's Social Inclusion Strategy," Isabelle Maquet and David Stanton discuss the EU's relative standard of poverty. They also discuss the relationship of the relative poverty measure to some of the other indicators developed by the EU to gauge the degree of social inclusion of citizens within the individual member countries. The actual production of these statistics is an impressive accomplishment.

The EU uses the Statistics on Income and Living Conditions (EU-SILC) for its official measure of being *at risk of poverty* and its other indicators of social inclusion data. These data make it possible to tabulate a number of social indicators across all 27 member states. The resource measure used in the at-risk measure is disposable household income excluding imputed rent, goods produced for consumption, and noncash income and transfers. Those whose equivalized disposable income falls below 60 percent of national equivalized median income are considered at risk of poverty.

Because the relative standard adopted by the EU refers to each individual state, and living standards vary widely across them, Maquet and Stanton explain that a decision was made to also publish the monetary thresholds that the relative standards represent in each country as well as other statistics regarding basic indicators of access to resources such as mean and median income. Moreover, as in the OECD statistics, measures of income dispersion such as the Gini coefficient are also provided. The intent is to provide a more complete depiction of the distribution of income in each country.

As with the OECD approach, a longstanding criticism of the EU's relative measure of poverty is that because the thresholds adjust upward every year, measured poverty can rise even when real incomes grow for everyone in the society. The EU understands that interested observers might like to know how the population at risk of poverty changes when measured against a fixed standard. Thus, like the OECD, they produce what are referred to as anchored measures. For those statistics, the relative poverty threshold for a given year is fixed, and the at-risk population is determined in subsequent years.

Maquet and Stanton also make use of the relative thresholds for being at risk of poverty, the resulting rates, and an index of material deprivation (which will be discussed in later chapters in detail) to demonstrate how multiple measures may better illustrate the situations of those with relatively low income than analyses based on individual variables can. Their analysis reveals that, because the relative poverty thresholds are a proxy for median income, countries with high thresholds tend to have little material deprivation. Also, countries with fairly low thresholds for determining who is at risk of poverty and the proportions of individuals at risk of poverty often have high rates of material deprivation. This phenomenon is explained by the relative dispersion of income across countries. A low-income country with a fairly tight income distribution will not have a large proportion of its population considered at risk of poverty, whereas a nation with high and widely dispersed incomes will have more people considered at risk of poverty. The indicator of material deprivation helps reveal underlying standards of living across countries with differing distributions of income.

The fourth chapter, "Deconstructing European Poverty Measures," by Richard V. Burkhauser, considers the implications for the EU of the American experience in measuring poverty. Burkhauser begins by considering different dimensions within which both the EU and the United States must make analytical decisions in order to operationalize an income-based measure of poverty.

Burkhauser then turns to the fundamental concepts that the EU's relative poverty measure and the US absolute measure seek to address. He argues that relative poverty rates emerge from a social context where reducing dispersion in income is seen as a primary social goal and that this tradition has been more prevalent in European history. Absolute poverty rates tend to emerge from consideration of the minimum income necessary to live at a subsistence level, which is consistent with the tradition of thinking on this issue in the United States.

At a technical level, Burkhauser agrees there are refinements to the US method of measuring poverty that could usefully be drawn from the EU approach. For example, in the EU, income is measured as disposable (net of taxes and cash transfers). In the United States, the income concept is pretax whereas expenditures on goods and services occur in posttax dollars, so the poverty threshold is stated in different terms than the resources available for spending are.

Burkhauser also makes the point that when the EU measure of being at risk of poverty is calculated for each member state relative to 50 percent of EU median income, there are some countries (Lithuania, Latvia, Poland, Estonia, Slovakia, Poland) where a majority of their population is below the income threshold that places them at risk of poverty. Thus, the official EU poverty measure, which is calculated within each individual country, obscures the depth of social inequality across member states.

II. BROADENING MEASURES OF INCOME AND OTHER FINANCIAL RESOURCES

This volume's second section explores additional forms of income and other resources that might be counted to determine the resources available to households, including (1) the valuation of housing, medical, and education benefits, currently excluded from the disposable income measure employed by both the OECD and the EU; (2) the imputed income from the rental value of housing and capital income from investments; and (3) the valuation of benefits provided by employers to employees. An American perspective on these efforts is also provided.

In the fifth chapter, "Accounting for the Distributional Effects of Noncash Public Benefits," Holly Sutherland and Panos Tsakloglou investigate the impact of valuing public housing subsidies, education, and health care on inequality in five European countries (Belgium, Greece, Germany, Italy, and the United Kingdom). These benefits represent transfers that account for a sizeable share of national resources and thus are likely to make significant contributions to the disposable incomes of beneficiaries.

The analysis contained in the chapter builds on the EU microsimulation model EUROMOD, developed under Sutherland's direction. EUROMOD provides a unified framework for calculating who bears the burden of taxes and who receives cash benefits. The value of beginning from the model in this analysis is that it provides conceptual rigor in thinking about differences in tax and transfer systems across countries. Although countries may each provide some form of public housing, free public education, and health care, the specific systems for determining who is eligible for those transfers and the extent to which individuals pay some portion of the cost themselves will vary across locations. These differences in institutional details across the five countries considered are modeled in the analysis.

Sutherland and Tsakoglou provide measures of income inequality before and after adding the value of these transfers to the standard EU definition of disposable income. They find that provision of these subsidies lowers inequality markedly in the countries considered. However, when they adjust the needs of households to reflect the benefits received, the impact of measuring these additional resources is not as dramatic.

To better understand Sutherland and Tsakoglou's results, consider the example of public education. The cost of education is high and the households that need it (having children present within the age range where it is compulsory) do not fully pay for the benefit themselves. Thus, valuing this resource adds a great deal to their incomes. Younger adults tend to have school age children and relatively lower incomes, so adding these resources has an equalizing impact on incomes. However, if the need to pay for education of their children is incorporated into the equivalence scale used to adjust the incomes of households into comparable units, children are more costly than when this expense is not included. Thus, once this additional adjustment is made in the equivalence scale, the net impact of adding educational expenditures into the transfer category is muted, as it meets an additional need. Nonetheless, providing an incidence analysis of both who is taxed to pay for the benefit and where the benefits flow illuminates the nature of the transfers involved.

In "Accounting for Imputed and Capital Income Flows," the sixth chapter, Joachim R. Frick and Markus M. Grabka develop methods for calculating imputed rent for home owners, as well as residents of social housing along with flows of income from wealth, and consider their impact on inequality. Their goal is to construct a more comprehensive measure of resources available to households than the measure of disposable income used by the OECD and the EU.

As Frick and Grabka explain, the reason that researchers feel it is appropriate to assign or impute income to households who are able to receive shelter for free whether through ownership or social provision is that they effectively have access to a resource for which they do not have to pay. Also, individuals often hold other assets that provide them with potential access to resources they have discretion in using. The most obvious example of this is liquid financial assets. Individuals can hold stocks of wealth. As the stock earns interest, it may simply be added to the existing principal. At the discretion of the individual, the interest and/or the principal can be spent. Thus, some argue that at least a conservative measure of the consumption possibilities that financial assets reflect should be imputed to individuals. Frick and Grabka consider the roles of both imputed rent and capital income on measured inequality.

Using data from the German Socio-Economic Panel (SOEP), Frick and Grabka find that imputing the value of housing to owner occupiers and residents of social housing tends to reduce measured inequality. In their empirical work, this imputed income tends to flow to older owner occupiers, thus improving their relative living standards. Imputation of capital income, because its recipients tend to be relatively well-off, tends to increase measured inequality.

In the seventh chapter, "Accounting for Employee Benefits," Neil Gilbert explores the different types of noncash benefits that can accompany employment, their share in total compensation, and the likely impact of including them in the measurement of resources available for consumption. Based on statistics provided in Gilbert's work, in European countries as well as the United States, a sizable share of compensation is not considered direct pay. In the United States, which lies at the low end of the observed range, nondirect compensation accounts for about 30 percent of the total in the most recently available data. Among European countries, nondirect pay usually accounts for 40 to 45 percent of the total.

Somewhat surprisingly, in the United States, expenses on health insurance and contributions to social insurance each represent relatively large shares of nondirect pay, but employer-provided pensions is the largest single category of benefit. This is significant, in part, because it is usually not considered part of taxable compensation. And because better pension plans are usually provided to higher earners, the inclusion of contributions to pensions as a component of income is most likely to raise measured cross-sectional inequality.

As Gilbert points out, in both the European and US approaches to measuring poverty, the key difficulty in measurement comes from benefits not currently counted as part of taxable income. If employers must report what is spent on a company car as part of worker compensation, then it is measured in pay. However, if contributions to pension plans below an allowable limit are not reflected in pay, then, as a significant part of nondirect compensation, it is desirable to have it reflected in a measure of resources available to households. The same can be said of employer-provided educational benefits, day care, and other forms of compensation not reflected in figures on worker pay. Each of these unmeasured benefits is also a marker of a better occupation. As is the case with employee pensions, the inclusion of each form of nondirect pay as an additional component of income is likely to contribute to higher measured inequality. As Gilbert notes, capturing these benefits across countries in a systematic manner would require data beyond what is currently available.

In the eighth chapter, "Impressionistic Realism: A European Focus on US Poverty Measurement," David S. Johnson places the work of the authors in this section of the volume in the perspective of US attempts to measure poverty as well as work carried out at the Census Bureau to implement an improved poverty measure. Johnson begins by noting that the research contained in this section of the book focuses on "details." Each of the authors in this section of the book considers additional noncash resources available to individuals. These are the important details in the construction of a more complete measure of resources for use in poverty and inequality analysis. However, Johnson argues that (p. 161), "In many cases, the details do not change our picture of the trend in poverty, or even the comparisons across countries, but they often change the composition of the poor."

Johnson acknowledges that the details considered by the authors are important to consider and that indeed, almost without exception, the Census Bureau has constructed alternative measures of poverty for the United States, which include either the same or similar adjustments to those considered by the authors. However, when many of these adjustments are made to the measure of resources available to individuals, they do not alter rankings of the extent of inequality across countries or change trends in poverty over time. Thus, a reasonable question given the technical difficulty of some of the proposed adjustments is whether the aim should be to have total and precise detail or a pretty good picture of what is happening.

One might also ask, what then is to be learned from all of these possible refinements to the measure of resources available to individuals? Johnson argues in concluding that the most important impact of these types of adjustments in the United States is on the distribution of the poor. Each modification of the method by which resources are measured is likely to differentially impact demographic subgroups. Johnson suggests that much will be learned about subgroup poverty by examining different hypothetical thresholds and resource measures and that, ultimately, this is the value of producing many alternative measures.

III. INCOME LEVELS FOR SOCIAL ASSISTANCE AND THEIR BEHAVIORAL EFFECTS

Although the most visible European poverty measures are relative in nature, when it comes to the distribution of social assistance, European countries use absolute measures to determine the distribution of means-tested benefits. This section of the volume explores the variety of methods by which social assistance benefits are distributed, the adequacy of benefits, and their behavioral impacts.

In the ninth chapter, "Minimum-Income Benefits in OECD Countries," Herwig Immervoll considers the range of income and near-income supports available to individuals in OECD countries. A large number of programs provide cash benefits or close substitutes in these countries. The benefits include payments to the unemployed, housing benefits, family benefits, special aid for lone-parent households, employment conditional benefits, and means-tested social assistance.

Of particular interest to Immervoll is how countries differ in the programs used to deliver cash to provide minimum-income benefits that are not targeted at any particular population. He explores the contrast between the United States where unemployment benefits are conditional on former earnings and job tenure with countries where unemployment assistance is not contingent on work history. In OECD countries where nonconditional unemployment benefits are offered, this is seen as a method of ensuring a minimal living standard for those not working. More similar to the American approach, many OECD countries also provide special support to lone-parent households. Some countries additionally provide universal family benefits.

Immervoll discusses the concern across member countries of the OECD regarding the disincentive effects of unconditional cash support for working-age adults, a view that is perhaps strongest in the United States. Even though many other OECD countries are now tying benefits to lone parents to conditions regarding participation in work or training activities, there is a larger commitment outside the United States to ensuring that even single, working-age adults, regardless of gender, have a minimum income floor they will not fall below.

Immervoll also explores the interaction between benefits that are conditional on prior behavior and those that are not. In unemployment insurance programs where benefit payments are tied to prior earnings and work history, time limits on receipt help motivate job search. Similarly, if benefits for lone parents such as medical insurance or child care are tied to their own work, this raises rewards for their efforts and encourages the activity. If minimum-income guarantees (and those for other social benefits) are set at a level near that of other behavior-contingent benefits, this may reduce the incentive effects embodied in the design of those programs. Thus, he concludes that unconditional benefits are often set below those of conditional supports in order not to totally undermine work incentives within the benefit structure of public assistance.

The tenth chapter examines similar issues (scope of social assistance programs, the means of targeting beneficiaries, and the relationship of benefit levels to work effort) in low-income and developing countries. In "Social Assistance Schemes in Developing Countries," Margaret Grosh, Carlo del Ninno, and Emil Tesliuc argue that in such countries, where the needs are more apparent and resources scarce, there is more urgency in delivering available benefits in the most effective manner.

Grosh, del Ninno, and Tesliuc provide data that show that spending on social assistance for basic subsistence as a fraction of gross domestic product varies surprisingly little across developing and developed countries, generally from 1 to 2 percent. Nonetheless, in less-developed countries, the amount of money is small and administrative systems are not as extensive. Once a political decision has been made to offer a form of social assistance (e.g., nutrition, health, schooling), two basic problems that administrators face are how to target benefits to achieve their intended impact and where to set the benefit level.

The authors' survey of the methods of targeting benefits in developing countries reminds us of the variety of methods available for ensuring efficient service delivery. In the developing context, where extensive administrative records are not available to track incomes and other aspects of individual and family life, other approaches are often employed. Using the case of nutrition, depending on the stability of the political system and the depth of need, targeting benefits can vary from providing assistance to large geographic areas (or an entire country) without qualification to specific targeting aimed at households with members unable to support themselves through work. This range is similar in character to the diversity seen in other societies in providing both unconditional and very specifically targeted benefits.

In setting benefit levels in developing countries, behavioral incentives are also a concern. As in other contexts, the basic desire is to provide benefits that fulfill an identified need and there is recognition that overly generous benefits can blunt the incentive for individuals to find work; however, the relatively low levels of support provided reduce the concern about induced dependency relative to more-developed countries. More commonly, the discussion centers on how transfers might be used to encourage other socially positive behaviors, such as school attendance by children, regular physical exams, and work participation by parents.

In looking at the levels and targeting of benefits employed in developing countries, a theme emerges that is consistent with that in more-developed economies. Benefits are often set based on perceived need. The generosity of the benefits is later compared, primarily for statistical purposes, to a standard such as the proportional subsidy it provides to pretransfer income. For example, children might be observed to be below weight or stunted relative to norms for their age and a food voucher is provided to their family. Subsequently, a study might be done of the types of families who received this type of benefit and the relative increase in their effective income that it represents.

From an American perspective, Richard Bavier revisits the themes of the design of benefits and their relationship to poverty measurement in the eleventh chapter, "Europe's Other Poverty Measures: Absolute Thresholds Underlying Social Assistance." As seen in the discussion of Immervoll, as well as that of Grosh, del Ninno, and Tesliuc, it is common throughout the world for social assistance benefit levels to be determined independent of poverty measurement per se. Instead, benefit levels are often based on expert assessments of need.

Bavier explains the role of experts in this process. In the area of nutrition, experts who understand human physiology and nutritional needs determine what constitutes an adequate diet but this may also require some judgments related to the manner in which individuals in a particular society actually consume food. Experts are often called on to assist in this weighing of basic needs and social context to determine benefit levels. Often, the implicit amount that would be spent to provide what experts determine is needed is larger than what official poverty measures imply.

The largely independent provision of benefits vis-à-vis poverty measurement is not simply a phenomena observed in European countries or in the context of developing nations. Bavier explains that many of the in-kind benefits provided in the United States are based on the judgment of experts. It is still sensible to gauge the assistance provided by various in-kind benefits to families who may be below the poverty line. However, the establishment of benefits throughout the world often moves independent of poverty measurement itself. Bavier argues that this is a phenomenon American observers should note.

IV. NONINCOME MEASURES

In discussions of poverty measurement among developed nations, it is often acknowledged that it would be desirable to measure consumption rather than income, because it is a better measure of well-being. Consumption measures the realized access to goods, whereas income (or assets) represents potential access. Moreover, some individuals with low incomes may be able to augment current consumption by accessing stocks of wealth.

In "Asset-Based Measurement of Poverty," the twelfth chapter, Andrea Brandolini, Silvia Magri, and Timothy M. Smeeding augment relative and absolute measures by annuitizing the values of housing for owner occupiers, as well as other financial assets. The motivation for reflecting the value of housing and net financial wealth in income is that each represents a resource that households may potentially draw from if they would like. Although current disposable income might indicate that a household with substantial assets holdings is below a poverty threshold, accounting for the flow value of these assets to households can present a different picture.

Brandolini, Magri, and Smeeding make use of the Luxembourg Wealth Study (LWS) in their analysis. The LWS is a recently developed database of existing cross-sectional surveys that include measures of wealth. Where necessary, the LWS staff work to make the measures comparable ex post. This particular study includes information for the countries of Canada, Finland, Germany, Italy, Norway, Sweden, the United Kingdom, and the United States.

The authors find that imputing an annuity value of housing and financial assets to individuals has palpable effects (15 to 20 percent) in reducing poverty in the population as a whole but a much larger impact among those living in households headed by individuals ages 55 years and over (about 50 percent). The large impact of valuing assets on poverty among that group occurs primarily because many own their homes or have sizeable equity that, if annuitized to a stream of income, would substantially raise their incomes.

Brandolini, Magri, and Smeeding go further to develop a measure of economic vulnerability that gauges the proportion of households that would have difficulty paying expenses for several months from liquid financial assets if there were an interruption in their incomes. They find that a sizeable portion of individuals is financially vulnerable and many of them are not the same people counted as being poor or at risk of poverty. This highlights that many families that are above the poverty threshold (or not considered at risk of poverty) are nonetheless financially vulnerable.

Peter Lanjouw, in Chapter 13, "Consumption-Based Measures in Developing Nations: Lessons from Brazil," demonstrates the difficulty of arriving at a consumption-based measure of well-being in the context of the rapidly developing economy of Brazil. It is often noted that consumption represents an achieved level of well-being, whereas income most likely represents an inaccurate measure of potential consumption. In most societies, individuals augment their current consumption by accessing credit markets, through intrafamily transfers, with home production, and so on. Thus, the interest in the development of consumption-based measures of economic well-being extends beyond developing economies.

Lanjouw orients his discussion of the development of a consumption-based measure of well-being around the *Pesquisa de Orçamentos Familiares* of 2002/2003 fielded by the Instituto Brasileiro de Geografia e Estatística. This consumption survey systematically collects information on expenditures by trying to match the segments of its questionnaire to the frequency with which different goods are likely to be purchased. Goods such as food are likely to be purchased at greater frequencies than items such as clothing or consumer durables. Thus, consumption surveys administered at a point in time are structured to elicit responses about purchases or consumption of broad categories of goods that have occurred during different time intervals in the past.

From the survey, one might think that once monetary values are assigned to the different consumption items, constructing an aggregate measure of household consumption would be fairly straightforward. However, Lanjouw explains that there are some types of consumption that pose analytical difficulties in aggregating. How to deal with goods that are purchased infrequently but are very large in size is one analytical problem. Relatively few households purchase a car in a year, but ownership may be common. Thus, to reflect infrequent large purchases in a consumption-based measure requires that ownership of the asset be elicited in the survey and that its flow value is imputed to the household, as was done for housing in the analysis by Brandolini, Magri, and Smeeding in Chapter 12. Other problems in constructing a consumption-based measure of economic well-being include distinguishing goods that households may purchase that are really an input to production or that are purchased for others.

Lanjouw discusses the construction of a consumption aggregate for Brazilian households by systematically tracing through the analytical decisions that have to be made for each of the major categories of spending included in its construction. What emerges from this discussion is that for many of the major components, there are analytical concerns about the accuracy of the measures. There are also major components that may be excluded (such as the value of some large consumer durables) due to the difficulty in collecting data about them and imputing their value. Thus, a consumption-based measure of economic well-being runs into some of the same analytical problems that are encountered in trying to construct a comprehensive measure of disposable household income. This leads Lanjouw (p. 287) to conclude, "In sum, the construction of a consumption aggregate is part science, part art."

Chapter 14, "Alternatives to Income-Based Measures of Poverty," by Kenneth A. Couch, discusses the symmetrical problems that arise in developing an income or consumption-based measure of economic well-being. In theory, direct measures of consumption are preferable as a measure of well-being, particularly for low-income households, because they are more likely to reflect the end result of the many paths individuals may take to sustain themselves. In practice, however, problems of valuation of nonmarket goods arise both when an analyst begins with income as a measure of resources but then wishes to augment it with unpurchased items, and when consumption expenditures is the ultimate analytical goal but individuals access goods in many ways other than market transactions.

Couch explains that the analytical problems encountered in constructing a comprehensive measure of disposable income begin with accurately measuring the components of the standard definition. There are basic components of the commonly used disposable income concept that are not measured accurately. One important component of disposable income most analysts think is not measured accurately is self-reported income, whereas excise and sales taxes are totally neglected both in the United States and Europe.

Beyond this, there is a recognition that even an idealized measure of disposable income would not fully capture living situations of many households, as discussed by Brandolini, Magri, and Smeeding. Valuing the consumption of in-kind transfers, the use of a house by owner occupiers, and the portion of financial wealth that might reasonably be viewed as available income are each difficult conceptual problems for which a consensus has not developed regarding how to incorporate them in a practical manner into a measure of disposable income.

Similarly, Couch argues that constructing a measure of total household consumption beginning with a survey such as the one discussed by Lanjouw poses a similar set of analytical problems. The measurement of consumption begins with expenditures on goods and has to augment that information by placing values on nonmarket consumption (e.g., use of durables such as housing and cars, value of intrafamily transfers). In consumption surveys, there are problems with whether some important investments households make in their own future by building assets such as livestock and housing are reflected in the survey. Similar to problems encountered in approaches to measuring well-being using income as the starting point, consensus methods do not yet exist regarding how the value of assets not reflected in current expenditures should be attributed to individuals and the households in which they live.

V. MULTIDIMENSIONAL MEASURES

The conceptual underpinnings of modern poverty measurement within the EU extend most directly from the work of the well-known sociologist Peter Townsend (1979). Townsend argued that poverty is a multidimensional construct related to the ability of individuals to participate in the social life of their own society. There are at least two important observations that can be drawn from this statement. First, being at risk of poverty is related in part to the lack of income necessary to participate in social life. Second, there are other important dimensions of an individual's experiences that may also leave them excluded from society's mainstream.

In Chapter 15, "Developing and Learning from EU Measures of Social Inclusion," Eric Marlier, Bea Cantillon, Brian Nolan, Karel Van den Bosch, and Tim Van Rie provide an empirical exploration of the EU measures of social inclusion, both individually and in relation to each other. They make use of an EU-sponsored data source, *Statistics on Income and Living Conditions* (EU-SILC), designed to support construction of a suite of social indicators in their analysis.

Beginning with the at-risk-of-poverty measure and the relevant poverty threshold of each country, they establish that some countries with low average incomes nonetheless have low proportions of individuals found to be at risk of poverty. What explains this somewhat counterintuitive finding is that countries with relatively high standards of living and wider dispersions of income will have more individuals who fall below 60 percent of median income (the EU poverty threshold) than countries with lower average incomes and relatively tight dispersions.

Extending from the conceptualization of Townsend but also in acknowledgement of the misleading inferences that might be drawn from the at-risk measure by itself, the EU produces a number of other social indicators. The indicators beyond those related to income capture aspects of labor market performance (unemployment and joblessness), low educational qualifications, the employment situation of immigrants, material deprivation, and access to health care. Construction of measures related to housing and child well-being is in progress.

These indicators are intended to provide a broader context within which to view exclusion from participation in society consistent with the thinking of Townsend. Marlier et al. report that for some of these measures (material deprivation), it is possible to find countries in Europe, such as Spain, with a relatively high proportion of individuals considered to be at risk of poverty yet with relatively low levels of deprivation. Similarly, one can find countries with low proportions of individuals at risk of poverty that have relatively high percentages reporting being materially deprived (Hungary and Slovakia). Thus, the additional social indicators allow analysts to obtain a more accurate picture of need in a society than would be allowed by examining a single indicator by itself.

"Using Nonmonetary Deprivation Indicators to Analyze European Poverty and Social Exclusion," Chapter 16, by Brian Nolan and Christopher T. Whelan, focuses exclusively on what can be learned from examination of these indicators of material deprivation in conjunction with measures of being at risk of poverty. A key difference in the EU perspective and that of the United States is that those below the relevant income threshold of 60 percent of the median are considered to be at risk of poverty rather than poor per se. Nolan and Whelan look at the relationship of the proportion of those measured as materially deprived by different standards as compared to the proportion at risk of poverty and usefully point out that in Europe, these measures are widely used in combination to focus scarce resources on the most deprived populations.

From this perspective, it is also useful to examine which categories of material need seem to most commonly account for the extent of deprivation (the count of individual items individuals can not afford). Nolan and Whelan, using data both from EU-SILC and the European Community Household Panel Survey in their analysis, demonstrate that this varies across countries and is likely related to the nature of social supports in each country. Some countries have virtually nonexistent levels of need with respect to housing but apparently significant levels of nutritional deprivation. Similarly, others appear to have nonexistent problems with respect to nutritional adequacy but housing and other needs are more commonly reported.

Nolan and Whelan find that, if policy were focused more tightly on those who are both at risk of poverty using the EU standard and who also report being materially deprived, the group for whom society might arguably be most concerned about shrinks tremendously. Put simply, for many countries within the EU, living standards are high and measured material deprivation even by European standards is quite low.

The most basic reason for the disconnect between the proportions at risk of poverty in the EU and those reporting material deprivation is that incomes, even below the at-risk standard, often provide enough for individuals to access the majority of goods whose consumption is detailed in the list used to gauge material deprivation. Thus, Nolan and Whelan conclude that the label of being at risk of poverty is appropriate and from that perspective, focusing policy on the intersection of groups at risk of poverty and reporting material deprivation is sensible. They argue that multiple measures of social inclusion allow "for new insights in making comparisons across countries and in tracking changes over time, and in framing policies to respond to the situation and needs of different groups" (p. 358).

Another potential reason more overlap is not observed between those who are labeled as at risk of poverty and those reporting material deprivation is that individuals with low incomes may access other resources to smooth their consumption. In Chapter 17, "Poverty Redefined as Low Consumption and Low Wealth, Not Just Low Income: Psychological Consequences in Australia and Germany," Bruce Headey, Peter Krause, and Gert G. Wagner make use of data from two panel data sets, the Household, Income, and Labour Dynamics in Australia and the German SOEP, to investigate the relationship between measures of being at risk of poverty based on relative income alone versus those that also consider low wealth and low consumption. Wagner, in his role as the leader of the SOEP data collection effort, and Headey, in the same role for Household, Income, and Labour Dynamics in Australia, have been international leaders in the collection of self-reported data on well-being. In their analysis, they highlight the relationship of different measures of poverty to a number of dimensions of individual well-being.

In the analysis of Headey, Krause, and Wagner, when the concept of poverty is redefined as existing when individuals are seen as at risk by multiple measures, the group that is of policy concern shrinks dramatically. In Australia, those who would be considered at risk of poverty in the EU (using a standard of 60 percent of the median income) are about 20 percent of the population. If poverty itself was defined to also require being below 60 percent of the median of consumption and having liquid assets insufficient to meet three months of expenses, the rate shrinks to 5 percent. In Germany, those at risk of poverty are about 18 percent of the population. Expanding that definition to also require low-wealth levels lowers the rate to 8 percent.

The authors also expand their analysis by requiring that their experimental measures of core poverty be sustained for three years. In Australia, this would lower the poverty rate to 2.2 percent. In Germany, the rate falls to 6.2 percent.

They further extend their analysis by examining responses to questions regarding life satisfaction in each country conditional on being defined as poor in Australia by having low relative income, consumption, and low assets and in Germany by having relatively low income and assets. They find that poverty defined in this way is highly related to responses on surveys regarding life satisfaction, partner satisfaction, physical health, and mental health in both countries. In the more general literature on life satisfaction, it has occasionally been argued that differences in satisfaction across income groups reflect nothing more than envy. Systematic variations in health that relate to income and assets extend beyond envy.

The discussion by American Neil Gilbert, in Chapter 18, "Anomalies in European Measures of Poverty and Social Exclusion," questions the usefulness of the measures of material deprivation chosen by the EU as part of their portfolio of social indicators. In several of the chapters in this volume, it is noted that there is not a large overlap between those who report not being able to afford some things and those who are below the relative poverty threshold of the EU. Gilbert points out that there is in fact a very strong negative correspondence between the relative poverty threshold each individual country employs and the proportion that report being materially deprived in some way. In other words, as the standard of living in the country rises, so does material well-being. Thus, it is fair to question the extent to which these measures of material deprivation yield useful knowledge about the nature and extent of poverty.

Gilbert presses this point further noting that the list of items that individuals are asked if they can afford (as components of material deprivation) include unexpected expenses and an annual holiday. There are no monetary values attached to the questions to anchor the responses across respondents, and this calls into question the reliability of the measures both in cross section and over time. Gilbert also points out that to some extent, the EU measure of relative poverty appears to fundamentally contradict the measures of material deprivation. Several chapters point toward countries where the proportion of the population at risk of poverty is relatively low yet the proportion of people who report being materially deprived is relatively high. Gilbert questions the utility of these incongruent and inconsistent measures and whether they really add useful information to our understanding of poverty beyond what is captured by more common monetary measures.

In contrast to the puzzling information that is contained in measures of material deprivation, Gilbert argues that traditional income-based measures of poverty are easily understood by most people and relate in clear ways to commonly understood concepts of well-being and what it means to be poor. In considering the expanded financial measures of poverty contained in the work of Headey, Krause, and Wagner, Gilbert notes that these are fairly direct extensions of existing concepts of poverty but with different implications for policy. According to Gilbert, "the data here show that the rates of income-related poverty as defined by many public agencies fall to very low levels when measured by empirical indicators of financial resources that are more comprehensive than the conventional measure of income" (p. 395).

Gilbert concludes his commentary by noting that, at a broad level, the EU's additional measures of social inclusion might be seen as reframing a progressive agenda for social transfers to address needs such as taking a vacation and having other material comforts beyond what most people would associate with poverty. When multiple financial indicators are employed in the analysis, the core group of those measured as poor shrinks considerably. This suggests that the lack of resources traditionally thought of as poverty has been adequately dealt with through existing transfer systems. It would be very difficult to gain political traction for expanding income transfers if measures of poverty based on multiple financial indicators were officially adopted.

* * *

Concluding Thoughts

In the last chapter of this volume, "New Comparative Measures of Income, Material Deprivation, and Well-Being," Timothy M. Smeeding provides an overview of the research contained in this book. Smeeding is a pioneer in international efforts to facilitate cross-national research on poverty and inequality through his work to develop LIS and LWS. Smeeding notes that 30 years ago, a collection of work such as that contained in this volume would not have been possible because the information on which it is based did not exist. Since that time, LIS and LWS were developed, as were the cross-national collections of panel data contained in the Cross National Equivalent File, the European Community Household Panel Survey, and the EU-SILC. These data sources provided the information used in almost all of the chapters in this volume.

Smeeding also points to the value of cross-national research efforts in providing the opportunity for those interested in social policy in an individual country to learn that indeed most countries face similar challenges. Although uniform policy responses across countries are not realistic, nonetheless, the work contained in the volume demonstrates that it is possible to organize the different approaches into conceptual groups that have evolved for the most part independently of each other.

Finally, Smeeding notes the opportunity that comparative work on social policy now provides for all countries. Whereas each country may have developed its own network of social programs largely on an independent basis, nonetheless, an innovative policy developed in an individual country may resonate with others, leading to more widespread adoption. This opportunity to learn from each other about approaches to common problems is the greatest benefit from comparative research on social policy. That seems like a fitting thought with which to conclude this introduction as well as the entire volume.

* * *

We hope that these chapters help spark a cross-Atlantic dialogue about how best to measure income, poverty, and material well-being. Just as important, we hope that this process will serve as a model for cross-national exchanges in other areas of social welfare policy.

Notes

1. Besides adjustments for inflation, the last changes to the poverty measure were in 1981, when the "farm" poverty threshold was eliminated and the largest family size category was increased from "seven persons or more" to "nine persons or more."

2. Heikki Hiilamo, Seppo Sallila, and Reijo Sund (2004, 5) in "Rethinking Relative Measures of Poverty" state: "Using a median threshold is also subject to well-grounded criticism. A median income threshold, as a standard, comes closer to the definitions of absolute poverty, which does not take account of the changes in the economic and social context of the upper half of the income distribution. On the other hand, the threshold defined by the mean reflects income equalities caused by changes in the upper end of the distribution, and it may well be criticized for obscuring the difference between inequality and poverty measures. However, the difference is already blurred as poverty measures correlate with inequality measures to a large degree. This does not mean that the measures should be kept in different categories. Actually, they focus on more or less the same phenomenon, though from a slightly different perspective (Yitzhaki 2002)."

3. The 1998 Eurostat Task Force on Poverty and Social Exclusion recommended the change from mean to median income because, due to the "special features of the income distributions (asymmetry, long tails, etc)," the median "is less affected by the extreme values of the income distribution and is less affected by sampling fluctuations" compared to the mean (European Statistical Systems 1998). The recommendation of 60 percent of median income (as opposed to 40, 50, or 70 percent) was apparently not designed to raise the poverty threshold or poverty rates, rather, it was chosen because the poverty rate at 60 percent of median income was, for most EU countries, about equal to the then-current poverty rate at 50 percent of mean income, so that there was no substantial change in poverty rates for most countries.

4. When determining overall poverty rates, household incomes are adjusted by the size and composition of the household using equivalency scales. Equivalency scales assign a different weight to each additional adult and child in the household, reflecting differences in consumption. These equivalency scales can skew absolute poverty rates. For example, if children are given similar weights as adults, then countries that have more children per household will have higher poverty rates than countries with fewer children per household will (Neubourg and Notten 2007; Smeeding 2005).

References

Atkinson, Anthony, Eric Marlier, and Brian Nolan. 2004. "Indicators and Targets for Social Inclusion in the European Union." *Journal of Common Market Studies* 42 (1): 47–75.

Besharov, Douglas J., and Douglas M. Call. 2009. "Income Transfers Alone Won't Eradicate Poverty." *Policy Studies Journal* 37 (4): 603.

Besharov, Douglas J., and Peter Germanis. 2004. *Reconsidering the Federal Poverty Measure.* College Park, MD: Welfare Reform Academy. http://www.welfareacademy.org/pubs/poverty/povmeasure.description.pdf.

Blank, Rebecca. 2008. "Presidential Address: How to Improve Poverty Measurement in the United States." *Journal of Policy Analysis and Management* 27 (2): 233–254.

Bradshaw, Jonathan. 2001. "Methodologies to Measure Poverty: More than One Is Best!" Presented at International Symposium Poverty: Concepts and Methodologies 5, Mexico City, March 28–29, 2001. http://www.bris.ac.uk/poverty/pse/conf_pap/mex01_jrb.pdf.

Bradshaw, Jonathan, Sue Middleton, Abigail Davis, Nina Oldfield, Noel Smith, Linda Cusworth, and Julie Williams. 2008. *A Minimum Income Standard for Britain: What People Think.* York: Joseph Roundtree Foundation. http://www.jrf.org.uk/sites/files/jrf/2226-income-poverty-standards.pdf.

Chen, Shaohua, and Martin Ravallion. 2008. *The Developing World Is Poorer than We Thought, But No Less Successful in the Fight against Poverty.* Policy Research Working Paper 4703. Washington, DC: World Bank. http://papers.ssrn.com/sol3/papers.cfm?abstract_id=1259575.

Citro, Constance F., and Robert T. Michael, eds. 1995. *Measuring Poverty: A New Approach.* Washington, DC: National Academy Press.

Dalaker, Joseph. 2001. *Poverty in the United States: 2000.* Washington, DC: US Census Bureau. http://www.census.gov/prod/2001pubs/p60-214.pdf.

European Commission. 2004. *Joint Report by the Commission and Council on Social Inclusion.* 8. Brussels: European Commission. http://ec.europa.eu/employment_social/soc-prot/soc-incl/final_joint_inclusion_report_2003_en.pdf.

European Statistical Systems. 1998. "Recommendations on Social Exclusion and Poverty Statistics." Presented at 31st Meeting of the Statistical Programme Committee, Luxembourg, November 26–27, 1998. http://www.ibge.gov.br/poverty/pdf/eurostat1.pdf.

Förster, Michael, and Marco Mira d'Ercole. 2005. *Income Distribution and Poverty in OECD Countries in the Second Half of the 1990s.* OECD Social, Employment, and Migration Working Paper Series 21. Paris: Organization for Economic Co-operation and Development. http://www.sourceoecd.org/10.1787/882106484586.

Headey, Bruce, Peter Krause, and Gert G. Wagner. 2012. "Poverty Redefined as Low Consumption and Low Wealth, Not Just Low Income: Psychological Consequences in Australia and Germany." In *Counting the Poor: New Thinking about the European Poverty Measures and Lessons for the United States.* Edited by D. J. Besharov and K. A. Couch, xx–xx. New York: Oxford University Press, Inc.

Hiilamo, Heikki, Seppo Sallila, and Reijo Sund. 2004. *Rethinking Relative Measures of Poverty.* Luxembourg Income Study Working Paper Series 368. Luxembourg: Luxembourg Income Study. http://www.lisproject.org/publications/liswps/368.pdf.

Neubourg, Chris de, and Geranda Notten. 2007. "Relative or Absolute Poverty in the US and EU? The Battle of the Rates." Working paper, Maastricht Graduate School of Governance, Maastricht. http://www.merit.unu.edu/publications/mgsog_wppdf/2007/wp2007-001.pdf.

Nolan, Brian. 2003. "Social Indicators in the European Union." Presented at the Statistics Users' Conference, London, November 13, 2003.

Nolan, Brian, and Christopher T. Whelan. 2010. "Using Non-Monetary Deprivation Indicators to Analyze Poverty and Social Exclusion: Lessons from Europe?" *Journal of Policy Analysis and Management* 29: 305–325.

Organization for Economic Co-operation and Development. 2008. *Growing Unequal: Income Distribution and Poverty in OECD Countries.* Paris: Organization for Economic Co-operation and Development.

Sallila, Seppot, Heikki Hiilamo, and Reijo Sund. 2006. "Rethinking Relative Measures of Poverty." *Journal of European Social Policy* 16 (2): 107–120.

Smeeding, Timothy. 2005. *Poor People in Rich Nations: The United States in Comparative Perspective.* Luxembourg Income Study Working Paper Series 419. Luxembourg: Luxembourg Income Study. http://www.lisproject.org/publications/liswps/419.pdf.

Townsend, P. 1979. *Poverty in the United Kingdom: A Survey of Household Resources and Standards of Living.* Harmondsworth, England: Penguin Books.

PART ONE

European Measures of Income, Poverty, and Inequality

The OECD Approach to Measuring Income Distribution and Poverty

MICHAEL F. FÖRSTER AND MARCO MIRA D'ERCOLE ■

INTRODUCTION

Inequalities and poverty matter in both poor and rich countries. Whereas inequality and poverty manifest themselves in a variety of dimensions, *income* is one of the most evident manifestations, and the one that better lends itself to periodic comparisons across countries and over time. Most people in Organization for Economic Co-operation and Development (OECD) countries[1] do care about income inequalities and are capable of articulating judgments on the shape of the income distribution. When asked about whether income inequalities in their country are "too high" or "too low," a majority of respondents in all OECD countries indicate the first option, even with large differences across countries in the size of this group.[2] Greater income inequality matters not only in itself—as a key element for the evaluation of overall well-being in society—but also instrumentally, that is, as a means of attaining other valuable goals. Politically, high inequality can fuel populist and protectionist sentiments, which may lead to policies inimical to economic growth and migration; economically, high inequality means a waste of human resources implied by a large portion of the population out of work or trapped in low-paid, low-skilled jobs.

In 2008, the OECD released a major report on trends and driving factors of income distribution in OECD countries: *Growing Unequal?* This report renewed a long tradition of OECD work on these issues and has generated much interest and debate. One of the main findings of the report was that, over the past two decades, income inequality has widened in more than three-quarters of OECD countries. Although this conclusion may seem obvious to most commentators and analysts monitoring developments in each individual country, it is not so in a comparative perspective and prompts a number of related questions. Has this trend affected all industrialized countries with similar intensity? Has it intensified over time? Does it reflect universal causes (e.g., linked to demographic factors, technical progress, or globalization) or do national circumstances make a difference?

To benchmark countries' performances in this field, over the years, the OECD has developed a statistical infrastructure that makes use of a number of standardized concepts and classifications. Even though inequalities and poverty are not only, or even mainly, about income, statistical information on the distribution of household incomes can be compared across all OECD member countries in a more reliable way than that for other monetary (e.g., wealth, consumption) and nonmonetary (e.g., health, education) dimensions. This is why a significant part of the OECD report focuses on incomes.

The first section of this chapter describes the OECD history of research into income distribution and poverty dating back to the mid-1970s. It also discusses some of the methodological and conceptual choices that have been made to construct more comparable indicators. The second section reviews some of the main findings from *Growing Unequal?*, the latest OECD study. The third section considers limits of the OECD approach and describes some of the steps that have, or could, be undertaken to overcome those. The fourth section concludes the discussion.

MAIN FEATURES OF THE DATA COLLECTION AND METHODOLOGY

The OECD has a long association with research on the distribution of household income. The first stage in OECD work on this issue is represented by Sawyer (1976) who, in an article for the OECD *Economic Outlook*, reviewed the performance of 12 OECD countries in the late 1960s and early 1970s. An important drawback of this study was that it was based on commonly used measures of inequality and poverty, measures that differed across countries. Because of this limit, the release of its findings led to many political controversies, and it took almost 20 years before the OECD ventured to analyze these issues again.

A true milestone in OECD work on these issues is represented by the report prepared by Atkinson, Rainwater, and Smeeding (1995), who presented results referring to 12 OECD countries in the second half of the 1980s. These results were based on unit record data from the Luxembourg Income Study (LIS) database, a standardized data environment that allows analysts to apply common definitions to microrecords from different national surveys. This study was critical in establishing that a reasonable degree of comparability across countries could be ensured by working on the unit record data of individual countries and that the patterns highlighted by these comparisons had the potential to enrich policy discussions. However, the discussion of the main results of the report with national authorities also highlighted areas where the "reclassified" LIS data departed from national sources. At about the same time, and based on the same microdata from LIS, the OECD also published a review of the methodological options for the measurement of low incomes and poverty for international comparisons between developed market economies (Förster 1994b) and applied these to a subset of 14 OECD countries (Förster 1994a).

The third phase of work began with the regular data collection undertaken by the OECD (at around five-year intervals) through a network of national consultants who provide standard tabulations based on comparable definitions and methodological approaches. This is done via a detailed data questionnaire and terms of reference available on the OECD home page (www.oecd.org/els/social/inequality). The first wave of this data collection was undertaken jointly by the OECD Employment, Labour, and Social Affairs Directorate and its Economic Department. It included 13 OECD countries in the mid-1980s and mid-1990s. Results were published in Burniaux et al. (1998) and Oxley et al. (1999). A second wave extended the coverage to 21 countries and included additional indicators (Förster and Pellizari 2000, Förster and Pearson 2002). The third wave of data collection added results for a year around 2000 for 27 OECD countries, with results summarized in Förster and Mira d'Ercole (2005). The latest wave of data collection, which served as one major input for the publication *Growing Unequal?* (2008), updated income information to the mid-2000s and included, for the first time, all 30 OECD member countries.

This approach to data collection, based on a network of national contact points, allows covering a broader range of OECD countries, based on information that is both more up-to-date relative to that available through other statistical sources and better suited for assessing changes in income distribution over time. Its disadvantage is that it does not allow accessing the original microdata, which constrains the analysis that can be performed.

The OECD data collection strives to achieve both comparability across countries and consistency over time.[3] The latter implies that discontinuities, due to either changes in the statistical source used or to changes in survey design or weighting, are generally addressed by collecting data for the same year both on a "new" and "old" basis, and then chain-linking the various indicators. This procedure for correcting breaks has been implemented, so far, for 10 countries. In other cases—notably 6 of the European Union (EU) countries that recently shifted to using the new EU Statistics on Income and Living Conditions survey and discontinued the national surveys previously used by the OECD—no common data year is available, so this constitutes a genuine break in the series.

A series of methodological choices have been made by the OECD to ensure the highest possible degree of comparability. The following sections describe some of their main features.

Income Rather than Consumption

Although economic analysis of poverty and inequality is ultimately interested in consumption possibilities, the OECD data focus on (disposable) household income. Indeed, the practice of comparing data on the distribution of income for some countries with data on the distribution of consumption for others is potentially misleading for reasons that are detailed by Atkinson and Brandolini (2001). There are several reasons why the socially necessary minimum income (Y^*) may differ from necessary minimum expenditure (E^*). A household may attain E^* with an income below Y^* by relying on the goods produced by the households, by dissaving or by borrowing. On the other hand, an income above Y^* may not be sufficient to attain E^* due to certain market failures (if access to housing, for instance, is typically rationed for newcomers, e.g., immigrants). Choosing income over consumption (or spending) as an indicator of the standard of living implies focusing on the capacities of individuals and households to participate in the mainstream of their society rather than on their actual consumption behavior. Income as a yardstick is also used by LIS as well as by the EU in the frame of the *at-risk-of-poverty indicators*.[4]

The definition of *income* at the microlevel, however, is not trivial. As a matter of fact, many countries use significantly different definitions for national publications on poverty and income inequality, for example, *gross* (i.e., before income and payroll taxes) income in the United States, *net* (i.e., after tax) income before housing costs in

Germany, *net* income after housing costs in the United Kingdom, or *net* income after income taxes but before payment of social contribution paid by workers in France.

The OECD definition of household income follows the definitions put forward by the Canberra Group[5] (Franz, Walton, and Ramprakash 1998, Canberra Group 2001) and by LIS (Smeeding, O'Higgins, and Rainwater 1990). Table 2.1 sets out the standard accounting framework that underlies these definitions. In this framework, income from wages and salaries, self-employment, and property sum up to *factor income;* factor income plus occupational and private pensions gives *market income;* market income plus public and private cash transfers, as well as other types of cash income, produces *gross income;* finally, gross income minus personal income and wealth taxes, as well as workers' social security contributions gives *cash disposable income.* This last concept is used as the main measure of household well-being. The approach set out in Figure 2.1 is an accounting framework that allows different

Table 2.1 THE INCOME ACCOUNTING FRAMEWORK

Income component
Gross wages and salaries from dependent employment
+
Self-employment income
+
Capital and property income
=
1. Factor income
+
Occupational and private pensions
=
2. Market income
+
Social security cash benefits (universal, income-related, contributory)
+
Private transfers
+
Other cash income
=
3. Gross income
−
Income tax (and employee social security contributions)
=
4. Cash disposable income

components of income to be related to each other and suitable aggregates to be derived; however, as will be discussed, the framework is both linear and static. These limits matter for the interpretation of results.

The time frame over which household income is assessed in the OECD question-naire is the year, rather than a week or a month. However, in some countries, the assessment period is shorter (often monthly and sometimes weekly income, which are then converted into annual values). Again, differences in the period over which income is assessed may influence comparative assessment: monthly (or weekly) income may be expected to fluctuate more than annual income, which would lead to an overestimation of income inequality and poverty.[6] Unfortunately, the cross-country differences that exist in this (and other) respects could only by addressed through greater ex ante standardization in survey practices. For a range of reasons (e.g., ease of recall), annual income seems the measure that is most suited to international com-parisons. A further advantage of adopting the year as the accounting period is that comparisons can readily be made with household income data from national accounts.

Counting People Rather than Households

Most European research on income inequality has traditionally looked at the distri-bution of disposable income among individuals while keeping the household (and, more rarely, the family) as the unit within which income is pooled and shared among its members. Conversely, most analyses in the United States have focused on the distribution of (pretax) income among families (and, more rarely, households). The OECD questionnaire describes the distribution of income among people rather than among households, in other words, taking the individual as the fundamental unit of analysis. This implies that the income of the household is attributed to each of its members irrespective of who in the household receives that income. Technically, this means (under the current OECD convention) that a couple with two children is counted as four units rather than only one.[7] In practice, taking the individual as the unit of analysis also assumes equal sharing of resources within a household. Even though this assumption may conceal inequalities in the distribution of income within the household (e.g., between men and women, or adults and children) it is obviously preferable than the alternative assumption of no sharing of resources within the household.[8] It has been shown, however, that differences between inequality mea-sures based on those two units of analysis are not very large, especially when assessed in a comparative perspective (Eurostat 1990).

Accounting for Economies of Scale

Taking the individual as the unit of reference requires adjusting income to reflect differences in needs for households of different sizes. With equivalence scales, each household type in the population is assigned a value in proportion to its needs. The factors commonly taken into account to assign these values are the size of the household and the age of its members (i.e., whether they are adults or children). A wide range of equivalence scales exist, many of which are reviewed in Atkinson,

Rainwater, and Smeeding (1995). Some of the most commonly used scales include the following:

- The *OECD equivalence scale*: This assigns a value of 1 to the first household member, of 0.7 to each additional adult, and of 0.5 to each child. This scale (also called the Oxford scale) was mentioned by OECD (1982) for "possible use in countries which have not established their own equivalence scale." For this reason, this scale is sometimes labeled the "(old) OECD scale."
- The *OECD-modified scale*: After having used the old OECD scale in the 1980s and the earlier 1990s, the statistical office of the European Union (Eurostat) adopted in the late 1990s the so-called *OECD-modified equivalence scale*. This scale, first proposed by Hagenaars, de Vos, and Zaidi (1994), assigns a value of 1 to the household head, of 0.5 to each additional adult member and of 0.3 to each child.[9]
- The *square root scale*: Recent OECD publications comparing income inequality and poverty across countries use a scale that divides household income by the square root of household size.[10] This scale implies that, for instance, a household of four persons has needs twice as large as one composed of a single person. However, some of the country reviews undertaken by the OECD, especially for nonmember economies, apply the equivalence scales that are in use in each country.

Table 2.2 illustrates how needs are assumed to change as household size increases, for the three equivalence scales just described and for the two "extreme" cases of no sharing of resources within household (per capita income) and full sharing (household income). In general, all equivalence scales are, to some extent, based on professional convention, rather than being developed through the analysis of consumption expenditure for various countries. There is no universally accepted method for determining equivalence scales and no equivalence scale is recommended by the OECD for general use.

The choice of a particular equivalence scale depends on technical assumptions about economies of scale in consumption as well as on value judgments about the priority assigned to the needs of different individuals such as children or the elderly. These judgments will affect results. For example, the poverty rate of the elderly will be lower (and that of children higher) when using scales that give greater weight to each additional household member. In selecting a particular equivalence scale, it is therefore important to be aware of its potential effect on the level of income inequality and poverty, on the size and composition of the poor population, and on the ranking of countries. Studies have documented that income poverty rates are higher when using the extreme assumptions of per capita income ($e = 0$) and household income ($e = 1$) than for intermediate elasticities, thus displaying a U-shaped function (Jenkins 1991 for the United Kingdom; Förster 1994b for a larger sample of OECD countries).[11] Sensitivity analyses also suggest that although both the level and, in particular, the composition of income poverty are affected by the use of different equivalence scales, trends over time and rankings across countries are much less affected (Burniaux et al. 1998). Whereas the choice of the most appropriate equivalence scale has been the subject of much discussion in individual countries (inter alia

Table 2.2 EQUIVALENCE SCALES AND CORRESPONDING ELASTICITIES

Household size	Equivalence scale				
	Per Capita Income	Oxford Scale (Old OECD Scale)	OECD-Modified Scale	Square Root Scale	Household Income
1 adult	1	1	1	1	1
2 adults	2	1.7	1.5	1.4	1
2 adults, 1 child	3	2.2	1.8	1.7	1
2 adults, 2 children	4	2.7	2.1	2.0	1
2 adults, 3 children	5	3.2	2.4	2.2	1
Elasticity[a]	1	0.73	0.53	0.50	0

[a]Using household size as the determinant, equivalence scales can be expressed through an *equivalence elasticity,* which is the power by which economic needs change with household size. The equivalence elasticity can range from 0 (when unadjusted household disposable income is taken as the income measure) to 1 (when per capita household income is used). The smaller the value for this elasticity, the higher the economies of scale in consumption.

because of its importance for access to welfare benefits), this choice is less critical for the purposes of benchmarking countries' performances.

Focusing on Relative Rather than Absolute Poverty

For the purposes of measuring poverty, the OECD questionnaire focuses on relative income indicators, as opposed to absolute income or subjective measures (i.e., the income level that people in each country would regard as "needed" to avoid poverty). Both absolute and subjective income thresholds pose difficult methodological issues for cross-country comparison of poverty (Förster 1994b), which the relative approach tries to overcome by comparing the incomes of each person to that of the resident population as a whole. This approach thus takes into account the different levels of well-being within a society and how it changes over time. Relative measures also allow one to compare income situations across countries because they are independent of a specific country's definition of basic needs.

An additional reason for focusing on relative poverty is that both psychological and economic analyses have suggested that income differences within a society have real significance for the well-being of each person: People assess their own conditions through comparisons with others (Paugman and Selz 2005; Boarini et al. 2006). This implies that information on relative income matters for the assessment of the living conditions of people independent of judgments of what is "fair" in society.

Income poverty is measured according to the so-called economic distance approach, namely as a fraction of typical (mean or median) income. The choice for one specific threshold is arbitrary but the presentation of results referring to a range of values (40 percent, 50 percent, and 60 percent of median income) allows users to benchmark country performance according to their own view. The main threshold used in the OECD framework is 50 percent of median equivalized household disposable income.[12] In addition to poverty rates (or headcounts), other measures of relative poverty (such as poverty gaps, i.e., the distance between the average income of the poor and the poverty threshold) are also collected.

That said, OECD reports have also included measures of the absolute income of the poor population. One way to illustrate how *absolute* poverty has changed over time is to use a relative threshold in a base year that is then kept unchanged in real terms in later years (i.e., it is adjusted only for changes in consumer price inflation, as measured by the consumer price index). In particular, measures of income poverty "anchored" to a specific year are calculated in *Growing Unequal?* based on a threshold set at one-half of median income in the mid-1990s.[13] In addition, the real values of poverty thresholds, expressed in purchasing power parities for actual consumption, are also presented. These various indicators allow placing the estimates of relative poverty in the context of overall income differentials between countries.

Static Rather than Dynamic Measures

The OECD income distribution questionnaire collects indicators referring to a benchmark year from the mid-1980s (mid-1970s for a few countries) until the mid-2000s, in approximate five-year periods (Table 2.3). The data are cross-sectional; in other words, households are not followed over time though some of the underlying surveys allow tracking changes over time in the income and living conditions of the same person. One problem for analysis of changes over time is that inequality and poverty indicators for individual countries refer to specific years that may differ in terms of the cyclical position of each country. In theory, changes between these years may not be fully representative of underlying trends. In practice, a comparison with "commonly used" measures of income inequality for several OECD countries suggests that this consideration is of limited practical importance for most countries.[14]

Nothing about these methodological choices and approaches is new or pathbreaking. On the contrary, most choices are rather "conservative" and not very controversial. The value of the OECD reporting system does not lie in its methodological assumptions, but rather in setting up an infrastructure that is maintained and updated over time.

MAIN RESULTS FROM THE ANALYSIS

This section reviews some of the patterns identified in analyses of past waves of the OECD data. Emphasis is given to those patterns that pertain to the OECD area as a whole rather than to highlighting country differences.

Table 2.3 Survey Sources and Income Years of OECD Income Distribution Questionnaire

Country	Source	Income Year					
					1994/1995	1999/2000	2003/2004
Australia	*Survey of Income and Housing*						
Austria	*Micro census*		1983		1993	1999	
	EU Survey of Income and Living Conditions						2004
Belgium	*Tax records*		1983		1995		
	European Community Household Panel				1995	2000	
	EU Survey of Income and Living Conditions						2004
Canada	*Survey of Consumer Finances*	1975	1985		1995	2000	2005
	Survey of Labour and Income Dynamics				1995		
Czech Republic	*Micro census*			1992	1996	2002	
	EU Survey of Income and Living Conditions						2004
Denmark	*Danish Law Model System*		1983		1994	2000	2005
Finland	*Household Budget Survey*	1976					
	Income Distribution Survey		1986		1995	2000	2004
France	*Enquête Revenus Fiscaux*		1984	1989	1994	2000	2005
	EU Survey of Income and Living Conditions						2004
Germany	*German Socio Economic Panel (old Länder)*		1985	1990	1995	2000	
	German Socio Economic Panel (all Länder)				1995	2000	2004
Greece	*Household Budget Survey*	1974			1994	1999	2004
Hungary	*Hungarian Household Panel/Household Monitor Survey*		1986	1991	1995	2000	2005

(Continued)

Table 2.3 Survey Sources and Income Years of OECD Income Distribution Questionnaire (Cont'd)

Country	Source	Income Year					
Iceland	EU Survey of Income and Living Conditions						
Ireland	Living in Ireland Survey		1987		1994	2000	
	EU Survey of Income and Living Conditions						2004
Italy	ITAXMOD95		1984	1991	1993		
	MASTRICT (microsimulation models based on Bank of Italy Survey of Household Income and Wealth)				1995	2000	2004
Japan	Comprehensive Survey of Living Condition of the People on Health and Welfare		1985		1995	2000	2003
Korea	Household Income and Expenditure Survey (combined with Farm Household Economy Survey)						2006
Luxembourg	Panel Socio-Economique Liewen zu Lëtzebuerg		1986/1987		1996	2001	2004
Mexico	Survey of Household Income and Expenditure		1984		1994	2000	2004
Netherlands	Income Panel Survey	1977	1985	1990	1995	2000	2004
New Zealand	Household Economic Survey		1986	1991	1996	2001	2004
Norway	Income Distribution Survey		1986		1995	2000	2004
Poland	Household Budget Survey					2000	2004
	EU Survey of Income and Living Conditions						
Portugal	Household Budget Survey		1980	1990	1995	2000	2004
	EU Survey of Income and Living Conditions						

Spain	*Continuous Survey of Household Budgets*		1985	1990	1995		
	European Community Household Panel				1995	2000	
	EU Survey of Income and Living Conditions						2004
Sweden	*Income Distribution Survey*	1975	1983	1991	1995	2000	2004
Switzerland	*Income and Consumption Survey*					2000–2001	2004–2005
Turkey	*Household Income and Consumption Survey*		1984		1994		2004
United Kingdom	*Family Expenditure Survey*	1975	1985	1991	1995	2000	
	Family Resources Survey						2004
United States	*Annual Social and Economic Supplement to the Current Population Survey*	1974	1984		1995	2000	2005

Large Differences in the Shape of the Income Distribution Across Countries

Differences in the overall shape of the distribution of household income across OECD counties are both large and persistent. The Gini coefficient of income inequality is twice as high in Mexico (the OECD country where income distribution is widest) as in Denmark (the country where income distribution is narrowest), and differences remain large when excluding from the analysis countries at both ends of the league table of OECD countries (Figure 2.1).[15] Significant cross-country differences in inequality are found regardless of the measure used with the ranking of countries little affected by which one is used.[16] When income distributions are compared betweens pairs of countries, in a large majority of cases, the Lorentz curves do not cross each other, which implies that these country rankings of the level of income inequality do not depend on the portion of the income distribution that is compared. There are uncertainties about the precise level of inequality in any country, because of small sample sizes, underreporting of certain types of income, and overrepresentation of some demographic groups. Different statistical sources for the same country may also sometimes provide a different picture of how household income is distributed. But these uncertainties are not so large as to give serious grounds for doubting the broad sweep of the findings in terms of cross-country differences in inequality.

Large cross-country differences are also evident when looking at income poverty. Whereas Figure 2.1 shows only one measure of relative income poverty (the poverty headcount, based on a threshold set at 50 percent of median income, shown as a

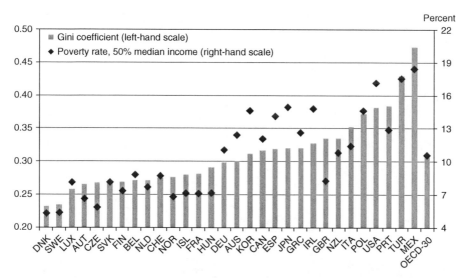

Figure 2.1 Levels of Income Inequality and Income Poverty in the Mid-2000s.
NOTE: Countries are ranked in increasing order of the Gini coefficient of income inequality. Data refer to the distribution of household disposable income in cash across people, with each person being attributed the income of the household where they live adjusted for household size. Poverty rates are defined as the share of individuals with equivalized disposable household income less than 50 percent of the median for the entire population.
SOURCE: OECD (2008).

diamond), cross-country patterns are fairly robust with respect to the choice of different thresholds.[17] Relative poverty rates are always among the lowest, whatever the threshold used, in Sweden, Denmark, and the Czech Republic and always among the highest in the United States, Turkey, and Mexico; they are below average in all Nordic and several Continental European countries, and above average in Southern European countries as well as Ireland, Poland, Japan, and Korea. A composite measure of poverty—constructed by combining information on both the number of poor people in each country and how much their income falls below the poverty line—ranged in the mid-2000s from around 1 percent in Sweden to around 7 percent in Mexico.

Availability of employment opportunities is a key factor for cross-country comparisons on the prevalence of income poverty: Countries where the share of people of working age in paid employment is higher also display lower poverty rates, and the same holds when looking at the relation between the level of employment of mothers and child poverty. At the same time, however, work is not the only factor shaping the risk of poverty: on average, people living in households with workers account for around 60 percent of the income poor (based on a 50 percent income threshold) across OECD countries, and for an even higher share in the United States.

Data on the absolute income level of individuals and households at different points of the distribution are also important for cross-country comparisons of economic welfare. Across countries, measures of mean equivalized household disposable income are highly correlated with conventional System of National Accounts' (SNA) aggregates (such as net national income per capita). There are, however, wide differences across countries in terms of:

- the income gap (in US dollars at purchasing power parity rates) between people in the top decile and in the bottom decile of the distribution (this gap ranges from US$20,000 in the Slovak Republic to more than US$85,000 in the United States).
- how people at similar points in a country's income distribution compare across countries:The United States tops the league by a wide margin in terms of the average income of people in the top decile, comes in fourth (after Luxembourg, the Netherlands and Switzerland) when looking at median income, and is twelfth when looking at the average income of the bottom decile (Figure 2.2).

A Widening in Income Inequality in a Large Majority of OECD Countries

The 20 years between the mid-1980s and mid-2000s have experienced a widening of the income distribution in most OECD countries. On average, the Gini coefficient of income inequality increased by around 2 percentage points, or 7 percent (Figure 2.3). This rise is equivalent to each person below the median hypothetically transferring around 7 percent of their own income to all those above the median, under the assumption that total household income is unchanged.[18] Other summary measures such as the standard coefficient of variation point to larger increases—by almost 30 percent since the mid-1980s—but these are more affected by developments

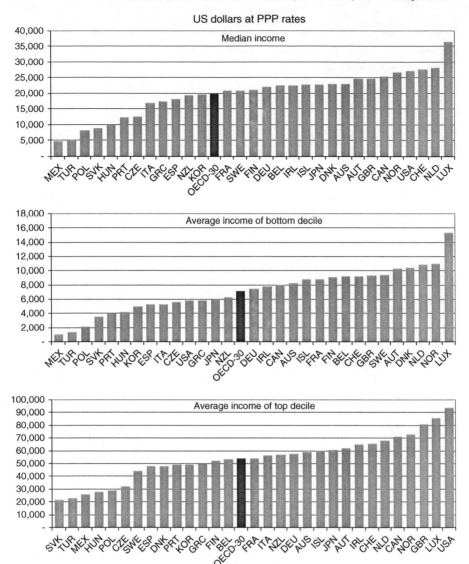

Figure 2.2 Income Levels for People at Different Points in the Distribution, Mid-2000s.
NOTE: The data refer to equivalized household disposable income of people at different points of the distribution. Income data for each country are adjusted for inflation (when they refer to a year different from 2005) and then converted into US dollars based on purchasing power parity rates for actual consumption in 2005. This exchange rate expresses the costs of a standard basket of consumer goods and services purchased on the market or provided for free (or at subsidized rates) by the public sector in different countries.
SOURCE: OECD (2008).

at the extremes of the distribution. In all cases, these increases—though significant—fall short of the sharp rises sometimes advanced in public discussion on the subject.

Further, this increase has not affected all countries—as witnessed by declines in France, as well as in Ireland and Spain (where consistent time series are limited up to

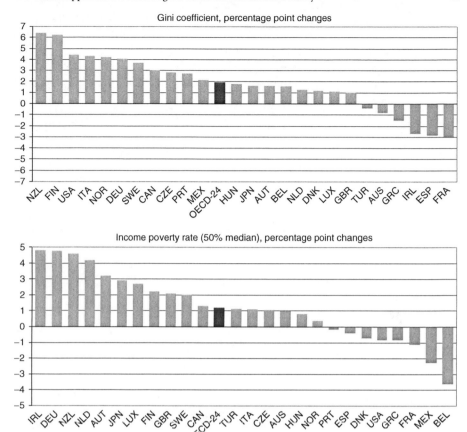

Figure 2.3 Changes in Income Inequality and Income Poverty over the Past 20 Years.
NOTE: Poverty rates are defined as the share of individuals with equivalized disposable household income below 50 percent of the median for the entire population. Data refer to percentage point changes between the mid-1980s and mid-2000s, except for Czech Republic, Hungary, and Portugal (from around 1990 to mid-2000s) and for Austria, Belgium, Czech Republic, Ireland, Portugal, and Spain (from mid-1980s to around 2000). SOURCE: OECD (2008).

the year 2000), with broad stability in many other countries. The increase in income inequality was also larger in the decade from the mid-1980s to the mid-1990s than in the more recent decade, with some countries (e.g., Mexico, Turkey) recording large swings in performance. In the early 2000s, income inequality has increased significantly in Canada, Germany, Norway, and the United States while declining in the United Kingdom, Mexico, Greece, and Australia. These differences in how income inequalities have changed over time are important, as they suggest that the importance of common drivers (whatever their exact nature, e.g., globalization) has not been large enough to offset the influence of country-specific factors.

The poverty headcount, based on a threshold set at one-half of median income, has also risen in most countries in the past 20 years, edging up by 0.6 percentage points in each of the two decades. While the increase in income poverty had been more moderate than for income inequality in the decade from the mid-1980s to the mid-1990s, the reverse applies to the most recent decade. Countries generally display consistent changes in terms of both income inequality and poverty over the entire period, although there are exceptions. For example, Ireland combined a significant increase in relative income poverty (up to the year 2000) and a small decline in income inequality.

Shift in the Relative Income and Poverty Risks of Various Population Groups

Aggregate trends in income distribution have affected people at various points of the distribution in different ways. In Ireland, Mexico, and Turkey, the decline of income inequality experienced over the past decade has mainly reflected falls in the income share accruing to people in the top quintile of the distribution and gains for people in the middle three quintiles. Conversely, in most of the countries where income inequality increased over the decade, this mainly reflected gains at the top of the distribution.

One consequence of these large gains at the top of the distribution has been that middle-class families have often lost ground relative to the economy-wide average—the so-called phenomenon of the hollowing out of the middle class. This is especially evident in New Zealand and the United Kingdom (in the decade from the mid-1980s to the mid-1990s), as well as Canada, Finland, and the United States (where the median-to-mean ratio fell by around 10 percent over the entire period). Conversely, the relative income of middle-class families has been stable in Denmark, France, and Sweden and has improved in the Netherlands and Greece throughout the period and in more countries since the mid-1990s.

Changes in economic conditions have also shifted poverty risks among various demographic groups. The most significant of these shifts has been away from the elderly and toward young adults and children (Figure 2.4). While the very old (people aged 75 years and over) continue to be exposed to a greater risk of (relative-income) poverty than other age groups, this risk has fallen from a level almost twice as high as that of the population average in the mid-1980s to 50 percent higher by the mid-2000s. For people aged 66 to 75 years, this risk is now lower than for children and young adults. Conversely, children and young adults experienced poverty rates that are today around 25 percent higher than the population average, whereas they were close to and below that average, respectively, 20 years ago. Changes have been smaller when looking at poverty risks across household types, with lone parents as the group exposed to the highest risk—three times higher than average—a disadvantage that increased further over the past decade.

Drivers of Changes in Income Distribution

Cross-country differences in income inequality and poverty reflect the interplay of many factors. Three in particular have figured prominently in discussions on the subject. These are changes in demography and living arrangements, labor market trends, and government tax and transfer policies. Although it is not always easy to

Poverty rate of the entire population in each year = 100

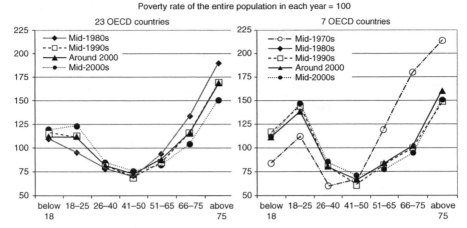

Figure 2.4 Risk of Relative Poverty by Age of Individuals, Mid-1970s to Mid-2000s, OECD Average.

NOTE: Relative poverty risk is the age-specific poverty rate divided by the poverty rate for the entire population times 100. The poverty threshold is set at 50 percent of median income of the entire population. OECD-23 is the average poverty rate across all OECD countries except Australia, Belgium, Iceland, Korea, Poland, the Slovak Republic, and Switzerland. OECD-7 is the average for Canada, Finland, Greece, the Netherlands, Sweden, the United Kingdom, and the United States. Data for mid-1980s refer to around 1990 for the Czech Republic, Hungary, and Portugal; those for mid-2000s refer to 2000 for Austria, Belgium, the Czech Republic, Ireland, Portugal, and Spain (where 2005 data, based on EU Statistics on Income and Living Conditions, are not comparable with those for earlier years). SOURCE: OECD (2008).

distinguish among these factors, the most recent OECD report on this subject highlights several patterns.

First, demographic factors have played an important role in shaping households' living conditions. The most direct way in which this has occurred is by reducing average household size, implying that economies of scale in consumption are lost and that a higher income is needed to ensure the same level of household well-being. The decline in household size (on average from about 2.8 to about 2.6) affected all OECD countries but was particularly large in Ireland, Italy, Japan, Mexico, Spain, and the United Kingdom.

Changes in demography and changes in living arrangements also affect income inequalities. The most important channel is by increasing the share in the total population of groups with below average income (e.g., the elderly or lone parents) or with higher within-group inequality. Comparing the actual change in income distribution to what would have occurred had the population structure (by both age of individuals and household type) remained "frozen" at the level prevailing some 10 years ago suggests that these structural factors have increased income inequality in a majority of countries, and significantly so in Australia, Canada, France, Germany, the Netherlands, and the United Kingdom. More important than population aging per se have been the changes in living arrangements with more people living alone and in lone-parent households. These changes, coupled with a trend toward positive "assortative mating" (the tendency for men and women with similar education and earnings potential to form a family) had a sizeable influence on increasing household income inequality in some countries (e.g., for the United States in the 1980s, Karoly and Burtless 1995; and Gottschalk and Danziger 2005).[19]

Second, labor markets are crucially important for income distribution. Personal earnings disparities among full-time workers have indeed increased rapidly since 1990, with most of the widening reflecting developments in the upper part of the distribution. This widening has also been sharper for men and women, considered separately, than for all workers, irrespective of their gender as the decline of the wage gap between men and women working full time has narrowed the "distance" between the earnings distributions of men and women.

Disparities in personal earnings among workers, however, do not necessarily translate into a wider distribution of household earnings among all people, whether working or not. This is because higher employment (especially of second earners) may spread earnings among a larger number of households. Despite this potential offset, the polarization of employment opportunities on income inequalities has played a significant role. In particular, the employment gains experienced throughout the OECD area since the second half of the 1990s have not led to significant declines in the share of people living in jobless households. The persistence of high household joblessness despite higher employment has partly reflected the concentration of employment gains among people with high and intermediate education, and the decline of employment rates among less-educated people. As a result of these contrasting developments, changes in the concentration of household earnings have been small in most OECD countries in the period from the mid-1990s to the mid-2000s.

At the same time, capital income and, to a lesser extent, self-employment income have become more concentrated in a much larger number of OECD countries. This suggests that nonwage income sources—whose measurement is subject to larger uncertainties than in the case of earnings—account for a significant part of the observed widening in the distribution of household disposable income. Taking all market income sources together (from earnings, self-employment, and capital income, as well as private and occupational pensions), their distribution has became more unequal than that of disposable incomes, especially between the mid-1980s and the mid-1990s and again since around 2000 (Figure 2.5).

Finally, cross-country differences in the shape of the income distribution partly reflect differences in how governments redistribute income across individuals through the cash benefits they provide and the household taxes they collect. The effect of government redistribution in lowering income inequality is largest in the Nordic countries and lowest in Korea and the United States. The country ranking is similar when looking at the effects of taxes and transfers in reducing income poverty. It appears that countries that redistribute more toward people with lower incomes achieve a narrower distribution of household income and lower poverty rates. Also, most of this redistribution toward people at the bottom of the income scale is generally achieved through public cash benefits—with the main exception of the United States, where a large part of the support provided to low-income families is administered through the income tax system.

These cross-country differences in the scale of redistribution among people with different incomes partly reflect differences in the size and structure of social spending—with spending toward people of working age achieving a larger reduction in

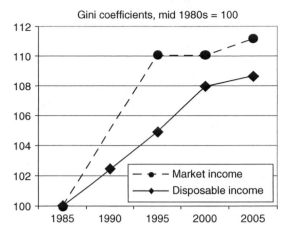

Figure 2.5 Trends in Market and Total Disposable Income Inequality, Working-Age
Population, OECD Average.
Note: OECD-15 is the average of countries for which information is available over the
entire period from the mid-1980s to the mid-2000s (Canada, Denmark, Finland, France,
Germany, Greece, Italy, Japan, Luxembourg, the Netherlands, New Zealand, Norway,
Sweden, the United Kingdom and the United States). Gini coefficients for market and
disposable income are based on people ranked based on each of the two income concepts.
Source: OECD (2008).

poverty than social spending toward the elderly (Figure 2.6). Differences in spending
levels and structure are, however, only part of the story. The OECD countries
redistribute in a variety of ways; some through universal benefits, others with more
targeted programs; some mainly rely on transfers, others mainly granting tax rebates
to low-income families. Also, redistribution across individuals with different income
levels always coexists with redistribution across the life course, with some evidence
that countries that redistribute more across the life cycle spend more, in the aggregate, than those that focus more on redistribution between rich and poor.

When looking at changes over the past decade in the size of redistribution from
rich to poor, such changes differ significantly across countries but are small on average. The reduction of income inequality achieved by the combined effect of household
taxes and public cash transfers declined over the past decade in around half of the
countries; these developments were mainly driven by changes in the redistribution
achieved by public cash transfers (which declined in most countries) that was partly
offset by stronger redistribution through household taxes (in particular in Denmark,
Germany, Italy, the Netherlands, and the United Kingdom). There is also some evidence that less redistribution toward people at the bottom of the income scale
increased the risks of poverty among people of both working and retirement age.[20]

LIMITS AND STATISTICAL ISSUES

Whereas the data outlined in the previous sections allow comparing trends and
drivers in income inequality across OECD countries, there are four types of
limitations in the current OECD reporting system on income distribution. First,

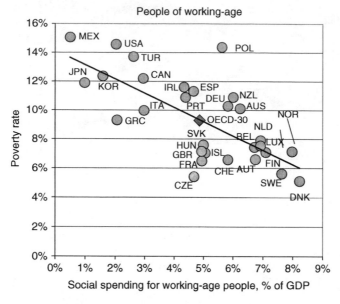

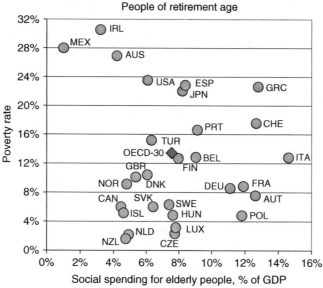

Figure 2.6 Poverty Rates and Social Spending for People of Working Age and Retirement Age, Mid-2000s.

Note: Poverty rates based on a threshold set at one-half of median household disposable income. Social spending includes both public and mandatory private spending in cash (i.e., excluding in-kind services). Social spending for people of working age is defined as the sum of outlays for incapacity, family, unemployment, housing, and other (i.e., social assistance) programs; social spending for people of retirement age is the sum of outlays for old-age and survivors benefits. Social spending is expressed in percentage of gross domestic product at factor costs. Data on poverty rates refer to the mid-2000s for all countries; data for social spending refer to 2003 for all countries except Turkey (1999). Source: OECD (2008).

there are limits due to the OECD data collection itself, such as the low frequency of data collection and the long time lags for processing and release. Second, there are limits embedded in the household surveys underlying OECD data collection, such as underreporting of particular income components. Third, the reporting system is limited to cash income measures, although it is clear that any serious assessment of economic inequality would have to consider whether other factors—noncash income, nonmonetary measures, dynamic measures—validate or invalidate conclusions based on static income measures alone. Fourth, there are other conceptual issues that will need to be tackled in future research, such as the issue of how to improve measures of the redistributive impact of taxes and transfers.

Underreporting of Cash Income Components

The OECD income concept includes all components that are regularly received in cash and quasi-cash forms.[21] As information on these items is collected through surveys (in most cases), these data are subject to underreporting that may bias assessments of how income inequality compares across countries. The degree of underreporting may also change over time within each country, which may distort assessments of trends.

Most of the income items that are covered in the OECD questionnaire have a counterpart in the SNA, which provide a natural external benchmark for assessing the quality of these estimates. In practice, it is not obvious that SNA aggregates are always superior and more comprehensive than survey data: SNA data for the household sector may reflect errors in other accounts and be affected by the statistical procedures used to ensure consistency across accounts. A comparison of information between the two sources in a given year highlights some significant differences between the two. The differences are generally small for the aggregate of household disposable income, but they are more significant when looking at individual components. Although several OECD countries regularly undertake such comparisons of survey and SNA aggregates, the task is much more challenging when undertaken in a comparative perspective. Despite these difficulties, achieving a better integration of survey and national accounts data is a critical research priority for the future, with some OECD countries (such as France) in the process of developing a household appropriation account for major socioeconomic groups (such as income and household type).

Other possible external benchmarks are available for other income components. Individual country studies that have compared information on public cash transfers to households from administrative sources with that available through household surveys have generally uncovered large underreporting. Similar comparative work on public cash transfers could rely on information on expenditures data from administrative sources (both for the total and for major program categories), as available from the OECD social expenditure database.

Noncash Income Components

The OECD income concept excludes various (imputed) income components that are not generally included in the household surveys that underlie the OECD tabulations.

The importance of these imputed components varies across countries, and they may be of differing importance for people at the top or bottom of the income scale. Some, such as goods produced for own consumption, are minor for most developed OECD economies but could be more important for less-developed OECD countries such as Mexico and Turkey and a fortiori for countries such as India and China; most of these income flows are also likely to be concentrated among subsistence farmers who are clustered at the bottom of the income scale. Other components, such as imputed rents and other capital income flows are more important in richer countries and are more likely to be concentrated at the top than at the bottom of the income distribution. Their exclusion from the income definition used by the OECD may then imply that, when the share of these components rise over time, trends in inequality are understated. With more OECD countries moving in the direction of collecting more comprehensive information on these items in their surveys, the issue that will have to be faced is whether the standard OECD income definition should be broadened in future work.

Other noncash income components omitted from the standard accounting framework shown in Table 2.1 are government activities that affect household well-being through the in-kind services they provide and the consumption taxes they collect. The value of publicly provided services for education, health, and other social services varies significantly across countries (from less than 10 percent of household disposable income in Turkey to more than 40 percent in Denmark and Sweden), as well as over time (mainly reflecting the expansion of publicly provided education and health services). This suggests that including these imputed items in a more comprehensive measure of households' economic resources could significantly affect any assessment of cross-country comparisons of levels of inequality and of changes in individual countries.[22]

The recent OECD report *Growing Unequal?* applies different approaches to assess the impact of public services on the distribution of broader measures of household income. Although some conclusions differ according to the techniques used, some general patterns also appear:

- Public in-kind services such as health and education are distributed rather uniformly across people belonging to various income groupings. This implies that they account for a larger share of household income at the bottom of the distribution than at the top. As a result, inclusion of these in-kind services narrows the Gini coefficient of income inequality at a point in time, by roughly one-quarter on average across OECD countries, and by larger amounts in Sweden, Norway, Australia, Denmark, New Zealand, Portugal, France, Italy, and the United States (Figure 2.7).
- This equalizing effect, however, differs among programs with large reductions due to compulsory education, nonspecialist health care and public housing, and negligible reductions for noncompulsory education. Indeed, noncompulsory education is more unequally distributed than income in approximately one in three countries.
- The effect of government services in narrowing the Gini coefficient of income inequality is quite large. It is equivalent to about two-thirds of the equalizing impact of household taxes and public cash benefits. In the United States, public services appear to have the same impact in reducing inequality as do taxes and transfers.

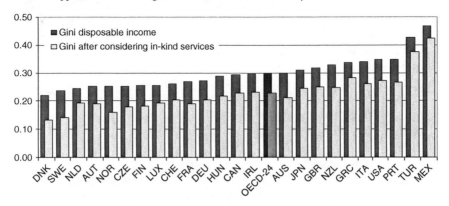

Figure 2.7 Influence of Publicly Provided Services on Income Inequality, around 2000.
NOTE: Countries are ranked from left to right in increasing order of the Gini coefficient of income inequality. Estimates of the effect of public in-kind services for health care, education, and other social services in narrowing income inequality.
SOURCE: OECD (2008).

Conversely, consumption taxes tend to increase income inequality, although their effect seems to be lower than that (in the opposite direction) of in-kind government transfers. Although quantitatively important, however, it seems that, at this stage, these additional factors should be brought into the picture through one-off analyses, rather than being integrated in the OECD periodic collection.

Nonmonetary Measures

Money income is only a partial indicator of living conditions and other measures are important in their own right. One of these measures is household wealth. Surveys measuring household assets and liabilities exist in several OECD countries, but differences in survey design in this field are much larger than in the case of income. *Growing Unequal?* draws some preliminary findings from comparative information on household wealth made available through the Luxembourg Wealth Study (LWS) project. The analysis is limited to eight OECD countries that are part of the LWS and to those types of assets for which information on their distribution is available for all these countries. In general, the importance of these excluded asset categories varies across countries, affecting assessments of both the levels of household wealth and the extent of inequality in their distribution. Findings include the following:

- The distribution of wealth is much more unequal than that of income: this reflects differences in saving patterns across the income distribution (with small savings among those at the bottom of the income scale and much larger savings for people at the top), and the importance of bequests for the transmission of wealth across generations.
- Alternative measures of wealth inequality (concentration coefficients, or the share of total wealth held by people in the top decile) and definitions of household wealth (i.e., excluding business equity) lead to different country rankings: The share of wealth held by the top decile is higher in the United

States than in the other OECD countries in the analysis, but this is not the case when considering the Gini coefficient.

- Country rankings also differ when comparing the absolute level of household assets and income, with Italy having the highest median net worth (followed by the United Kingdom) despite having the lowest equivalized household income among the OECD countries included in the LWS. Sweden has the lowest median net worth (equivalized) despite an income that is above that of many other OECD countries.
- Median net wealth varies with the age of the household head, generally rising until the end of working life and then declining during retirement. This inverted-U profile is, however, less steep than for income, with only small declines taking place in Canada and a continued increase by age of the household head in the United States.
- Across individuals, income and net worth are highly correlated, but the correlation is not perfect. In general, income-poor people have fewer assets than the rest of the population, with a net worth generally less than one-half of that of the population as a whole.

Nonincome measures are also important for poverty measurement. *Material deprivation* is often used in the European literature to refer to the extent to which people can afford those items and activities that are typical in their society. Studies of the size and features of material deprivation are typically undertaken for individual countries and in a regional (i.e., European) context but can also be extended (with a number of caveats) to a broader range of European and non-European countries. An analysis of this type is undertaken in *Growing Unequal?*, highlighting large differences in the extent of material deprivation across OECD countries. The prevalence of material deprivation is higher in countries characterized by lower national income, suggesting that relative income poverty rates are a poor proxy for hardship in countries with a relatively low, but equally distributed, standard of living.

Other general patterns in material deprivation also emerge. Within countries, the likelihood of experiencing deprivation declines monotonically as income rises. It also declines with age, in contrast to the U-shaped relation between relative-income poverty and age found in most countries, suggesting that older people with low relative income are not necessarily "poor" in the sense of experiencing material hardship. Results also suggest that, although there is some overlap between low income and deprivation, a large share of income-poor people are not materially deprived and that, conversely, a large share of those materially deprived are not income-poor.

Information on these nonincome measures of economic well-being is important for social policies. This is most evident when considering ways of improving the targeting of social programs to reach those with greater needs. Income may be a poor proxy of economic needs. Moreover, equity concerns may relate to a range of inequalities (e.g., in education and health) that have not been addressed in the OECD report. Indirectly, the nonincome measures considered in this report also point to the importance of looking at factors that go beyond the earnings capacity of people to other constituents of an acceptable standard of living. More comprehensive information on asset holdings would also allow assessing the impact of asset tests embodied in social programs on the behavior of social assistance clients. These are important issues for future research.

Measuring the Redistributive Effects of Welfare States

A standard approach to account for the redistributive effect of the welfare state is to compare the income distribution before and after transfers (mostly public cash transfers) and taxes (mostly income taxes and workers social security contributions). Most of the comparative studies based on LIS, as well as earlier OECD work on this issue relied on this standard approach. However, as the situation that would prevail in the absence of redistribution cannot be directly observed, the *counterfactual* situation used in this pre/post approach is problematic in three respects. First, taxes and transfers redistribute both vertically (between individuals) as well as horizontally (between generations). This is important insofar as the social protection systems of various countries put more emphasis on one or the other of these dimensions. Social insurance–based systems, for instance, focus primarily on horizontal redistribution.[23] Second, welfare state policies affect both the pre- and posttax/transfer distribution, not only the latter: active labor market programs, for instance, will have an effect on the earnings distribution, to the extent that they help individuals with low earnings potential to move into jobs. Third, the standard approach assumes away behavioral changes, notably labor supply responses to taxes and transfers. These responses will vary between population and income groups. Bergh (2005) summarizes the various biases embedded in the standard pre/post approach as "the counterfactual problem of welfare state research."

Growing Unequal? calculates two measures of the effect of income taxes and cash benefits in reducing income inequality. These are shown in Figure 2.8:

- In the first approach (shown as diamonds), inequality in the distribution of market income is computed by ranking people by their level of market income. This closely corresponds to the standard approach used by most comparative studies. With this measure, on average, across the 24 countries covered, the tax and transfer systems lower income inequality by approximately one-third (i.e., around 15 percentage points), with declines ranging from around 45 percent in Denmark, Sweden, and Belgium to less than 8 percent in Korea.
- In the second approach (shown as bars), the Gini coefficient for market income is based on people ranked by their disposable income; in other words, individuals are ranked by where they end up after redistribution, rather than where they were placed before redistribution. With this second measure, the reduction of inequality achieved by taxes and transfers is a little more than one-fourth (i.e., around 11 percentage points), with declines ranging from around 40 percent in Sweden and Denmark to 5 percent in Korea.

The difference between the two measures of redistribution across countries can be seen as a result of the reranking of some households as a consequence of welfare state programs. In particular, in countries with generous public pensions, the standard approach implies that middle-class individuals are plunged into market-income poverty on retirement, simply because it is the government, rather than the market, that provides their pensions: Generous earnings-related public pensions are then measured as being very effective at reducing inequality, in part because they restore middle-income retirees to their preretirement ranking. A comparison between the

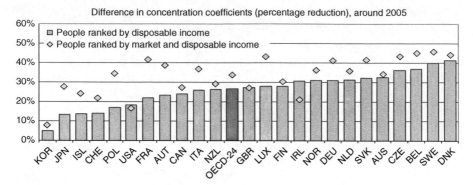

Figure 2.8 Differences in Inequality before and after Taxes and Transfers in OECD Countries.
NOTE: Countries are ranked, from left to right, in increasing order of the percentage reduction in the concentration coefficient achieved by household taxes and public cash transfers, based on people ranked by their household disposable income. Bars are computed based on grouped data for average market and disposable income, by deciles of people ranked by their household disposable income. Diamonds are computed based on individual data, with people ranked by market income (for the Gini coefficient of market income) and ranked by disposable income (for the Gini coefficient of disposable income). SOURCE: OECD (2008).

two alternative measures suggests that, in some OECD countries, a significant part of the redistribution measured by the standard approach reflects such a reranking of people. In particular, the countries where the reranking effect is most significant are precisely those where public pensions account for more than 90 percent of the total disposable income of the retirement-age population—Austria, Belgium, France, Italy, Luxembourg, and Sweden. In contrast, reranking is lower in Korea, the United States, Canada, Finland, the United Kingdom, Ireland, and Australia, where public pensions are 50 percent or less of the disposable income of the retired.

The use of two different benchmarks for the counterfactual distribution gives some important insights. Nonetheless, the problem of taking into account behavioral changes in a comparative assessment of redistribution remains an important issue for future research on income distribution and social policies.[24]

Conclusive Summary

This chapter has described and discussed the strengths and limits of the approach used by the OECD to measure and compare household income distribution across countries. The objective of the OECD work in this area has been to anchor inequality and poverty concerns in the policy agenda of member countries. The monitoring of distributive and antipoverty goals and policies requires adequate indicators and a statistical infrastructure: We believe that the efforts undertaken so far have built the basis for such infrastructure. Though the scope of "measurement errors" surely exists, this is not unique of income distribution analysis. Further, we believe that comparative work along the lines pursued by the OECD and other international organizations is a powerful tool to achieve greater convergence in statistical practices.

For approximately 15 years now, the OECD has conducted a regular data collection (at around 5-year intervals) through a network of national consultants who provide standard tabulations based on common definitions and methodological approaches. In that frame, a series of methodological choices have been made to ensure the highest possible degree of comparability. Some of their features are:

- Using income rather than consumption as a yardstick, with the benchmark concept defined as annual cash disposable income;
- Counting individuals rather than households or families;
- Accounting for economies of scale by applying a square root equivalence scale;
- Focusing on relative rather than on absolute poverty;
- Collecting static rather than dynamic measures.

Whereas several of these choices are clearly linked to issues of data availability and coverage—the prime aim being to describe comparable trends—other choices are rooted in conceptual and theoretical considerations. There remain, however, four types of limitations in the current OECD reporting system on income distribution:

1. Limits linked to the OECD data collection itself: The low frequency of data collection, the long time lags for collecting and processing, as well as the fact that tabulations on specific aspects can only be undertaken by the data providers themselves are examples of these limits.
2. Limits embedded in the household surveys underlying the OECD questionnaire data collection: These include breaks in series and underreporting of particular income components.
3. Limits in the monetary income concept: This concept disregards the sometimes growing importance of items such as owner-occupied housing and life insurance claims, as well as publicly provided services or consumption taxes.
4. Conceptual limitations: These are the accurate measurement of government redistribution, as well as the correct treatment of extended monetary and nonmonetary measures of economic resources. The question arises whether and to what extent these additional factors should be integrated in the OECD periodic data collection.

Finally, the scope of this work has for a long time been limited to constructing comparable indicators across the most developed industrialized countries. With the ongoing OECD enlargement process, enhanced cooperation with a number of large but significantly less-developed countries will require adaptation and extension of the OECD set of indicators on household income distribution.

Notes

1. The OECD, which traces its roots to the Marshall Plan, was founded in 1961 and, at the time of writing, groups 30 countries (today, 34 countries) committed to democratic government and the market economy (for a list of countries, see Table 2.3). It provides a forum where governments can compare and

exchange policy experiences, identify good practices and promote decisions and recommendations. Its mission is to work for a "stronger, cleaner and fairer" world economy (www.oecd.org).

2. These differences ranged from two-thirds in the United States to nine-tenths in a number of European countries. See Förster and Mira d'Ercole (2005), which is based on surveys undertaken in 1999 under the aegis of the International Social Science Programme. More recent data for individual countries suggest, if anything, that these sentiments have increased further in the 2000s, both in the boom years that preceded the "bubble" and in those that followed its bust.

3. For instance, the choice of the statistical sources to use for the OECD income distribution questionnaire is made in consultation with national authorities and consultants. A key criterion for that choice is that of temporal consistency between years.

4. Before changing to income in the mid-1990s, the European Union relied on consumption as a yardstick for poverty measurement (namely 50 percent of the mean equivalent household expenditure), arguing that "household expenditure is a more reliable indicator for permanent income" (Eurostat 1990).

5. The Canberra Group on Household Income Statistics (1996–2000) was established to enhance the quality of household income statistics by developing relevant standards on conceptual and practical issues. To improve international comparability, the group developed and recommended a set of international guidelines. These guidelines led, in 2003, to the adoption of a resolution concerning household income and expenditure statistics by the 17th International Conference of Labour Statisticians.

6. Some evidence exists. For example, Gibson, Huang, and Rozelle (2001) analyze 1992 microdata for two urban areas in Hebei and Sichuan, in China, to demonstrate that various measures of income inequality are higher (by 17 percent for the percentile ratio, and by 23 percent for the Gini coefficient) when relying on a measure for monthly, rather than annual, income.

7. Focusing on individuals rather than households has also been based on the argument according to which each individual in society should be treated as "equal citizen" in the distribution (Jarvis and Micklewright 1995). It also has been included in recommendation 9 in Atkinson et al. (2002) with the argument that "individuals are at the heart of our concern."

8. For a discussion of intrahousehold and intrafamily inequality and possible effects on poverty and distribution estimates, see for example Haddad and Kanbur (1990), Jenkins (1991), Sutherland (1997) or Orsini and Spadaro (2005).

9. As a matter of fact, an early OECD study included income comparisons on the basis of a scale very close to the OECD-modified scale (OECD 1976).

10. This means an equivalence elasticity of 0.5. In its initial methodological paper, OECD proposed and applied a similar but somewhat steeper equivalence scale with an elasticity of 0.55, labeled the "policy-based scale," as it was derived as the median value of elasticities inherent in social assistance programs of 22 OECD countries (Förster1994b).

11. This relates to the fact that both small households (e.g., single elderly) and large households (e.g., families with many children) tend to have above average poverty risks.

12. The (absolute) poverty line used in the United States is closer to 40 percent of median income, whereas a threshold of 60 percent of median income is used as

a benchmark for the at-risk-of-poverty rate at the EU level. Eurostat had previously used 50 percent of the average consumption as a poverty benchmark. It should be noted that poverty rates based on these latter two benchmarks are very similar. Therefore, one of the reasons to adopt the 60 percent–median benchmark was to ensure a certain comparability of published poverty estimates in EU countries over time. Another reason was to avoid the poverty estimates to be sensitive to few very low incomes.

13. The EU set of social inclusion indicators includes a similar measure, namely the at-risk-of-poverty rate "anchored" in year $t - 3$ and uprated by inflation over the following three years.

14. Annual time series of "commonly used" measures of income inequality in nine OECD countries—shown in Atkinson (2002)—display relatively minor variations around the trend (with the exception of Italy).

15. The Gini coefficient is a common measure of equality and ranges from 0 in the case of *perfect equality* (each share of the population gets the same share of income) to 100 in the case of *perfect inequality* (all income goes to the share of the population with the highest income).

16. This refers to five alternative inequality indicators: the mean log deviation, the squared coefficient of variation, the ratio between the upper limit of the ninth income decile and the upper limit of the first decile (P90/P10), the ratio between median income and the upper limit of the first decile (P50/P10), and the ratio between the share in total income of the top quintile and that of the bottom quintile (S80/S20, see *Growing Unequal?*, Annex 1.A2).

17. Income poverty rates for additional thresholds—40 percent and 60 percent of median income—are shown in Chapter 5 (Figure 5.1) of *Growing Unequal?*.

18. When total household income rises, inequality can increase, despite real income growth for everyone, as long as the dispersion in growth rates across the distribution rises over time.

19. Conversely, there is little evidence of strong links between changes in the relative income of various groups and changes in their population size, suggesting that shifts in the relative income of various groups have been driven more by changes in access to jobs and support from the welfare system than by demographic factors per se.

20. For results of a simple decomposition of changes in the poverty head counts over the past decade, based on shift-share analysis, see Tables 5.4 and 5.5 of *Growing Unequal?*.

21. The notion of quasi-cash income includes items such as Food Stamps.

22. The SNA already foresees a concept of "adjusted" household disposable income, which includes the value of those publicly provided public services that benefit individual users.

23. Ståhlberg (2007) shows that the horizontal dimension of redistribution makes up about one-half of all redistribution in Australia but some 80 percent in Sweden.

24. Bergh (2005) uses theoretical simulations based on artificially generated data to show that the behavioral feedback induced by taxes and transfers will increase pre-redistribution inequality when taxes are proportional and benefits are flat-rate, whereas it will decrease pre-redistribution inequality when taxes are progressive and benefits are positively income-related. He concludes that the

standard approach is "biased towards exaggerating the redistributive effect of flat-rate benefits and underestimating the redistributive effect of systems with progressive taxes and positively income-related benefits." Esping-Andersen and Myles (2009) propose to rely on partial empirical simulation models of the EUROMOD type to develop a more comprehensive methodology that includes the modeling of behavioral changes.

References

Atkinson, Anthony B. 2002. "Income Inequality in OECD Countries: Data and Explanations," CESifo Working Paper 881, CESifo, Munich.

Atkinson, Anthony B., and Andrea Brandolini. 2001. "Promise and Pitfalls in the Use of 'Secondary' Data-Sets: Income Inequality in OECD Countries," Temi di discussion del Servizio Studi 379, Banca d'Italia, Rome.

Atkinson, Anothony B., Bea Cantillon, Eric Marlier, and Brian Nolan. 2002. *Social Indicators—The EU and Social Inclusion*. Oxford: Oxford University Press.

Atkinson, Anthony B., Lee Rainwater, and Timothy M. Smeeding. 1995. *Income Distribution in OECD Countries*. OECD Social Policy Studies 18. Paris: Organization for Economic Co-operation and Development.

Bergh, Andreas 2005. "On the Counterfactual Problem of Welfare State Research: How Can We Measure Redistribution?" *European Sociological Review* 21: 345–357.

Boarini, Romina, Asa Johansson, and Marco Mira d'Ercole. 2006. "Alternative Measures of Well-Being." Social, Employment and Migration Working Papers 33. Organization for Economic Co-operation and Development, Paris. http://dx.doi.org/10.1787/713222332167.

Burniaux, Jean Marc, Thai Thanh Dang, Douglas Fore, Michael F. Förster, Marco Mira d'Ercole, and Howard Oxley. 1998. "Income Distribution and Poverty in Selected OECD Countries." OECD Economics Department Working Paper 189, Organization for Economic Co-operation and Development, Paris. http://www.oecd.org/dataoecd/34/37/1864447.pdf.

Canberra Group. 2001. *Expert Group on Household Income Statistics: Final Report and Recommendations*. Ottawa: Statistics Canada. http://www.lisproject.org/links/canberra/finalreport.pdf.

Esping-Andersen, Gøsta, and John Myles. 2009. "Economic Inequality and the Welfare State." In: *Oxford Handbook of Income Distribution*. Edited by Weimer Salverda, Brian Nolan, and Timothy Smeeding, 639–664. Oxford: Oxford University Press.

Eurostat. 1990. *Poverty in Figures: Europe in the Early 1980s*. Study carried out by the Institute of Social Studies Advisory Service (ISSAS). Luxembourg: Eurostat.

Förster, Michael F. 1994a. "The Effects of Net Transfers on Low Incomes Among Non-Elderly Families." *OECD Economic Studies* 22: 181–221. http://www.oecd.org/dataoecd/47/56/33941184.pdf.

———. 1994b. "Measurement of Low Incomes and Poverty in a Perspective of International Comparisons." OECD Labour Market and Social Policy Occasional Paper 14, Organization for Economic Co-operation and Development, Paris. http://dx.doi.org/10.1787/112854878327.

Förster, Michael F., and Marco Mira d'Ercole. 2005. "Income Distribution and Poverty in OECD Countries in the Second Half of the 1990s." OECD Social, Employment and Migration Working Paper 22, Organization for Economic Co-operation and Development, Paris. http://dx.doi.org/10.1787/882106484586.

Förster, Michael F., and Mark Pearson. 2002. "Income Distribution and Poverty in the OECD Area: Trends and Driving Forces." OECD Economic Studies 34: 7–39. http://www.oecd.org/dataoecd/16/33/2968109.pdf.

Förster, Michael F., and Michele Pellizzari. 2000. "Trends and Driving Factors in Income Inequality and Poverty in the OECD Area." OECD Labour Market and Social Policy Occasional Paper 42, Organization for Economic Co-operation and Development, Paris. http://dx.doi.org/10.1787/488747757407.

Franz, Alfred, John Walton, and Deo Ramprakash. 1998. "Preliminary Report on the Distribution of Income, Consumption and Accumulation of Households (DICAH)." Preliminary report, Eurostat, Luxembourg.

Gibson, John, Jikun Huang, and Scott Rozelle. 2001. "Why Is Inequality So Low in China Compared to Other Countries? The Effect of Household Survey Methods." Economics Letters 71: 329–333.

Gottschalk, Peter, and Sheldon Danziger. 2005. "Inequality of Wage Rates, Earnings and Family Income in the United States, 1975–2005." Review of Income and Wealth 51 (2): 231–254.

Haddad, Lawrence, and Ravi Kanbur. 1990. "How Serious is the Neglect of Intra Household Inequality?" The Economic Journal 100: 866–881.

Hagenaars, Aldi, Klaas de Vos, and Ashgar M. Zaidi. 1994. Poverty Statistics in the Late 1980s: Research Based on Micro-Data. Luxembourg: Office for Official Publications of the European Communities.

Jarvis, Sarah, and John Micklewright. 1995. "The Targeting of Family Allowances in Hungary." In Public Spending and the Poor: Theory and Evidence. Edited by D. van de Walle and K. Nead, 294–320. Baltimore, MD: The Johns Hopkins University Press.

Jenkins, Stephen P. 1991. "Poverty Measurement and the Within-Household Distribution: Agenda for Action." Journal of Social Policy 20: 457–483.

Karoly, Lynn, and Gary Burtless. 1995. "Demographic Change, Rising Earnings Inequality and the Distribution of Personal Well-Being, 1959–1989." Demography 32: 379–406.

OECD. 1976. Public Expenditure on Income Maintenance Programmes. Paris: Organization for Economic Co-operation and Development.

———. 1982. The OECD List of Social Indicators. Paris: Organization for Economic Co-operation and Development.

———. 2008. Growing Unequal? Income Distribution and Poverty in OECD Countries. Paris: Organization for Economic Co-operation and Development.

Orsini, Kristian, and Amedeo Spadaro. 2005. "Sharing Resources within the Household: a Multi-Country Microsimulation Analysis of the Determinants of Intrahousehold 'Strategic Weight' Differentials and Their Distributional Outcomes." EUROMOD Working Paper EM3/05, EUROMOD, Essex.

Oxley, Howard, Jean Marc Burniaux, Thai Thanh Dang, and Marco Mira d'Ercole. 1999. "Income Distribution and Poverty in 13 OECD Countries." OECD Economic Studies 29: 55–94.

Paugman, Serge, and Marion Selz. 2005. "La perception de la pauvreté en Europe depuis le milieu des années 1970." Economie et Statistique 383: 384–385.

Sawyer, Malcolm. 1976. *Income Distribution in OECD Countries.* OECD Economic Outlook: Occasional Studies. Paris: Organization for Economic Co-operation and Development.

Smeeding, Timothy, Michael O'Higgins, and Lee Rainwater, eds. 1990. *Poverty, Inequality, and Income Distribution in Comparative Perspective.* Hemel Hempstead, UK: Harvester Wheatsheaf.

Ståhlberg, Ann-Chalotte. 2007. "Redistribution across the Life Course in Social Protection Systems." In *Modernising Social Policy for the New Life Course.* 201–222. Paris: Organization for Economic Co-operation and Development.

Sutherland, Holly. 1997. "Women, Men and the Redistribution of Income." *Fiscal Studies* 18: 1–22.

Income Indicators for the EU's Social Inclusion Strategy

ISABELLE MAQUET AND DAVID STANTON ■

This chapter concentrates on the income indicators used in the social inclusion strategy used by the European Union (EU), considers the strength of the way in which we measure poverty and make use of the portfolio of agreed indicators, and looks at other supplementary ways of understanding the differences in the number of people living on low incomes.

THE OPEN METHOD OF COORDINATION

The fight against poverty is a long-term commitment of the member states of the EU and an essential element of the union's 10-year strategic goal of sustained economic growth, more and better jobs, and greater social cohesion. When the Lisbon strategy was launched in 2000, European governments had very different views on how to conduct the structural reforms needed to reach this goal. Heads of states, therefore, opted for a voluntary, flexible, and decentralized form of cooperation—the so-called open method of coordination (OMC). Cooperation in the fight against poverty rests on regular reporting, peer pressure, and mutual learning. (See Box 3.1.) It involves:

Agreeing on common objectives;
Agreeing on a set of common indicators;
Preparing national strategic reports;
Evaluating these strategies jointly with the European Commission and the member states; and
Learning from each other through a series of tools supported by the Commission such as peer reviews, study programs, networks, etc.

In the absence of any binding mechanism, a large part of the effectiveness of the method relies on the capacity to analyze thoroughly the situation of member states in an international context. It is also crucial to be able to assess whether the policy priorities and corresponding policy tools they have identified at the national level are appropriate to meet the commonly agreed upon objectives.

Box 3.1

THE OPEN METHOD OF COORDINATION IN THE FIELD OF SOCIAL PROTECTION AND SOCIAL INCLUSION

In the context of the OMC, social policy remains under the full competency of member states. To coordinate their action, member states agree on common goals (e.g., making a decisive impact on the eradication of poverty)[a] and on common indicators used to monitor progress and compare best practices. Member states translate the common goals into their own strategic objectives and regularly report on the policies they put in place to reach these objectives. The National Strategy Reports are analyzed and assessed at the EU level, and common policy conclusions drawn from this analysis are jointly adopted by the European Commission and member states in the yearly Joint Report on Social Protection and Social Inclusion. The EU runs an action program to support mutual learning through a variety of instruments: financing of EU stakeholder networks, peer reviews on specific policy issues, independent experts network, round table, EU meeting of people experiencing poverty, transnational and awareness raising projects, studies, data collection, etc.

Action at the EU level has increased political awareness of poverty and exclusion and placed the fight against poverty higher on national political agendas. It encouraged member states to critically examine their policies. It highlighted how countries perform well in certain areas, spurring on other member states to perform better. It also created a better basis for policy making by involving a range of actors such as nongovernmental organizations, social partners, local and regional authorities, and those working with people in poverty. The method also allowed for creating a clear consensus about a number of common key priorities in the fight against poverty and social exclusion: child poverty, active inclusion, decent housing for all, etc.

[a]A full description of the agreed common objectives in European Commission (2005).

This analytical capacity rests on the commonly agreed upon indicators that member states have identified through a collective and consensual process to reflect their situation vis-à-vis their common objectives. To ensure the transparency and legitimacy of the assessment, EU's analytical capacity also needs a common and agreed upon framework of how to use and interpret the common EU indicators.

The development of indicators and of the analytical framework is carried out by the Indicators Sub-Group (ISG) of the Social Protection Committee. It was set up in 2001, and it gathers representatives of the 27 national governments that are experts in monitoring policies in the field of social inclusion.[1] The work of the group is supported by the European Commission's policy analysts (Directorate General for Employment, Social Affairs, and Inclusion) and statisticians (Eurostat). Finally, it draws on academic expertise, notably on the 2001 and 2007 reports on indicators for the EU social inclusion strategy by Atkinson et al. (2001, 2007). The ISG is also a key stakeholder in the development of EU-level statistical capacity and especially in the development of the EU's Survey on Income and Living Conditions (SILC) (see next section).

Indicators are developed with the help of the ISG's expertise and following strict quality criteria.[2] They are also subject to empirical validation using available data and then consensually adopted by all 27 member states. The political endorsement of the indicators by the Social Protection Committee or by the 2001 Laeken Council of Ministers constitutes the specific strength of the EU portfolio of social indicators.

This chapter does not cover all the indicators used but concentrates on the income indicators only.[3] Before discussing the income indicators and how they have worked in the OMC, we need to say something about the EU's Survey of Income and Living Conditions (also SILC).

EU-SILC

EU-SILC is a household-based survey organized under a framework regulation of the European Parliament and the European Council (number 1177/2003). It is the reference source at EU level for statistics on income and living conditions and for common indicators for social inclusion in particular.

EU-SILC was launched in 2003 on the basis of a "gentleman's agreement" in six member states (Belgium, Denmark, Greece, Ireland, Luxembourg, and Austria), as well as in Norway. Since 2005, EU-SILC has covered the 25 EU member states that were members at that time plus Norway and Iceland. Bulgaria, Romania, Switzerland, and Turkey launched EU-SILC in 2007.

A key objective of EU-SILC is to deliver robust and comparable data on total disposable household income. Income components were defined to follow as closely as possible the international recommendations of the Canberra Group report (2001). The EU-SILC definition of *total household disposable income* excludes imputed rent as well as nonmonetary income components and, in particular, the value of goods produced for own consumption and noncash employee income except for company cars.

The income reference period is a fixed 12-month period (such as the previous calendar or tax year) for all countries except the United Kingdom for which the income reference period is the current year and Ireland for which the survey is continuous and income is collected for the last 12 months.

In the so-called register countries (Denmark, Norway, Iceland, Netherlands, Sweden, Finland, and Slovenia), most income components and some demographic information are obtained through administrative data whereas other personal information is collected through interviews. In all other countries, the full information is obtained through surveys.

EU-SILC provides two types of annual data: cross-sectional (pertaining to a given time or a certain time period) and longitudinal (pertaining to individual-level changes over time usually over a four-year period). For most countries, the 2007 survey this refers to income received in 2006. The 2009 survey was the first year that there was 4 years of panel data for the 15 countries that implemented SILC in 2004 and 3 years of panels for the others. At that time, the achieved sample size equaled 200,000 households (around 440,000 adults) for the EU as a whole (including Norway and Iceland). In all countries, standard errors have been calculated and the quality measured by 95 percent confidence intervals for the key indicator—the at-risk-poverty rate—is impressive, at around 1 percentage point.

A full description of the progress made with EU-SILC can be found in a report to the European Parliament.[4] There are areas that need some attention: Two countries have two income surveys: EU-SILC and a separate one that is used for policy analysis and policy monitoring and evaluation.

An important determinant of future improvements will be the extent to which the data gets used not only in the OMC, but also in the research and academic world. In this context, it is worth noting the value of forums or research networks involving both data producers and data users (e.g., the Eurostat-funded Network for the Analysis of EU-SILC). The work program covers eight broad areas. The areas that are most relevant to income indicators are methodological issues, income distribution, and poverty and deprivation.

The quality of the data will continue to improve. Nevertheless, it is important to remember what the survey cannot do even if all efforts at improving the data exceed expectations. First, and perhaps most important for monitoring social exclusion, the data by definition does not cover people not living in households—those in institutions and those who are homeless and outside the sampling frame for a household survey. These people are the most socially excluded but no household-based survey can monitor the welfare of this group. Second, there is a need to further improve the timeliness of the data as explained before. Finally, in most of the member states, the income data refers to year $t - 1$ and the household information to year t. If households remain unchanged, there is no problem, but where households are newly formed, the income collected is relevant to the household in the previous year not the household in the survey year.

INCOME INDICATORS IN THE OMC

In 1975, the European Council defined the *poor* as "those individuals or households whose resources are so low as to exclude them from the minimum acceptable way of life in the country where they live." This definition is rooted in academic work that aimed at defining poverty in developed countries. In these countries, the aim of governments goes beyond ensuring minimum subsistence levels for their citizens: It is also to ensure that all benefit from the general level of prosperity of the society.

This concept differs from those referring to "deprivation of basic human needs" (United Nations 1995) that are more appropriate to measure poverty in developing countries, or to an "accumulation of disadvantages that is beyond reach of macroeconomic policies" (Dahrendorf 1990), or to "permanent dependence on the State" (Engbersen 1991).

According to the EU concept, poverty is relative, graduated, and multidimensional with an important temporal dimension. This definition of poverty is also responsive to a range of macroeconomic policies such as redistribution and employment policies.

The current portfolio of agreed indicators to monitor the EU social inclusion strategy allows covering these key characteristics to a large extent. With reference to this politically agreed definition of *poverty,* the "at-risk-of-poverty rate" was adopted as the headline poverty indicator. It measures relative poverty at a point in time in a country. It is the share of persons aged 0+ years with an equivalized disposable income[5] below 60 percent of the national equivalized median income. The key breakdowns are the indicator for households with children and the indicator for households 65+ years. The data from 2007 are summarized in Figure 3.1.

This "overarching" indicator should be presented and used together with the other income indicators related to social inclusion that help with capturing the multiple facets of income poverty.

THE AT-RISK-OF-POVERTY RATE IS RELATED TO THE OVERALL LEVEL OF INCOME INEQUALITIES

An important element of context to analyze the at-risk-of-poverty rate is the overall level of inequality of the income distribution in the country. Two indicators relate to this: the Gini coefficient and the ratio of the shares of income enjoyed by the top and bottom quintiles (S80/S20). On average in the EU, the total income received by the 20 percent richest is five times higher than the total income received by the 20 percent poorest. However, the ratio varies greatly across EU member states, from less than 4 to more than 6 in four countries. Although most of the wealthy member states are among those with the lowest levels of inequalities, countries with lower gross domestic product (GDP) per capita can be found among both the most equal and unequal income distributions (Figure 3.2).

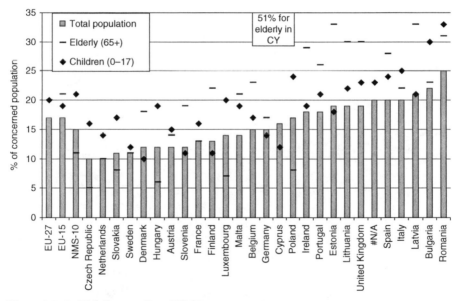

Figure 3.1 At-Risk Poverty Rate EU-27.
EU-27: weighted average for the 27 member states of the European Union. EU-15: weighted average for the 15 old members (members before 2004: Belgium, Denmark, Germany, Ireland, Greece, Spain, France, Italy, Luxembourg, the Netherlands, Austria, Portugal, Finland, Sweden, the United Kingdom). NMW-10: weighted average for the 10 new members (joined the EU in 2004: Czech Republic, Estonia, Cyprus, Latvia, Lithuania, Hungary, Malta, Poland, Slovakia, Slovenia).
SOURCE: EU-SILC (2007); income data for 2006, except for the United Kingdom (income year 2007) and Ireland (moving income reference period 2006–2007).

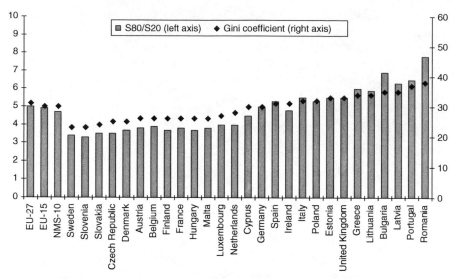

Figure 3.2 Income Inequalities: Gini Coefficients and Income Quintile Share Ratio, EU-27. SOURCE: EU-SILC (2007); income data for 2006, except for the United Kingdom (income year 2007) and Ireland (moving income reference period 2006–2007).

Poverty is Graduated

The at-risk-of-poverty rate needs to be interpreted together with an indicator that helps us understand the shape of the income distribution around the 60 percent threshold, and this is why in the "strand" indicators, there is the risk of poverty rates using 40 percent, 50 percent, and 70 percent of the median income. Figure 3.3 shows these different indicators of the depth of the poverty rate for the EU-27.

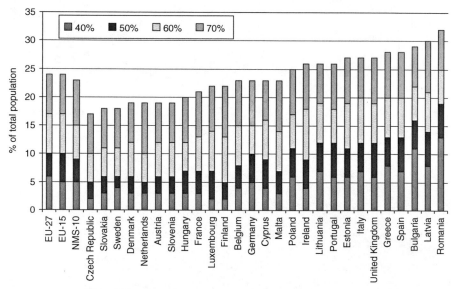

Figure 3.3 At-Risk Poverty Rate EU-27 at Different Thresholds. SOURCE: EU-SILC (2007); income data for 2006, except for the United Kingdom (income year 2007) and Ireland (moving income reference period 2006–2007).

In the EU as a whole, 5 percent of the total population (or one-third of the poor population) live on an income below 40 percent of the median income in their country, 10 percent live below 50 percent, and 24 percent live below 70 percent. This shows that nearly two-thirds of the population at risk of poverty would need a significant increase of at least 20 percent in their equivalized income to lift them out of poverty, and for one-third, an increase of at least 50 percent would be necessary. Countries with similar at-risk-of-poverty rates calculated in relation to the 60 percent thresholds show significant variations in the number of people who are poor when more severe criteria (lower thresholds) are used. Among the countries with poverty rates below 15 percent, the Czech Republic, the Netherlands, Denmark, and Austria have the lowest shares of very poor people. Ireland has the lowest share of very poor people among the countries with higher poverty rates.

The depth of poverty is measured by the gap between the 60 percent threshold and the median income of the poor. In 2007, in the EU, the median income of people at risk of poverty was 22 percent lower than the poverty threshold. As illustrated in Figure 3.4, poverty tends to be more severe in countries where the shares of people at risk of poverty are highest (countries in the top right-hand corner of the graph).

Poverty has an Important Temporal Dimension

Finally, these income indicators need to be augmented to reflect a key aspect of poverty—duration. EU-SILC does have the capacity to follow a panel over four years and this allows us to have a measure of duration—the proportion of people living below the poverty threshold in any three of four years (the data was not available at the time the chapter was written). The persistent risk of poverty measures the percentage of total population who are *poor* (with an income under the poverty threshold) and were

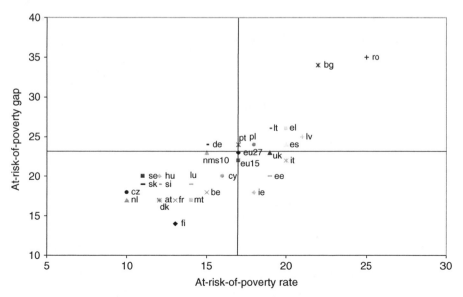

Figure 3.4 At-Risk-of-Poverty Gap against At-Risk-of-Poverty Rate.
SOURCE: EU-SILC (2007); income data for 2006, except for the United Kingdom (income year 2007) and Ireland (moving income reference period 2006–2007).

also poor at least two out of the previous three years. The value of this will depend on an evaluation of the data quality. The panel sample in some countries will be small and the attrition rate is usually high among low-income groups and is thus likely to be biased against low-income households, especially those living in precarious accommodation. This indicator became available in 2010 on the basis of EU-SILC. According to the European Community Household Panel, the rate was 9 percent for the EU-15 in 2001 while the at-risk-of-poverty rate was 15 percent, meaning that nearly two-thirds of the people considered at risk of poverty were durably living on low income.

Another indicator takes account of the evolution of the living standards of the population defined as *relatively poor*. This is often thought of as the at-risk-of-poverty rate anchored at a point in time. This asks how many people in time t are below the at risk poverty threshold calculated for $t - n$. If the at-risk-of-poverty rate does not improve against the contemporary poverty threshold, it is still important to ask if poor households are enjoying increases in real income that raise their command over resources compared with the real incomes received in previous years. The *anchored poverty rate* is defined as the risk of poverty associated with a 60 percent threshold fixed at a point in time and adjusted for inflation.

In Figure 3.5, the indicator is put in relation to the average GDP growth prevailing in each country from 2004 to 2006 relative to its rate of GDP growth over that period. This illustrates that in all countries (except Luxembourg) with high GDP growth (>5 percent per year) over the three-year period, the anchored poverty rate was dramatically reduced. In these countries, the benefits of growth also reached those

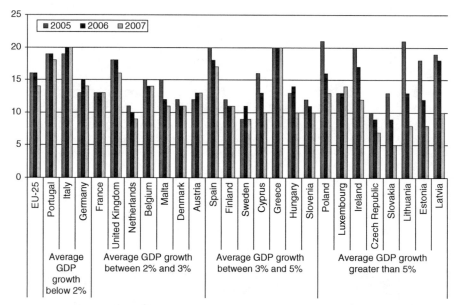

Figure 3.5 At-risk-of-Poverty Rate Anchored at a Point in Time (2005) by Average GDP Growth, 2005–2007.
SOURCE: European Commission AMECO database (GDP) and EU-SILC (2007, 2006, and 2005); income data for 2006, 2005, 2004, except for the United Kingdom (income years 2007, 2006, 2005) and Ireland (moving income reference period 2006–2007, 2005–2006, 2004–2005); Bulgaria and Romania missing.

that were at the bottom of the income distribution in the base year by raising their living standards in comparison to previous years. However, because high growth tends to raise median income in a country, the relative position of the poor does not necessarily improve. In this group of countries, the number of people living under the current poverty threshold only decreased in Poland (from 21 percent to 17 percent), Slovakia (from 13 percent to 11 percent), and Lithuania (from 21 percent to 19 percent). In all other high-growth countries, relative poverty remained stable. The impact of growth on real incomes of the people at risk of poverty is less clear for the second group of countries with average GDP growth rates between 3 and 5 percent. In Greece, Finland, and Sweden, for instance, the anchored poverty rate remain virtually unchanged despite a fair level of GDP growth.

The Main Determinants of the Risk of Poverty

Stark comparisons in the data raise questions worth answering. Why can the Nordic countries with high household incomes achieve low at-risk poverty rates? Why does the United Kingdom have one of the highest at-risk poverty rates for households with children when its household income is also high? What drives the comparatively favorable position of the elderly in Poland, Slovakia, and Hungary?

Because this indicator in isolation has raised important questions, it is clear that other indicators related to the overall picture are needed. The importance of employment led to the addition of two employment-related indicators: the proportion of people living in jobless households (shown in Figure 3.6) and the at-risk poverty rate (shown in Figure 3.7) for households with at least one person who worked. By comparing Figure 3.7 to Figure 3.6, it can be seen that households in which no one works are at much higher risk of poverty; however, it is also usually true

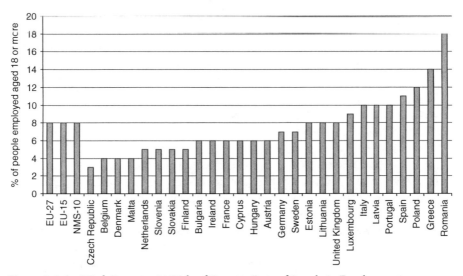

Figure 3.6 In-Work Poverty: At-Risk-of-Poverty Rate of People in Employment.
SOURCE: EU-SILC (2007); income data for 2006, except for the United Kingdom (income year 2007) and Ireland (moving income reference period 2006–2007).

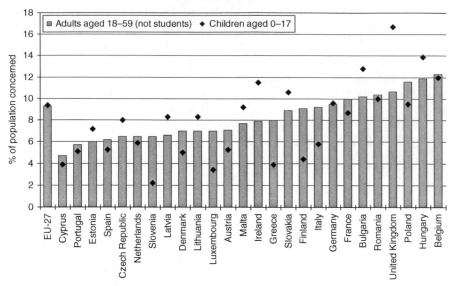

Figure 3.7 People Living in Jobless Households, 2007.
SOURCE: Eurostat Labour Force Survey, spring results.

that the raw number of those at risk of poverty in work is greater. The indicator of jobless households is not strictly an income indicator, but it is a complement to the working-poor indicator.

Another determinant of the cross-country differences in poverty risk is the extent to which welfare systems assist in reducing the risk of poverty faced by households before the receipt of social transfers. A context indicator helps with measuring this impact: the at-risk-of-poverty rate before social transfers (excluding pensions).[6] In the absence of all social transfers, the average poverty risk for EU member states would be 26 percent[7] (against 16 percent after receipt of government support). Figure 3.8 shows the percentage drop in the at-risk-of-poverty rate as a result of social transfers. It illustrates the great variation of the impact of social transfers across EU countries and the generally greater impact on families with children.

At-Risk-of-Poverty Rates and the Diversity of Living Standards Across EU Member States

When the indicators were first developed, it was agreed that the poverty threshold used in each member state should be national. Social exclusion is about how you compare yourself with others in the society in which you live. Pragmatically, this also resonated with the acceptance that social policy is a member state responsibility rather than a policy area determined at the EU level. Nevertheless, it was felt that the different at-risk-of-poverty rates needed to be put in context by the use of another indicator: the poverty threshold in each country. The threshold for each member state is shown in Figure 3.9 for an illustrative one-person household. Even if the values are expressed in purchasing power standards to take account of the differences in the cost of living across countries, and if we consider Luxembourg as an

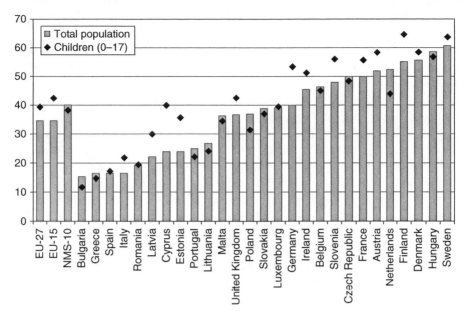

Figure 3.8 Impact of Social Transfers (Excluding Pensions): Reduction in At-Risk-of-Poverty Rate in Percentage of Poverty Rate before Transfers, 2007.
Source: EU-SILC (2007); income data for 2006, except for the United Kingdom (income year 2007) and Ireland (moving income reference period 2006–2007).

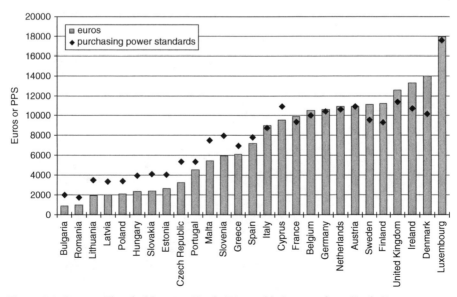

Figure 3.9 Poverty Threshold—2007 Yearly Disposable Income for a Single-Person Household, in Euros and in Purchasing Power Standards.
SOURCE: SILC (2007); income data for 2006, except for the United Kingdom (income year 2007) and Ireland (moving income reference period 2006–2007).

outlier, the value of the poverty threshold in the richest countries is nearly five times higher than it is in the poorest.

This information goes a long way toward addressing concerns of many people that the at-risk-of-poverty indicator was in danger of being discredited. An at-risk poverty rate for Luxembourg that is higher than that in the Czech and Slovak Republics requires information about the level of median household income in each country and, therefore, of the poverty threshold.

Others have also argued for the use of material deprivation indicators to illustrate the same point. In February 2009, the Social Protection Committee adopted an EU indicator of material deprivation. This adoption was the result of a long process. Even in 2001, the Social Protection Committee had already recommended the development of indicators of material deprivation in its Laeken report on social inclusion indicators. It acknowledged the need to supplement the income-based indicators with nonmonetary measures of poverty. Such measures help assess the availability of accumulated resources (e.g., durable goods, housing) that are not captured by current income. If it is based on a common basket of basic deprivation items, it also highlights the disparities in living standards across countries.

This recommendation became even more relevant after the accession of 12 new member states in 2004 and 2007. The new indicator measures the proportion of people whose living conditions are severely affected by a lack of resources. For instance, these people cannot afford to pay their rent, mortgage, or utility bills; keep their home adequately warm; face unexpected expenses; eat meat or proteins regularly; go on holiday; or cannot afford to buy a television, a fridge, a car, or a telephone.[8]

Figure 3.10 illustrates how the material deprivation indicator complements the at-risk-of-poverty rate and its threshold. While the EU average is the same

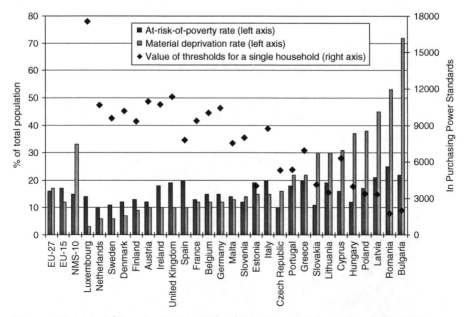

Figure 3.10 Material Deprivation, At-Risk-of-Poverty and Poverty Thresholds, 2007.
SOURCE: EU-SILC (2007); income data for 2006, except for the United Kingdom (income year 2006) and Ireland (moving income reference period 2006–2007).

(16 percent), the ranking of countries is very different and the variability of the material deprivation rate is much higher than, but similar to, the variability of the poverty threshold.

The material deprivation indicator reflects better the "geography" of poverty across the EU. This is because it depends as much on the level of development of the country as on the social policies that are supposed to redistribute the benefits of growth. One important observation that can be drawn from Figure 3.10 is that in countries, such as Sweden and Denmark, with high thresholds for households to be at risk of poverty, rates of material deprivation are low. However, for others with very low income thresholds for being at risk of poverty, such as Romania and Bulgaria, the extent of material deprivation is very high. Because the poverty thresholds are set as a proportion of median income, high-income countries with relatively high living standards tend to have relatively few people who are materially deprived within their populations. However, the at-risk-of-poverty rate relating to the national median income remains the most pertinent indicator to monitor the impact of social policies that are conducted at the national level, such as redistribution and employment policies.

The combined use of the two indicators should allow us to better explain the EU's integrated approach to the fight against poverty that relies on a positive interaction between the growth and jobs strategy and the social inclusion strategy. The material deprivation rate highlights better the disparities in living conditions across Europe and thereby the need for a greater territorial, social, and economic cohesion within the EU. Disparities in the material deprivation rate reflect the large differences that remain between EU countries.

Figure 3.11 shows that over the three-year period from 2005 to 2007,[9] in the 15 old EU member states, both the risk of poverty and the material deprivation rates remained stable. These countries are characterized by a high level of development and a rather moderate growth over the period. On the contrary, in the 10 new member states from Central and Eastern Europe, relative poverty remained stable while material deprivation rates were significantly reduced. This partly reflects the rapid growth that was observed in many of these countries over the period. These are very preliminary trends but they are consistent with the analysis of the anchored poverty rate presented earlier.

ASSESSING THE INCOME INDICATORS IN THE OMC

Main Achievements

The first and most important point is to acknowledge what an achievement it is to have a set of income-based poverty indicators for all 27 EU member states that can be used in the OMC. The indicators are based on a data set that allows comparison across member states and data are also available for Iceland, Switzerland, Norway, and Turkey. The range of indicators gives a rounded assessment of the situation of people on low incomes in the member states. The regular reporting cycle of the OMC has given all member states an opportunity for mutual understanding and learning from the experience of others.

Set in the context of a full analysis of the determinants of differences in poverty rates, a powerfully strong evidence-based policy tool is available to member states in monitoring and evaluating their special concerns in the fight against poverty.

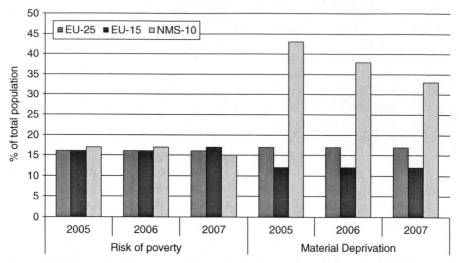

Figure 3.11 Three-Year Evolution of the At-Risk-of-Poverty and Material Deprivation Rates, in the EU, EU-15, and NMS-10, 2005–2007.
EU-15: members before 2004: Belgium, Denmark, Germany, Ireland, Greece, Spain, France, Italy, Luxembourg, the Netherlands, Austria, Portugal, Finland, Sweden, the United Kingdom. NMW-10: members the joined the EU in 2004: Czech Republic, Estonia, Cyprus, Latvia, Lithuania, Hungary, Malta, Poland, Slovakia, Slovenia.
SOURCE EU-SILC (2007); income data for 2006, except for the United Kingdom (income year 2006) and Ireland (moving income reference period 2006–2007); Bulgaria and Romania not included.

At the EU level, the use of an agreed analytical framework relying on common indicators increases the transparency and legitimacy of the diagnosis of the determinants of poverty. This framework provides a useful basis for highlighting not just the relative outcomes of each country, but also for identifying the main causes of poverty in each country. It can help identify in which areas action is most needed and can provide a basis for defining policy priorities.

At the national level, a common analytical framework can help policy makers because it allows for benchmarking the performance of each country against that of countries sharing the same challenges. It also allows for a better appreciation of the true magnitude of those challenges and in some instances to pinpoint emerging trends. Mutual learning—one of the key features of OMC—becomes easier when countries are able to compare their respective strengths and weaknesses on the basis of a common framework.

Issues for Consideration

Some issues need consideration. The first is transparency. The original plan involved a commitment to use the 60-percent median income poverty rate only in the context of all the other related indicators. This commitment to perfection has proven difficult to adhere to in practice. Too often, the result is that the at-risk poverty rate is used on its own, which at times can leave the press and general public confused and misled.

The lack of timeliness of the data has already been mentioned. In the autumn of 2009, a full year after the financial crisis, the then-latest data referred to incomes from 2006. There is probably little scope for improvement in timeliness given that the data has to come from 27 EU member states.

A more technical issue is that household income has to be equivalized and the EU has adopted the Organization for Economic Co-operation and Development (OECD) equivalence scales. Where the pattern of households remains constant or changes slowly over time, the scale does not affect the monitoring of changes in household income–based indicators over time. But the choice of scale will affect cross-sectional comparisons whether they are across countries or across different sections of the population within a country. A particular problem can arise with social security transfers that vary with household type. These benefits have an implied equivalence scale that is not necessarily the same as the OECD scale. For example in the United Kingdom, the income-related benefit, Pension Credit, given to pensioners who do not have a second pension or only a very small one, lifts single households above the poverty threshold but leaves couple households just below. Some sensitivity testing to the impact of the use of the OECD equivalence scale relative to those implied by the structure of payments within individual transfer systems may be sensible.

A key test of the success of the EU approach is whether the income indicators are aligned with overarching objectives. These are:

- The first main objective to which member states are committed under the social inclusion and social protection strategy is the promotion of social cohesion, equality between men and women, and equal opportunities for all through adequate, accessible, financially sustainable, adaptable, and efficient social protection systems and social inclusion systems.
- The second overarching objective is to promote effective, mutual interaction between the Lisbon objectives of greater economic growth, more and better jobs, and greater social cohesion and the EU's sustainable development strategy.

The first objective is the most relevant to the role of the income indicators in OMC. Any EU government's first and main weapon against poverty is the tax and benefit system. Although all governments make transfers in kind, the main engine of redistribution is through the tax and benefit system. There is little direct reference to the social protection system in the battery of income indicators. Total social expenditure net and gross as a percentage of GDP is used as a measure of the resources transferred by governments. We have also started developing, with the OECD, a measure that compares net income of social assistance recipients as a percent of the relevant poverty threshold. Figure 3.12 shows the preliminary results for those countries where it has been possible to calculate the ratio (countries where noncategorical social assistance schemes are in place).

A key problem is the estimates made for special benefits related to social assistance, such as housing benefits. The OECD has used 20 percent of average earnings as a proxy measure for housing benefits that cover all the rent paid by households receiving social assistance. In the United Kingdom, this is too high and gives the wrong impression that most household types on social assistance are on incomes above the

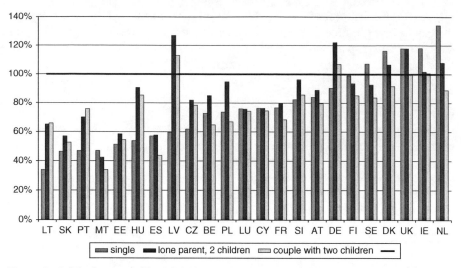

Figure 3.12 Net Income of Social Assistance Recipients, 2006. As a Percentage of the At-Risk-of-Poverty Threshold for Three Jobless Family Types, Including Housing Benefits.
NOTE: Only countries where noncategorical social assistance benefits are in place are considered.
SOURCE: Author's calculation using OECD tax-benefit models, and Eurostat.

poverty threshold. More work is needed as it is important to have a measure of whether safety net benefits are lifting households above the poverty threshold.

The other area where benefit expenditure is used is the calculation of the at-risk-of-poverty rate before and after social transfers (see Figure 3.8). This indicator on its own can only measure the effectiveness of social transfers in combating poverty if household structure is exogenous to the structure and administration of social transfers. It is unlikely that this assumption holds in practice.

Extensive benefit data exist in many EU countries. Social assistance levels are in some sense the democratically determined poverty level; they are meant to be a safety net below which no one falls. The data can be timely and duration is easily and accurately calculated. Data of this type can also be used to assess repeated spells of dependency on social protection benefits. In addition, with modern computing power, 100 percent counts are possible, and this brings the possibility of having social protection data down to very small areas. Household survey data always exclude those not in households but people not in households can receive social security benefits. Measuring the number of people dependent on benefits and whether that is growing is easily understood by the general public who often struggle with at-risk poverty rates.

There have always been objections. First the introduction of a new benefit or a change in eligibility can result in a surge in numbers dependent on the new benefit. Second, decisions to raise the generosity of social assistance can lead to an automatic growth in the number falling below this social assistance–determined poverty rate. But this should not be a problem. If society decides the national poverty level or safety net should be higher, then initially, the numbers falling below it may be higher.

The financial crisis may accelerate the use of benefit data across the EU. The ISG is currently contributing to the Social Protection Committee's monitoring of the social impact of the crisis. We have realized that data on social security benefits are going to be more timely even if there may not be comparable availability across all member states, and we are going to use what data exists to give a more up-to-date picture of the social consequences of the recession across the EU.

LESSONS FOR OTHER OECD COUNTRIES

We have argued that these indicators have been useful within the EU in understanding the way that social policy operates across member states. This raises the question of whether the method could be relevant outside the EU in the rest of the OECD. The OECD's (2008) publication *Growing Unequal? Income Distribution and Poverty in OECD Countries* shows clearly that the EU's approach is part of a well-established analytical tradition for analyzing inequality. The OECD's work will have been harder because outside the EU there is no common database. The more difficult question is whether the EU's experience has special lessons for countries with a strong federal structure to their government. In the EU, social policy is the responsibility of member states, although there are common objectives aimed at encouraging coordination. Where a country has a federal structure with social policy delegated to the federal level, then the EU's experience as described in this chapter is relevant. The framework allows comparisons and analyses of poverty across units of government and uses poverty thresholds that are specific to each unit.

CONCLUSIONS

The adoption and use of income indicators together with the successful launch of a comparable database across the EU-27 and beyond to Turkey, Iceland, Switzerland, and Norway is a major achievement. Although a newly adopted indicator of material deprivation reflects better the geography of poverty across Europe, the at-risk-of-poverty rate relating to the national median income remains the most pertinent indicator to monitor the overall impact of social policies that are conducted at the national level, such as redistribution and employment policies. Investing further in the development of sound analytical frameworks is crucial to ensure that the EU indicators are used in policy making, both at EU and national levels. However, there is a need for better information to monitor the main policy instrument in combating poverty—the social protection system operating in each member state. Benefit data would be easily understood by the public; it would be more timely; and it would allow more accurate measures of duration on minimum incomes. The need to monitor the impact of the financial crisis will probably accelerate the adoption of this source of information.

Notes

1. When the OMC was extended to the field of pensions and health care reforms, indicators experts in these two areas also joined the subgroup.
2. See quality criteria and list of indicators in European Commission (2009b).
3. The latest analysis of the complete list of OMC indicators is available in European Commission (2008c).

4. Report from the Commission to the Council and to the European Parliament on the implementation of Regulation (EC) No. 1177/2003 of the European Parliament and of the Council of June 16, 2003, or latest assessment available at http://circa.europa.eu/Public/irc/dsis/eusilc/library?l=/quality_assessment/comparative_quality_1/comparative_2005/_EN_1.0_&a=d.

5. *Equivalized median income* is defined as the household's total disposable income divided by its "equivalent size," to take account of the size and composition of the household, and is attributed to each household member. Equivalization is made on the basis of the OECD modified scale.

6. For the purpose of this analysis, pensions are considered primary income because their role is not only to redistribute resources across income groups, but also, and primarily, over the life cycle of individuals and/or across generations.

7. The indicator for the poverty risk before social transfers must be interpreted with caution for a number of reasons. First, no account is taken of other measures that, like social cash transfers, can have the effect of raising the disposable incomes of households and individuals, namely transfers in kind, tax credits, and tax allowances. Second, the pretransfer poverty risk is compared to the posttransfer risk with all other things being equal—namely, assuming unchanged household and labor market structures, thus disregarding any possible behavioral changes that the absence of social transfers might entail.

8. The indicator measures the percentage of the population that cannot afford at least three of the nine quoted items.

9. Three years is the longest series available for most countries.

References

Atkinson, Anthony B., Bea Cantillon, Eric Marlier, and Brian Nolan. 2001. *Social Indicators: the EU and Social Inclusion.* Oxford: Oxford University Press.

———. 2007. *The EU and Social Inclusion: Facing the Challenges.* Bristol, UK: The Policy Press.

Canberra Group. 2001. *Expert Group on Household Income Statistics: Final Report and Recommendations.* Ottawa: Statistics Canada. http://www.lisproject.org/links/canberra/finalreport.pdf.

Dahrendorf, Ralf. 1990. *Reflections on the Revolution in Europe: In a Letter Intended To Have Been Sent to a Gentleman in Warsaw.* New York: Random House.

Engbersen, G. 1991. "Moderne armoede: feit en fictie." *De Sociologische Gids* 38 (1): 7–23.

European Commission. 2005. "Working Together, Working Better: A New Framework for the Open Coordination of Social Protection and Inclusion Policies in the European Union." Communication of the European Commission to the Council, the European Parliament, the European Economic and Social Committee and the Committee of the Regions COM(2005) 706 final.

———. 2008. *Child Poverty and Well-Being in the EU: Current Status and Way Forward.* Luxembourg: Office for Official Publications of the European Communities.

———. 2009a. *Joint Report on Social Protection and Social Inclusion 2009.* Luxembourg: Office for Official Publications of the European Communities.

———. 2009b. *Portfolio of Indicators for the Monitoring of the European Strategy for Social Protection and Social Inclusion—2009 Update.* Opinion of the Social Protection Committee.

European Commission ECFIN - AMECO: Annual macroeconomic database, http://ec.europa.eu/economy_finance/db_indicators/ameco/index_en.htm Eurostat EU-SILC: European Union Statistics on Income and Living Condition, http://epp.euro-stat.ec.europa.eu/portal/page/portal/income_social_inclusion_living_conditions/introduction#.

OECD. 2008. *Growing Unequal? Income Distribution and Poverty in OECD Countries.* Paris: Organization for Economic Co-operation and Development publications. OECD tax-benefit model, http://www.oecd.org/els/social/workincentives.

United Nations. 1995. *The Copenhagen Declaration and Programme of Action. World Summit for Social Development.* New York: UN Department of Publications.

4

Deconstructing European
Poverty Measures

RICHARD V. BURKHAUSER ■

The movement toward evidence-based policy making in the United States owes much to politicians and scholars such as Daniel Patrick Moynihan, who once said: "In policy debates everyone is entitled to his own opinion but not his own facts." But facts do not "droppeth as the gentle rain from heaven," but rather are the difficult-to-obtain first step in the empirical process that allows policy makers to establish social success indicators for their policies, understand the causal relationships between those policies and social outcomes, and thus more effectively carry out policies that best achieve future social successes.

The United States and the European Union (EU) share the common goal of alleviating poverty. The chapters in this volume demonstrate that the European scholars whose business it is to establish the necessary facts to measure poverty, how it changes over time, and what policies best reduce it share a great deal with their American colleagues. This is especially so with respect to their need to both conceptualize poverty and how they choose to operationalize it in collecting the data necessary for its measure.

Within the EU, each state's statistical agency has been increasingly asked to coordinate its microdata gatherings along EU guidelines. The first major success of this effort is the EU-SILC (European Union—Survey of Income and Living Conditions). Hence, it is useful to consider the poverty concepts this European-based data set captures. Förster and Mira d'Ercole (2012, Chapter 2) provide exactly the kind of information necessary to do so. They outline the dominant method of conceptualizing and operationalizing European poverty measures used in the development of the EU-SILC questionnaire. They do so in the context of their explanation of how the OECD tracks its individual member country poverty rates and trends, including those in the United States. Maquet and Stanton (2012, Chapter 3), in their discussion of official EU member state poverty rates using EU-SILC, show that the measurement concepts outlined by Förster and Mira d'Ercole (2012, Chapter 2) are, with minor differences, the same as the ones used by the EU in their official poverty statistics.

What is surprising is that for the most part, the US Census Bureau uses similar data and methods to measure US poverty rates; but with a fundamental difference that has important implications for those interested in cross-national comparisons of poverty and the methods used to alleviate it. That difference is not the one most commonly associated with European and US poverty measures—that one is an absolute measure and the other relative. It is more fundamental. The United States is 200 years ahead of the EU in recognizing that member states that agree to share a common economic market, in which capital and labor are free to move from one state to another, and a common currency will inevitably share a common set of values and social policies.

Chief among them is that solidarity does not end at a state's border. It is telling that neither Förster and Mira d'Ercole (2012, Chapter 2) nor Maquet and Stanton (2012, Chapter 3) provide any poverty measure in which relative poverty is based on the economic well-being of the average EU citizen. Instead, all official EU poverty statistics, as well as Organization for the Economic Co-operation and Development's (OECD) official measures of poverty within the EU, are provided as if each state was a completely separate social entity. Hence, the economic well-being of an EU citizen in a given state depends on his or her income relative to only those EU citizens who happen to live in that member state.

Although such a relative concept makes sense for government entities based on blood or tribal relationships, it is far less appropriate when these government entities have embraced the free movement of capital and labor across their borders and the free market mechanisms that will make such archaic relationships increasingly less important in the day-to-day market activities of their citizens. In contrast, in the United States of America, even though we certainly provide official (Census Bureau) information on poverty rates at the state level, it is always in the context of a single poverty concept directly linking the well-being of a given citizen with all other US citizens rather than only to members of their same blood, tribe, or state of residence.

In the following section, I use the expositional model of Förster and Mira d'Ercole (2012, Chapter 2) to more systematically compare and contrast EU and US poverty measurement methods and the implications they have for understanding the fundamental differences between us.

THE NUTS AND BOLTS OF POVERTY MEASUREMENT

Income Rather than Consumption

Although economics-based conceptualizations of individual economic well-being focus on those things individuals consume—goods, services, and leisure—data collection issues have forced European and American researchers to focus instead on income. Income consists of both private and government transfer cash income; that is, on the ability of individuals to purchase goods and services. Income includes wages and salaries, self-employment income, property income (such as interest, dividends, and net rental income), and government in-cash transfers. It excludes capital gains, imputed rent, or in-kind government (e.g., Food Stamps, Medicaid) or private benefits (e.g., employer health insurance). Also, it takes no account of the time and energy—work or reduction in leisure—required to earn it.

The limits of such measures are well understood in the literature. Although alternative overall consumption measures have been proposed, as well as measures of material deprivation or social exclusion, all official OECD, EU, and US poverty measures are cash income–based. The major difference is that the Europeans explicitly remove income tax and social security contributions from gross cash income and make all comparisons using the resultant disposable cash income measure. Disposable income is clearly a more accurate measure of one's ability to purchase goods and services and is superior to the gross cash income measure used in official US poverty measures.

Counting People Rather than Households

The EU-SILC, like other European and American data sets, collects information on the income of all household members. Households can contain families (those related by blood or marriage) and those families contain individuals. European poverty measures assume all household income is shared equally among its members and that there are some economics of scale in its use, so that they can focus on poverty at the individual level. Official US poverty statistics make the same assumptions but at the family level, and their economics of scale assumptions are somewhat different.

Whereas the choices of sharing unit and scale economies can have substantial impacts on the characteristics of the poor—for example, the greater the economies of scale, the more likely that those in smaller households (widows, older persons) will be counted as poor—these choices do not appear to seriously affect trends in poverty within or across countries (see Burkhauser, Smeeding, and Merz 1996).

Static Versus Dynamic

The EU-SILC, like the US Survey of Income and Program Participation, is a short panel design that allows for dynamic analysis of poverty. For some OECD countries, much longer panels are available. These panels are vital for understanding persistent poverty and its causes. But until recently, only a few OECD countries (e.g., the United States, Germany, and Great Britain) had either a short- or a long-term panel. Hence, official poverty statistics in both Europe and the United States are based on cross-sectional data. So there is not much difference here (see Burkhauser 2001).

Relative vs. Absolute

The single most discussed difference between European and American poverty measures is that Europeans use a relative poverty scale and the United States uses an absolute scale. What becomes clearer once these two scales are more carefully considered is that they both address two fundamental issues with respect to poverty measurement: (1) What is the initial level of poverty that best represents the social minimum level of access to resources for a given society? (2) How should this social minimum level change over time? It is in how our two poverty scales relate to these two fundamental issues that our differences are best seen.

THE EUROPEAN APPROACH
Europeans have historically made the reduction of overall income inequality one of their major social success goals. Hence, it is not surprising that the intellectual underpinnings of their concept of poverty rest entirely on income distribution grounds—poverty is defined as having income below some percentage of median income. (The OECD uses a 50 percent cutoff point, whereas the EU uses a 60 percent cutoff point.) Furthermore, this is made explicit in some European-style models of

economic well-being, in which a person's individual well-being is considered not only a positive function of his or her own consumption, but is also positively associated with his or her place in the distribution (see Ravallion and Chen 2009).

Such a concept of poverty not only resolves the first fundamental issue, but also the second, because as median income rises over time (both because of increases in inflation and because of real productivity gains), so will the poverty line. Doing so, in principle, commits governments that use this type of relative poverty line to guarantee sufficient additional revenue to lower income groups each year to keep them above a constant real social minimum level of economic well-being and enough additional revenues so that they do not fall behind the rest of the population when real economic growth occurs. Under such scoring rules, all persons, including the poor, in the population could improve their economic well-being, but poverty rates could still rise—income distribution goals could trump improvement in personal consumption goals. Such social success scales do not recognize success in reducing poverty unless economic growth increases poor peoples' income faster than that of the median person's income.

The US approach
The United States has historically focused less official attention on overall income inequality issues, instead concentrating on the lower end of the income distribution. Hence, it is no accident that the intellectual underpinnings of our concept of poverty do not rest explicitly on income distribution grounds but rather on the amount of income necessary to purchase some social minimum basket of goods and services. Unlike simply taking some percentage of median income, it is much more difficult to establish what should be included in that basket of goods and its cost. Originally, the US social minimum was based solely on the cost of a healthy diet for a family of three. Later, economies of scale values were introduced again based on food consumption.

That takes care of the first fundamental question; but not the second. In fact, our poverty line is increased each year by the inflation rate alone. Governments, like that of the United States, that use the level of income necessary to purchase a fixed basket of goods and services as their poverty alleviation goal would only have to transfer sufficient revenues to lower income groups each year to maintain their original level of consumption. Under a scoring rule such as this, poverty rates could fall to 0 with no change or possibly even an increase in income inequality. That is, economic growth would reduce poverty as long as poor people received at least a share of that growth.

Why do these approaches continue to differ?
In reality, the initial official poverty line set by European or American policy makers was more a political than a scientific one, as is the degree that the poverty thresholds should be sensitive to average real growth. It would have been possible, for instance, for Europeans to have chosen a conceptual social minimum based on a basket of goods that ended up equaling 50 or 60 percent of the income of the median person and then have argued that this basket should grow with real median income, and the result would have been the same.

It is likely that when President Lyndon Johnson accepted our initial conceptual social minimum in the United States based on food consumption, he was more interested in the percentage of poor Americans such an initial standard captured—not too few as to suggest that poverty was not a serious problem, but not too many as to make doing anything about it too daunting—than in the scientific justification for such a standard.

The limitations of using data on a healthy diet as a measure of the acceptable social standard of a minimum basket of goods and services and of holding that level constant in real terms for very long time periods have been discussed in detail in Citro and Michael (1995), as have many other problems with the current US poverty scale—for example, using disposable income, using a household rather than a family as the sharing unit, and more consistent scale economies—that would make it closer in design to European-style measures. But as Lerman (2009) points out, the unwillingness of US government officials to make any of these changes in the official poverty scales over the last decade and a half since the Citro and Michael (1995) report may have more to do with the fact that many federal programs have come to use the official state poverty rate to allocate funds rather than because of their ignorance of the scientific arguments for doing so. Hence, any reforms in our flawed poverty measure will have immediate implications for the size and distribution of those federal funds to the states.

Furthermore, the initial unwillingness of President Johnson to commit the United States to a poverty scale that automatically increases with economic growth may also have been based on the pragmatic argument that future federal government officials might not want to automatically ensure that such funds be committed to low-income transfers but rather that it be left to future generations of citizens to explicitly decide how to distribute the fruit of additional growth and hence to explicitly decide when the real social minimum level should be raised.

In contrast with the very close relationship between changes in our official poverty rate and in the level and distribution of federal expenditures to the states, there appears to be no direct relationship between the relative poverty line detailed by Förster and Mira d'Ercole (2012, Chapter 2) and Maquet and Stanton (2012, Chapter 3) and actual EU social policies or the policies of its state members. So, even though the European measure of the social minimum rises with real growth in each state, there is no requirement that funds from those states or the EU be allocated based on this increase. Hence, the policy consequences of such a poverty scale are somewhat lower in terms of its real impact on people than would be the case in the United States.

INCLUDING THE VALUE OF NONCASH TRANSFERS

Förster and Mira d'Ercole (2012, Chapter 2) mention current issues in poverty measurement that are also of interest in the United States. Of most interest is the importance of taking into consideration noncash transfers from government and noncash benefits from employers as additional sources of income. (See, Sutherland, and Tsakloglou [2012, Chapter 5] and Frick and Grabka [2012, Chapter 6] for examples of the value of including noncash government transfers and Gilbert [2012, Chapter 7] for an example of the value of including private nonwage compensation, in measures of income.) In the United States, the failure to take into account the value of in-kind government transfers that are primarily targeted to low-income people in our official poverty calculations understates the resources available to them. But it also understates the degree that, for instance, the $35 billion in government expenditures spent on an in-kind transfer program such as Food Stamps or the $116 billion spent on Medicaid improved the economic well-being of low-income people. (Figures are for 2008 for Food Stamps and 2006 for Medicaid. See Burkhauser and Daly 2011.)

WHAT CAN WE LEARN FROM THE EUROPEAN APPROACH TO POVERTY MEASUREMENT?

Certain aspects of the European style of poverty measurement should be seriously considered as we think about reforms in our official poverty measures. Several are noncontroversial. Disposable income is a better measure of purchasing power and is more consistent with the income-based measure of poverty we both use. Including the effect of government tax policies will account for the degree that taxes reduce personal consumption and would also take account of the degree that tax credits, such as the Earned Income Tax Credit, increase the effective wages and disposable income of workers in low-income households.[1] Counting families without considering the number of people within them, which is still done in some Census Bureau official statistics, fails to take into account the number of mouths that a given family's income must feed and should also be more uniformly done here. Also, we should look to Europe for a more sensible way of controlling for economics of scale.

More controversially, using a household rather than a family sharing unit may make sense given the number of nonmarried, nonblood relatives who are now sharing resources but who under current rules are counted as not doing so. Even more controversially, it may be time to reevaluate the appropriateness of the current implicit goal embedded in our poverty line measures. Because we have only adjusted our poverty line for inflation over the nearly half a century since President Johnson first established our social minimum level, it is still set at the same real 1960s War on Poverty income level. Given the considerable economic growth we have experienced as a country since then, it now may be time to explicitly raise our social minimum. But in doing so, it is far less clear that we should use a European-style approach.

There are some aspects of current European-style poverty lines that make much less sense for the United States, and even for the EU. Chief among them is the official OECD and EU choice of solidarity reference group in measuring member state poverty. Column 1 and Column 2 of Table 4.1 are based, respectively, on Figures 3 and 8 from Tóth and Medgyesi (2009). The values in these columns differ in part because Column 1 uses a poverty measure based on 60 percent (EU standard) of median income whereas Column 2 uses a poverty measure based on 50 percent (OECD standard) of median income. But the real difference between them is that, apparently, this European team of researchers did not get the memo that one should never provide alternative measures of relative poverty for EU countries in the same paper, even if you never connect the dots.[2] Doing so provides a nice example of the dramatic difference in member state–measured poverty rates made by one's choice of solidarity reference group, and more broadly, why it is important to make explicit the social goal toward which the success indicator is being used to measure progress.

Column 1 reports poverty rates by EU state using standard EU methods—60 percent of the household size-adjusted median income of persons in that state—for establishing a poverty threshold. The data come from the first (income year 2005) wave of EU-SILC data, and Tóth and Medgyesi (2009) use the OECD2 equivalent

Table 4.1 EUROPEAN POVERTY RATES BY MEMBER STATE USING
ALTERNATIVE SOLIDARITY GROUP MEDIANS

Alternative Solidarity Group Poverty Rates

Member State	0.6 of Median Income of Member State[a]	0.5 of Median Income of EU Population[b]
Lithuania	20	68
Latvia	23	63
Poland	18	58
Estonia	18	52
Slovakia	12	50
Hungary	16	50
Portugal	18	28
Czech Republic	10	22
Greece	20	25
Spain	20	12
Italy	19	7
Slovenia	12	5
United Kingdom	19	4
Germany	12	3
Sweden	12	3
France	13	3
Ireland	18	3
Cyprus	16	3
Belgium	15	2
Denmark	11	2
Austria	13	2
Netherlands	9	2
Finland	12	2
Luxembourg	13	1
EU Average	16	20

[a]Sixty percent of the household size-adjusted income of the median person in that state using the OECD2 equivalence scale.
[b]Fifty percent of the household size-adjusted income of the median person in the EU using a per capita equivalence scale.

SOURCES: Adapted from Tóth and Medgyesi (2009, Figures 3 and 8).

income scale to account for differences in household size. These resulting state poverty rates are very close to those reported by Maquet and Stanton (2012, Chapter 3) that are based on official EU measures for income year 2006 in their Table 3.2.

What is the message from using this Column 1's kind of social success indicator for EU member states? Poverty remains a significant problem in all EU member states with a group bunched at the extreme low end (around 10 to 13 percent)—the Netherlands, Czech Republic, Denmark, Germany, Slovenia, Spain, Finland, Luxembourg, and Austria; several more in the middle; and another set of member states bunched around the extreme high of around 20 percent—United Kingdom, Italy, Greece, Spain, Lithuania, and Latvia. But somewhat surprisingly, Column 1 suggests that there is not all that much difference in the risk of poverty across EU member states, including comparisons of old and new member states.

But the poverty numbers are quite different when we change the social success indicator by extending the solidarity reference group from the median person in the state to the median person in the EU. In Column 2 of Table 4.1, EU member states are arrayed in descending order of their poverty rates using an EU-wide solidarity group measure. That is, in addition to shifting from an EU standard 60 percent to an OECD standard 50 percent of median income threshold for poverty, Tóth and Medgyesi (2009) also shift from the EU and OECD practice of determining a unique poverty threshold for each EU state—only considering the median income of persons living in a given EU state to measure the poverty threshold for persons in that state—to using the median income of all persons in the EU to establish a single poverty threshold for every EU state and for every EU citizen, regardless of where they live.

This change in solidarity reference group dramatically changes the message Column 2 provides with respect to the incidence of poverty across member states. In Column 1, the cluster of states with the highest poverty rates had about twice the poverty rates of the states with the lowest poverty rates. In contrast, in Column 2, the majority of the population in 6 member states—Lithuania, Latvia, Poland, Estonia, Slovakia, and Hungary—is below the EU-wide poverty line, whereas 12 member states have poverty rates below 5 percent of the EU-wide poverty line. That is, poverty rates in the high-poverty states are now shown to be 10 times those in the low-poverty states. Hence, Column 2's takeaway message is that there is an enormous difference between the extremely high poverty rates in the mostly new lower median income states of the EU and the extremely low poverty rates in most of the original higher median income EU member states.[3]

What is driving this dramatic difference in messages? Fundamentally, by focusing solely on a state median, the first measure completely ignores cross-state differences in income levels. Hence, approximately 20 percent of the citizens of Lithuania, Greece, and the United Kingdom are considered to live in poverty, even though there are substantial differences in median income in these states and, hence, in access to the goods and services available to those with only 0.6 or 0.5 of that income across those states. When solidarity is extended across state borders by using a single EU-wide social minimum, this disparity becomes much clearer as these states' poverty rates change to 68, 25, and 4 percent, respectively.

Following on the Table 4.1 comparisons, Table 4.2 shows the differences in state poverty rates in the United States as normally estimated and those same states if we adopted the EU's solidarity reference group approach. States are arrayed from highest to lowest based on their child poverty rate using Current Population Survey

Table 4.2 STATE CHILD POVERTY RATES IN THE UNITED STATES USING ALTERNATIVE SOLIDARITY GROUP MEDIANS

State	Standard US method[a]	0.5 of median income of state[b]
District of Columbia	33	18.8
Mississippi	31	18.9
Louisiana	24	22.8
Texas	23	20.7
Alabama	22	20.3
Kentucky	22	20.5
New Mexico	22	21.6
West Virginia	22	18.5
Arkansas	21	14.1
Georgia	21	18.8
Arizona	20	23.6
New York	20	26.3
North Carolina	20	17.2
Oklahoma	20	17.6
Tennessee	20	18.2
Missouri	19	13.8
South Carolina	19	18.0
California	18	25.7
Kansas	18	13.0
Ohio	18	18.6
Indiana	17	13.8
Michigan	17	19.5
Montana	17	13.9
Florida	16	21.2
Oregon	16	16.2
Pennsylvania	16	18.4
Rhode Island	16	22.7
Illinois	15	21.7
South Dakota	15	12.3
Wisconsin	15	15.1
Colorado	14	13.1

(*Continued*)

Table 4.2. STATE CHILD POVERTY RATES IN THE UNITED STATES
USING ALTERNATIVE SOLIDARITY GROUP MEDIANS (*CONT'D*)

State	Standard US method[a]	0.5 of median income of state[b]
Iowa	14	13.0
Maine	14	13.7
Massachusetts	14	24.2
North Dakota	14	12.3
Delaware	13	18.8
Idaho	13	13.9
Nebraska	13	13.0
Nevada	13	13.1
Virginia	13	18.8
Wyoming	13	13.9
Connecticut	12	22.7
Maryland	12	18.8
Minnesota	12	15.8
Utah	12	13.1
Washington	12	19.0
Alaska	11	16.1
Hawaii	11	16.1
New Jersey	11	21.8
Vermont	9	13.7
New Hampshire	6	13.7

[a]Official US poverty measure.
[b]Poverty measure based on OECD guidelines with state as solidarity reference group.

SOURCES: Column 1 based on National Center for Children in Poverty (2009), using Current Population Survey for 2006–2008. Column 2 based on Rainwater, Smeeding, and Coder (2001, Table 2.4, p. 61), using Current Population Survey for 1995–1997.

data from 2006 to 2008, as reported on the National Center for Children in Poverty Web site using the standard American social minimum approach. The results in Column 1 are unsurprising. Official child poverty is most severe in lower-income states—the top 10 poverty states include 8 from the South as well as the District of Columbia and New Mexico.

Although US studies using the European approach to estimate poverty on a state basis are rare, Column 2 of Table 4.2 provides one such estimate (Rainwater, Smeeding, and Coder 2001) using the OECD/EU approach—0.5 of the household size-adjusted income of the median income person in the state. The results substantially change the states with the greatest poverty problem. Of the top 10 highest-poverty states under our official measure of poverty, only New Mexico and Louisiana remain. The three states whose children are most likely to be in poverty live in New York, California, and Massachusetts.

Because federal dollar allocations to the states are directly tied to our official state poverty rates, such a change would have profound effects on this allocation. It is hard to imagine the coalition of American child welfare experts who would argue for a change that would shift federal dollars from the poor children of Alabama, Mississippi, and Kentucky to their higher-income counterparts in New York, California, and Massachusetts because they were more relatively deprived.

But why is this so in America and not in the EU? In my view, in 1789, when our 13 states formally agreed on the rules under which they would become the United States of America, there were profound differences among those states, including laws governing slavery that took a civil war to resolve. But over time, an increasing share of Americans began to think of themselves as Americans first and citizens of a state second. Nonetheless, more than 200 years later, there are significant state and regional, as well as racial and ethnic, differences that come into play in the allocation of federal and state resources, and it is still difficult to convince citizens of higher-income states to subsidize their poorer state cousins. Hence, we still tolerate some degree of difference in poverty rates across states as Column 1 of Table 4.2 demonstrates using our standard poverty measures.

Because of our heterogeneity of interests, Americans may be less willing to share individual resources and to provide a higher social minimum for all Americans than is the case for some of the individual states of the EU that are more homogeneous by blood or tribal bonds. Nonetheless, it would be laughable to propose that federal government poverty reduction policy in the United States be based on a state solidarity group measure like the one currently used in the OECD or EU to capture poverty across its EU member states. And, as a comparison of Column 2 of Table 4.1 and Column 1 of Table 4.2 shows, our cross-state differences in poverty using an American-wide solidarity group poverty measure are much smaller than those in the EU using an EU-wide solidarity group measure.[4]

My guess is that it will become increasingly difficult for the EU to maintain its goal of a fully integrated EU market economy of the type that we have enjoyed in the United States since our inception, while continuing to measure the risk of poverty of fellow EU citizens based solely on poverty scales that implicitly argue that solidarity stops at state borders. That is, how much longer will the dramatic difference in state poverty rates found in Column 2 of Table 4.1 be tolerated before reducing these differences becomes a social goal toward which this type of success indicator measures progress?[5]

Notes

1. More controversial, but of value in capturing the resources available to households, would be including in-kind government transfers and the nonwage compensation paid to workers by firms.

2. Someone must have eventually given them the memo since in their published version of this paper (Toth and Medgyesi, 2011) Figure 8 and all discussion of it is gone.

3. Beblo and Knaus (2001) were the first to conceptualize the EU as a single entity and empirically show when doing so that residents of Italy, Spain, and Portugal made up a disproportionate share of the bottom decile of the overall EU population in 1995.

4. In a similar vein, Burkhauser and Couch (2010) review the income distribution literature comparing the United States and EU countries and make the point that although income inequality in the United States is greater than income inequality for most of the EU countries individually, when income inequality is measured across all EU citizens, overall income inequality in the EU is much closer to that found in the United States as first shown by Brandolini (2007).

5. A careful reading of Nolan and Whelan (2012, Chapter 16) offers a hint that the problems associated with using a single relative poverty scale, set at state borders, to capture both within-state income inequality and the enormous differences in access to consumption across EU state borders, are becoming clearer to European-style poverty experts. Nolan and Whelan (2012, Chapter 16) provide the intellectual justification for a "material deprivation" measure of poverty that is entirely separate from standard income distribution–based European poverty scales. Instead, the intellectual origin of material deprivation poverty scales, at least as formulated from the 17 items taken from questions on the EU-SILC, appear to be coming from the American minimum basket of goods and services tradition of poverty measurement. This is a tradition in which the items in the basket do not vary relative to the average income of the state in which the questions are asked. More generally, this suggests that when a society has more than one social success goal with respect to its lower income populations, it may be necessary to have more than one measure of social program success.

References

Beblo, Miriam, and Thomas Knaus. 2001. "Measuring Income Inequality in Euroland." *Review of Income and Wealth* 47 (3): 301–320.

Brandolini, Andrea. 2007. "Measurement of Income Distribution in Supranational Entities: The Case of the European Union." In *Inequality and Poverty Re-Examined*. Edited by Steven Jenkins and John Micklewright, 62–83. Oxford: Oxford University Press.

Burkhauser, Richard V. 2001. "What Policymakers Need To Know about Poverty Dynamics." *Journal of Policy Analysis and Management* 20 (4): 757–759.

Burkhauser, Richard V., and Kenneth A. Couch. 2010. "Are the Inequality and Mobility Trends of the United States in the European Union's Future?" In *United in Diversity*. Edited by Jens Alber and Neil Gilbert, 280–307. Oxford: Oxford University Press.

Burkhauser, Richard V., and Mary C. Daly. 2011. *The Declining Work and Welfare of People with Disabilities: What Went Wrong and a Strategy for Change*. Washington, DC: American Enterprise Institute Press.

Burkhauser, Richard V., Timothy M. Smeeding, and Jochim Merz. 1996. "Relative Inequality and Poverty in Germany and the United States Using Alternative Equivalency Scales." *Review of Income and Wealth* 42 (4): 381–400.

Citro, Connie F., and Robert T. Michael, eds. 1995. *Measuring Poverty: A New Approach*. Washington, DC: National Academy Press.

Förster, Michael, and Marco Mira d'Ercole. 2012. "The OECD Approach to Measuring Income Distribution and Poverty." In *Counting the Poor: New Thinking about European Poverty Measures and Lessons for the United States*. Edited by Douglas J. Besharov and Kenneth A. Couch, 25–58. New York: Oxford University Press.

Frick, Joachim R., and Markus M. Grabka. 2012. "Accounting for Imputed and Capital Income Flows." In *Counting the Poor: New Thinking about European Poverty Measures and Lessons for the United States*. Edited by Douglas J. Besharov and Kenneth A. Couch, 117–142. New York: Oxford University Press.

Gilbert, Neil. 2012. "Accounting for Employee Benefits." In *Counting the Poor: New Thinking about European Poverty Measures and Lessons for the United States*. Edited by Douglas J. Besharov and Kenneth A. Couch, 143–160. New York: Oxford University Press.

Lerman, Robert. 2009. "Discussion of Income Levels and Benefits Programs." Paper presented at Measuring Poverty, Income Inequality, and Social Exclusion: Lessons from Europe Conference, Paris, March 16–17, 2009. http://umdcipe.org/conferences/oecdumd/conf_papers/index.shtml.

Maquet, Isabelle, and David Stanton. 2012. "Income Indicators for the EU's Social Inclusion Strategy." In *Counting the Poor: New Thinking about European Poverty Measures and Lessons for the United States*. Edited by Douglas J. Besharov and Kenneth A. Couch, 59–77. New York: Oxford University Press.

National Center for Children in Poverty. 2009. "50-State Demographics Wizard." Accessed May 6, 2009. http://www.nccp.org/tools/demographics/.

Nolan, Brian, and Christopher T. Whelan. 2012. "Using Nonmonetary Deprivation Indicators To Analyze European Poverty and Social Exclusion." In *Counting the Poor: New Thinking about European Poverty Measures and Lessons for the United States*. Edited by Douglas J. Besharov and Kenneth A. Couch, 343–362. New York: Oxford University Press.

Rainwater, Lee, Timothy M. Smeeding, and John Coder. 2001. "Poverty across States, Nations, and Continents." In *Child Well-Being, Child Poverty, and Child Policy in Modern Nations: What Do We Know?* Edited by Koen Vleminckx and Timothy M. Smeeding, 33–74. Bristol, UK: Policy Press / Toronto: University of Toronto Press.

Ravallion, Martin, and Shaohua Chen. 2009. "Weakly Relative Poverty." Paper presented at Measuring Poverty, Income Inequality and Social Exclusion: Lessons from Europe Conference, Paris, March 16–17, 2009. http://umdcipe.org/conferences/oecdumd/conf_papers/index.shtml.

Sutherland, Holly, and Panos Tsakloglou. 2012. "Accounting for the Distributional Effects of Noncash Public Benefits." In *Counting the Poor: New Thinking about European Poverty Measures and Lessons for the United States*. Edited by Douglas J. Besharov and Kenneth A. Couch, 95–116. New York: Oxford University Press.

Toth, Istvan Gyorgy and Marton Medgyesi. 2009. "Income Distribution in New (and Old) EU Member States." Paper presented at Measuring Poverty, Income Inequality, and Social Exclusion: Lessions from Europe Conference, Paris, March 16-17, 2009. http://umdcipe.org/conferences/oecdumd/conf_papers/index.shtml.

Tóth, István György, and Márton Medgyesi. 2011. "Income distribution in new (and old) EU member states." *Corvinus Journal of Sociology and Social Policy* 2 (1): 3–31.

PART TWO

Broadening Measures of Income and Other Financial Resources

5

Accounting for the Distributional Effects of Noncash Public Benefits

HOLLY SUTHERLAND AND PANOS TSAKLOGLOU ∎

INTRODUCTION

A household's command over resources is determined not only by its spending power over commodities it can buy, but also by resources available to the members of the household through in-kind provision of the welfare state as well as private noncash incomes. The omission of noncash incomes from the concept of resources used in distributional studies may call into question the validity of comparisons, both time series within a particular country and cross-sectional ones across countries. For example, comparing the income distributions of two countries, one where health services are primarily covered by private out-of-pocket payments and another where such services are provided free of charge by the state to the citizens is likely to lead to invalid conclusions about the relative degree of inequality and, perhaps, policy implications. Further, this omission could have important implications for the efficient targeting of resources aiming to reduce inequality or mitigate poverty.

Previous studies suggest that in-kind transfers are more equally distributed than disposable income and, thus, reduce aggregate inequality.[1] In quantitative terms, cross-country differences seem to be substantial, but it is not always clear whether such differences are genuine or can be attributed to underlying data or methodological choices made by the researchers.

The aim of this chapter is to extend previous analyses of the distributional effects of welfare programs in rich countries; focus on three of the most important public transfers in kind, namely, public education services, public health care services, and public housing; and analyze their short-term distributional effects in a strictly comparable framework in five European Union (EU) countries (Belgium, Germany, Greece, Italy, and the United Kingdom).[2] Unlike other publicly provided services, such as those in the fields of national defense and public order, the benefits of health care, housing, and education are relatively easy to quantify and allocate to particular members of the population.

The methods of calculating the value of each of the three sources of in-kind benefits and identifying beneficiaries are described in the next section. This is followed by a presentation of the main results of the distributional analysis, showing the effects of the three noncash elements of income in terms of their relative importance in aggregate and across the cash income distribution. Their effects are compared with those of the cash benefits systems, and their overall impact on measures of inequality and poverty are estimated. The following section discusses the welfare interpretation of the empirical findings and outlines an alternative approach using different sets of equivalent scales, providing some empirical illustrations. A final section concludes.

METHODS AND DATA

A guiding principle that is adopted in calculating the monetary value of each of the three in-kind transfers, and in allocating them to households, is to do so in a manner that is comparable across the five countries considered. The microdata used to provide information on household characteristics and cash income are taken from survey sources that are broadly comparable in terms of methods used to collect them, period in time, and content (Table 5.1). These data were chosen because they also provide the input data for EUROMOD, the EU tax-benefit microsimulation model (Sutherland 2007; Lietz and Mantovani 2007). Using our estimates of the three noncash benefits within EUROMOD enables their size and impacts to be compared with those of cash benefits and direct taxes, as included in standard measures of disposable income and simulated by EUROMOD.

Table 5.1 INCOME DATA SETS USED IN THE ANALYSIS

Country	Data Set	Date of Collection	Reference Time Period for Incomes	Tax-benefit System
Belgium	EU-SILC	2004	2003	2003
Germany	German Socio-Economic Panel	2002	2001	2001
Greece	Household Budget Survey	2004/2005	2004	2004
Italy	Italian version of EU-SILC	2004	2003	2003
UK	Family Resources Survey	2003/2004	2003/2004	2003

SOURCE: EUROMOD data sources are the EU Statistics on Incomes and Living Conditions (EU-SILC) made available by Eurostat (under contract EU-SILC/2007/03); the public use version of the German Socio-Economic Panel Study made available by the German Institute for Economic Research, Berlin; the Greek Household Budget Survey made available by the National Statistical Service of Greece; the Italian version of the EU-SILC made available by the Italian National Institute of Statistics; and the Family Resources Survey, made available by the UK Department for Work and Pensions through the Data Archive. Material from the Family Resources Survey is Crown copyright and is used by permission. None of the data providers bears any responsibility for the analysis or interpretation of the data reported here.

The usual measuring stick employed in studies of poverty and income distribution in Europe and most other developed counties is disposable income measured at the household level and equivalized to account for differences in household size and composition. It consists of gross market income plus private transfers less income taxes and social insurance contributions (paid by employees and the self-employed), plus cash benefits. Because this concept of income omits the incidence of indirect and corporate taxes and employer social contributions as well as the effects of noncash public expenditure, it provides only a partial picture of the effect of the public sector on household welfare. Our analysis improves the comprehensiveness as well as the comparability of the income measure by including noncash public transfers in the fields of education, health care, and housing but still remains partial.

The estimates of inequality indices derived in the later sections of the chapter rely on static incidence analysis under the assumption that public transfers in kind do not create externalities. It is assumed that the beneficiaries of the public transfers are exclusively the recipients of the transfers (and the members of their households) and that these services do not create any benefits (such as a healthy and educated workforce) or losses to the nonrecipients. The presence of noncash benefits means that taxes and contributions paid by both recipients and nonrecipients are higher than they otherwise would be.[3]

Moreover, in the cases of public education and public health care, it is assumed that the value of the transfer to the beneficiary is equal to the average cost of producing the corresponding services. Similar assumptions are standard practice in the analysis of the distributional impact of publicly provided services (Jones, Annan, and Shah 2008; Marical et al. 2008; Smeeding et al. 1993).

The following three subsections describe how the estimates of noncash income were derived for each of the three components.

Education

Information on spending per student in primary, secondary, and tertiary education is derived from the Organization for Economic Co-operation and Development (OECD) (2006) as shown in Table 5.2.[4] Each student in a public education institution (or a heavily subsidized private education institution) identified in the income survey (see Table 5.1) is assigned a public education transfer equal to the average cost of producing these services in the corresponding level of education. Then, this benefit is assumed to be shared by all household members. In other words, it is implicitly assumed that in the absence of public transfers, the students and their families would have to undertake the expenditures themselves.

Because of limitations regarding the information available on education in some of the income surveys, we focus on three levels of education (primary, secondary, and tertiary), leaving aside other levels such as preprimary and nontertiary postsecondary education and suppressing distinctions such as those between different types of secondary and tertiary education, which may be important in some countries.

In all countries, public spending per secondary education student is higher than the corresponding figure for primary education. In some countries, such as Germany and Belgium, the differences are quite large, whereas in others, such as Italy and Greece, the differences appear to be relatively small. Because their main beneficiaries

Table 5.2 PUBLIC SPENDING PER STUDENT IN THREE EDUCATIONAL LEVELS
(IN CURRENT EUROS)

Country/Year	Level of education		
	Primary	Secondary	Tertiary (without research and development)
Belgium 2003	4,662	5,814	5,809
Germany 2001	3,131	4,857	5,410
Greece 2004	2,541	2,984	2,772
Italy 2003	5,310	5,723	3,264
United Kingdom 2003	3,989	4,972	5,207

SOURCE: OECD (2006).

are not the students, estimates of public transfers to tertiary education students are calculated net of research and development public expenditures.

Tertiary education students living away from their parental homes pose the broader question of whether household income is a good approximation of their standard of living. Analyses that simply look at all students risk attributing an unwarranted benefit to students who appear to have low incomes simply because they moved temporarily away from high-income parental homes for the period of their studies. The literature on the returns to education indicates that their likely positions in the earnings distribution will be toward the top. Moreover, the living arrangements of tertiary education students differ substantially across countries while their treatment in the national surveys is not always the same. For example, most of tertiary education students in Greece live with their parents, whereas this is the case for relatively few students in the United Kingdom. In Belgium and Italy, students living in student accommodation are treated as members of their parental households in the income surveys; in the United Kingdom, they are not included at all. Therefore, the corresponding results should be treated with caution. It should be noted that in the United Kingdom, there is a substantially more important role for student fees in funding tertiary education than in other countries.[5]

Figure 5.1 shows the position of the individual beneficiaries of public education subsidies in the distribution of equivalized household disposable income[6] for primary, secondary, and tertiary education. Bars higher (lower) than 20 percent indicate that the quintile groups under consideration contain proportionally more (fewer) beneficiaries than their population shares. The top left graph depicts the situation regarding primary education. In Belgium and Germany, the beneficiaries of public primary education transfers appear to be fairly evenly distributed across the first four quintiles, whereas in the rest of the countries, they seem to be disproportionately concentrated lower down the cash income distribution. In all countries, especially in Germany and the United Kingdom, they are substantially underrepresented in the top quintile. A similar picture emerges in the top right graph, which shows that in all countries, there is a negative relationship between the share of beneficiaries of public secondary education and the quintile of the income distribution.

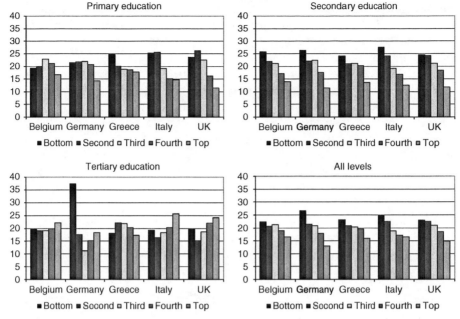

Figure 5.1 Distribution of Public Education Beneficiaries by Quintile of Household Disposable Income and by Level of Education.
SOURCE: EUROMOD.

In the cases of Greece and the United Kingdom, this can be partly attributed to the fact that the (relatively few) private education students are concentrated to the upper part of the cash income distribution (especially the top quintile). Such students cannot be identified in the income surveys of the remaining countries. Moreover, in all countries, high-earning childless households are overrepresented in the top quintiles.

The bottom left graph shows the location of public tertiary education beneficiaries in the income distribution. No clear cross-country pattern emerges, although with the exception of Greece there is a U-shaped pattern with more beneficiaries at the top and the bottom than in the middle. The higher shares of beneficiaries at the bottom, especially notable in Germany, can be attributed to a large number of single-person (student-only) households, naturally with low levels of current income. As previously explained, cross-country differences in the living circumstances of tertiary-level students and the exclusion of students living in institutional accommodation may explain the observed effects. The bottom right chart combines all levels of education and shows how, in all countries, beneficiaries are underrepresented in the top and, in most cases, the fourth quintile, while they are overrepresented in the three lowest quintiles.

Health

The most often used method in the literature of the distributive evaluation of health care services accounts for the distributional impact of health care services by increasing household income by the sum of the corresponding public expenditures. Three approaches can be distinguished in this context: (1) the actual consumption approach, (2) the insurance value approach, and (3) the use of equivalence scales that incorporate health care needs.

The *actual consumption approach* uses detailed data on the effective use of health care services by individuals (see, for example, Evandrou et al. [1993] and Sefton [2002] for the United Kingdom). The problem with this approach is that it ignores the greater needs that are associated with being ill (Aaberge and Langørgen 2006). It implies that, ceteris paribus, sick people are better off than healthy persons just because they receive more health care services. In fact, it has been clearly demonstrated that poorer individuals tend to have lower health levels and, consequently, greater needs for health care (see, for example, Hernandez-Quevedo et al. [2006] and Berloffa, Brugiavini, and Rizzi [2006]).

Using the *insurance value approach,* the "insurance value" of coverage for each person is imputed based on specific characteristics (such as age, sex, socioeconomic status). The insurance value is the amount that an insured person would have to pay in each category so that the third-party provider (government, employer, other insurer) would have just enough revenue to cover all claims for such people (Smeeding 1982). It is based on the notion that what the public health care services provide is equivalent to funding an insurance policy where the value of the premium is the same for everybody sharing the same characteristics, such as age (Marical et al. 2008). Nevertheless, a problem remains because the relative needs of individuals for health care are not the same as for commodities bought in the market. Different equivalence scales should be used in the two distributions (disposable income and disposable income plus the value of public health care services).

Therefore, a third approach, which has considerable informational requirements, is to use the insurance-based approach and introduce an equivalence scale that corrects for differences in health care needs between individuals. The problem with this approach, however, lies in the choice of the equivalence scale. No attempt to construct sets of equivalence scales covering differences in needs for the entire population exists, although a number of empirical studies focusing on particular population groups or specific situations can be found in the literature (Jones and O'Donnell 1995; Klavus 1999; Zaidi and Burchardt 2005; Berloffa, Brugiavini, and Rizzi 2006). Nevertheless, the welfare foundations of these studies are not always straightforward (Radner 1997). The problem of the appropriate equivalence scales and the welfare interpretation of the corresponding incidence analysis are discussed further in the penultimate section of this chapter.

The present chapter uses the risk-related insurance value approach. Following this approach, each individual is assumed to receive a public benefit determined by the average spending on his/her age group, irrespective of whether use of public health services was actually made. Then, this benefit is added to the resources of the household to which this individual belongs. We calculate per capita expenditures for each age group using the OECD (2007) Social Expenditure database (SOCX), which provides data that are comparable across countries.[7]

The age pattern is the same as that used in Marical et al. (2008) and is shown in Figure 5.2. As expected, spending per capita is considerably higher for older people. The distributional impact of health care spending is, therefore, likely to be determined to a considerable extent by the location of older people in the income distribution.

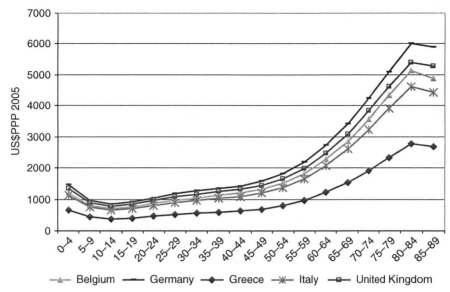

Figure 5.2 Public Health Care Expenditures Per Capita for Each Age Group.
SOURCE: Calculations based on the OECD SOCX database.

As shown in Table 5.3, which reports the relative mean per capita public health care expenditure by quintile of equivalized household disposable income, health care spending is higher (lower) than average for lower (higher) income households. The cross-country pattern by income is similar in all cases but less marked in Italy and Germany than in the other countries.

Housing Subsidies

Public support for housing costs can take many forms. Some of these are captured in the measurement of cash household disposable income. Housing benefits paid in cash and tax relief on mortgage interest are examples of common forms that are

Table 5.3 RELATIVE MEAN PER CAPITA PUBLIC HEALTH CARE TRANSFER PER QUINTILE OF HOUSEHOLD CASH DISPOSABLE INCOME

Quintile	Belgium	Germany	Greece	Italy	United Kingdom
1 (bottom)	1.17	1.05	1.11	0.98	1.10
2	1.17	1.06	1.11	1.03	1.10
3	0.95	0.99	1.00	1.04	1.02
4	0.87	0.95	0.90	0.99	0.92
5 (top)	0.84	0.96	0.88	0.96	0.85
All	1.00	1.00	1.00	1.00	1.00

SOURCE: EUROMOD.

usually accounted for in cash income measures. However, cross-country (or inter-temporal) comparisons of the extent and incidence of public housing support are compromised if these forms of assistance are captured and direct subsidies are not. To redress this situation, we estimate the extent to which tenants in the social rented sector are paying rent below the amount they would pay if they were renting the same accommodation in the private market. Actual rent paid (calculated gross of any cash housing benefit) by social sector tenants is recorded in the income survey data sets underlying our analysis. Market rents must be estimated. We adopt the method developed to estimate the value of imputed rents for owner occupiers (Frick and Grabka 2003). The approach, known as the rental equivalence method, considers the opportunity cost of housing in nonsubsidized rental markets. It is based on a hedonic regression approach, following a two-step procedure. First, a regression model is estimated for the population of tenants (or rented accommodations) in the private, nonsubsidized market with rent as the dependent variable. Explanatory variables may include characteristics of the dwelling and the occupants.[8] The second stage applies the resulting coefficients to otherwise similar social tenants (see Frick et al. [2010] for further discussion). Table 5.4 shows that the proportion of households in the social rented sector varies considerably from almost none in Greece and very few in Italy to almost 20 percent in the United Kingdom. In all countries, they are concentrated, but not located exclusively, in the lower income quintiles.

Incidence of Public Noncash Transfers

In this section, we consider the effects of the combination of the three public transfers across the income distribution. First, we consider the size of each of the three components, measured relative to cash disposable income. Figure 5.3 shows that public rent subsidies make up a tiny proportion of the combined noncash transfers that we consider, even in the countries where they affect a significant number of households. Their largest effect is in the United Kingdom, where they are equal to 1 percent of disposable income. Public spending on education and health each has a much bigger effect in all countries. Education transfers in kind are equal to nearly 10 percent of disposable income in Belgium, which has the highest spending relative to

Table 5.4 SOCIAL TENANTS (PERCENTAGE OF ALL HOUSEHOLDS) BY QUINTILE OF HOUSEHOLD CASH DISPOSABLE INCOME

Quintile	Belgium	Germany	Greece	Italy	United Kingdom
1 (bottom)	10.3	10.8	0.2	1.5	30.6
2	7.3	7.9	0.0	0.8	35.5
3	3.1	5.9	0.1	0.4	19.3
4	2.4	5.2	0.1	0.4	9.6
5 (top)	1.8	2.2	0.1	0.1	1.9
All	5.2	6.5	0.1	0.7	19.5

SOURCE: EUROMOD.

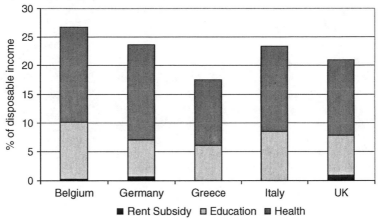

Figure 5.3 Noncash Income Components as a Proportion of Household Disposable Cash Income.
SOURCE: EUROMOD.

disposable income, whereas the lowest percentage is 6 percent in Germany. Health makes a larger aggregate contribution than education in all five countries. It contributes most in Belgium and Germany (16 to 17 percent), followed by Italy (15 percent), the United Kingdom (13 percent), and Greece (12 percent). Added together, the three noncash transfers that we consider represent the largest proportional addition to cash income in Belgium (27 percent) followed by Germany and Italy (23 to 24 percent), and the United Kingdom (21 percent), with the addition in Greece being the lowest (18 percent).

The scale of the transfer via noncash benefits, contrasted with that of cash benefits is illustrated in Figure 5.4. The left-hand chart shows the composition, across all households, of "augmented" income (cash disposable income plus noncash income), in terms of the average size of each income component as a percentage of augmented household income as a whole. As such, it shows how much market income is necessary on average to achieve a given level of augmented income; how much is added as cash and noncash benefits and deducted as income taxes and social insurance contributions. Cash benefits are subdivided in Figure 5.4 into (1) public pensions and (2) other cash benefits. In all five countries, cash benefits, taking the two types together, play a larger role in augmented income than noncash benefits do, but the extent to which this is so varies. At one extreme, in the United Kingdom, the proportions are similar with cash making up 19 percent and noncash 17 percent. At the other extreme (Greece and Italy), the contribution of noncash transfers considered here is much smaller than that of cash transfers, largely because of the importance of public pensions on the cash side. In Belgium and Germany, both cash and noncash benefits are relatively large components of income, but cash benefits including pensions make up the larger share.

The middle chart shown in Figure 5.4 illustrates the composition of augmented income in the bottom decile group (using equivalized augmented income to rank households). Both cash and noncash benefits are more important at low levels of income. Cash benefits are more closely (but inversely) related to income than are

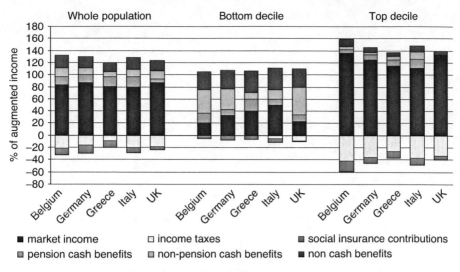

Figure 5.4 Composition of Augmented Household Incomes, Including Noncash Benefits (Housing Subsidies, Education, and Health).
NOTE: Decile groups are defined using household disposable income augmented with noncash benefits and equivalized using the modified OECD scale.

noncash benefits—so the share of noncash in all benefits is lower in the bottom decile group than overall. In the top decile group, shown on the right of Figure 5.4, both cash and noncash benefits are clearly less important. In the case of the United Kingdom, noncash benefits are larger than cash benefits. In all the other countries, mainly because of the role of public pensions, cash maintains the same relative role in benefits as a whole in the top income group as it does for all households. Figure 5.4 also shows the relative size of direct taxes and contributions paid by households. Whereas the top decile group pays more in these taxes than it receives back in cash and noncash benefits, the reverse is strongly the case in the bottom decile group, with the contrast being particularly clear for Belgium.

The relative contribution of each source of noncash benefit in reducing inequality as we move from the distribution of disposable income to the distribution of augmented income is shown in Table 5.5 in terms of the effect on quintile shares. Noncash benefits as a whole have a rather similar and common absolute effect on quintile shares across the five countries considered, in each case increasing the share of the bottom two quintiles and reducing the share of the top quintile, whereas the effect on the third is slightly positive and on the fourth slightly negative. The relative contributions of health and education are similar across countries, although education seems to play a larger and more strongly redistributive role in Italy than in other countries, increasing the share of the bottom quintile group by 1.7 percentage points and reducing that of the top quintile group by 2.1 points. To a lesser extent, the same applies to health in Belgium, where the share of the bottom quintile group increased by 1.6 percentage points, compared with 1.4 to 1.5 points in all other countries. As expected from earlier results, the contribution of housing subsidies to changing quintile shares is small in all countries with the largest effects being an increase in the share of the bottom quintile group in the United Kingdom of 0.3 points (corresponding to a transfer equivalent to 5 percent of the income of the quintile).

Table 5.5 Quintile Shares (Percentage) for Cash and Augmented Equivalized Household Income

		Household Income				
	Quintiles	Cash Only	+ In-kind Rent Subsidy	+ Education	+ Health	+ All Three Public Noncash Transfers
Belgium	1	10.3	10.3	11.5	11.9	12.9
	2	15.0	15.1	15.7	16.1	16.6
	3	18.8	18.7	19.1	18.9	19.1
	4	23.1	23.0	22.7	22.4	22.1
	5	32.9	32.8	31.1	30.7	29.3
Germany	1	9.3	9.5	10.4	10.8	11.9
	2	13.8	13.9	14.4	14.9	15.3
	3	17.6	17.6	17.9	18.0	18.2
	4	23.0	22.9	22.6	22.4	22.2
	5	36.3	36.1	34.7	33.9	32.5
Greece	1	7.3	7.3	8.3	8.7	9.6
	2	12.9	12.9	13.4	13.8	14.2
	3	17.3	17.3	17.5	17.6	17.8
	4	23.1	23.1	22.9	22.6	22.5
	5	39.4	39.4	37.9	37.2	36.0
Italy	1	7.7	7.7	9.3	9.2	10.5
	2	13.4	13.4	14.3	14.3	15.0
	3	17.8	17.8	17.9	18.2	18.2
	4	23.3	23.3	22.7	22.9	22.4
	5	37.8	37.8	35.8	35.5	33.8
UK	1	8.3	8.6	9.5	9.8	11.0
	2	12.3	12.5	13.2	13.4	14.3
	3	16.6	16.6	17.0	17.1	17.3
	4	22.7	22.5	22.3	22.2	21.8
	5	40.1	39.7	38.0	37.5	35.6

NOTE: Quintiles are fixed and based on equivalized cash household disposable income.

SOURCE: EUROMOD.

Not surprisingly, the effect of adding noncash transfers to cash income is to reduce inequality. (We consider the welfare interpretation of such a measure in the next section.) As shown in Table 5.6, inequality using the augmented measure is lower in all countries than for cash income alone for each of the three inequality indexes considered (the Gini coefficient and the Atkinson index with inequality aversion parameters set to 0.5 and 1.5). The proportional reduction in inequality is largest in Belgium and smallest in Greece and is, generally, in line with the relative sizes of the noncash transfers and cash income (shown in Figure 5.3).

Finally, we consider the effect of the inclusion of public in-kind transfers in the concept of resources on the risk of poverty, as measured using the proportion of the population with an equivalized income below 60 percent of the median. Figure 5.5 contrasts the effect of using the standard cash measure of disposable income with that using income augmented by noncash transfers. The approach adopted is explicitly relative and the poverty threshold is calculated using each income concept under analysis. It is worth noting that adding noncash income increases the median (and hence the threshold) by most in Belgium (31 percent), slightly less in Germany (30 percent), less in Italy and the United Kingdom (29 percent and 28 percent, respectively), and substantially less in Greece (22 percent). However, as clearly demonstrated in Figure 5.5, the proportion of people below the relevant threshold is much lower in all countries, when using the augmented income measure. The effect is particularly strong in the United Kingdom, where the "poverty" rate is reduced by

Table 5.6 INEQUALITY INDICATORS FOR CASH AND AUGMENTED EQUIVALIZED HOUSEHOLD INCOME

		Cash Income	Augmented Income
Belgium	Gini	0.2279	0.1760
	Atkinson (0.5)	0.0452	0.0266
	Atkinson (1.5)	0.2165	0.0855
Germany	Gini	0.2697	0.2124
	Atkinson (0.5)	0.0587	0.0368
	Atkinson (1.5)	0.1681	0.1042
Greece	Gini	0.3197	0.2672
	Atkinson (0.5)	0.0879	0.0595
	Atkinson (1.5)	0.2732	0.1738
Italy	Gini	0.3020	0.2408
	Atkinson (0.5)	0.0791	0.0501
	Atkinson (1.5)	0.2419	0.1514
UK	Gini	0.3178	0.2510
	Atkinson (0.5)	0.0832	0.0539
	Atkinson (1.5)	0.2414	0.1437

SOURCE: EUROMOD.

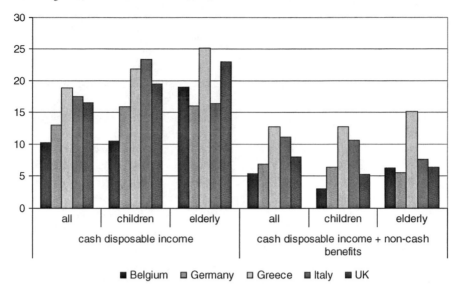

Figure 5.5 Percentage of Population Groups with Cash Disposable Income and Augmented (Cash + Noncash) Income Less than 60 Percent of the Median.
NOTE: Incomes are equivalized using the modified OECD scale.
SOURCE: EUROMOD.

more than one-half and least strong in Greece where it is, nevertheless, reduced by one-third. In all countries, the reduction in the proportion of people in households with an income below the thresholds is larger for children and older people. This is not surprising because the incidence of public spending for education and health care, respectively, is particularly concentrated on these two groups. The proportions of children below the threshold using the augmented measure are just a little over one-quarter of those using the cash measure in Belgium and the United Kingdom and only one-third of the number of elderly below the cash income threshold are below the augmented income threshold in Belgium, Germany, and the United Kingdom.

However, it is doubtful whether these results should be interpreted as having a bearing on the assessment of poverty or inequality from a welfare perspective. They are simply of interest because they show the scale of noncash incomes relative to cash incomes without taking into account the needs of individuals for health care or education. The next section attempts to address this issue.

WELFARE INTERPRETATION AND EQUIVALENCE SCALES

The practice adopted in the analysis so far is in line with most studies found in the relevant empirical literature in the sense that the same equivalence scales are used to construct the distribution of augmented income, as well as for the distribution of disposable income. This may be problematic, particularly in the case of public education and public health care, where needs are characterized by strong life-cycle patterns. The reason is that the equivalence scales used to measure inequality in disposable income are "conditional" on the existence of free public education and free public health care (Pollak and Wales 1979; Blundell and Lewbel 1991). By introducing the latter in the concept of resources in the augmented income distribution, we treat them like private commodities that households must pay for in order to obtain them. Therefore, the equivalence scales should be modified accordingly (Aaberge et al. 2010).

This is not an easy task. Both education and health care have some rather unique characteristics. Their consumption is absolutely necessary for the individuals involved and it does not involve any economies of scale at the household level. Needs for education and health care are likely to vary far more with individual characteristics such as age rather than with income. At the limit, we can adopt a "fixed cost" approach, assuming that the needs of the recipients of these services are equal to a specific sum of money. For example, we could assume that the per capita amounts spent by the state for age-specific population groups on public education and public health care depict accurately the corresponding needs of these groups. Then, the recalculation of equivalence scales is straightforward.

Assuming that y is household disposable income, k is the amount of extra needs of the household members for health and education (or each of them separately), e the OECD scale, and e' the new scale, the following should be valid for the household to remain in the same welfare level:

$$\frac{y}{e} = \frac{y+k}{e'} \tag{5.1}$$

and e' should be equal to

$$e' = \frac{e(y+k)}{y} \tag{5.2}$$

As an illustration of the implications of this approach, in Table 5.7, we exploit cross-country spending variations in EU-15 and adjust k accordingly. In each country, the value of k used in the equivalence scales is adjusted in order to be equal as a share of gross domestic product (GDP) per capita to the EU-15 unweighted average public spending for the corresponding educational level (primary, secondary, tertiary) and health care spending per age group (18 age groups). Therefore, for each household with n members ($i = 1, \ldots, n$) with different characteristics (such as age), the needs for education and health care are assumed to be:

$$k = \sum_{i=1}^{n} \left[k_{ENi} \frac{S_{EEUi}}{S_{ENi}} + k_{HNi} \frac{S_{HEUi}}{S_{HNi}} \right], \tag{5.3}$$

where k_{ENi} and k_{EHi} are, respectively, national spending for public education and public health care for persons with characteristics i; S_{ENi} and S_{HNi} are national spending figures for public education and public health care expressed as a share of the country's GDP per capita (i.e., they are equal to k_{ENi}/GDP_{pcN} and k_{EHi}/GDP_{pcN}, respectively); and S_{EEUi} and S_{HEUi} are the corresponding (unweighted) averages for EU-15.

Table 5.7 reports proportional changes in inequality indices when public education, health care, and housing services are included in the concept of resources.

Table 5.7 Proportional Changes in Inequality Indices as a Result of Noncash Public Transfers in the Fields of Housing, Education, and Health Care Using Alternative Equivalence Scales

	Belgium			Germany			Greece			Italy			United Kingdom		
	G	A0.5	A1.5	G	A0.5	A1.5	G	A0.5	A1.5	G	A0.5	A1.5	G	A0.5	A1.5
Baseline	-22.8	-40.6	-62.9	-21.2	-37.2	-38.1	-16.5	-31.4	-39.6	-20.3	-35.6	-40.7	-21.0	-35.1	-40.7
Scenario 1	-0.9	-2.0	-3.2	-2.3	-4.6	-5.1	-1.6	-3.0	-2.8	-1.4	-2.8	-3.3	-1.0	-4.0	-7.5
Scenario 2	-0.3	-0.7	-1.4	-0.8	-1.5	-1.8	-0.1	-0.2	0.0	0.0	0.0	0.0	-1.1	-2.0	-1.6

Scenario 1: only people in compulsory education age groups have education needs.
Scenario 2: all students have education needs.

SOURCE: EUROMOD.

Two alternative assumptions are used about which age groups have education needs. First (Scenario 1), it is assumed that only people in age groups for whom education is compulsory have educational needs. School-leaving age varies in the five countries under consideration: 14.5 years in Greece, 15 in Italy, 16 in the United Kingdom, and 18 in Belgium and Germany (OECD 2006, Table C1.2). All people below these age thresholds and above the compulsory primary education enrolment age are considered to have educational needs (including those who do not receive any public transfers such as dropouts and private education students), whereas the rest of the students in noncompulsory stages of the education system may receive public transfers but are assumed not to have the corresponding needs. Scenario 2 assumes that all students have needs for education services, irrespective of their educational level, as do dropouts below the official school leaving age of the country under consideration.

The first line of the table ("Baseline") reports the proportional changes of the inequality indices between the estimates derived from the distribution of disposable income and the same distribution augmented by the value of in-kind public education, health care, and housing services using the modified OECD scales, as shown in Table 5.6. The impact of the transfers appears to be very large. In the next two lines, the distribution of equivalized income is derived using the equivalence scales in Equation (5.2) and the proportional changes from the baseline distribution (distribution of equivalized disposable income using the modified OECD equivalence scales) are reported. This time, the changes appear to be modest, albeit inequality-reducing, in most cases. In the first scenario, the decline is due to the transfers to households with members in the noncompulsory stages of education (who are assumed to receive transfers in kind without having corresponding needs), to the effects of public housing subsidies, and to differences in the national levels of spending on health and education (included in income) and those at the EU average (providing our illustrative measure of needs). These factors are on balance inequality-reducing, especially in the United Kingdom and Germany and when using inequality indices sensitive to changes close to the bottom of the distribution, such as Atkinson (1.5). In the second scenario, all students and people of compulsory school age are considered to have education needs. In this case, the net effect on inequality is negligible in most cases, with small reductions remaining in Germany, Belgium, and the United Kingdom.

We believe that the approach outlined here can contribute to a better understanding of the distributional effects of noncash public transfers. At this stage, it may still be relatively crude, but it can be improved in several ways, either by capturing variations in the quality of services directed to particular segments of the population or by identifying systematic under- or overusers of such services. For example, in countries with federal rather than national education or health systems, it may be possible to identify regions with higher spending per capita (provided there is evidence that the higher spending is translated in higher quality of services). In the case of education, we can identify people who do not use public services, and we can bring pre-primary education into the picture. In the case of health care, we can differentiate between males and females, identify private health insurance holders who may systematically underuse the public health care system, or groups that make excessive use of public services (Le Grand and Winter 1985). Likewise, we can also identify people with disabilities or chronic illness whose needs are likely to be higher than the rest of the population. Finally, k may be made to vary with y, albeit less slowly than the conventional equivalence scales assume.

CONCLUSIONS

Standard microeconomic theory suggests that cash transfers are superior to noncash transfers, because using cash transfers, individuals may be able to allocate their budgets to commodities freely, so as to maximize their welfare. However, there are many theoretical arguments in favor of transfers in kind (Nelson 1987); in practice, governments use them extensively and, as Knetsch (1995) points out, in many circumstances, people seem to prefer noncash to cash transfers of equal value. Noncash benefits in the form of publicly provided education, health, and housing subsidies together make up an important supplement to cash incomes in Europe, and in particular, in the five countries that we consider. Nevertheless, even in combination, they are smaller in size, on average, than cash benefits.

Noncash benefits add a larger proportion to the resources available to households with low disposable incomes than they do to households with high income. Their absolute size also tends to be larger for households with low cash incomes. To the extent that the size and incidence of these noncash incomes differ across countries, it is important that they are accounted for—or considered in some way—in cross-national comparisons of income inequality and poverty. Among the countries we consider, the differences in size and distributional effect are small, relative to those we would observe if we compared EU countries with the United States or other developed countries outside Europe. However, there are important differences that can be summarized as follows. First, public housing subsidies, though relatively small in all cases and almost nonexistent in some, nonetheless add 1 percent to incomes as a whole in the United Kingdom and somewhat less than this in Germany. The aggregate effect of public education ranges from 6 percent of disposable income in Greece and Germany to 10 percent in Belgium, and for health the range is between 12 percent in Greece and 17 percent in Belgium and Germany. Given the differences in scale of spending, the distributional effect is quite similar in all five countries, but with education having a somewhat more pronounced effect on inequality measures in Italy than in other countries, and public health having a larger effect in Belgium.

Two further points remain. First, it is doubtful whether results derived using the standard approach in the field of static incidence analysis can have a straightforward welfare interpretation. Using this approach, we incorporate the value of the public services in the concept of household resources but ignore the problem of extra needs of public services recipients. Once these needs are taken into account with appropriate changes in the household equivalence scales used in the analysis, the distributional effects of noncash transfers appear to be far more modest and, under particular circumstances, may even appear to increase inequality.

Second, the practical lessons from this comparative empirical exercise should not be forgotten. The results presented in this chapter are as comparable as possible, but, nevertheless, there are some factors that may apply in different ways across countries and these should not only be borne in mind, but they should also provide the basis for future improvements in data and methods for the type of exercise we have carried out. Publicly provided education, health care, and housing are organized differently across countries and common analytical choices—for example, in the inclusion or otherwise of preprimary education or tertiary students living on their own—have different implications across countries. Furthermore, the available comparable data on spending by subgroup (e.g., pupils by sublevel of education or health care by gender) may be insufficient to capture differential levels of spending that may be important in some countries but not in others. Microdata from income surveys may not carry enough information about the use of private alternatives to public services (or co-payments) for the private components of spending to be captured properly. Again, the importance of these will vary with national context. Although we believe that we have made a contribution to the comparative evidence on the distributional effects of noncash benefits, many challenges remain.

ACKNOWLEDGMENTS

The analysis on which this chapter is based was carried out as part of the Accurate Income Measurement for the Assessment of Public Policies (AIM-AP) project, which was funded by the European Commission Framework Programme 6, 2006-09 under Priority 7 *Citizens and Governance in a Knowledge-Based Society* [Project no. 028412]. Estimating the value and incidence of noncash incomes—private as well as public— was one of three related objectives of the project as a whole. See http://www.iser. essex.ac.uk/euromod/research-and-policy-analysis-using-euromod/aim-ap for more information. We are particularly grateful to Alari Paulus for his help with this chapter and also to Tim Callan, Francesco Figari, late Joachim Frick, Tim Smeeding, Gerlinde Verbist, and Francesca Zantomio, on whose work we draw heavily. We also thank the other project participants for their contributions of national-level analysis, as well as for valuable discussions and insights: Conchita d'Ambrosio, Kieran Coleman, Chiara Gigliarano, Tim Goedemé, Markus Grabka, Olaf Groh-Samberg, Claire Keane, Christos Koutsambelas, Stijn Lefebure, Mattia Makovec, Killian Mullen, and Klaas De Vos. We are also indebted to all past and current members of the EUROMOD consortium for the construction and development of EUROMOD. However, any errors and the views expressed in this chapter are the authors' responsibility.

Notes

1. See, for example, O'Higgins and Ruggles (1981); James and Benjamin (1987); Lampman (1984); Smeeding et al. (1993); Evandrou et al. (1993); Tsakloglou and Antoninis (1999); Antoninis and Tsakloglou (2001); Sefton (2002); Caussat, Le Minez, and Raynaud (2005); Harding, Lloyd, and Warren (2006); Aaberge and Langørgen (2006); Garfinkel, Rainwater, and Smeeding (2006); Wolff and Zacharias (2006); Jones, Annan, and Shah (2008); and Marical et al. (2008).
2. These countries vary substantially in their standard of living as approximated by GDP per capita and represent three of the four welfare state regimes encountered in developed countries: liberal (United Kingdom), continental (Germany, Belgium), and southern (Italy, Greece) (Esping-Andersen 1990; Ferrera 1996).

National expertise was an essential input into the analysis reported here. The AIM-AP project did not include expertise on any country belonging to the "social democratic" welfare state regime; hence, no such example is included in our analysis.

3. Taxes are not earmarked in the countries we consider, and it would be misleading to allocate taxes to particular items of spending within a partial analysis.

4. More specifically, figures from Table X2.5 (p. 434) (Annual Expenditure on Educational Institutions per Student for All Services [2003] in Equivalent Euros Converted Using PPP, by Level of Education Based on Full-Time Equivalents) were multiplied by the estimates of the share of public expenditures in total educational expenditures (separately for tertiary and nontertiary education) reported in Table B2.1b (p. 206) (Expenditure on Educational Institutions as a Percentage of GDP by Level of Education [1995, 2000, 2003] from Public and Private Sources by Source of Funds and Year) and euro purchasing power parity conversion rates as reported in Table X2.2 (p. 431) (Basic Reference Statistics [Reference Period: Calendar Year 2003, 2003 Current Prices]). Then, in order to derive the corresponding estimates for years other than 2003, these estimates were inflated or deflated using country-specific nominal GDP per capita conversion factors derived from the data of the online OECD database (using real GDP growth rates, GDP deflators, and population growth rates).

5. For a detailed discussion see Callan, Smeeding, and Tsakloglou (2008).

6. Following the practice of Eurostat, in the main body of the chapter, income is equivalized using the modified OECD equivalence scale—with weights of 1.0, 0.5, and 0.3 assigned to the household head, each other household member aged above 13 years, and each member aged below 14, respectively.

7. The health care expenditures are taken from the OECD Health Data and include all public expenditure on health care, including among other things, expenditure on inpatient care, ambulatory medical services, pharmaceutical goods, and prevention. They do not include nonreimbursed individual health expenditures or cash benefits related to sickness. One drawback of the SOCX database arises from the fact that it does not distinguish differences in the use of health care by men and women, although there is evidence that spending patterns differ across sexes (Costello and Bains 2001; Carone et al. 2005). Another issue is that research and development spending is included. It may be argued that this component is not relevant for current welfare, but the SOCX database does not allow its deduction from the concept of public health care transfers (see Smeeding, Tsakloglou, and Verbist [2008] for further discussion).

8. This straightforward approach can be further improved by correcting for potential selectivity into the owner status (e.g., by applying a Heckman selection correction), as well as by considering measurement error in the imputation process; in other words, by adding an error term to the imputed rental value, thus maintaining the variance in the final construct. The practical solution found for the five countries considered here varied both in terms of the precise method (the Heckman correction was not successfully employed for the United Kingdom and Italy) and the explanatory variables that were chosen. Each country used broadly the same approach, while using the available variables that were most applicable to national housing markets.

References

Aaberge, Rolf, Manudeep Bhuller, Audun Langørgen, and Magne Mogstad. 2010. "The Distributional Impact of Public Services when Needs Differ." *Journal of Public Economics* 94: 549–562.

Aaberge, Rolf, and Audun Langørgen. 2006. "Measuring the Benefits from Public Services: The Effects of Local Government Spending on the Distribution of Income in Norway." *Review of Income and Wealth* 52: 61–83.

Antoninis, Manos, and Panos Tsakloglou. 2001. "Who Benefits from Public Education in Greece? Evidence and Policy Implications." *Education Economics* 9: 197–222.

Berloffa, Gabriella, Agar Brugiavini, and Dino Rizzi. 2006. "Health, Welfare and Inequality." Department of Economics Research Paper Series 41/06, University Ca' Foscari of Venice, Venice.

Blundell, Richard, and Arthur Lewbel. 1991. "The Information Content of Equivalence Scales." *Journal of Econometrics* 50: 49–68.

Callan, Tim, Timothy M. Smeeding, and Panos Tsakloglou. 2008. "Short Run Distributional Effects of Public Education Transfers in Seven European Countries." *Education Economics* 16: 277–290.

Carone, Giuseppe, Declan Costello, Nuria Diez Guardia, Gilles Mourre, Bartosz Przywara, and Aino Salomaki. 2005. "The Economic Impact of Ageing Populations in the EU25 Member States." Special edition, *European Economy* 236.

Caussat, Laurent, Silvie Le Minez, and Denis, Raynaud. 2005. "L'assurance-maladie contribue-t-elle à redistribuer les revenus?" *Dossiers solidarité et santé* 1: 7–41.

Costello, Declan, and Mandeep Bains. 2001. *Budgetary Challenges Posed by Aging Populations.* Directorate General for Economic and Financial Affairs of the European Commission, Economic Policy Committee Document EPC/ECFIN/655/01-EN final. Brussels: Directorate General for Economic and Financial Affairs of the European Commission.

Esping-Andersen, Gosta 1990. *The Three Worlds of Welfare Capitalism.* Princeton, NJ: Princeton University Press.

Evandrou, Maria, Jane Falkingham, John Hills, and Julian Le Grand. 1993. "Welfare Benefits in Kind and Income Distribution." *Fiscal Studies* 14: 57–76.

Ferrera, Maurizio 1996. "The 'Southern Model' of Welfare in Social Europe." *Journal of European Social Policy* 6: 17–37.

Frick, Joachim R., and Markus M. Grabka. 2003. "Imputed Rent and Income Inequality: A Decomposition Analysis for the U.K., West Germany, and the USA." *Review of Income and Wealth* 49(4): 513–537.

Frick, Joachim R., Markus M. Grabka, Timothy M. Smeeding, and Panos Tsakloglou. 2010. "Distributional Effects of Imputed Rents in Five European Countries." *Journal of Housing Economics* 19: 167–179.

Garfinkel, Irwin, Lee Rainwater, and Timothy M. Smeeding. 2006. "A Reexamination of Welfare State and Inequality in Rich Nations: How In-Kind Transfers and Indirect Taxes Change the Story." *Journal of Policy Analysis and Management* 25: 855–919.

Harding, Ann, Rachel Lloyd, and Neil Warren. 2006. "Moving Beyond Traditional Cash Measures of Economic Well-Being: Including Indirect Benefits and Indirect Taxes." Discussion Paper 61, National Centre for Social and Economic Modelling, University of Canberra, Canberra, Australia.

Hernández-Quevado, Cristina, Andrew M. Jones, Ángel López Nicolás, and Nigel Rice. 2006. "Socio-Economic Inequalities in Health: A Comparative Longitudinal Analysis Using the European Community Household Panel." *Social Science and Medicine* 63: 1246–1261.

James, Estelle, and Gail Benjamin. 1987. "Educational Distribution and Income Redistribution Through Education in Japan." *Journal of Human Resources* 22: 469–489.

Jones, Andrew, and Owen O'Donnell. 1995. "Equivalence Scales and the Costs of Disability." *Journal of Public Economics* 56: 273–289.

Jones, Francis, Daniel Annan, and Saef Shah. 2008 "The Redistribution of Household Income, 1997 to 2006/7." *Economic and Labour Market Review* 2: 18–31.

Klavus, Jan 1999. "Health Care and Economic Well-Being: Estimating Equivalence Scales for Public Health Care Utilization." *Health Economics* 8: 613–625.

Knetsch, Jack L. 1995. "Assumptions, Behavioural Findings and Policy Analysis." *Journal of Policy Analysis and Management* 14: 68–78.

Lampman, Robert J. 1984. *Social Welfare Spending.* New York: Academic Press.

Le Grand, Julian, and David Winter. 1985. "The Middle Classes and the Welfare State under Conservative and Labour Governments." *Journal of Public Policy* 6: 399–430.

Lietz, Christine, and Daniela Mantovani. 2007. "A Short Introduction to EUROMOD: An Integrated European Tax-Benefit Model." In *Micro-Simulation in Action: Policy Analysis in Europe Using EUROMOD.* Edited by Olivier Bargain. Research in Labor Economics. 25. New York: Elsevier.

Marical, François, Marco Mira d'Ercole, Maria Vaalavuo, and Gerlinde Verbist. 2008. "Publicly-Provided Services and the Distribution of Households' Economic Resources." *OECD Economic Studies* 44: 1–38.

Nelson, Richard R. 1987. "Roles of Government in a Mixed Economy." *Journal of Policy Analysis and Management* 6: 541–557.

O'Higgins, Michael, and Patricia Ruggles. 1981. "The Distribution of Public Expenditures and Taxes among Households in the United Kingdom." *Review of Income and Wealth* 27: 298–326.

OECD. 2006. *Education at a Glance 2006.* Paris: Organization for Economic Co-operation and Development.

———. 2007. Health Expenditure and Financing. http://stats.oecd.org/Index. aspx?datasetcode=SOCX_REF.

Pollak, Robert A., and Terrence J. Wales. 1979. "Welfare Comparisons and Equivalence Scales." *American Economic Review* 69 (Papers and Proceedings): 216–221.

Radner, Daniel B. 1997. "Noncash Income, Equivalence Scales and the Measurement of Economic Well-Being." *Review of Income and Wealth* 43: 71–88.

Sefton, Tom 2002. "Recent Changes in the Distribution of the Social Wage." CASE Paper 62, Centre for Analysis of Social Exclusion, London School of Economics, London.

Smeeding, Timothy M. 1982. *Alternative Methods for Valuing Selected In-Kind Transfer Benefits and Measuring Their Effect on Poverty.* US Bureau of Census Technical Paper 50. Washington, DC: US Government Printing Office.

Smeeding, Timothy M., Peter Saunders, John Coder, Stephen P. Jenkins, Johan Fritzell, Aldi J. M. Hagenaars, Richard Hauser, and Michael Wolfson. 1993. "Poverty, Inequality and Living Standard Impacts across Seven Nations:

The Effects of Non-Cash Subsidies for Health, Education and Housing." *Review of Income and Wealth* 39: 229–256.

Smeeding, Timothy M, Panos Tsakloglou, and Gerlinde Verbist. 2008. "Distributional Effects of Public Health Care Transfers in Seven European Countries." AIM-AP report, Institute for Social and Economic Research, Essex. www.iser.essex.ac.uk/files/msu/emod/aim-ap/deliverables/AIM-AP1.3.pdf.

Sutherland, Holly 2007. "EUROMOD: The Tax-Benefit Microsimulation Model for the European Union." In *Modelling Our Future: Population Ageing, Health and Aged Care*. Edited by Anil Gupta and Ann Harding, 483–488. International Symposia in Economic Theory and Econometrics 16. New York: Elsevier.

Tsakloglou, Panos, and Manos Antoninis. 1999. "On the Distributional Impact of Public Education: Evidence from Greece." *Economics of Education Review* 18: 439–452.

Wolff, Edward, and Ajit Zacharias. 2006. "An Overall Assessment of the Distributional Consequences of Government Spending and Taxation in the United States, 1989 and 2000." In *The Distributional Effects of Government Spending and Taxation*. Edited by Dimitris Papadimitriou, 15–68. New York: Palgrave/Macmillan.

Zaidi, Asghar, and Tania Burchardt. 2005. "Comparing Incomes When Needs Differ: Equivalization for the Extra Costs of Disability in the UK." *Review of Income and Wealth* 51: 89–114.

6

Accounting for Imputed and Capital Income Flows

JOACHIM R. FRICK† AND MARKUS M. GRABKA ∎

MOTIVATION

Income inequality has clearly increased in the majority of OECD countries over the past 20 years (see OECD 2008). Various factors have contributed to this general trend, such as increasing unemployment, growing wage inequality induced by skilled-based technological change (see Card and DiNardo 2002) and immigration (for the United States, see, e.g., Borjas 2006). Recent literature on growing inequality focusing on the upper tail of the distribution (Atkinson and Piketty 2007) has shown that, for example, the superstar phenomenon (i.e., the compensation for chief executive officers) had an independent effect on increased inequality (Bebchuk and Grinstein 2005). Above and beyond the impact of such processes on the labor market, changing demographic structures also exert an independent effect on the income distribution: These include increasing shares of single-person households and lone-parent families and the aging phenomenon, together with selective mortality and lower fertility rates (see Reed 2006 for an analysis of the British case).

Whereas the impact of increased earnings inequality on the overall level has been described in depth, less is known about the impact of other specific income components, in particular investment income. This research gap is considerable given that returns on investment and income from self-employment have clearly increased in importance compared to labor's share in domestic income in nearly all Organization for Economic Co-operation and Development (OECD) countries over the past 20 years (OECD 2008). In Germany, this development was clearly in favor of net investment income (see Figure 6.1). While net investment income more than doubled over the period 1991–2007, employees' compensation, as well as profits and income from self-employment, increased by less than 40 percent. Existing literature on the increasing importance of investment income (at the microlevel) includes Jäntti (1997) for Great Britain and the United States, as well as Frässdorf, Grabka, and Schwarze (2008) and Becker (2000) for Germany. All of these authors consistently report that the impact of property income on overall inequality is about two to three times higher than its contribution to income itself. However, all those

---

† Dr. Joachim R. Frick unfortunately passed on December 16, 2011 before the book went to press.

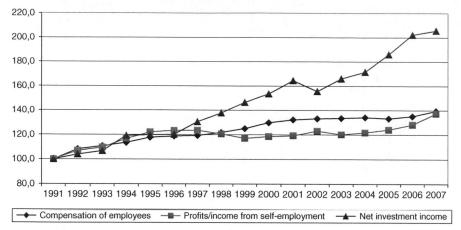

Figure 6.1 The Development of Income Aggregates in the German SNA (1991 = 100).
SOURCE: Authors' calculations based on the German Council of Economic Experts (SVR 2007).

papers consider only monetary returns on investments, thus ignoring (fictitious) income advantages arising from investments in owner-occupied housing. This appears to be inconsistent with the fact that buying one's own home is just an alternative to reaping benefits from investments in the capital market, that is, receiving interests and dividends. However, there is a separate strand of literature focusing on the impact of nonmonetary income components on income inequality and cross-national inequality analyses (see Canberra Group 2001). Imputed rent for owner-occupied housing is the most prominent example (see, e.g., Yates 1994 for Australia; Frick and Grabka 2003 for the United States, the United Kingdom, and Germany).[1] Typically the *net* value of imputed rent increases in age due to the nature of mortgage repayment schemes, thus yielding a decrease in income inequality and especially in relative income poverty among the elderly and providing a possible means of old-age provision.

Nevertheless, there appears to be no comprehensive analysis to date on the joint impact of monetary and nonmonetary returns on capital investments. This lack appears even more crucial given that increased income inequality is typically accompanied by increased wealth inequality (see Frick and Grabka 2009). Both economic outcome measures interact, with high-income earners typically having greater saving rates and thus accumulating more wealth than low-income groups do. Wealth, and financial wealth in particular, can be a distinct source of income. One might hypothesize that this interaction is of specific relevance in aging societies. Although the standard life-cycle theory (Jappelli and Modigliani 2005) predicts a consumption of capital in old age, (significant) dissaving cannot be observed in many countries, including Germany, where the median elderly household showed a saving rate of above 4 percent (savings defined as additions to the physical capital stock, see Börsch-Supan, Reil-Held, and Schnabel 2003). Thus, elderly individuals tend to remain in a preferable wealth position, continuously receiving returns on their investments.[2] At the same time, elderly homeowners tend to profit above the average from the consideration of imputed rent.

The increased importance of investment income can partly be explained by a shift in favor of a private coverage of old-age insurance, particularly in nonliberal welfare systems. Due to the significant reduction in benefits from statutory pension insurance, employees increasingly need to participate in occupational and private programs. As a consequence of this reorientation of the public old-age insurance system, individuals in general will enjoy higher claims from investment income, although most likely in a rather unequal manner.

The aim of this chapter is to give a comprehensive view of the joint impact of two components of investment income, namely (monetary) *capital income* (CI) and (nonmonetary) *imputed rent* (IR). We make use of more than 20 waves of consistently measured income data from the German Socio-Economic Panel (SOEP). After describing the microdata used and the methods applied to investigate the impact of investment income on overall inequality and poverty in "Data and Methods," "Empirical Results" presents the empirical findings with respect to the incidence and relevance, separately, of the two components of investment income, CI and IR. We consider these components in our "full" income concept relative to a "baseline" income concept net of investment income in order to investigate their respective impacts on inequality and poverty. Decomposition by subgroup is used to identify beneficiaries of investment income. The final section concludes.

DATA AND METHODS

The German SOEP

The German SOEP is a representative longitudinal survey of individuals living in private households in Germany (Wagner, Frick, and Schupp 2007). The survey was started in 1984 in West Germany and was extended to East Germany in June 1990, somewhat more than half a year after the fall of the Berlin Wall. The initial sample included over 12,000 respondents, with everyone aged 17 years and over in the sample households being interviewed. In recent years, new subsamples have been drawn, which approximately doubled the initial sample size. Due to the high concentration of economic resources (income and wealth) at the top of the distribution, welfare analyses based on representative population surveys are often confronted with the lack of information on rich individuals. To overcome this problem, the SOEP introduced a high-income sample in 2002, overrepresenting the top 3 percent of the income distribution—this sample is thus included in the more recent years of our time series. The sample analyzed in the "Empirical Results" section employs all available observation years up to survey year 2007.

One of the main problems when asking for (specific) income and wealth information in any population survey is nonresponse, and the SOEP is no exception to this concern. Due to the rather irregular and volatile nature of capital income, questions targeted at this income component are severely hampered by measurement problems, clearly imposing a threat to the explanatory power and validity of the data. Making effective use of the panel nature of SOEP, item nonresponse is corrected by applying longitudinal (and cross-sectional) imputation techniques, thus reducing bias arising from selectivity among the group of survey respondents (see Frick and Grabka 2005).

Another problem in the empirical assessment of the impact of capital income on inequality lies in the volatility of this income component (even before the recent financial crisis). Single cross-sectional analyses of capital income can suffer from discretionary changes and fluctuations in the value of an asset and the implicit returns. Thus, it seems crucial to use repeated and consistently surveyed information about capital income over a longer period to isolate the independent effect of that income component on overall inequality. Again, the time series information collected in the SOEP from the same households does help to assess the quality of the income information and possible measurement error.

Definition of Income Measures

BASELINE INCOME
We assess the impact of CI and IR on inequality by comparing results from a more comprehensive (or full) income concept, including these two components, with results derived from a baseline income excluding any investment income. Our analyses focus on economic well-being *after* redistribution through government and social security schemes. Thus, we apply a measure of equivalent annual postgovernment income.[3] We correct for income needs of households with different sizes and age compositions by calculating equivalent incomes using the modified OECD scale, which assigns a value of 1 to the head of household, 0.5 to all adult household members aged 14 years and over, and a value of 0.3 to children below 14 years of age. To allow for comparability across time, all incomes are expressed in euros (introduced only in 2002) and are deflated to 2000 prices (including a correction of purchasing power differences between East and West Germany).

COMPONENTS OF INVESTMENT INCOME
In the following section, we briefly describe the two types of investment income that are at the heart of the empirical analyses in the "Empirical Results" section, namely capital income and imputed rent.

Capital Income
The definition of *capital income* is anything but clear-cut, and reconciling macro- and microdata requires harmonization of measurement concepts. In the System of National Accounts (SNA), capital income is being used as a synonym for investment and property income, and extends to income derived from a resident entity's ownership of domestic and foreign assets. The most common types of investment income arise from equities (e.g., dividends, distributed income of corporations, branch profits, reinvested earnings) and income on debt (interest), as well as income from rentals and leasing, and royalties. Investment *income* includes the components of direct investment income, portfolio investment, and other investment income (OECD2001/2003) and also covers income imputed to households from net equity in life insurance reserves and in pension funds. A complication comes with the fact that rent from land (less expenses from rentals) is counted as investment income in the SNA, whereas rental housing or equipment is regarded as a production activity, and the respective income received is treated as part of *mixed income* (as recommended in the 1968 SNA, see United Nations 1968).

However, an investment in real estate rather than in the capital market yields returns for the investor, thus this separation raises the question of whether the measurement of capital income may be biased when considering rent from land only. This general problem also applies to the fictitious imputed rental value for owner-occupied housing (IR). Again, in the SNA, IRs are counted as a production activity, although all household members enjoy a fictitious income advantage from this investment. If the same household had invested in the capital market rather than in real estate, a direct income flow of capital income would have been observed as part of the household's investment income.

This—from a layman's point of view, artificial—differentiation hampers the analysis of CI and its impact on overall inequality on the basis of population surveys. Obviously, the various subcomponents of investment income mentioned are subject to specific measurement problems, especially for comparative research. A typical simplification is to lump together rent from land and other rental income. For example, to enhance comparability across various national data sets, the Luxembourg Income Study does not separate these income types and includes income from renting as part of property income.

Information about investment income in the SOEP is collected at the household level for all household members. At first, the SOEP questionnaire asks separately for income from renting and leasing and for accompanying expenses. The final measure of total capital income is net of any expenses that are related to rentals.[4] The SOEP does not differentiate between rentals from land and other rental income as the SNA does, but instead follows the procedure employed in the Luxembourg Income Study. Each household also has to specify whether assets, such as saving accounts, building savings contracts, life insurance policies, bonds, stocks, or business assets, are held by any household member. Each household is also asked to report the sum of all returns on the various investments received over the previous year. If the exact amount is not known, the respondents can give a rough assessment in six income categories—these values are transformed into metric information for the analyses to follow.[5] Other property incomes such as royalties are not covered by the SOEP questionnaire.

Another problem when trying to collect information about capital income in population surveys is the lack of detailed information about imputed income from investments, for example, in life insurance reserves. Even though investors regularly (typically on an annual basis) receive information about the accumulated stock on their investments, this information usually does not report the portion attributable to interest only. Thus, respondents are not able to provide information about the return on that investment. This is one reason why population surveys, compared with the SNA, typically underestimate investment income. The measure of capital income in the SOEP similarly does not cover income imputed to households from net equity in life insurance reserves and pension funds.

According to Smeeding and Weinberg (2001), it is advisable to extend the concept of capital income to returns on private retirement pensions—as is done in the SNA. However, the concept of "private retirement income" can consist of various forms of old-age provision. Private pensions could either be linked to an employment relationship, making them occupational pension plans, or they may be based on a contract between an individual and an insurance company, making them personal pension plans (e.g., cash-value life insurance contracts). Whereas occupational pensions can be interpreted as deferred labor compensation, and thus should not be counted as capital income, personal pensions can be seen as an alternative form of investment in insurance plans instead of in the capital market. However, some occupational pension schemes—at least in Germany—allow employees to make voluntary contributions to a pension account, thus also yielding returns on private investment. It is therefore difficult to separate the pure private portion from the deferred labor compensation. Although SOEP tries to collect detailed information about pension incomes, it still faces this separation problem. Thus, even though any pension payments received are part of our standard income measure, we refrain from considering returns derived from private pension plans in the measure of CI.

When dealing with CI, one might also think of capital gains. The Canberra Group (2001, 17) argues that "the theoretical argument for including capital gains in an extended measure of income is that this would be in line with the definition of income leaving a household as well off at the end of the accounting period as at the beginning. Capital gains or losses do have an effect on the economic behaviour of households and may affect their decisions on consumption." However, capital gains are not included in disposable income in the SNA, and the Canberra Group also does not recommended that they be considered (2001). Although earnings on capital (such as dividends) are counted as income from an SNA perspective, capital gains (or losses) are not regarded as the result of a productive activity that affects gross national product or total household income. Households almost certainly consider capital gains as a form of implicit saving, thus as a change in the value of an asset. This might be one reason why population surveys typically do not provide information about capital gains, as is the case with the SOEP.[6] Above and beyond this data limitation, we are not interested in changes in stocks but rather in changes in income flows, thus we refrain from considering capital gains in this chapter, following the recommendation of the Canberra Group (2001, 28).

Imputed Rent

Imputed rent is a fictitious income advantage from owner-occupied housing. A household's decision to move into homeownership represents a trade-off in which the opportunity to invest in financial assets that would create real income flows through interest or dividends is foregone; thus, the welfare position of owner occupiers would be biased as long as the fictitious return from housing is not considered in an extended income concept. Based on such considerations, European Commission (EC) Regulation No. 1980/2003 provides an accurate definition of IR to be used to harmonize income measurement in the context of the European Union Statistics on Income and Living Conditions (EU-SILC):

> The imputed rent refers to the value that shall be imputed for all households that do not report paying full rent, either because they are owner-occupiers or they live in accommodation rented at a lower price than the market price, or because the accommodation is provided rent-free. The imputed rent shall be estimated only for those dwellings (and any associated buildings such [as] a garage) used as a main residence by the households. The value to impute shall be the equivalent market rent that would be paid for a similar dwelling as that occupied, less any rent actually paid (in the case where the accommodation is rented at a lower price than the market price), less any subsidies received from

the government or from a non-profit institution (if owner-occupied or the accommodation is rented at a lower price than the market price), less any minor repairs or refurbishment expenditure which the owner-occupier households make on the property of the type that would normally be carried out by land-lords. The market rent is the rent due for the right to use an unfurnished dwell-ing on the private market, excluding charges for heating, water, electricity, etc.[7]

According to the EC regulation, potential beneficiaries of IR include owner occupi-ers, rent-free tenants, and tenants with below-market rent, including those who live in public or social housing, as well as those who have been granted a rent reduction by their respective landlords (e.g., relatives or employer).

Whereas this general definition of IR can be seen as a blueprint for population surveys, one problem exists in determining the exact measure of an equivalent market rent. This is of particular importance for countries such as the United Kingdom with a relatively low share of tenants in the private housing market.[8] Another problem is the accurate consideration of owner-specific costs that need to be deducted to derive a measure of *net* IR.

The SOEP measure of IR employed in the following has been defined along the lines of the EC regulation using the *opportunity cost approach*.[9] This procedure also includes advantages of living in subsidized rented accommodation or living rent-free (the latter group may indeed include former owner occupiers [often outright owners], who hand over the deeds to their property to their children in exchange for a usufructuary right to remain in their current dwelling).

The opportunity cost approach applied in the SOEP is based on a regression of gross rent per square meter (not including heating costs) actually paid by main tenants in the private market. Independent variables include the year of construc-tion, condition of dwelling, size of dwelling, length of occupancy, community size, and disposable income. Applying these regression coefficients to the population of otherwise comparable owner occupiers and individuals living in households with reduced rent yields a gross measure of imputed rents. After deducting all owner-related costs, such as operating, maintenance, and interest payments on mortgages, as well as property taxes, one arrives at a net value of IR that can be interpreted as the income advantage of owner-occupied housing. For rent-free households and per-sons living in households with below-market rent, no further deductions have to be made. The most important owner-specific costs are interest payments on mort-gages.[10] Assuming a standard (German) mortgage with regular payments over a period of 30 years, we find an increasing income advantage for owners over the entire period. At the beginning of the payment period, interest payments clearly exceed the mortgage payments. As times goes by, the share of the mortgage that is paid off increases, leaving an increasing income advantage from owner-occupied housing (for more details on the imputation of IR in SOEP, as well as for sensitivity analyses showing the variation in the distributional impact by the choice of the method used to derive IR, see Frick, Grabka, and Groh-Samberg 2007).

Imputed rents are approximated in the SNA as well as in population surveys. Whereas IR in the SNA is counted as a production activity, thus not as investment income, population surveys typically provide IR as a separate piece of fictitious income information. Thus, a user can decide whether IR should be counted as investment income or not. In the following, we describe the impact of the monetary component of investment income (CI) separately from the nonmonetary, fictitious income advantage (IR) on overall inequality.

Methodology

Following standard procedures in inequality research, and in order to check the robustness and sensitivity of our findings, we employ various indicators of inequality: the Gini coefficient, which is more sensitive to changes in the middle of the income distribution, as well as the half-squared coefficient of variation (HSCV), which belongs to the family of generalized entropy measures and is also referred to as the I_2 measure.

$$HSCV = \frac{C(y)^2}{2} = \left(\frac{1}{2n\bar{y}^2}\right)\sum_{i=1}^{n}(y_i - \bar{y})^2 \qquad (6.1)$$

This index is more sensitive to changes at the top end of the income hierarchy. Comparing time series on inequality results obtained from such measures when applied to income with and without CI and IR will help to identify where in the income distribution these two components matter most.

To analyze which population subgroups are most affected by the consideration of investment income in the final (full) outcome measure of disposable income, we make use of the decomposition by subgroups as described in Shorrocks (1984), based on the mean log deviation (MLD). The MLD also belongs to the family of generalized entropy measures and is sensitive to changes at the lower tail of the income distribution. The MLD is also referred to as the I_0-Measure.

$$MLD = \frac{1}{N}\sum_{i=1}^{N}\ln\left(\frac{\bar{y}}{y_i}\right). \qquad (6.2)$$

Relative income poverty is calculated based on a threshold given by 60 percent of the national median of equivalent disposable income. We employ the family of poverty measures described by Foster, Greer, and Thorbecke (1984), using three different values for the poverty aversion parameter α, thus giving different weights to the individual's poverty intensity. This allows us to control for whether the incorporation of investment income has different impacts depending on the proximity of different individuals to the poverty line.

$$FGT(a) = \frac{1}{n}\sum_{i=1}^{q}\left(\frac{z-y_i}{z}\right)^a. \qquad (6.3)$$

EMPIRICAL RESULTS

In addition to describing what has been going on with respect to different types of investment income in Germany since the mid-1980s, we are especially interested to see which subgroups of the population might be affected most by these types of income.[11] The German pay-as-you-go public pension system is clearly under pressure to cut back, mostly due to increasing longevity and decreasing fertility rates, while a range of newly established publicly co-funded financial instruments (e.g., *Riester-Rente*) are driving increasing numbers of people to invest in private old-age provision. Thus, age is a crucial structural variable in the following analyses. Among other issues, we will address the question of whether inequality decomposition by age (within-/between-group inequality) has also changed over time due to the inclusion of CI and IR. At least for IR, this is to be expected from the literature (e.g., Yates 1994). However, the picture for CI may be less clear. On the one hand, the elderly are typically more risk-averse and "conservative" in their investment behavior, which should yield lower interest. On the other hand, due to their longer periods of accumulation, their financial holdings (wealth stock) should be higher, thus also improving their chances for risk diversification.

The following section contains time-consistent estimates for Germany based on annual income data from the SOEP.[12] The time series shown in the following analyses refer to the year of the observation; thus, the income refers to the previous calendar year. That is, the most recent measure used here is from 2007 and gives the annual income as of 2006. Due to sweeping changes in the income distribution in the early years after the end of the German Democratic Republic, annual figures for the East German subsample of the SOEP can only be provided starting with income year 1991. Thus, all time series on income, inequality, and poverty give results based on West Germany until 1991 and results for unified Germany thereafter.[13]

Incidence and Relevance of IR and CI

The *incidence* of a given income component is measured by the share of individuals receiving a given income component (here IR and CI), whereas the *relevance* of IR and CI is defined as the percent of each in baseline income. Figure 6.2 reveals that by and large, there is a rather stable share of about 40 percent of the population receiving IR. There is an expected dip after German unification caused by the considerably lower share of owner occupiers in the new federal states of East Germany. Similarly, the share of individuals receiving some type of capital income ranges between 80 and nearly 90 percent over the entire period with a slight reduction in the years since 2000.

Obviously, these figures do not reveal how much of a given income source a person actually receives. Thus, Figure 6.3 gives the relevance of both income sources as a share of our augmented equivalent annual postgovernment income. Separating IR and CI from the baseline income reveals that these two components doubled from the mid-1980s to 2007. This is true in absolute as well as in relative terms. For example, IR as a share of baseline disposable income went from 2.9 percent in 1985 to more than 5 percent in 2007; similarly, the relevance of CI increased from 3.4 percent to 5.7 percent. Finally, it should be noted that although the incidence of IR is lower than that of CI, it constitutes a larger fraction of income among the households who receive IR, because the percentage of total income is similar for CI and IR.

Analyzing the incidence of the two components across baseline income quintiles shows very little variation in the distribution of beneficiaries from IR over the

Population share holding CI and IR (in %)

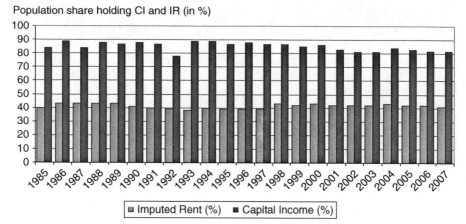

Figure 6.2 Incidence of CI and IR in Germany, 1985 to 2007.
NOTE: Population: individuals in private households. Up to 1991, West Germany only.
SOURCE: SOEP (1985–2007).

income hierarchy (see Table 6.1), whereas the beneficiaries of CI are clearly more concentrated at the top of the distribution. This pattern is even more pronounced when looking at the relevance—the share of income coming from the respective components. When moving up the income ladder, the amount of equivalent income derived from CI is less than €500 among households in the first quintile in 2007, whereas this value is five times higher among households in the top quintile.

The rise in magnitude of both income components is in line with macrostatistics, revealing a clear reduction in the share of gross domestic product coming from labor income (this share peaked in 1993 at almost 68 percent and sunk to 61 percent in 2007, see Frick and Grabka 2008).

CI and IR as a share of total disposable income (in %)

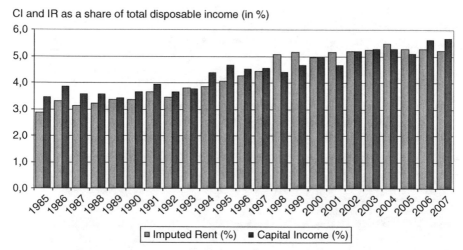

Figure 6.3 Relevance of CI and IR in Germany, 1985 to 2007.
NOTES: Population: individuals in private households. Up to 1991, West Germany only.
SOURCE: SOEP (1985–2007).

Income Inequality

Turning to the effects of IR and CI on disposable income inequality, Figure 6.4 compares inequality indices (Gini and HSCV) for baseline income with those for augmented full income measures including IR, CI, and both at the same time. We observe a consistent inequality-reducing effect arising from the consideration of IR, which is in line with the literature (see, e.g., Yates 1994 for the case of Australia; Frick and Grabka 2003 for the United States and United Kingdom, as well as Germany; and Frick et al. 2009 for various EU countries) although one should keep in mind that our baseline income measure does not include capital income as typically is

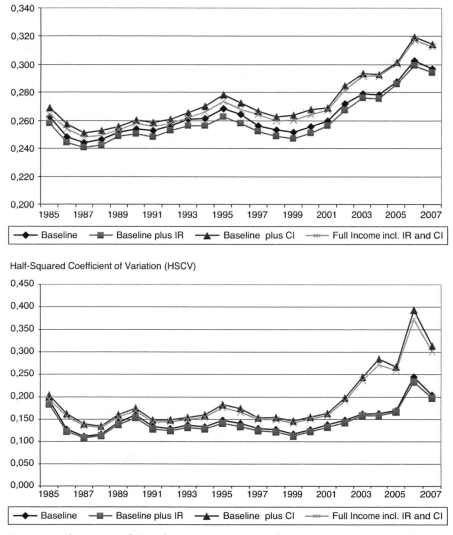

Figure 6.4 The Impact of CI and IR on Income Inequality in Germany, 1985 to 2007. NOTES: Population: individuals in private households. Up to 1991, West Germany only. SOURCE: SOEP (1985–2007).

the case. The incorporation of IR into the baseline equivalent disposable income reduces income inequality according to the Gini coefficient by about 1 to 2 percent, which appears related to the fact that the beneficiaries from IR are more equally distributed across the income distribution.[14] At the same time, the top-sensitive HSCV shows a considerably larger inequality reduction effect up to 5 percent, which is of the same magnitude when looking at the bottom-sensitive MLD. These somewhat stronger effects at the tails of the income distribution are the result of two aspects: homeowners in general tend to be higher up in the income hierarchy, however, due to the nature of the typical mortgage repayment schemes, the *net* IR measure—which we apply here—is supposedly more concentrated among the elderly, who are typically associated with somewhat lower baseline incomes.

A very different finding arises for CI, where disposable income inequality clearly increases due to the inclusion of this income component, which disproportionately goes to high earners. First, as expected, this increase is much stronger when looking at the top-sensitive HSCV than in the case of the Gini coefficient. The respective relative changes are 3 to 6 percent for the Gini coefficient, whereas the relative change using the HSCV is about 10 times higher. Second, the change resulting from the incorporation of CI, though volatile, does increase over time. Whereas the HSCV increased due to the inclusion of CI by 10 to 20 percent in the 1980s and 1990s, this relative change has more than doubled in recent years. Obviously, omitting CI and IR from an extended income measure would severely bias long time series on income inequality in Germany.

Summing up, income inequality in Germany has increased significantly from the mid-1980s to the most recent years. Using a comprehensive disposable income measure (including IR and CI), the Gini coefficient moves up from around 0.26 to more than 0.31. This increase in inequality has been paralleled by shrinking incomes among the middle class (see Grabka and Frick 2008). Irrespective of an overall inequality-reducing effect arising from IR, there was a massive prorich growth of CI during the financial boom period of the late 1990s to 2007, which overall has resulted in increased income concentration. This is confirmed by the even stronger increase in the top-sensitive HSCV measure, which moves from 0.195 in 1985 to more than 0.300 in 2007.

Relative Poverty

Throughout the period under investigation and in line with the above-mentioned development of inequality, the relative poverty risk rate in Germany reached record levels in 2006 (about 18 percent), followed by a minor reduction in 2007, which was mainly due to improved labor market conditions and reduced unemployment in the economic upswing until 2008 (see Frick and Grabka 2008). To adequately show the effect on poverty of incorporating IR and CI into the income measure, we dynamically adjust the poverty threshold when including each of the aforementioned income components (see Figure 6.5).

With respect to the inclusion of IR, our results are strongly supportive of the inequality-dampening effect of IR: The poverty reduction effect as measured by the change in the poverty risk rate (i.e., FGT0 in the top panel of Figure 6.5) is clearly visible during the 1980s and 1990s and levels off over the first decade of the new

Poverty risk rate (FGT0)

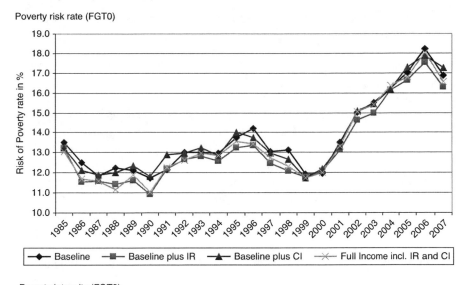

Poverty intensity (FGT2)

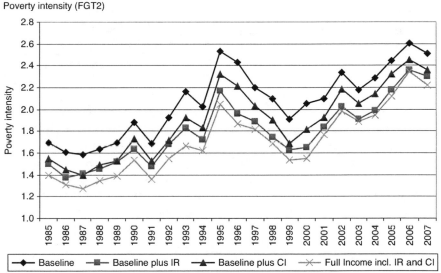

Figure 6.5 The Impact of CI and IR on the Risk of Relative Poverty in Germany, 1985 to 2007.
NOTES: Population: individuals in private households. Up to 1991, West Germany only.
SOURCE: SOEP (1985–2007).

century. However, when giving more weight to inequality among the poor by applying the FGT2 index ($\alpha = 2$) in the lower panel in Figure 6.5, the reduction effect arising from IR becomes clearly more pronounced (around 20 percent).

Including CI in the income measure does not show a similarly clear-cut picture with respect to the poverty head-count ratio (FGT0); however, there is a more pronounced poverty-reduction effect from increasing α. The overall effect arising from including both IR and CI is a clear reduction in poverty. However, it should be noted that these reductions appear to dwindle over time; for example, up to the end of the last century, the poverty-reduction effect for FGT2 was in the range of 20 percent, whereas this effect was only 10 percent in more recent years.

Subgroup Analyses

INVESTMENT INCOME BY INCOME QUINTILE AND AGE GROUPS

Having analyzed these time trends on the basis of the entire population in private households, we now turn to the question of where in the income distribution these effects matter most, as well as which socioeconomic characteristics are likely to be most associated with the inclusion of IR and CI. Thus, we compare the incidence and relevance of IR and CI across baseline disposable income quintiles (Table 6.1), as well as across age groups (Table 6.2). Due to the above-mentioned changes over time, we run these analyses separately for 1997 and 2007. While the share of the population with IR is modified only slightly across baseline income quintiles, there is a pronounced positive relationship between CI and baseline income (see top panel in Table 6.1). For both income components, we see that these relationships become stronger from 1997 to 2007.

Adding IR and CI to baseline income (second panel in Table 6.1) and analyzing the relative change shows that for 1997, each of the two components adds about 5 percent to baseline income, although this increase is much stronger among the poorest quintile (plus 20 percent once we add IR and CI), whereas the richest quintile increases its baseline income by less than 10 percent. However, for the latter, this is in part due to higher baseline income and masks the fact that the absolute average amount of IR and CI added in each quintile is positively correlated with baseline income. The only exception appears to be the very lowest income group: This is most likely a reflection of the higher probability of poor people enjoying the fictitious income advantage of subsidized social housing, which is included in our measure of IR. When looking at the absolute figures for CI and IR, we observe that in 1997, the highest income quintile had 1.7 times more investment income than the poorest quintile, and that by 2007, this ratio had more than doubled, showing the former to have 3.5 times more investment income than the latter (€4,208 vs. €1,183).

The lowest panel in Table 6.1 reports the share of overall income held per quintile for each of the four definitions: In 1997, the poorest fifth of the population had only 9.1 percent of baseline income, but the richest possessed over 34.9 percent. Adding IR to baseline income made the distribution slightly less unequal, whereas adding CI again increased the inequality somewhat. Considering both components of property income at the same time yielded more or less the same picture. Apparently, for all indicators shown in this table, there is a consistent change from 1997 to 2007 toward rising inequality. This can be exemplified by the even more pronounced increase in CI among the highest income groups, the reduced (increased) share of property income among the poorest (richest), and finally by the fact that in 2007, 39.3 percent of full disposable income was in the hands of the top 20 percent, as compared to only 37.8 percent of baseline income.

Table 6.2 reports similar information for age groups rather than for income quintiles. There is the expected positive relationship between the probability of enjoying IR and age with the exception of the youngest age group: That group's somewhat higher share of IR recipients does not so much reflect early homeownership as

Table 6.1 The Impact of IR and CI by Baseline Income Quintile

Population Share (%) Holding . . .

Quintile	1997		2007	
	IR	CI	IR	CI
1 (bottom)	38	69	35	60
2	37	86	38	76
3	37	91	42	86
4	42	95	44	91
5 (top)	42	95	49	96
All	39	87	41	82

Equivalent Income (euro)

Quintile	1997				2007			
	Baseline	IR	CI	IR and CI	Baseline	IR	CI	IR and CI
1 (bottom)	7,140	724	726	1,450	6,661	690	494	1,183
2	11,638	625	386	1,012	11,468	778	581	1,359
3	14,416	681	461	1,142	14,871	879	627	1,506
4	17,937	815	834	1,650	19,466	1,055	1,012	2,067
5 (top)	27,467	995	1,524	2,519	31,826	1,548	2,659	4,208
All	15,714	768	786	1,554	16,856	990	1,075	2,064

(Continued)

Table 6.1 The Impact of IR and CI by Baseline Income Quintile (Cont'd)

	Income from IR and CI as a percentage of baseline income							
Quintile	Baseline	Baseline Plus IR	Baseline Plus CI	Full Income Including IR and CI	Baseline	Baseline Plus IR	Baseline Plus CI	Full Income Including IR and CI
1 (bottom)	—	10.1	10.2	20.3	—	10.4	7.4	17.8
2	—	5.4	3.3	8.7	—	6.8	5.1	11.9
3	—	4.7	3.2	7.9	—	5.9	4.2	10.1
4	—	4.5	4.7	9.2	—	5.4	5.2	10.6
5 (top)	—	3.6	5.5	9.2	—	4.9	8.4	13.2
All	—	4.9	5.0	9.9	—	5.9	6.4	12.2

	Income share (%)							
Quintile	Baseline	Baseline Plus IR	Baseline Plus CI	Full Income Including IR and CI	Baseline	Baseline Plus IR	Baseline Plus CI	Full Income Including IR and CI
1 (bottom)	9.1	9.3	9.0	9.1	7.9	8.1	7.7	7.8
2	14.8	14.8	14.5	14.4	13.6	13.6	13.1	13.1
3	18.4	18.4	18.0	18.0	17.7	17.7	17.1	17.2
4	22.9	22.8	22.6	22.7	23.1	23.0	22.7	22.6
5 (top)	34.9	34.7	35.9	35.8	37.8	37.6	39.4	39.3
All	100.0	100.0	100.0	100.0	100.0	100.0	100.0	100.0

NOTES: Population: individuals in private households. Income in 2000 prices. Up to 1991, West Germany only.

SOURCE: SOEP (1997, 2007).

it does young adults still living with their parents. On the other hand, we do not find a strong correlation between age and the probability of getting returns on CI (top panel of Table 6.2).

Nevertheless, for those with IR from owner-occupied housing, we see the well-known strong increase in that type of income across age groups, which simply reflects the degree to which mortgages are paid off and equity is increased. For example, in 1997, 25- to 40-year-olds had €468 in IR on average, whereas those aged 65 years and over had about three times this amount (€1,324). In line with a standard age profile of wealth, the absolute amount of CI peaked among the 50- to 65-year-olds (1997: €1,222) and diminished slightly in the oldest cohort (€999) due to dissaving and transfers to younger generations, among other things. However, considering both types of income together, the oldest enjoy the highest average amount of (all types of) investment income. Comparing again the situation in 2007 with the situation 10 years earlier, it appears that the oldest profited most from the aforementioned increase in inequality: Although considering IR and CI pushed baseline incomes of those aged 65 years and over up 17 percent in 1997, their incomes rose further to almost 24 percent in 2007, compared to a much lower impact among the middle age groups.

INEQUALITY DECOMPOSITION BY SUBGROUP

The extent to which these differences across subgroups impact income inequality can be assessed by means of inequality decomposition analysis. Based on the MLD, which exhibits the necessary criteria of being an additively decomposable inequality measure, Table 6.3 gives the respective results for decomposition by household/family type and socioeconomic status of the household head, as well as by individual age. The latter appears to be an important structural variable in light of our hypothesis on the increasing relevance of returns on private investment (i.e., CI and IR) as an alternative income source in old age. To provide evidence of possible changes in the relative concentration of inequality over time, we repeat this analysis for the years 1997 and 2007.

The inclusion of IR and CI increases the baseline income measure by about 10 percent in 1997 and by more than 12 percent in 2007. However, this increase is not evenly spread. It accrues disproportionately to the elderly (especially due to IR), individuals living in households headed by pensioners (due to IR), and the self-employed (mostly due to CI). Again, young adults who are still living at home profit from their parents' IR and CI (due to the standard assumption of pooling and sharing of resources across all household members). In line with the results mentioned in earlier sections, all those effects are much stronger in 2007.

With respect to inequality, the change induced by investment income in the overall MLD is 15.6 percent in 1997 and 47.4 percent in 2007. Even though this huge change may be somewhat related to the volatility of CI, it is perfectly in line with the general increase in inequality in Germany over this period, which is strongly related to massive unemployment (Frick and Grabka 2008). One of the advantages of inequality decomposition by subgroup is the opportunity to evaluate changes of within- and between-group inequality related to the incorporation of both sources of investment income. In general, we find that within-group inequality increases significantly when considering returns on private investments in absolute as well as in relative terms. On the other hand, the contribution of between-group inequality

Table 6.2 The Impact of IR and CI by Age Group

Age Group	1997				2007		
	Population Share (%) Holding . . .						
	IR	CI		IR	CI		
<25	35	86		34	79		
25–<40	28	88		25	82		
40–<50	38	88		36	83		
50–<65	49	89		54	82		
≥65	53	87		61	83		
All	39	87		41	82		

Equivalent Income (Euro)

Age Group	Baseline	IR	CI	IR and CI	Baseline	IR	CI	IR and CI
< 25	14,320	529	583	1,112	14,865	619	675	1,293
25–<40	16,130	468	465	933	16,803	527	583	1,109
40–<50	17,642	675	853	1,528	18,445	668	1,036	1,704
50–<65	17,130	1,061	1,222	2,283	19,881	1,428	1,442	2,871
≥65	14,027	1,324	999	2,323	15,254	1,810	1,788	3,598
All	15,714	768	786	1,554	16,856	990	1,075	2,064

Income from IR and CI as a percentage of baseline income

Age group	Baseline	Baseline Plus IR	Baseline Plus CI	Full Income Including IR and CI	Baseline	Baseline Plus IR	Baseline Plus CI	Full Income Including IR and CI
< 25	—	3.7	4.1	7.8	—	4.2	4.5	8.7
25–<40	—	2.9	2.9	5.8	—	3.1	3.5	6.6
40–<50	—	3.8	4.8	8.7	—	3.6	5.6	9.2
50–<65	—	6.2	7.1	13.3	—	7.2	7.3	14.4
≥65	—	9.4	7.1	16.6	—	11.9	11.7	23.6
All	—	4.9	5.0	9.9	—	5.9	6.4	12.2

NOTES: Population: individuals in private households. Income in 2000 prices. Until 1991, West Germany only.

SOURCE: SOEP (1997, 2007).

Table 6.3 THE INEQUALITY DECOMPOSITION BY SUBGROUP

			1997		
	Population Share (%)	Increase in Mean Equivalized Income. Due to IR and CI (%)	MLD		Change in Inequality Due to IR and CI (%)
			Baseline	Including IR and CI	
Household/family type					
Single ≤60	9.1	12	0.1789	0.2671	49.3
Couple no kids ≤60	13.6	8	0.1060	0.1179	11.2
HH with children up to 17	38.7	7	0.1332	0.1482	11.2
HH with adult children	15.4	9	0.1012	0.1113	10.0
HH head aged >60	23.2	15	0.1088	0.1259	15.7
Within-groups inequality (%)	—	—	0.1231	0.1440	17.0
Between groups inequality (%)	—	—	0.0067	0.0060	−9.8
Socioeconomic group of HH head					
Blue-collar worker	19.8	5	0.0567	0.0597	5.4
White-collar worker	33.8	8	0.1090	0.1169	7.3
Self-employed	7.1	15	0.1393	0.1542	10.7
Unemployed	7.6	7	0.1080	0.1087	0.6
Pensioner	23.7	17	0.1071	0.1645	53.5
Other	8.0	9	0.1476	0.1549	4.9
Within-groups inequality (%)	—	—	0.1098	0.1295	17.9
Between groups inequality (%)	—	—	0.0200	0.0205	2.9
Age of HH member					
<25	26.9	8	0.1352	0.1496	10.7
25–<40	23.4	6	0.1059	0.1092	3.0
40–<50	13.9	9	0.1169	0.1401	19.8
50–<65	19.8	13	0.1422	0.1778	25.1
≥65	16.0	17	0.1225	0.1418	15.8
Within-groups inequality (%)	—	—	0.1259	0.1459	15.9
Between groups inequality (%)	—	—	0.0039	0.0041	5.6
All	100.0	10	0.1298	0.1501	15.6

NOTES: Population: individuals in private households. Up to 1991, West Germany only. HH is household.

SOURCE: SOEP (1997, 2007).

	2007								
	Percentage Contribution to Aggregate Inequality		Population Share (%)	Increase in Mean Equivalized Income. Due to IR and CI (%)	MLD		Change in Inequality Due to IR and CI (%)	Percentage Contribution to Aggregate Inequality	
	Baseline	Including IR and CI			Baseline	Including IR & CI		Baseline	Including IR and CI
	12.5	16.2	10.7	9	0.2086	0.3826	83.4	10.9	13.6
	11.1	10.7	14.1	10	0.2549	0.3335	30.8	17.6	15.6
	39.7	38.2	36.9	8	0.1865	0.2339	25.4	33.7	28.7
	12.0	11.4	13.8	11	0.1766	0.2440	38.2	11.9	11.2
	19.5	19.5	24.5	23	0.1513	0.3135	107.2	18.2	25.5
	94.9	96.0	—	—	0.1978	0.2950	49.2	96.9	98.0
	5.1	4.0	—	—	0.0064	0.0059	−7.2	3.1	2.0
	8.7	7.9	16.9	6	0.0651	0.0704	8.1	5.4	3.9
	28.4	26.3	35.2	8	0.1234	0.1426	15.6	21.3	16.7
	7.6	7.3	7.9	18	0.3315	0.5115	54.3	12.8	13.4
	6.3	5.5	7.6	5	0.1756	0.1901	8.3	6.6	4.8
	19.6	26.0	23.5	22	0.1184	0.2199	85.8	13.6	17.2
	9.0	8.2	8.8	15	0.2928	0.7147	144.1	12.7	21.0
	84.6	86.3	—	—	0.1720	0.2669	55.2	84.3	88.7
	15.4	13.7	—	—	0.0321	0.0340	5.9	15.7	11.3
	28.0	26.8	25.7	9	0.1919	0.2441	27.2	24.2	20.8
	19.1	17.0	19.8	7	0.1509	0.1722	14.2	14.6	11.3
	12.5	13.0	16.5	9	0.1696	0.2958	74.4	13.7	16.2
	21.7	23.5	18.8	14	0.2765	0.3757	35.9	25.5	23.5
	15.1	15.1	19.2	24	0.1524	0.3149	106.6	14.3	20.1
	97.0	97.2	—	—	0.1978	0.2938	48.6	96.9	97.6
	3.0	2.8	—	—	0.0064	0.0072	12.3	3.1	2.4
	100.0	100.0	100.0	12	0.2042	0.3010	47.4	100.0	100.0

declines when considering investment income—and it drops even in absolute terms when decomposing by household/family type. This is mostly driven by the fact that households with elderly heads (aged 60 years and over), who represent about one-quarter of the population, exhibit a rather low baseline inequality. In 2007, the MLD for this group was 0.151 compared with 0.204 in the overall population; however, for the full income measure, the MLD was 0.314 as compared to 0.301—this overproportional change causes the share of aggregate inequality that can be attributed to this group to increase from 18 percent in the baseline model to 26 percent in the full model. In contrast, in 1997, this group did not change its contribution to overall inequality when comparing baseline and full income. Similarly, persons in households headed by a self-employed person who make up less than 8 percent of the population in both years, contributed only 7 percent to aggregate inequality in 1997, but to more than 13 percent of aggregate inequality in 2007. In other words, for all subgroups where we observe an above-average incidence of investment income, the within-group inequality also shows an above-average increase over time, outweighing changes in inequality across groups.

CONCLUSIONS

There have been a number of papers seeking to explain the general trend of increased income inequality in the majority of the OECD countries. Whereas many of these papers discuss (structural) changes in the labor market and earnings as well as in the population as the driving forces behind income inequality, this chapter focuses on the scope and structure of investment income. This type of income not only consists of monetary CI (such as interest and dividends), but should also include fictitious returns from investments in real estate (IR). We demonstrate the separate impacts of these two types of investment income, and we provide evidence underscoring the need to consider their joint impact. Our definition of IR follows a regulation by the EC, which is currently being used to harmonize income measurement for EU-SILC in Europe.

Using representative microdata from the German SOEP, the incorporation of CI and IR (for owner-occupied housing as well as for rent-free and otherwise subsidized tenants) into the measure of investment income clearly indicates the increasing relevance of these income sources for economic inequality in Germany over the last two decades. Even though the two components can be commonly defined as returns on alternative private investments (CI = return on financial investments, IR = return on investments in owner-occupied housing), they do not necessarily coincide with respect to their impact on income inequality and poverty. We find that, in line with the literature, whereas IR tends to exert a dampening effect on inequality and relative poverty, CI tends to accentuate inequality. In recent years, as the German public pension scheme has proven itself ever less capable of maintaining people's living standards into retirement, we find these effects to be of increasing magnitude.

Both incomes, IR and CI, are strongly related to age. In case of *net* IR—the most prevalent means of old-age provision outside the public pension system—this effect simply results from the increasing share of outright ownership among the elderly. For CI, there is a savings-related accumulation of capital in higher age groups, supported by the increased probability of inheritances around the age of 50 to 60 years. The relationship of the processes of accumulation with aging again yields higher financial returns for older citizens, such as interest and dividend; however, one should also consider that the investment behavior of the elderly most likely is more risk-averse due to the smaller chances for recovering from large financial losses by means of alternative incomes.

Another important issue from a social policy standpoint is that income decomposition by subgroup confirms the established fact for most Western countries that private investment in owner-occupied housing is a very effective means of reducing the risk of old-age poverty as well as inequality (see Zaidi et al. 2006). Thus, any age-related income analysis will be biased if the fictitious income advantage arising from owner-occupied housing was not considered. This argument will be of much more relevance when performing cross-country comparisons where different structures of housing tenure will affect the magnitude of this income component over the whole income distribution.

The analyses presented here make a clear case for the joint consideration of all components of private investment income (this should also systematically include income from private pensions, which are currently included in our baseline income measure) for the purpose of welfare analysis, be they of a monetary or nonmonetary nature. This appears to be relevant in at least three dimensions of comparative research: (1) across time; (2) across space and welfare systems, thus also accounting for differences in the incentive structure to choose from different sorts of private investments (e.g., self-employed vs. dependent employed employees); and (3) across the individual life course, thus analyzing the impact of investment income on intrapersonal mobility patterns. Obviously, the panel nature of the data used in this chapter, will help to address the latter point in future research. Against the background of aging societies and a shift from the pay-as-you-go old-age pension systems to increased private coverage, accounting for the role of these financial assets available to households will become increasingly important in the analysis of inequality in the future.

Notes

1. The EU-funded project Accurate Income Measurement for the Assessment of Public Policies (AIM-AP) provides a series of papers on the distributional impact of noncash incomes from private sources (including IR) as well as from public provision of services (in the domains of health, housing, and education) for a variety of EU countries (see http://www.iser.essex.ac.uk/euromod/research-and-policy-analysis-using-euromod/aim-ap). All of those empirical analyses clearly support the claim of considering noncash incomes in the measurement of economic well-being.

2. However, the empirical analyses of the process of dissaving should not be evaluated simply on the basis of repeated cross-sectional and cohort-specific data but rather using panel data in order to effectively control for selectivity in mortality (see DeNardi, French, and Jones 2009). In other words, comparing wealth endowments across age cohorts in a given point in time and inferring from this how well-off the future elderly will be may not adequately reflect the process of individual (dis)saving behavior.

3. When analyzing CI in the context of disposable equivalent income (i.e., after taxes and public transfers), we use a *net* measure of CI by applying the individual average tax rate of the household to the originally collected gross measure of CI.

4. Due to the specific way in which this information is collected in SOEP, there is a lower limit of 0; thus, possible losses from renting and leasing are not considered.

5. Although SOEP collects information on irregular income inflows (windfall income), such as one-time transfers, winnings, inheritances, and gifts of money or goods, these are not considered in the measure of CI employed here.

6. One exemption is the US Bureau of the Census, which has published experimental measures of income that include, among other things, realized capital gains (see also Wolff and Zacharias 2009).

7. See EC Regulation No. 1980/2003 of October 21, 2003, implementing Regulation (EC) No. 1177/2003 of the European Parliament and of the European Council concerning EU-SILC as regards definitions and updated definitions.

8. For a detailed discussion about measurement problems when deriving a fictitious income advantage from IRs, see the various country reports that were published in the context of the EU-funded AIM-AP project.

9. Other methods to derive IR, such as the market-value approach and the self-assessment approach, as well as differences in the final outcome measure of IR arising from the choice of the method used to derive IR, are described in detail in Frick and Grabka (2003) and Frick et al. (2009).

10. Interest payments on mortgages are not tax-deductible in Germany. This is different from most of other European countries, where home ownership is explicitly promoted through various tax-favored treatments.

11. Finally, it should be noted that all of the following analyses refer to the population in private households only: We exclude individuals living in institutions such as nursing homes.

12. The following calculations are based on version SOEPv24. Since SOEPv26 any missing income information due to partial unit non-response (PUNR, non-responding individuals in households with at least one successful interview) has been imputed (see Frick, Grabka and Groh-Samberg, 2010). The data still support the previously identified long-term trends in income inequality and poverty, although on a somewhat lower level.

13. All empirical analyses have been conducted using Stata, version 9.2 (StataCorp, College Station, Texas). For the analyses of inequality, we drew heavily on add-ons for measurement and decomposition of inequality and poverty by subgroup as provided by Philippe van Kerm (CEPS/Instead, Luxembourg) and Stephen P. Jenkins (University of Essex).

14. However, this inequality-reducing effect arising from the inclusion of IR may vary considerably with the share of individuals living in owner-occupied housing. According to Frick et al. (2009), the Gini coefficient drops by more than 5 percent when including IR in cases of Greece and Italy, where ownership rates are above 70 percent.

References

Atkinson, Anthony B., and Thomas Piketty, eds. 2007. *Top Incomes over the Twentieth Century: A Contrast between European and English-Speaking Countries*. Oxford: Oxford University Press.

Bebchuk, Lucian A., and Yaniv Grinstein. 2005. "The Growth of Executive Pay." *Oxford Review of Economic Policy* 21 (2): 283–303.

Becker, Irene 2000. "Einkommensverteilung in Deutschland—Strukturanalyse der Ungleichheit nach Einkommenskomponenten." *Jahrbücher für Nationalökonomie und Statistik* 220 (4): 400–418.

Borjas, George J. 2006. "Native Internal Migration and the Labor Market Impact of Immigration." *Journal of Human Resources* 41 (2): 221–258.

Börsch-Supan Axel, Anette Reil-Held, and Reinhold Schnabel. 2003. "Household Saving in Germany." In *Life Cycle Savings and Public Policy*. Edited by Axel Börsch-Supan, 57–99. Amsterdam: Academic Press.

Canberra Group. 2001. *Expert Group on Household Statistics: Final Report and Recommendations*. Ottawa: Statistics Canada. http://www.lisproject.org/links/canberra/finalreport.pdf.

Card, David, and John E. DiNardo. 2002. "Skill-Biased Technological Change and Rising Wage Inequality: Some Problems and Puzzles." *Journal of Labor Economics* 20 (4): 733–783.

DeNardi, Mariacristina, Eric French, and John B. Jones. 2009. "Life Expectancy and Old Age Savings." NBER Working Paper 14653, National Bureau of Economic Research, Cambridge, Massachusetts. http://www.nber.org/papers/w14653.

Foster, James, Joel Greer, and Erik Thorbecke. 1984. "A Class of Decomposable Poverty Measures." *Econometrica* 52 (3): 761–766.

Frässdorf, Anna, Markus M. Grabka, and Johannes Schwarze. 2008. "The Impact of Household Capital Income on Income Inequality–A Factor Decomposition Analysis for Great Britain, Germany and the USA." ECINEQ WP 2008–89. Working paper, Society for the Study of Economic Inequality, Palma de Mallorca, Spain.

Frick, Joachim R., Jan Goebel, and Markus M. Grabka. 2007. "Assessing the Distributional Impact of 'Imputed Rent' and 'Non-Cash Employee Income' in Microdata: Case Studies Based on EU-SILC (2004) and SOEP (2002)." *SOEP Papers on Multidisciplinary Panel Data Research at DIW Berlin 2, February*. Berlin: DIW Berlin.

Frick, Joachim R., and Markus M. Grabka. 2003. "Imputed Rent and Income Inequality: A Decomposition Analysis for the U.K., West Germany, and the USA." *Review of Income and Wealth* 49 (4): 513–537.

———.2005. "Item Non-Response on Income Questions in Panel Surveys: Incidence, Imputation and the Impact on Inequality and Mobility." *Allgemeines Statistisches Archiv* 89: 49–61.

———.2008. "Niedrigere Arbeitslosigkeit sorgt für weniger Armutsrisiko und Ungleichheit." *DIW-Wochenbericht* 38: 556–566.

———. 2009. "Wealth Inequality Rises in Germany." *DIW Berlin Weekly Report* 10: 62–73.

Frick, Joachim R., Markus M. Grabka, and Olaf Groh-Samberg. 2007. *Estimates of Imputed Rent and Analysis of Their Distributional Impact in Germany*. Luxembourg: European Commission. (National Report. Research project "Accurate Income Measurement for the Assessment of Public Policies" [AIM-AP], funded by European Commission, 6th Framework Programme, 2006–2009, Contract No. CIT5-CT-2005–028412).

———. 2012. "Imputation of annual income in panel surveys with partially non-responding households." *Sociological Methods and Research*, (in press).

Frick, Joachim R., Markus M.Grabka, Panos Tsakloglou, and Tim M. Smeeding. 2009. "Distributional Effects of Imputed Rents in Five European Countries." *Journal of Housing Economics* 19: 167–179.

Grabka, Markus M., and Joachim R. Frick. 2008. "The Shrinking German Middle Class—Signs of Long-Term Polarization in Disposable Income?" *DIW Berlin Weekly Report* 4 (2008): 21–27.

Jäntti, Markus 1997. "Inequality in Five Countries in the 1980s: The Role of Demographic Shifts, Markets and Government Policies." *Economica* 64: 415–440.

Jappelli, Tullio, and Franco Modigliani. 2005. "The Age-Saving Profile and the Life-Cycle Hypothesis." In *The Collected Papers of Franco Modigliani—Vol. 6*. Edited by Francesco Franco, 141–172. Cambridge: The MIT Press.

Jenkins, Stephen. P. 1995. "Accounting for Inequality Trends: Decomposition Analyses for the U.K., 1971–1986." *Economica* 62: 29–63.

OECD. 2001/2003. "Balance of Payments, Investment Income." Glossary of Statistical Terms. http://stats.oecd.org/glossary/detail.asp?ID=162.

———.2008. *Growing Unequal? Income Distribution and Poverty in OECD Countries.* Paris: Organization for Economic Co-operation and Development Publishing.

Reed, Howard 2006. "Appendix 2: Modelling Demographic Pressure on Poverty and Inequality." In *Population Politics.* Edited by Mike Dixon and Julia Margo, 155–160. London: Institute for Public Policy Research.

Shorrocks, Anthony F. 1984. "Inequality Decomposition by Population Subgroups." *Econometrica* 52: 1369–1388.

Smeeding, Tim M., and Daniel H. Weinberg. 2001. "Toward a Uniform Definition of Household Income." *Review of Income and Wealth* 47 (1): 1–24.

Sozio-oekonomisches Panel (SOEP). Daten der Jahre 1984–2007. doi: 10.5684/soep.v24.

SVR (The German Council of Economic Experts). 2007. "Jahresgutachten: 2007/08." *Das Erreichte nicht verspielen.* Wiesbaden: Statistisches Bundesamt.

United Nations. 1968. *A System of National Accounts: Studies in Methods.* 3rd ed. Series F, 2. New York: United Nations.

Wagner, Gert G., Joachim R. Frick, and Jürgen Schupp. 2007. "The German Socio-Economic Panel Study (SOEP)—Evolution, Scope and Enhancements." *Schmoller's Jahrbuch—Journal of Applied Social Science Studies* 127 (1): 139–169.

Wolff, Edward., and Ajit Zacharias. 2009. "Household Wealth and the Measurement of Economic Well-Being in the United States." *Journal of Economic Inequality* 7 (2): 83–115.

Yates, Judith 1994. "Imputed Rent and Income Distribution." *Review of Income and Wealth* 40 (1): 43–66.

Zaidi, Ashgar, Mattia Makovec, Michael Fuchs, Barbara Lipszyc, Orsolya Lelkes, Marius Rummel, Bernd Marin, and Klaas de Voos. 2006. *Poverty of Elderly People in EU25.* Vienna: European Centre for Social Welfare Policy and Research.

Zaidi, Ashagr, Joachim R. Frick, and Felix Büchel. 2005. "Income Mobility in Old Age in Britain and Germany." *Ageing and Society* 25 (4): 543–565.

7

Accounting for Employee Benefits

NEIL GILBERT ■

Employee benefits encompass all of the supplemental compensations beyond direct pay for time worked in the employee's remuneration package. These add-ons are often characterized as "fringe" benefits because they supplement salary and wages for time worked, which represent the monetary core of the employee remuneration package (see Table 7.1). Some of the fringe benefits are voluntarily offered by employers; others are mandated by government. These benefits include a wide range of cash and in-kind allocations, such as chauffeured limousines and company cars, parking, education, free lunches and dinners, private pensions and mandated employer contributions to public pensions, day care, health and disability insurance, massage therapy, club memberships, vacations, family leave, and subsidized housing—all of which can contribute to an employee's standard of living.

Many (though not all) of these benefits receive favorable tax treatment, which varies among different countries—a matter to which we shall return in due course. Given the wide range of employee benefits and the rising number of two-earner families, in the 1970s, working families in the United States increasingly began to experience a duplication of benefits, particularly health insurance coverage, which is one of the most expensive benefits offered by employers. This spurred the development of flexible benefit packages, sometimes called "cafeteria plans," under which employees are permitted to select a package of benefits tailored to their needs. These plans allow employees to make the best use of available funds according to their individual situations, which might involve the presence of children and coverage by a spouse's health care benefits. By 1997, these plans covered about 13 percent of workers employed in medium and large private establishments (Moehrle 2001).

There are gray areas concerning exactly what supplemental compensations to include under the rubric of fringe benefits. A high-profile case in point was Thomas Daschle's (President Obama's Secretary of Health and Human Services nominee) failure to treat the receipt of a car and driver as a form of supplemental compensation, which in this case was taxable. Mr. Daschle said he considered the transportation service a gift from a wealthy friend with whom he also happened to do business. Gifts are normally not considered remuneration for services rendered. Yet, the line begins to blur when an employer gives a worker (or his spouse) a gift.

Efforts to assess the value of employee benefits tend to focus on their costs to the employer. National data on the costs and distribution of these benefits are usually reported as a percentage of the employer's hourly compensation costs under the functional categories in Table 7.1, which are used by the US Department of Labor, Bureau of Labor Statistics (BLS). Although not exhaustive, these categories illustrate the variety and range of benefits. (A more detailed classification of labor costs adopted by the International Labour Organization is shown in Appendix 7.A.) According to the International Labour Office (2007), data compiled by the BLS are the most reliable series available for making international comparisons.

Much of the gray area in benefit calculations resides in categories such as pay in kind, which covers numerous possibilities. The hourly direct pay for time worked in Table 7.1 (shown as direct wages and salaries in Appendix 7.A) represents the monetary core of the remuneration package. All the other costs are fringe benefits.

Table 7.1 HOURLY COMPENSATION COSTS

* Hourly direct pay

Pay for time worked

    Basic wages

    Piece rate

    Overtime premiums

    Shift differentials

    Bonuses and premiums paid regularly

    Cost-of-living adjustments

Other direct pay

    Pay for time not worked (vacations, holidays, and other leave, except sick leave)

    Seasonal and irregular bonuses

    Social allowances

    Pay in kind

* Employer social insurance expenditures (both legally required and contractual and private) and other labor taxes

Retirement and disability pensions

Health insurance

Income guarantee insurance and sick leave

Life and accident insurance

Occupational injury and illness compensation

Unemployment insurance

Family allowances

Other social insurance expenditures

Taxes (or subsidies) on payrolls or employment

SOURCE: US Department of Labor, Bureau of Labor Statistics, *International Comparisons of Hourly Compensation Costs in Manufacturing, 1975–2006.*

How do employee benefits affect existing income-based measures of poverty and inequality? In considering this issue, the analytic focus is on those benefits that are currently excluded from these measures (i.e., they are not counted as employee income). On certain aspects of this issue, the evidence is relatively unambiguous; on others, it is more equivocal. To frame the broader context of this analysis, the first two sections of this paper review the relatively clear-cut data, which show that: (1) employee benefits have come to form an increasingly significant part of remuneration, accounting for a higher proportion of the costs of hourly compensation in Europe than in the United States; and (2) these benefits tend to disproportionately favor those already earning high incomes. To pin down the actual impact of these benefits is a more complicated issue. In the two sections on "Computing Distributional Effects," we turn to the thorny questions of exactly what benefits to count and how to value them for inclusion in measures of poverty and inequality. The concluding section examines some of the broader implications for the treatment of functionally equivalent social benefits. This analysis draws on the BLS series on employee benefits for production workers in manufacturing to illustrate the measurement issues. The discussion is limited to this occupational category mainly because it is the group for which comparative international data are most readily available.

AN INCREASING PROPORTION OF TOTAL EMPLOYEE COMPENSATION

In the United States, employee benefits date back well over a century. Voluntary employee pensions, among the most costly and important of these benefits, were first established by the American Express Company in 1875 (Stein 1980). Before the 1940s, employee pension plans were prevalent in only a few industries, primarily railroads, banking, and public utilities. After World War II, these private schemes began to spread, rising in number to 489,000 pension plans by 1980. Between 1980 and 1995, participation in private pension plans climbed by over 50 percent, from 57.9 to 87.5 million people (US Census Bureau 1999).[1] By the mid-1990s, more than one-half of the civilian labor force participated in private occupational-based pensions. Although employers have much discretion in how they structure private plans, to receive favorable tax treatment, these plans must meet both the terms of the Internal Revenue Code and minimum standards of the 1974 Employee Retirement Income Security Act regarding participation, vesting, nondiscrimination against lower paid workers, and other criteria (Pension Benefit Guarantee Corporation 1992).[2]

Occupational pensions also constitute an increasingly significant portion of employee benefits in European countries. Between 1980 and 1995, the percentage of pensioner households with income from private pensions climbed throughout most of western Europe. By the mid-1990s more than half of the pensioner households received occupational pensions in Norway, Sweden, Finland, the Netherlands, and the United Kingdom (Behrendt 2000).Occupational pensions rose significantly as a share of the aggregate income of old-age pensioners in Norway, the United Kingdom, Germany, and Denmark. In Norway, the share of income in this group almost doubled from 11 to 20 percent: In the Netherlands, occupational pensions accounted for about 30 percent of the retirement income throughout this period (Pedersen 2004).

Private pensions, however, are just one of many provisions in the overall package of employee benefits, which has expanded considerably over the last three decades in

Table 7.2 EMPLOYEE BENEFITS AS A PERCENTAGE OF HOURLY COMPENSATION
COSTS FOR PRODUCTION WORKERS IN MANUFACTURING, 1975–2006

	1975	1980	1985	1990	1995	2000	2006
United States	23.6	25.8	26	27.2	28.1	27.1	29.5
Austria	46	47.7	49.7	49.9	49.4	48.6	48.5
Denmark	14.9	16.5	17.7	16.3	21.4	26.1	28
Finland	28.2	32.7	33.7	38.2	38.8	37.6	40.6
France	40	41.5	44.7	46.3	45.7	45.3	44.3
Germany	—	—	—	—	43.6	42.2	42.1
Netherlands	40.9	42.3	42.6	42.5	42.6	40.3	41.8
Norway	28.3	30.7	31.3	31.4	29.2	29.8	32.9
Spain	48.1	44.6	43.8	46.2	47.3	44.1	45.5
Sweden	31	38.1	40.5	40.8	39.7	41.6	43.5
United Kingdom	21.1	27.9	26.2	25.8	26.2	31.1	30.3

NOTE: Employee benefits include the employer's costs of all compensation minus pay for time worked.

SOURCE: Calculated from US Department of Labor, Bureau of Labor Statistics, *International Comparisons of Hourly Compensation Costs in Manufacturing, 1975–2006,* Table 13.

the United States and throughout Europe. From 1975 to 2006, for example, employee benefits as a proportion of total compensation for production workers in manufacturing rose from 31 to 44 percent in Sweden and 23 to 30 percent in the United States. Among nine of the major European countries in Table 7.2, the average employee benefits in manufacturing climbed from 33 percent in 1975 to 40 percent in 2006. The pattern of growth in Table 7.2 shows that between 1975 and 1985, the level of employee benefits rose in every country except Spain. After 1990, the level of benefits varied only a few percent in most countries, except for steeper increases in the United Kingdom and Denmark. In 2006, employee benefits for production workers in the United States accounted for a smaller proportion (in most cases a substantially lower percentage) of hourly compensation than that of all of the major European countries in Table 7.2, except Denmark (Pedersen 2004).

DISPROPORTIONATELY FAVORING THOSE
WITH HIGHER INCOMES

Although it is difficult to get comprehensive data on the distributional impact of fringe benefits in Europe and the United States, it is generally the case that the greatest benefits go to those with the highest incomes (Organization for Economic Cooperation and Development 1988).[3] Private pensions account for a major portion of the standard costs in the basic fringe benefit package. A number of studies show

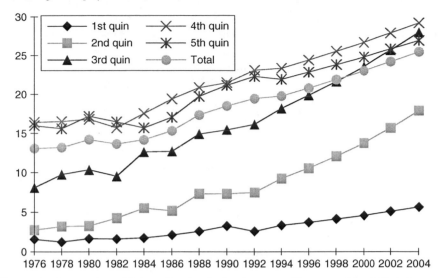

Figure 7.1 Proportion of Private Pension in the Aggregated Income of Aged Units by Income Quintile: 1976–2004.
SOURCE: Gilbert and Park (1996).

that private pensions have been a growing component of retirement income and are associated with income inequality among retired households (Pestieau 1992). Studying the United States, Chung (2003) found that even though compensations for employee pensions increase inequality, the disproportionate decline in health insurance for less skilled workers from 1987 to 1994 also contributed to growing inequality. Analyzing the period from 1987 to 2007, Pierce (forthcoming) found that high-end wages grew the most over this span at the same time that employee benefits rose more in high-wage than low-wage jobs, indicating an increase in inequality in both wages and compensation more broadly defined.[4]

Along similar lines, a study of the United States shows that not only is an increasing proportion of the population coming to rely on private pensions as a primary source of retirement income, but also, that the shifting mix of support from public and private pensions is quite different for people in the upper-, middle-, and lower-income groups. By 1990, private retirement benefits had risen to account for more of the aggregate income than social security benefits among elderly people within the top 20 percent of incomes. As illustrated in Figure 7.1, the elderly in the bottom 40 percent of the income distribution continue to remain highly dependent on social security, while reliance on private pensions is climbing for those at the middle and upper-middle levels (Gilbert and Park 1996). Overall, estimates point to the emergence of a two-tiered system of pensions in the not-too-distant future with a resulting widening inequality of retirement income (Park and Gilbert 1999).

COMPUTING DISTRIBUTIONAL EFFECTS: WHAT BENEFITS TO COUNT?

In general, it can be said that employee benefits significantly and differentially supplement the resources and standard of living derived from wages received directly for time worked. The differential in these supplements not only favors those with higher incomes, but also it varies by factors such as occupational categories, union versus nonunion status, establishment size, and public versus private sector (BLS 2007). In the United States, for example, benefits in 2007 for all private industry employees amounted to 29.3 percent compared to 33.6 percent for public employees (Employee Benefits Research Institute 2008).

A precise calculation of how the distributional effects of employee benefits modify conventional income-based measures of poverty and inequality in Europe and the United States requires countries to formulate comprehensive measures of how much these benefits add to household incomes. Although some rough estimates might be made by focusing on one or two major benefits (e.g., see Chung 2003), reasonably precise comprehensive measures currently do not exist and are difficult to construct. They entail decisions regarding conceptual issues about what benefits to count and how to assess their value.

Taxable Benefits

The question of what to count refers to the fact that certain employee cash benefits, such as paid vacations, and some in-kind benefits, such as free lunches, are incorporated into their basic wage as part of a worker's taxable income. Although pay for vacations, rest periods, and special bonuses are part of the fringe benefit package of compensation for employees that goes beyond direct pay for time worked, these fringe benefits already are normally taken into account as part of a worker's taxable income used to compute income-based measures of poverty and inequality. Payments for time not worked comprise almost the entire costs of fringe benefits in the broad category of "other direct pay." As shown in Table 7.3, other direct pay ranges from a low of 7.6 percent of hourly compensation costs for production workers in the United States to a high of 21.5 percent in Austria (or between almost 25 to 50 percent of the total employee benefits among the sample of 11 countries). The US position at the bottom of the rank largely reflects the fact that European countries have much more liberal policies mandating paid vacation days (for example, 30 days in France, Austria, Spain, and Denmark) than does the United States, which has no mandated policy for paid vacations.

Benefits in Kind: Diverse Tax Treatment

In trying to interpret the impact of the BLS measure for the hourly compensation costs of other direct pay, it is important to bear in mind that this figure excludes many, if not most, of the in-kind benefits involving facilities, employee training, and services such as child care, legal assistance, and on-site doctors provided by employers. These benefits are omitted because systematic data are not available for many countries. The BLS estimates that the excluded in-kind compensations can account for up to 2 percent of the total hourly labor costs, a small, but not trivial proportion of employee benefits.

As noted earlier, in-kind employee benefits comprise a broad gray area of compensation that provides additional resources and services, from housing and vehicles

Table 7.3 PRIMARY CATEGORIES OF EMPLOYEE BENEFITS

2006
Employee benefits for production workers

	Total Benefits	Other Direct Pay	Social Insurance and Related Costs
United States	29.5	7.6	21.9
Austria	48.5	21.5	27.0
Denmark	28	17.6	10.4
Finland	40.6	19.6	21.0
France	44.3	12.2	32.1
Germany	42.1	19.1	23.0
Netherlands	41.8	19.4	22.4
Norway	32.9	12.9	20.0
Spain	45.5	19.9	25.6
Sweden	43.5	10.4	33.1
United Kingdom	30.3	9.0	21.3

SOURCE: Calculated from US Department of Labor, Bureau of Labor Statistics, *International Comparisons of Hourly Compensation Costs Manufacturing, 1975–2006,* Tables 13, 14, 15.

to day care and legal assistance, which supplement the recipient's standard of living. These benefits are subject to tax treatments that vary widely among different countries. The values of employer-provided automobiles and free or subsidized housing are usually taxable (with some exceptions for cases in which the worksite is particularly remote or inconvenient). Other benefits are sometimes taxable only when they exceed a certain cash value. In some cases, benefits, such as free plane tickets to airline employees, are not taxable because they incur no (market) cost to the employer (Organization for Economic Cooperation and Development 1988). Many in-kind fringe benefits are not taxed as income, but this is more often the case in the United States than in Europe. In the United States, tax-free benefits include: day care, tuition, and other educational assistance, on-site health facilities, adoption assistance, meals on business premises, lodging on business premises, commuting and parking benefits, group term life insurance, accident and health benefits, certain awards, and discounts (Turner 1999).

Professionals and managerial workers have disproportionate access to in-kind benefits including child care assistance, adoption assistance, subsidized commuting, education, fitness, centers, and the like. Recent data from the National Compensation Survey (Appendixes 7.B and 7.C) in the United States, for example, show that whereas 52 percent of all employees in private industry have access to work-related educational assistance, 70 to 78 percent of those in the professional and managerial categories have access to these benefits. Similar differentials favoring white collar employees appear for access to adoption assistance, child care, subsidized commuting, long-term care insurance, and other benefits in kind. As already discussed, educational assistance and dependent care in the United States are tax exempt up to a certain level. In some cases, these benefits are quite substantial. Google, one of the US companies most highly rated for employee benefits, provides up to $8,000 per year in tuition reimbursement (but only if the employee receives a grade of "B" or better). Beyond basic items, such as health insurance and pensions, the list of employee quality-of-life benefits covered in the BLS National Compensation Survey changes periodically, with new benefits being added and those that showed no growth or limited user interest dropped. Thus, for example, items related to educational assistance, adoption assistance, and fitness centers were dropped from the survey between 2008 and 2009 (Buckely 2009).

Untaxed and Tax Deferred Benefits

Because the vast majority of additional compensation included in the BLS measures of other direct pay is already counted as taxable income, these benefits have no additional bearing on the outcome of current income-based measures of poverty and inequality. Thus, for the purpose of estimating the impact of uncounted fringe benefits on poverty and inequality, we would concentrate on the category of social insurance and related expenditures. This is the main source of additional compensations (on which data are available) that should be taken into account for comprehensive measures of poverty and inequality. Examining this category in Table 7.3, we find that the United States, which had next to the lowest percentage of hourly costs for the total employee benefits, is now virtually in the middle of the pack among the European countries.

Looking at the total costs of fringe benefits, one might have concluded that employee benefits would have the least impact on current measures of poverty and inequality in the United States and Denmark, because their total employee benefits (29.5 and 28 percent of hourly costs) amounted to considerably lower proportions of hourly compensation than in the other countries and that the largest impact would be found in Spain and Austria. But these rankings shift when the focus narrows to include only the benefits of social insurance and related expenditures. Whereas Denmark remains at the bottom joined now by Norway, France and Sweden rise to the top of the group, and the United States falls close to the middle. (Denmark's relatively low level of employee benefits in this category is due to the fact that in comparison to other European countries employer contributions to statutory and occupational pensions are exceptionally low because a considerable share of national pensions is financed by tax revenues [Bach, Laitinen-Kuikka, and Vidlund 2004].)

Tax treatments of social insurance and related benefits vary. Some benefits, such as employer-provided health insurance are exempt from taxation in the United States but not in the United Kingdom. Employer-provided health benefits to workers, their dependents, and retirees in the United States were estimated as amounting to $480 billion (or 5 percent of the gross domestic product) in 2001 (Adema and Ladaique 2005). Over the last decade, the idea of taxing employees on these benefits has been put forth periodically. If such a reform came to pass, it would be accompanied by a substantial rise in the taxable incomes of the 53 percent of workers in private industry and 73 percent of state and local government workers participating in employer-provided health insurance schemes in 2008 (BLS 2008). Other major benefits involving employer contributions to a variety of occupational pension and old-age savings schemes are exempt at the contribution stage and during the investment period but are taxed throughout the payout period during retirement.

Although employer contributions to occupational pensions should be taken into account in formulating comprehensive income-based measures of poverty and inequality, it is important to consider when they are counted. For example, occupational pensions have been used to show how fringe benefits contribute to growing inequality in total compensation among workers, as well as how income from occupational schemes contribute to inequality in retirement income (e.g., see Chung 2003; Behrendt 2000). This suggests that inclusion of employee tax deferred benefits produced by employer contributions to occupational pensions poses a complicating issue for measuring long-term national trends in income-related poverty and inequality. One must watch that employer pension contributions to the workers' benefits do not get counted twice. That is, when measuring rates of poverty or inequality over time, employer contributions might initially be counted as workers' deferred income (a nontaxable share of their current gross income), which in the case of defined benefit schemes cannot be consumed or accessed. In later years, the same contributions might again be included as part of the occupational pension benefits that provide the same workers' retirement income. Employer contributions to individual retirement account plans present a somewhat different situation because workers are permitted access to the money contributed into their accounts before the age of retirement. But they must pay income taxes and a penalty for early access to individual retirement account funds, which then are no longer deferred income.

COMPUTING DISTRIBUTIONAL EFFECTS: HOW TO VALUE EMPLOYEE BENEFITS?

Once issues about which employee benefits to count are resolved, the question arises of how best to calculate their monetary value. There are several methods for valuing employee benefits, each of which can result in a different value for the same benefit. The BLS data presented in this chapter are based on the costs of benefits to the employer. The advantages of this approach is that it draws on the most easily established and readily available figures. The primary problem is that there can be large discrepancies between costs to the employer and the value of the benefits to the employee. As noted earlier, some types of fringe benefits that would be of tangible value to the employee (e.g., airline passage for United Airlines' employees or private schools giving free enrollment to its teachers' children) may entail no or limited costs for the employer. An employer's hourly costs per worker for providing access to certain types of benefits, such as health centers, meals, and on-site day care, are most easily calculated by averaging the total expenditure per worker. The real value of such benefits to employees, however, is not a matter of access, but of actual use. Benefits only accrue to those who regularly eat the meals, exercise in the gym, and place their children in the day care center.

An alternative to the employer's cost involves using the market value of employee benefits. As with the method of employer costs, the market value of a benefit does not always coincide with its value to employees. A vegan employee would not pay much for a steak dinner in the company cafeteria. Moreover, the market values of some benefits, such as a company car that can only be used to drive to and from work, are difficult to ascertain. Rather than the market value, for tax purposes, some countries administratively establish low-end standard values for popular employee benefits such as company cars and meals.

Arguably the fairest measure for calculating the value of fringe benefits is their value to the employees. This approach is somewhat subjective and circumstantial. With the increasing number of two-earner households, duplication of coverage often negates the value of duplicated benefits. Employer contributions for health insurance, for example, are of little or no value to an employee who is already covered by his working spouse's more comprehensive family health plan benefits. The same is true for services such as day care and legal assistance. On the other hand, group health care coverage through an employee benefit plan is of immense value to a single employee with a record of chronic illness, who otherwise might be unable to qualify for any health insurance. A variety of these methods are used by different countries to calculate the value of fringe benefits for tax purposes (Organization for Economic Cooperation and Development 1988).

Implications for Functionally Equivalent Social Benefits

Once we begin to consider how reframing the conventional measure of income impacts poverty and inequality, the question arises of where to draw the new lines, particularly in relation to the cash value and distribution of functionally equivalent social benefits. If the untaxed value of employer subsidies for low-interest housing loans should be added to the conventional measure of employee's income, for example, then it would seem to follow that the value of publicly subsidized housing should also be included in measuring the income of residents, whose standard of living is augmented by this social benefit.

There are two main differences between untaxed employee benefits in Europe and the United States. Employee health insurance in the United States constitutes a much larger portion of the social insurance-related benefits than it does in Europe. European countries tax a considerably larger number of employee in-kind benefits than the United States does. According to one survey, the United States taxes only 5 of the 16 most popular fringe benefits compared to an average of 9.5 benefits taxed among 10 western European countries in Table 7.3 (Organization for Economic Cooperation and Development 1988).

A few illustrative examples of how reframing the conventional accounting may affect poverty and inequality can be drawn from analyses conducted in the United States using alternative definitions of income, which include benefits in kind. One study shows a decrease in the degree of income inequality (Gini index declines from 0.450 to 0.418) as the definition of aggregate household income shifts from the standard measure of *money* income (all cash received by individuals over age 15) to *disposable* income, which includes money income (minus major taxes and work expenses) plus the imputed values of rent, capital gains, and noncash social benefit transfers involving Food Stamps, public or subsidized housing, and school lunches (US Census Bureau 2007). Although the inclusion of in-kind social benefits in the broader definition contributes to greater equality, the results remain inconclusive in the absence of employee in-kind benefits such as the cash value of day care, meals, subsidized housing loans, education tuition, commuting and others, along with the monetary values of both public and private health insurance.

Another study finds the rate of poverty according to the official US poverty measure declines from 12.5 to 9.7 percent when the definition shifts from money income to an alternative measure that includes money income (minus major taxes) plus a broader range of noncash transfers, which take account of employer-provided health benefits along with Medicare and Medicaid, in addition to Food Stamps, public or subsidized housing, and school lunches (Dalker 2005).

When a poverty line is drawn according to a specified level of need (adjusted for family size) as in the United States, the official rates of poverty would be expected to decline as in-kind benefits, both public and private, are included in the definition of family income (unless the poverty line was adjusted upward to reflect a higher level of need). In contrast, the impact of these in-kind benefits on poverty as defined in many European countries as 60 percent of the median income would depend on how the untaxed employee benefits were actually distributed throughout the population.

In conclusion, whereas employer-provided benefits constitute a significant stream of resources that enhance the employees' standard of living, much of their cash value remains uncounted in measures of poverty and inequality. Efforts to estimate the impact of employee benefits on income-based measures of poverty and inequality encounter at least three fundamental tasks, which have yet to be accomplished: (1) decisions have to be made about conceptual and methodological issues concerning what to count and how to value employee benefits; (2) once decisions are made, the consistent application of these measures is needed to obtain reliable and comparable data; and (3) before the value of these additional benefits are incorporated into the measure of poverty and inequality, questions about the treatment of functionally equivalent social benefits have to be systematically addressed.

Notes

1. This figure does not include those covered by private individual plans, such as individual retirement accounts—the value of which multiplied from $200 billion to $1.3 trillion between 1985 and 1996—and Keogh plans.
2. Even with mandatory minimum funding standards, however, private sponsors have considerable leeway in funding contributions, which leaves some schemes poorly funded. According to the Pension Guarantee Corporation, underfunding among private pensions has more than doubled from $18 billion in 1982 to about $40 billion in 1991 for single-employer plans. Another $11 billion in underfunding among multiemployer plans brought the 1991 total underfunding in the federally insured pensions to about $51 billion. Although most of the underfunding is concentrated in a relatively small number of companies, public liability is substantial and warrants reforms that strengthen the funding rules for private plans.
3. Data from the United Kingdom indicate that in 1983–1984, directors accounted for 25 percent of the recipients, but received 45 percent of the total taxable value of fringe benefits.

4. Pierce notes that the data are based on estimates of employer costs, which for several reasons, including tax considerations, will differ from employee valuations.

References

Adema, Willem, and Maxime Ladaique. 2005. *Net Social Expenditures, 2005 Edition.* OECD Social, Employment and Migration Working Papers No. 29. Paris: Organization for Economic Co-operation and Development.

Bach, Jarna, Sini Laitinen-Kuikka, and Mika Vidlund, eds. 2004. *Pension Contribution Level in Certain EU Countries, Intergroup Reviews,* 14. Helsinki: Finnish Center for Pensions.

Behrendt, Christina. 2000. "Private Pensions—a Viable Alternative? Their Distributional Effects in a Comparative Perspective." *International Social Security Review* 53 (3): 3–26.

Buckely, John. 2009. "Beyond Basic Benefits: Employee Access to Other Types of Benefits, 1979–2008." US Bureau of Labor Statistics, Compensation and Working Conditions Online. http://www.bls.gov/opub/cwc/print/cm20090527ar01p1.htm.

Chung, Wankyo. 2003. "Fringe Benefits and Inequality in the Labor Market." *Economic Inquiry* 41 (3): 517–529.

Dalker, Joe. 2005. *Alternative Poverty Estimates in the United States: 2003.* US Census Bureau Current Population Reports P60–227. Washington, DC: US Census Bureau.

Employee Benefits Research Institute. 2008. *EBRI Databook on Employee Benefits.* Washington DC: Employee Benefits Research Institute. http://www.EBRI.org/publications/books/index. (Updated December 2008.)

Gilbert, Neil, and Neung Hoo Park. 1996. "Privatization, Provision, and Targeting: Trends and Policy Implications for Social Security in the United States." *International Social Security Review* 49 (1): 19–29.

International Labour Office. 2007. *Key Indicators of the Labour Market.* 5th ed., chap. 17. Geneva: International Labour Organization.

Moehrle, Thomas. 2001. "The Evolution of Compensation in a Changing Economy." US Bureau of Labor Statistics Compensation and Working Conditions, available online at: http://www.bls.gov/opub/cwc/cm20030124ar01p1.htm.

Organization for Economic Cooperation and Development. 1988. *The Taxation of Fringe Benefits.* Paris: Organization for Economic Co-operation and Development.

Park, Neung Hoo, and Neil Gilbert. 1999. "Social Security and the Incremental Privatization of Retirement Income." *Journal of Sociology and Social Welfare* 26 (2): 187–202.

Pedersen, Axel W. 2004. "The Privatization of Retirement Income? Variations and Trends in the Income Packages of Old Age Pensioners." *Journal of European Social Policy* 14 (1): 5–23.

Pension Benefit Guarantee Corporation. 1992. *Annual Report, 1992.* Washington, DC: Pension Benefit Guarantee Corporation.

Pestieau, P. 1992. "The Distribution of Private Pension Benefits: How Fair is It?" In *Private Pensions and Public Policy.* Edited by E. Duskins, 31–52. Paris: Organization for Economic Co-operation and Development.

Pierce, Brooks. 2010. "Recent Trends in Compensation Inequality." In *Labor in the New Economy*. Edited by Katherine Abraham, James Spietzer, and Michael Harper, pages 63–98. Chicago: University of Chicago Press.

Stein, B. 1980. *Social Security and Pensions in Transition: Understanding the American Retirement System*. New York: The Free Press.

Turner, Robert. 1999. "Fringe Benefits." In *The Encyclopedia of Taxation and Tax Policy*. 2nd ed. Edited by Joseph J. Cordes, Robert D. Ebel, and Jane G. Gravelle, 159–162. Washington, DC: Urban Institute Press.

US Bureau of Labor Statistics. 2007. "Employer Costs for Employee Compensation: Supplemental Tables December 2006." Available online at: www.bls.gov/schedule/archives/ecec_nr.htm.

———. 2008. "Recent Data on Employers' Costs and Employees' Access." *Program Perspectives on Health Benefits* 1 (October).

US Census Bureau. 1999. *Statistical Abstract of the United States:1999*, 394. Washington, DC: Government Printing Office.

———. 2007. *The Effect of Taxes and Transfers on Income and Poverty in the United States: 2005*. Current Population Reports P60–232. Washington, DC: US Census Bureau.

US Department of Labor, Bureau of Labor Statistics. 2008a. *International Comparisons of Hourly Compensation Costs in Manufacturing, 1975–2006*. Washington, DC: Bureau of Labor Statistics.

———. 2008b. *National Compensation Survey, 2008*. Washington, DC: Bureau of Labor Statistics.

International Labor Organization Standard
Classification of Labor Cost

I. **Direct wages and salaries**
   1. Straight-time pay of time-rated workers
   2. Incentive pay of time-rated workers
   3. Earnings of pieceworkers (excluding overtime premiums)
   4. Premium pay for overtime, late shift, and holiday work
II. **Remuneration for time not worked**
   1. Annual vacation, other paid leave, including long-service leave
   2. Public holidays and other recognized holidays
   3. Other time off granted with pay (e.g., birth or death of family members, marriage of employees, functions of titular office, union activities)
   4. Severance and termination pay where not regarded as social security expenditure
III. **Bonuses and gratuities**
   1. Year-end and seasonal bonuses
   2. Profit-sharing bonuses
   3. Additional payments in respect of vacation, supplementary to normal vacation pay and other bonuses and gratuities
IV. **Food, drink, fuel, and other payments in kind**
V. **Cost of workers' housing borne by employers**
   1. Cost for establishment-owned dwellings
   2. Cost for dwellings not establishment-owned (e.g., allowances, grants)
   3. Other housing costs
VI. **Employers' social security expenditure**
   1. Statutory social security contributions (for schemes covering old age, invalidity and survivors; sickness; maternity; employment injury; unemployment; and family allowances)
   2. Collectively agreed, contractual and nonobligatory contributions to private social security schemes and insurances (for schemes covering old age, invalidity and survivors; sickness; maternity; employment injury; unemployment, and family allowances)
   3a. Direct payments to employees in respect of absence from work due to sickness, maternity, or employment injury to compensate for loss of earnings
   3b. Other direct payments to employees regarded as social security benefits

      4. Cost of medical care and health services

      5. Severance and termination pay where regarded as social security expenditure

VII. **Cost of vocational training,** including fees and other payments for services of outside instructors, training institutions, teaching material, reimbursements of school fees to workers.

VIII. **Cost of welfare services**

      1. Cost of canteens and other food services

      2. Cost of education, cultural, recreational, and related facilities and services

      3. Grants to credit unions and cost of related services for employees

IX. **Labor cost not elsewhere classified,** such as costs of transport of workers to and from work undertaken by employer (including reimbursement of fares), cost of work clothes, cost of recruitment, and other labor costs

X. **Taxes regarded as labor cost,** such as taxes on employment or payrolls, included on a net basis, that is, after deduction of allowances or rebates made by the state

SOURCE: Adapted from International Labour Office, *Key Indicators of the Labour Market* (2007).

Quality of Life Benefits: Access, Civilian Workers

Percent of Workers

Characteristics	Total 2	Employer Assistance for Childcare								
		Employer-Provided Funds	On-site and Off-site	Resource and Referral Services	Adoption Assistance	Long-term Care Insurance	Flexible Workplace	Employer-Provided Home Computer	Subsidized Commuting
All workers	16	3	6	11	11	15	4	2	6
Worker characteristics									
Management, professional, and related	26	5	11	18	17	24	9	5	10
Management, business, and financial	27	6	10	22	23	26	14	7	12
Professional and related	25	5	12	17	14	23	7	4	10

SOURCE: Adapted from US Department of Labor, US Bureau of Labor Statistics, "National Compensation Survey, 2008."

APPENDIX 7.C

Selected Benefits: Access, Civilian Workers

Percent of Workers						
		Education Assistance				
Characteristics	Job-related Travel Accident Insurance	Work-related	Non-Work-related	Wellness Programs	Fitness Centers	Employee Assistance Programs
All workers	21	52	16	29	15	47
Worker characteristics						
Management, professional, and related	30	72	24	46	25	64
Management, business, and financial	40	78	27	45	25	64
Professional and related	26	70	22	47	25	64

SOURCE: Adapted from US Department of Labor, US Bureau of Labor Statistics, "National Compensation Survey, 2008."

8

Impressionistic Realism

A European Focus on US Poverty Measurement

DAVID S. JOHNSON* ■

"In the art of communicating impressions lies the power of generalizing without losing that logical connection of parts to the whole which satisfies the mind."
— CAMILLE PISSARO

Viewed from afar, the picture is clear. As one examines more closely, the details are blurred. Inequality and poverty measurement require focusing on the details—the "logical connection of parts"—while examining the overall picture. It is this attention to measurement that the United States can learn from the European research and experience.

At the Joint OECD/University of Maryland Conference held in Paris on "Measuring Poverty, Income Inequality, and Social Exclusion: Lessons from Europe," many of the conference papers focused on alternative measures of income and evaluated their impacts on inequality and poverty. The conference papers highlight the impact of making detailed changes that affect measurement. These details, in turn, provide insight for the larger context of determining the "best" resource measure to use for poverty and inequality measurement. In many cases, the details do not change our picture of the trend in poverty, or even the comparisons across countries (see OECD 2008), but they often change the composition of the poor. Examining the details helps to logically connect the parts to form a satisfactory whole or picture. As it is often difficult to clarify all of the details and obtain the best measure, the main focus should be on obtaining a sufficient statistic that reflects a country's poverty or inequality and can be compared over time and across countries.

* The views expressed in this research, including those related to statistical, methodological, technical, or operational issues, are solely those of the author and do not necessarily reflect the official positions or policies of the Census Bureau, or the views of other staff members. This paper is released to inform interested parties of ongoing research and to encourage discussion of work in progress.

To evaluate how the logical connection of parts affects the overall picture of poverty, one must answer the *who, what, where, when, why,* and *how* of poverty measurement: Who is the unit of analysis (and the choice of equivalence scale)? What resource measure will be used? Where is poverty measured (and does it differ by geographic location)? When is poverty measured, and does it change over time? Why is poverty measured, and what is the purpose? How is the poverty threshold constructed and used?

THE US EXPERIENCE

As in Europe, the United States continues to evaluate alternative income measures and thresholds in determining a head-count poverty measure. Thirty-one years ago in the United States, the Office of Management and Budget issued Statistical Policy Directive 14 prescribing the method for estimating official poverty statistics.[1] Since then, there have been a number of evaluations of the poverty measure, including suggestions for changes and improvements. In 1995, the National Academy of Sciences (NAS) issued a report, *Measuring Poverty: A New Approach* (Citro and Michael 1995), that recommended making significant changes to the methods used to measure poverty in the United States. Over the past decade, the Census Bureau, other federal agencies, and the poverty research community have examined virtually every aspect of the NAS recommendations and, in many cases, have updated them. Recently, there has been renewed interest in the poverty measure recommended by the NAS report (see Blank 2008; Blank and Greenberg 2008; CEO 2008).

The Census Bureau has been producing NAS-type measures for a number of years.[2] For these measures, the poverty thresholds are constructed using the expenditures on a basic bundle of food, clothing, shelter, utilities, and a "little more" (the *how*). These thresholds are based on families and modified for various family types using a three-parameter equivalence scale (the *who*), adjusted for differences in the cost of living across states using a geographic adjustment (the *where*) that depends on the cost of housing, and updated over time using the change in median expenditures on the basic bundle (the *when*).

The calculation of resources (the *what*) for this measure starts with current money income, which is used to calculate official poverty statistics. This includes cash income received on a regular basis, such as income from earnings, any cash transfers, and property income.[3] Federal and state income taxes (along with social security taxes) are subtracted to obtain after-tax income. Taxes are estimated using a tax calculator; to improve the estimate of taxes, net realized capital gains are simulated and added to income. Added to after-tax income are the near-cash benefits that are available to meet spending needs defined in the thresholds (such as Food Stamps and housing subsidies), and necessary expenses, such as work-related expenses (including child care), are subtracted. Finally, to account for differences in health care needs, medical out-of-pocket (MOOP) expenses are subtracted to obtain the final resource measure used in determining the NAS-type poverty measure. By constructing both sides of the NAS-type poverty measure together, we ensure that the thresholds and resources are consistent and that they logically connect the parts to the whole.

Table 8.1 shows the overall poverty rates using the NAS-type measure as compared to the official poverty measure. In 2007, this measure is much higher than the

Table 8.1 OFFICIAL AND NAS-TYPE POVERTY RATES: 1999 TO 2010

Poverty Measure (percent)	1999	2000	2001	2002[a]	2003[a]	2004[a]	2005[a]	2006	2007	2008	2009	2010
Official measure	11.9	11.3	11.7	12.1	12.5	12.8	12.6	12.3	12.5	13.2	14.3	15.1
NAS[b]	12.1	12.3	12.9	13.2	13.4	13.4	13.3	13.6	15.3[c]	15.8[c]	15.7[c]	15.5[c]
NAS-CPI[b]	12.1	12.0	12.2	12.1	12.3	12.5	12.5	12.2	12.6	12.8	12.9	13.4

[a] The Census Bureau changed the way it modeled taxes and other items, which affects annual comparisons. For further information see http://www.census.gov/hhes/www/povmeas/altmeas07/nas_measures_historical.xls.

[b] This NAS-type measure is MSI-GA-CE produced by the Census Bureau and means medical out-of-pocket expenses (MOOP) subtracted from income; geographic adjustment (of poverty thresholds); thresholds were recomputed since 1999 using data from the Consumer Expenditure Survey.
The NAS-CPI measure is MSI-GA-CPI, which means medical out-of-pocket expenses (MOOP) subtracted from income; geographic adjustment (of poverty thresholds); thresholds were adjusted since 1999 using the CPI-U.

[c] See note 3.

SOURCE: US Census Bureau, Current Population Survey, 2000 to 2008 Annual Social and Economic Supplements.

official measure (15.3 percent compared with 12.5 percent).[4] This table also demonstrates the importance of the updating method (the *when*) and the impact of using a quasi-relative updating method. Using the CPI to update the thresholds, in Table 8.1, the NAS-CPI measure (see Table 8.1 for explanation) is 12.6 percent compared with the official measure of 12.5 percent. Results also suggest that while the geographic adjustments affect the relationship of state poverty rates, the other adjustments (the *what, who,* and *how*) taken separately do not substantially change the comparison between state poverty rates. The most dramatic effects occur in the changes in the composition of the poor (see Short 2001), and also Blank and Greenberg (2008) and CEO (2008).

ALTERNATIVE MEASURES OF INCOME (THE WHAT)

Many of the income definitions presented in the conference use components of income recommended by the Canberra Group (an international group of household income experts convened under the auspices of the United Nations Statistics Division). The Canberra Group's definition of adjusted disposable income includes the standard cash money income components, in-kind government transfers, cash value of fringe benefits, imputed rent, value of home production, and excludes taxes paid (see Table 2.1 in Canberra Group 2001). However, none of the papers follow a strict implementation of this income definition.

Most papers begin with a measure of after-tax cash income and include some in-kind transfers. The main issues for the NAS poverty measure are the measurement of health care expenditures and benefits and the imputed services from home ownership. Other issues include the methodology for calculating taxes and imputing in-kind benefits, the inclusion of employer-provided noncash benefits and of realized capital gains. As shown at this conference, most studies do not include all employer-provided benefits (see Gilbert 2012, Chapter 7), many do not include imputed rent, and none include the value of home production.

Using an after-tax income measure, the Organization for Economic Co-operation and Development (OECD) report—*Growing Unequal?* (OECD 2008; Förster and Mira d'Ercole 2012, Chapter 2), examines the impact of including various alternative income sources (for example, in-kind transfers, imputed rent). This report, together with conference papers, demonstrates that most additions to income (such as education, housing, health benefits, and imputed rent) decrease inequality and poverty, whereas sales taxes and capital income increase inequality. However, many of the impacts discussed are similar over time and across countries. In examining the US income distribution, many of the income components change inequality and poverty in ways similar to that shown in the OECD report. In addition, the changes do not affect the trends over time.[5] With similar effects, one wonders whether all of these components need to be taken into account, especially because many are difficult to measure and are not available in all countries.[6]

Sutherland, Taskloglou, and Paulus (2010) specifically evaluate the effects of the in-kind social benefits of housing, education, and health care. Each of these components is added to after-tax income, and their results confirm those from the OECD report that public benefits are equalizing (and poverty reducing). These benefits, however, do not change rankings across countries. The authors suggest that the different benefit structures across countries need to be considered when comparing poverty and inequality across countries. If health care services are provided in one country, and privately paid for in another, this could affect the cross-country comparisons of poverty. In addition, the composition of the poor can be affected by different benefits, such as education for children versus health care for the elderly.

The in-kind benefits examined in Sutherland, Taskloglou, and Paulus (2010) (and included in the Canberra report and the NAS poverty measure) must be imputed using additional information (and data). These imputations can affect not only the level of poverty, but also the composition of the poor, depending on which demographic variables are included in the imputation. Similar to Sutherland, Taskloglou, and Paulus (2010), the NAS income measure includes housing subsidies (as they are directed specifically to households); however, it does not include the social benefits of education and health care (and the Canberra report suggests including all social transfers in kind). As previously discussed, the NAS poverty measure actually subtracts MOOP from the resources and does not include the social benefit as imputed in Sutherland, Taskloglou, and Paulus (2010). The different treatment of MOOP and health care benefits can have a substantial impact on the level and composition of poverty.

With regard to housing, the NAS poverty measure does not include imputed rent. However, there have been discussions about how to handle home ownership in a poverty measure (see Citro and Michael 1995; Blank and Greenberg 2008). The Census Bureau does produce an "imputed rent" calculation using the net return on home equity. Using this measure decreases poverty, especially elderly poverty. Garner and Short (2001) further describe the alternative effects of measures of imputed rent.

Frick and Grabka (2012, Chapter 6) similarly examine capital income and imputed rents from housing. They show that imputed rent is equalizing and poverty-reducing, whereas capital income increases inequality. They highlight one of the problems with using relative poverty in comparing various income definitions: The inclusion of capital income actually increases poverty in some years. This is mainly due to the relative impact of the receipt of capital income on the elderly and suggests that the key issue again is the composition of the poor under alternative definitions. Whereas Frick and Grabka (2012, Chapter 6) focus on capital income, they do not discuss the inclusion of realized capital gains.

As the conference papers demonstrate, changes in measurement affect various demographic groups (e.g., children and elderly) in different ways. Because the main impacts are on the composition of the poor, this should be the focus of the evaluation of alternative income measures. In order to more fully examine these effects, the Census Bureau has released a Web-based table creator so that users can create their own poverty measures. This table creator can assist in evaluating each component of income or it can show the changes in composition between the official US poverty measure and alternatives. Most important, it can provide the impact on the composition of the poor by the inclusion of various income components.[7] Sutherland, Taskloglou, and Paulus (2010) use a more sophisticated modeling program to evaluate their impacts—EUROMOD.[8] A program like this would be useful for the United States and would allow more detailed examinations of the impact of changes on the composition of the poor.

VARIATIONS ON EQUIVALENCE SCALES (THE WHO)

Sutherland, Taskloglou, and Paulus (2010) also raise important measurement issues regarding the *who*; Do we need different equivalence scales for medical care and education, which are important for US poverty measurement? They construct an alternative scale for health care, and they evaluate allowing educational needs (and benefits) to vary for different households. Because most of the in-kind benefits are imputed to households, and these imputations vary by household composition, this creates an interaction between the income component and the equivalence scales— the *what* and the *who*. The NAS measure uses an imputation for MOOP that depends on the family types and sizes. This causes an interaction between the imputation and the equivalence scale. An alternative method presented in Short (2001) modifies the threshold and creates an additional equivalence scale adjustment for health care needs, which is similar to the method discussed in Sutherland, Taskloglou, and Paulus (2010). This points to the similarity across countries in the technical issues that different researchers are working to resolve.

Most studies use common arbitrary scales (such as the square root of household size) and fix them to be the same for all analyses—whether it be the choice of income, country, or time period (i.e., use the same *who* for the *what, where,* and *when*). As with changes in the components of income, the main impact of using various equivalence scales again is on the composition of the poor and not on the overall level or trend in poverty (see Short et al. 1999). As suggested herein, however, there can be interactions between the *who* and the *what*, and this could extend to interactions with the *where* and *when*.

Given the difference in "conditions" across countries, a "conditional" equivalence scale may need to be different for different countries.[9] Just as there may be reasons to alter the scale for health care, it may be useful to alter the scale over time. As the OECD report shows, the falling of average household size is one of the main drivers of changes in inequality. It could be that the "true scale" actually changes over time to reflect these choices, which could change our picture of the trend in inequality (or poverty). The framework discussed in Sutherland, Taskloglou, and Paulus (2010) can be applied to almost any in-kind benefit program. They suggest that including many of these benefits in an augmented income distribution means that they are like private commodities that households need, and hence, equivalence scales should be modified accordingly.

Gilbert (2012, Chapter 7) also raises some interesting measurement issues regarding the interaction of the *what* and the *who* in his examination of employer benefits, and in particular, those related to our ability to account for noncash employer benefits, such as paid vacations, sick days, and telecommuting. Many of these benefits could have different affects across family types, again demonstrating the interaction between the *what* and the *who*, suggesting the appropriateness of alternative equivalence scales for these types of benefits.

CONNECTING THE LOGICAL PARTS

Although examining the alternative components of an income measure is important, the main focus should be on obtaining a sufficient measure that reflects a country's poverty and can be compared over time and across countries. One issue is whether after-tax cash income tracks changes and differences across states or countries in a similar manner to the other measures presented here. Another issue is whether there need to be multiple measures for multiple purposes. Whereas the Canberra Group recommends one measure for income distribution, it could be that there is also a preferable income measure for poverty (as in the NAS measure) and yet another preferable income measure for program evaluation.

The impressionistic picture of poverty may look complete from a distance, but as one examines the details, many measurement issues remain. In particular, we need to examine the impact that changes in the income measure have on poverty rates of various demographic groups. We need to evaluate the "logical connection of the parts to the whole" to ensure that the composition of the picture "satisfies the mind." Though there may not be sufficient information to make all of the details clear, research in the United States and Europe must examine these details to understand if and how they change the picture of poverty. We must work together to maintain the big picture of comparability and determine a sufficient measure that provides enough information to measure poverty consistently over time, across countries (and states), and between demographic groups.

Notes

1. This directive stated that the basis of these measures is "the classification of income data collected by the Bureau of the Census in accordance with a definition of poverty developed by the Social Security Administration and revised by a Federal Interagency Committee in 1969." The full text of Office of Management and Budget Statistical Policy Directive 14 can be found at http://www.census.gov/hhes/povmeas/methodology/ombdir14.html.
2. See Table 8.1 for NAS; for details, see Short (2001) and Garner and Short (2008). More tables can be found at http://www.census.gov/hhes/www/povmeas/tables.html.
3. Before-tax income, regularly received, does not include net realized capital gains, gifts, lump sum inheritances, or insurance payments.
4. The Bureau of Labor Statistics implemented questionnaire improvements about expenditures on food away from home and type of mortgage in the Consumer Expenditure Interview Survey (CE) beginning in the second quarter of 2007. Consequently, comparisons with earlier years for the MSI-GA-CE measure may be affected.
5. See tables at http://www.census.gov/macro/032008/rdcall/1_001.htm.
6. See Table 2 in Smeeding and Weinberg (2001) for an inventory of income components for various countries.
7. See Johnson et al. (2008) for a description. The table creator can be accessed at http://www.census.gov/hhes/www/cpstc/apm/cpstc_altpov.html.
8. For information of EUROMOD, see http://www.iser.essex.ac.uk/research/euromod.
9. For example, using a constant elasticity equivalence scale (e.g., square root of household size), one could choose the scale elasticity that minimizes inequality within a country and then make intercountry comparisons.

References

Blank, Rebecca M. 2008. "How To Improve Poverty Measurement in the United States." *Journal of Policy Analysis and Management* 27 (2): 233–254.

Blank, Rebecca M., and Mark H. Greenberg. 2008. *Improving the Measurement of Poverty.* Hamilton Project Discussion Paper 2008–17. Washington, DC: Brookings Institution.

Canberra Group. 2001. Expert Group on Household Income Statistics: Final Report and Recommendations. Ottawa: Statistics Canada.

Center for Economic Opportunity. 2008. "The CEO Poverty Measure." Working paper, New York City Center for Economic Opportunity, New York.

Citro, Connie F., and Robert T. Michael. 1995. *Measuring Poverty: A New Approach.* Washington, DC: National Academy Press.

Förster, Michael, and Marco Mira d'Ercole. 2012. "The OECD Approach to Measuring Income Distribution and Poverty." In *Counting the Poor: New Thinking about European Poverty Measures and Lessons for the United States.* Edited by Douglas J. Besharov and Kenneth A. Couch, 25–58. New York: Oxford University Press.

Frick, Joachim, and Markus M. Grabka. 2012. "Accounting for Imputed and Capital Income Flows." In *Counting the Poor: New Thinking about European Poverty Measures and Lessons for the United States.* Edited by Douglas J. Besharov and Kenneth A. Couch, 117–142. New York: Oxford University Press.

Garner, Thesia, and Kathleen Short. 2001. "Owner-Occupied Shelter in Experimental Poverty Measures." Poverty Measurement Working Paper, Census Bureau, Washington, DC.

———.2008. "Creating a Consistent Poverty Measure over Time Using NAS Procedures:1996–2005." Poverty Measurement Working Paper, Census Bureau, Washington, DC.

Gilbert, Neil. 2012. "Accounting for Employee Benefits." In *Counting the Poor: New Thinking about European poverty Measures and Lessons for the United States.* Edited by Douglas J. Besharov and Kenneth A. Couch, 143–160. New York: Oxford University Press.

Johnson, David, Charles Nelson, Kathleen Short, and Sharon Stern. 2008. "Progress toward Improving the U.S. Poverty Measure." Paper presented at the Annual APPAM Research Conference, November 2008, Washington, DC.

OECD. 2008. *Growing Unequal? Income Distribution and Poverty in OECD Countries.* Paris: Organization for Economic Cooperation and Development.

Short, Kathleen. 2001. *Experimental Poverty Measures: 1999.* US Census Bureau, Current Population Reports, Consumer Income, P60–216. Washington, DC: US Government Printing Office.

Short, Kathleen, Thesia Garner, David Johnson, and Patricia Doyle. 1999. *Experimental Poverty Measures: 1990 to 1997.* US Census Bureau, Current Population Reports, Consumer Income, P60–205. Washington, DC: US Government Printing Office.

Smeeding, Timothy, and Daniel Weinberg. 2001. "Toward a Uniform Definition of Household Income." *Review of Income and Wealth* 47 (1): 1–24.

Sutherland, Hollly, Panos Tsakloglou, and A. Paulus. 2010. "The Distributional Impact of In-Kind Public Benefits in European Countries." *Journal of Public Analysis and Management* 29: 243–266.

PART THREE

Income Levels for Social Assistance and Their Behavioral Effects

9

Minimum-Income Benefits in OECD Countries

HERWIG IMMERVOLL ■

Almost all Organization for Economic Co-operation and Development (OECD) countries operate comprehensive minimum-income programs for working-age individuals and their families, either as last-resort safety nets alongside primary income replacement benefits or as the principal instrument for delivering social protection. These safety-net benefits aim at providing an acceptable standard of living for families unable to earn sufficient incomes from other sources. As antipoverty measures, they reduce income disparities at the bottom of the income spectrum and, as such, they represent important building blocks of redistribution policies. Equally important, they act as safety nets for individuals experiencing low-income spells and, hence, help to smooth income levels over time.

This chapter provides a broad overview of contemporary minimum-income transfers in OECD countries.[1] In the policy debate, as well as in economic models, such transfers are occasionally characterized as simple income floors. Yet, even though benefit levels are important, the extent to which they shape distributional outcomes depends on a multitude of other factors. To appreciate country differences in the role of minimum-income benefits, and in the situation of benefit recipients, it is necessary to look at a range of policy parameters in combination.

One important factor is the way in which benefits of last resort are embedded in the wider social policy framework. For example, their significance as a redistribution instrument evidently differs between countries where they complement other benefits that provide powerful first-tier safety nets (as in much of continental Europe) and those where they represent the main benefit (as in Australia and New Zealand). Consequently, reforms of higher-tier benefits will often have implications for minimum-income programs in terms of spending levels, the number and characteristics of benefit recipients, as well as optimal strategies for supporting them.

Since the 1990s, social policy debates in OECD countries have increasingly emphasized the need for "active" and "activating" support. Although the balance varies very much between countries and policy areas, such support includes assistance for those making efforts toward regaining self-sufficiency, allied to the possibility of benefit sanctions if a client's own efforts are considered inadequate. Attempts to rebalance policies from passive income assistance toward strengthening self-sufficiency have, at least in principle, been a central element of reform initiatives across a broad range of social policy areas. Nevertheless, the successes of such efforts have been uneven. Whereas those who are, in some sense, closest to the labor market are in a good position to benefit from work-oriented support, achieving lasting labor market integration and adequate incomes has proved much more difficult for other social policy clients, including recipients of social assistance and other benefits of last resort. The question of how to maintain active social policies in a context of weak labor markets, as experienced during the recent economic crisis, brings renewed momentum to this debate.

The chapter starts out by proposing a simple typology for situating different types of minimum-income benefits as elements of the overall redistribution system. The third section summarizes the generosity of benefit payments and the structure of health care–related support measures that complement them. The fourth section describes the limited available comparative data on the number of benefit claimants and considers to what extent they matter when assessing the relevance of social assistance measures as safety nets. The fifth section provides a condensed overview of the "mutual obligations" debate, discussing, in turn, the rationale of back-to-work and other activation measures and the main results from the evaluation literature. The last section concludes by highlighting some challenges for minimum-income programs posed by the recent economic downturn.

A TYPOLOGY OF MINIMUM-INCOME BENEFITS: SCOPE AND LINKS WITH OTHER TRANSFER PROGRAMS

Benefits of last resort mean different things in different countries and for different population groups. For the purpose of this chapter, they are defined as cash or in-kind transfers that aim at preventing extreme hardship and employ a low-income criterion as the central entitlement condition. Benefits of last resort, therefore, include social assistance benefits, as well as other means-tested assistance payments that are typically received by families with no other income sources (although, as we shall discuss, the same benefits can to some extent also top up the incomes of low-paid workers and other low-income groups). Examples are means-tested lone-parent benefits, as well as unemployment assistance benefits that are not conditional on work or contribution histories (as in Australia, Finland, Germany, Ireland, New Zealand, the United Kingdom). In what follows, *social assistance* refers to minimum-income benefits that are generally available and, thus, not targeted to specific population groups. *Minimum-income benefit* is a broader concept that includes social assistance and other, more targeted, programs with a similar function (e.g., means-tested lone-parent benefits). I use the terms *minimum-income benefit, minimum safety-net benefits, welfare benefits,* and *last-resort benefits* synonymously. To focus the discussion, it is limited to benefits targeted at *able-bodied working-age* individuals and their families.[2]

In most areas of social spending, overall expenditure data are a good starting point for appreciating country variations in terms of the importance of policies that address different contingencies. Such spending patterns are illustrated in Table 9.1 using recent social expenditure data compiled by the OECD. The columns on the right show breakdowns of total public spending across nine social policy domains, whereas the first three columns report total spending levels, as well as spending on cash

Table 9.1 PUBLIC SOCIAL EXPENDITURE IN OECD COUNTRIES: LEVELS AND COMPOSITION, 2005

	Total	Cash	Income-Tested	Old Age	Survivors	Incapacity Related	Health	Family	Active Labor Market Program	Unemployment	Housing	Other Social Policy Areas
	In Percentage of GDP			In Percentage of Total Spending								
Australia	17.1	8.1	6.3	26.0	1.2	14.2	34.3	16.5	2.2	3.2	1.5	0.8
Austria	27.2	18.4	1.1	46.5	1.3	8.8	25.1	10.4	2.3	4.2	0.4	1.1
Belgium	26.4	16.2	0.9	27.2	7.7	8.9	27.8	9.9	4.1	12.6	0.3	1.7
Canada	16.5	6.8	3.3	22.6	2.4	5.6	41.5	6.4	1.8	3.8	2.7	13.3
Czech Republic	19.5	11.4	1.6	38.3	0.9	12.4	32.4	8.9	1.3	3.2	0.4	2.3
Denmark	27.1	13.6	1.0	26.8	0.0	15.9	21.6	12.5	6.5	10.4	2.6	3.7
Finland	26.1	15.3	2.6	32.6	3.4	14.7	23.8	11.4	3.4	7.7	1.1	1.9
France	29.2	17.5	1.9	37.4	6.1	6.3	26.9	10.3	3.1	5.9	2.8	1.2
Germany	26.7	15.9	1.5	42.0	1.4	7.0	28.7	8.1	3.6	6.2	2.3	0.8
Greece	20.5	13.4	1.3	52.5	3.9	4.4	27.4	5.3	0.3	1.9	2.5	1.8
Hungary	22.5	13.6	0.6	39.2	1.2	12.5	26.6	13.8	1.3	2.5	2.3	0.7
Iceland	16.9	5.7	1.0	22.6	0.2	15.9	37.4	17.6	0.5	1.8	1.2	2.9
Ireland	16.7	8.4	2.6	17.3	5.0	9.7	38.8	14.9	3.8	5.4	3.1	2.1
Italy	25.0	16.7	0.7	46.4	9.9	6.8	27.3	5.2	2.3	2.0	0.1	0.1

(Continued)

Table 9.1 Public Social Expenditure in OECD Countries: Levels and Composition, 2005 (Cont'd)

	Total	Cash	Income-Tested	Old Age	Survivors	Incapacity Related	Health	Family	Active Labor Market Program	Unemployment	Housing	Other Social Policy Areas
	In percentage of GDP			In Percentage of Total Spending								
Japan	18.6	10.2	0.5	46.4	6.9	3.8	34.0	4.4	1.4	1.8	—	1.4
Korea	6.9	2.9	0.7	22.3	3.6	8.2	46.2	4.0	1.9	3.1	—	10.7
Luxembourg	23.2	13.9	0.5	22.6	8.7	14.1	30.1	15.5	2.2	4.2	0.7	1.9
Mexico	7.4	2.5	0.5	13.8	4.0	0.9	39.2	13.5	0.3	—	14.9	13.4
Netherlands	20.9	11.1	1.1	26.5	1.4	17.3	28.5	7.9	6.4	7.3	1.6	3.0
New Zealand	18.5	9.7	3.4	22.8	0.8	15.5	37.2	14.2	2.1	2.4	4.3	0.8
Norway	21.6	10.9	1.1	29.2	1.3	20.3	26.7	13.1	3.4	2.5	0.7	2.8
Poland	21.0	15.7	1.1	49.7	4.8	12.8	20.5	5.4	2.0	2.6	0.6	1.7
Portugal	22.9	13.9	1.7	36.3	6.6	10.5	31.0	6.5	2.9	4.7	0.0	1.4
Slovak Republic	16.6	10.2	0.6	37.3	1.3	10.1	31.9	12.8	2.1	1.6	0.0	3.0
Spain	21.2	13.1	1.6	37.1	2.6	11.7	27.5	5.4	3.6	10.4	0.8	0.9
Sweden	29.4	14.5	0.6	32.6	2.1	19.0	23.0	10.9	4.4	4.1	1.8	2.0
Switzerland	20.3	11.8	1.1	32.7	1.8	16.3	29.9	6.6	3.7	4.6	0.8	3.7

Turkey	13.7	8.1	0.5	46.7	11.5	1.5	39.6	0.2	0.0	0.4	—	—
United Kingdom	21.3	10.3	2.7	28.6	0.9	11.2	32.9	15.0	2.5	1.2	6.8	0.9
United States	15.9	8.0	1.2	33.3	4.8	8.1	43.7	3.9	0.8	1.9	—	3.6
OECD-Total	20.6	11.6	1.5	33.2	3.6	10.8	31.4	9.7	2.5	4.3	2.2	2.9

NOTES: Data are before tax and account neither for the tax treatment of social benefits nor for tax expenditures (e.g., tax deductions for children), although tax credits paid in cash are included. Alternative data report net spending data, which address these issues (see link shown under source).

Dashes indicate that data are not available. Data for Portugal are for 2003. The following income-tested spending items are included in the "income-tested" category: spending on "other social policy areas," income-tested spending on the unemployed (e.g., unemployment assistance payments for Germany), income-tested support payments to elderly and disabled (e.g., Belgium, and the United Kingdom), other income tested payments (e.g., family cash transfers). Excluded are earmarked housing subsidies, active labor market polices, and income-tested ,medical support. GDP is gross domestic product.

SOURCE: Extracted from the preliminary 2005 wave of the OECD SOCX database.

benefits and on income-tested programs. It is apparent that targeting low-income groups is a central design feature of cash transfer programs in several OECD countries, including the United Kingdom, Ireland, New Zealand, Canada, and, most notably, Australia. In countries with extensive social insurance benefits, the budgetary relevance of means-tested transfers is correspondingly lower.

However, for a number of reasons, these numbers are likely to portray a distorted picture of spending on minimum-income benefits as defined previously. First, program-level spending data are not always available, so the decision whether or not to count broader benefit categories as means-tested can be ambiguous. For the same reason, it is not straightforward to exclude programs that employ means testing but are not minimum-income benefits (e.g., unemployment assistance that depends on previous work status and/or contribution payments, family benefits that are withdrawn only at higher income levels). Second, data quality for the main social assistance benefits is generally lower than it is for other spending categories.[3] Finally, aggregate spending data cannot be broken down by age group; therefore, expenditures for the working-age population are not available.

Because of these limitations, a more detailed look at institutional policy parameters is useful for assessing the roles minimum-income benefits play across countries. In general, it is difficult to draw conclusions from looking at isolated measures without considering the full policy package affecting incomes and employment incentives: Similar measures can have very different effects depending on the institutional context in which they are used. To give a flavor of this context, Table 9.2 lists the most important working-age cash transfers using a functional classification.[4]

Unemployment benefits are the main support measures for job losers and other individuals without employment. *Unemployment insurance* programs exist in most OECD countries and offer compensation for lost earnings subject to work-related conditions. Reflecting insurance principles, claimants must have contributed to the insurance fund or have been employed over certain periods in order to be eligible. Claimants must also be actively looking for work and, in many cases, unemployment has to be involuntary. Benefit durations are limited in most, but not all, countries. Insurance is mandatory for most employees, but voluntary in some Nordic countries.

Job searchers whose entitlement to unemployment insurance benefits has expired, or who are ineligible in the first place, may be entitled to *unemployment assistance*. In some countries, unemployment assistance is the main unemployment benefit. Eligibility is often, but not always, conditional on previous employment. As unemployment benefits, they are only available to those who are available and actively looking for work. Benefit durations may or may not be limited. Although both insurance and assistance benefit schemes are typically (but, again, not universally) financed by contributions to unemployment insurance funds, the main purpose of assistance benefits is the provision of a minimum level of resources during unemployment rather than insurance against lost earnings. As a result, benefit levels tend to be lower and links to previous earnings tend to be weaker. They are reduced if other incomes are available, but means-testing tends to be less comprehensive than for social assistance benefits.

Finally, those who do not qualify for any unemployment benefit may receive *social assistance*, with central or subcentral governments acting as providers of last resort. The main eligibility criteria relating available incomes and assets to entitlements do not depend specifically on claimants' work history. Income and asset tests can be

Table 9.2 MAIN CASH BENEFITS FOR ABLE-BODIED WORKING-AGE INDIVIDUALS AND THEIR FAMILIES, 2007

	Unemployment		Social Assistance (SA)ᵃ	Housing Benefits	Family Benefits (FB)		Lone-parent benefits	Employment Conditional Benefits
	Insurance	Assistance			Universal	Means-tested		
Australia		•	•	•		•	•	•
Austria	•	•	•	•	•		T	•
Belgium	•	•	•	•	•		FB	
Canada	•		•	•		•	T	•
Czech Republic	•		•	•		•	•	
Denmark	•		•	•	•		FB	
Finland	•	•	•	•	•		FB	
France	•	•	•	•	•	•	T	•
Germany	•	•	•	•	•		T	
Greece	•	•			•			
Hungary	•	•	•	•	•		FB	•
Iceland	•				•	•	•	•
Ireland		•		SA			•	
Italy	•			•		•	FB	
Japan	•		•	•		•	•	•

(Continued)

Table 9.2 MAIN CASH BENEFITS FOR ABLE-BODIED WORKING-AGE INDIVIDUALS AND THEIR FAMILIES, 2007 (*CONT'D*)

	Unemployment		Social Assistance (SA)[a]	Housing Benefits	Family Benefits (FB)		Lone-parent benefits	Employment Conditional Benefits
	Insurance	Assistance			Universal	Means-tested		
Korea	•		•	•	•		•	•
Luxembourg	•		•	•	•		T	•
Netherlands	•		•	•	•		T	•
New Zealand		•	•	•		•	•	•
Norway	•	•	•	•	•		•	
Poland	•		•	•			FB	
Portugal	•	•	•	•		•	T	
Slovak Republic	•		•		•			
Spain	•	•	•	•		•	T	•
Sweden	•	•	•	•	•		•	•
Switzerland	•		•	•	•			
United Kingdom	•	•	•	•	•	•		•
United States	•		•				T	•

NOTES: • indicates that the specific benefit or tax credit exists in this country. Where no specific housing or lone-parent benefit is available, SA (social assistance), or FB (family benefit) or T (income tax) indicate that housing or lone-parent specific provisions exist as part of these schemes.
[a]Cash social assistance benefits only. Because of its importance, the US Food Stamps, a "near-cash" benefit program, is indicated as well.

SOURCE: OECD Benefits and Wages policy database (www.oecd.org/els/social/workincentives).

very restrictive and always take account of the resources of other persons living with the benefit claimant. Eligibility may be conditional on the claimant's effort to regain self-sufficiency. But whereas rules and practices vary substantially across countries, job-search and other activity requirements can be much less demanding than in the case of unemployment benefits.[5] Social assistance is typically not subject to explicit time limits but is paid for as long as relevant conditions are met. Benefits often "top-up" income from other sources (including other benefits). Because bigger families require more resources to secure a given living standard, top-ups are more likely for benefit claimants with dependent family members.

In addition to the main social assistance benefits, there are other government transfers that have similar characteristics or can complement or substitute for social assistance payments:

- Low-income households may also qualify for cash *housing benefits,* which employ similar forms of means-testing. They may be administered as separate programs or may be payable as part of social assistance entitlements. Unlike social assistance payments, dedicated housing benefit programs typically do not employ work-related requirements or interventions that seek to reestablish self-sufficiency.
- Families with children can claim *family benefits* in most countries (although the definition of what constitutes a "dependent child" varies considerably). Most countries provide special *benefits for lone parents* either in the form of additions to regular family or child care benefits or as separate programs. Where benefits for children or lone parents are means-tested, they can resemble social assistance benefits in all but name.[6] One difference concerns work-related activity requirements. Means-tested family benefits are frequently designed as temporary payments that enable one of the parents to spend time with their children. Apart from time limits (which can be generous and are often implicit, e.g., by specifying a maximum age for a dependent child: see Table 7 in Immervoll 2009), work-related requirements may therefore be minimal or nonexistent.
- Targeted income support is increasingly made available to those in work and can, to some extent, substitute for income top-ups provided by social assistance and other minimum-income benefits. Around half the OECD countries now operate employment-conditional benefits, or *in-work benefits* of one type or another. Like minimum-income benefits, some of these programs employ family-based low-income criteria. But because they are conditional on work, they are not payable to those with zero incomes and are therefore not benefits of last resort.[7]

It is clear from this overview that minimum-income benefits can be provided under a range of different policy headings. What they have in common is that they are received by those with no or very limited other resources and can provide fall-back safety nets for low-income families not entitled to other income replacement transfers. Figure 9.1 situates countries' programs along two dimensions:

1. *Rank:* Main income support program *or* lower-tier benefit.
2. *Scope:* Broad safety net *or* targeted program (notably to lone parents).

In most countries, they take the form of lower-tier fallback benefits for those not receiving other types of support. Last-resort benefits with a broad scope are shown in the upper right-hand corner in Figure 9.1. The biggest group in this category are social assistance programs providing cash and near-cash support (US Food Stamps, since 2008 Supplemental Nutrition Assistance Program). In addition, unemployment assistance benefits in Finland, Germany, Ireland, and the United Kingdom are available independently of contribution records or previous employment history and can be counted as broad-scope lower-tier benefits.[8] There are further last-resort benefits targeted at lone parents in France, the United Kingdom, and the United States (lower right-hand corner; the benefit for Norwegian lone parents is formally an insurance benefit, but is also included here as eligibility is subject to an income test and does not require an employment record).

In a few cases, minimum-income benefits are the main income support program for the majority of the working-age population (upper left-hand quadrant) or for individual groups (younger individuals in Australia and lone parents in Australia, Ireland, and New Zealand[9]). In addition to these first-tier programs, Australia and New Zealand also operate lower-tier emergency benefits, but these are much less common and are not shown here.

A small number of countries also operate targeted lower-tier minimum-income benefits that are not considered here, notably for individuals who are not able to work due to a disability, such as the US Supplemental Security Income and the Irish Disability Allowance. In both cases, non-means-tested insurance-based programs act as first-tier benefits. The New Zealand Invalid's Benefit and the Australian Disability Support Pension are examples of means-tested first-tier benefits for this group.

Main out-of-work safety-net benefits for able-bodied working-age individuals and their families, 2007

	first-tier benefit	lower-tier benefit
broad scope	nzl (*unemployment benefit*) aus (*newstart allowance*)	*Social Assistance*: aus aut bel can che cze dnk esp fin fra hun irl isl jpn kor lux nld nor nzl pol prt swe usa *Unemployment Assistance:* deu fin irl uk
targeted	aus (*parenting payment, youth allowance*) irl (*one-parent family payment*) nzl (*domestic purposes benefit*)	fra* (*allocation de parent isolé*) nor (*transitional benefit*) uk (*income support*) usa (*TANF, SSP* programs)

* As of mid-2009, the French *Allocation de Parent Isolé* (API) was abolished as the new Active Solidarity Income (*Revenue de Solidarité Active*, RSA) was extended to all low-income families, including lone parents.

Figure 9.1 A Typology: Rank and Scope of Minimum-Income Benefits.
NOTE: As of mid-2009, the French *Allocation de Parent Isolé* (was abolished as the new Active Solidarity Income (*Revenue de Solidarité Active*) was extended to all low-income families, including lone parents.

Generosity: Benefit Levels and Related Support Measures

BENEFIT LEVELS IN RELATION TO MEDIAN INCOMES
AND RELATIVE POVERTY THRESHOLDS

Poverty avoidance or alleviation are primary objectives of minimum-income benefits. When comparing benefit generosity across countries, a useful starting point is to
look at benefit levels relative to commonly used poverty thresholds. Figure 9.2 presents model calculations using the OECD tax-benefit calculator and relates the resulting net income levels of benefit recipients to median incomes from income
distribution data. In a large majority of OECD countries for which such calculations
are available, benefits of last resort can be significantly lower than the three alternative *relative* poverty lines (40 percent, 50 percent, and 60 percent of median income).
Individual poverty gaps are very large in some countries (there is no generally applicable social assistance benefit in Greece, Italy, and Turkey), and other income sources
are needed everywhere to avoid substantial poverty risks.

In a number of countries, the range of possible benefit entitlements can be very
wide, however. This is illustrated using error bars, which show the difference in benefit entitlements between a situation where the recipient claims no housing costs and
one where they live in privately rented accommodation and obtains partial or full
compensation for housing expenditures. Housing benefit calculations in this latter
case are based on a simple common rent assumption across countries (20 percent of
the average gross wage of a full-time worker).[10] For many benefit recipients, payment
levels will be somewhere in-between the "with housing costs" and "without housing
costs" scenarios. In about half of the countries, benefit rates show in fact little or no
variation with housing costs as housing support is not available at all, is modest (for
instance, there is no separate mechanism to provide cash housing support in the US
Food Stamp/Supplemental Nutrition Assistance Program program, but housing
costs slightly reduce reckonable income in some states), or is provided on a flat-rate
basis (for instance, social assistance entitlements may be designed in a way to cover
housing costs together with other expenditures).

Comparing across family types, it turns out that net incomes of minimum-income
recipients with children (second and third panels of Figure 9.2) tend to be higher
relative to the respective poverty thresholds than for single persons (first panel).
Consistent with heightened policy concerns about child poverty in many countries,
this indicates that benefit provisions for children and other family members are, at
least for poor households, typically more generous than would be implied by the
equivalence scales typically used in income distribution studies.

However, the distributional impact of minimum-income benefits is, not limited to
recipient families with incomes below the levels indicated in Figure 9.2. Because
concerns about the efficiency costs of work disincentives lead many countries to
employ gradual benefit phaseouts, those with nonbenefit incomes above the maximum benefit amounts can often still receive income top-ups.[11] Table 9.3 illustrates
this by showing the approximate earnings levels, as well as the associated net incomes,
where minimum-income benefits are fully phased out.

Less than half the countries shown fully deduct earned incomes from benefit entitlements, with marginal effective tax rates (METRs) exceeding 90 percent. Where
benefits are withdrawn at a much slower rate, minimum-income benefits can extend
support to nonpoor recipients even if they do not lift the lowest income groups out

Net income value in % of median household incomes, 2007

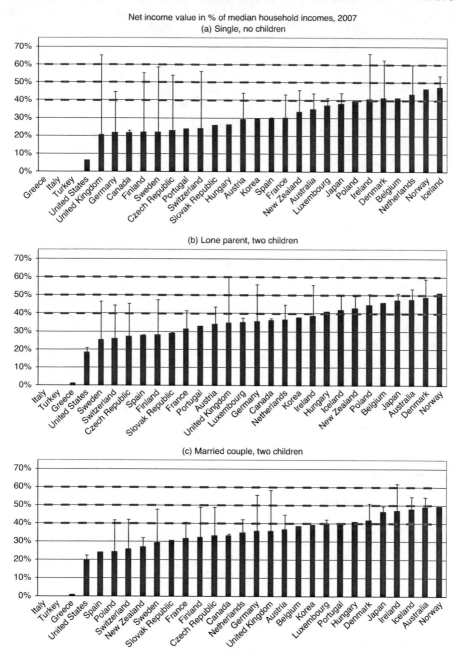

Figure 9.2 Income Levels Provided by Cash Minimum-Income Benefits.
NOTES: Median net household incomes are for a year around 2005 expressed in 2007
prices and are before housing costs (or other forms of "committed" expenditure). Results
are shown on an equivalized basis (equivalence scale is the square root of the household
size) and account for all relevant cash benefits (social assistance, family benefits, housing-
related cash support as indicated). The US results also include the value of Food Stamps, a
near-cash benefit. Income levels account for all cash benefit entitlements of a family with a
working-age head and assume no entitlement to primary benefits such as unemployment
insurance and the absence of other income sources. They are net of any income taxes and

of poverty. Results are only shown for singles, but phaseout *rates* tend to be similar for other family types. Because benefit amounts are higher for larger families, the phaseout points tend to be correspondingly higher up the earnings distribution. In some countries, and for some family types, income-tested in-work benefits may start being available around the earnings level where minimum-income benefits are fully phased out. In these cases, high METRs caused by benefit tapers can continue beyond the phaseout points shown in Table 9.3.

BENEFIT LEVELS RELATIVE TO IN-WORK INCOMES

As illustrated by the METRs shown in the preceding section, benefits are a key determinant of whether work "pays," especially for those with limited earnings potential. Because benefit recipients without any earned income mostly have net incomes below commonly used poverty thresholds, a relevant question is how much they would need to earn in order to escape poverty. This amount will depend on two factors. First, more earnings are required in countries with sizable individual "poverty gaps" (the distance between benefit entitlements and the chosen poverty line). The second factor is the METR, as it determines how much of the in-work earnings ends up adding to household net income.

One way of showing the situation of low-wage earners is by reference to statutory minimum wages, which exist in around two-thirds of the OECD countries. Comparisons based on gross minimum wage levels do not take into account differences in taxes and benefits and, therefore, can give only a partial indication about the true value of wage floors. Figure 9.3 shows incomes of full-time employees earning the statutory minimum wage after taxes and benefits and, as in Figure 9.2, relates those to median household disposable income.[12] In the majority of countries, a full-time minimum-wage earner in a single-person household makes enough to put themselves above 50 percent of median household income and, with the exception of the United States, full-time minimum-wage earnings are everywhere sufficient to ensure incomes above the 40 percent threshold (net incomes are higher in the considerable number of states that operate statutory minima exceeding the US federal minimum wage).

For families, one minimum-wage job is typically not enough to escape relative poverty using the 50 percent threshold. However, in-work benefits and/or gradual benefit phaseout rates for families with children can provide a significant income boost. For instance, a lone-parent full-time minimum-wage worker in New Zealand,

---

social contributions. Where benefit rules are not determined on a national level but vary by region or municipality, results refer to a "typical" case (e.g., Michigan in the United States, the capital in some other countries). Calculations for families with children assume two children aged four and six years. "Error" bars indicate the range of benefit levels in countries where they depend on actual housing expenditure. The bottom end of the error bar shows the situation where no housing costs are claimed, whereas the top end represents cash benefits for someone in privately rented accommodation with rent plus other charges amounting to 20 percent of average gross full-time wages. SOURCES: OECD tax-benefit models (www.oecd.org/els/social/workincentives) and OECD income distribution database (www.oecd.org/els/social/inequality).

Table 9.3 Benefit Phaseout Points and Benefit Withdrawal Rates

	Single-person Household, 2007 Minimum-income Benefits Assuming That Housing Expenditures are not Claimed or are Zero			Benefits Include Claims for Privately Rented Accommodation Expenditures, Where Relevant		
	Earnings, Percentage of Average Wage	Net Income at This Earnings Level, Percentage of Median Household Income	Marginal Effective Tax Rate Over Phaseout Range	Earnings, Percentage of Average Wage	Net Income at This Earnings Level, Percentage of Median Household Income	Marginal Effective Tax Rate Over Phaseout Range
United Kingdom	11	24	86	52	91	78
Sweden	14	23	97	41	59	100
Canada	17	24	90	17	25	90
Czech Republic	17	23	100	86	105	62
Switzerland	17	24	100	41	56	100
Hungary	17	25	105	23	34	82
Portugal	19	31	80	19	31	80
Finland	19	28	82	44	61	88
Spain	19	30	100	19	30	100
Germany	20	37	67	38	63	79
France[a]	20	32	95	37	57	80
Austria	20	31	97	30	46	98
Korea	22	40	76	22	40	76
Belgium	22	44	94	22	44	94

Ireland	23	42	98	41	75	100
Slovak Republic	24	35	77	24	35	77
Poland	24	41	97	39	65	71
United States	25	30	32	33	38	30
Iceland[b]	31	48	100	>150		
Japan	32	51	79	32	51	89
Netherlands	33	45	98	47	61	98
Norway	34	48	98	34	48	98
Australia	37	61	61	45	73	65
Luxembourg	39	45	86	42	48	88
New Zealand	45	59	66	70	90	61
Denmark[b]	46	51	38	106	109	45

NOTES: See explanatory notes to Figure 9.2. The marginal effective tax rate (METR) is calculated over an earnings interval from zero to the respective phaseout point. It is the fraction of any additional employment incomes that is "taxed away" by the combined effects of taxes and benefits withdrawals and therefore accounts for benefit tapers as well as income taxes and social contributions payable by the benefit recipient.

[a]Unlike the *Revenu Minimum d'Insertion* program shown in the table, the *Revenue de Solidarité Active*, which replaced it in 2009, uses a flat phaseout range with marginal deduction rates of about 38 percent. At just 120 percent of the full-time minimum wage, the phaseout point for a single person is almost three times higher than under the previous programs.

[b]For Iceland, METRs are not shown in the right-hand half of the table because housing benefits are withdrawn over a very wide earnings range and METRs, therefore, are more driven by the tax system than by the benefit taper. To a lesser extent, the same argument can also be made in the case of Denmark.

SOURCES: OECD tax-benefit models (www.oecd.org/els/social/workincentives) and OECD income distribution database (www.oecd.org/els/social/inequality).

in % of median household incomes, 2007

(a) Single, no children

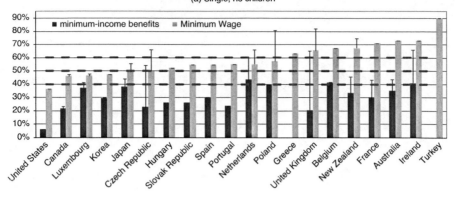

(b) Lone parent, two children

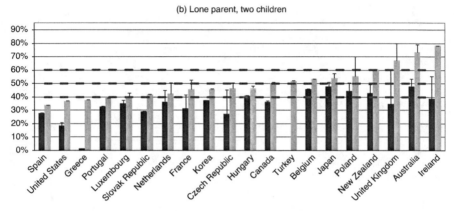

(c) Married couple, two children

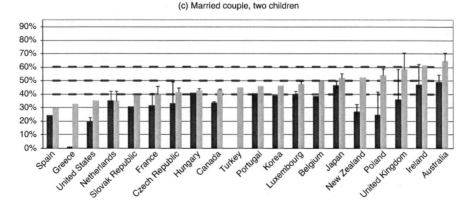

Figure 9.3 Net Incomes of Benefit Recipients and Full-Time Minimum-Wage Earners.
NOTE: See explanatory notes to Figure 9.2. Hourly minimum wages are converted to monthly earnings based on 40 working hours per week. Where minimum wages depend on age, profession, or sector, figures relate to the adult rate for white-collar workers in the private sector (Belgium, Greece, Portugal). The federal minimum is used for the United States. Where there is no country-wide minimum, weighted averages of regional minimum wages are used (Japan). Incomes in the married-couple case are calculated assuming that there is only one earner.
SOURCES: OECD tax-benefit models (www.oecd.org/els/social/workincentives), OECD income distribution database, and OECD minimum wage database.

the United Kingdom, Australia, and Ireland takes home net income at or above 60 percent of median incomes. The net income gain from working in a full-time job typically exceeds 20 percent. But in a number of cases, gains are quite limited, even if minimum wages are high (e.g., France, Luxembourg, the Netherlands). Work-incentive problems can be a problem especially for those entitled to housing-related benefits (as in Figure 9.2, such entitlements are indicated by the error bars). Finally, it is important to note that these income figures are before child care costs. Even with relatively large income gains, lone parents with children requiring care may still consider that a full-time job does little to improve the family budget and that they are financially better off on benefits (OECD [2007a] discusses child care costs and work incentives in detail).

In general, the earnings needed to escape poverty increase with family size, so that net incomes of lone-parent minimum-wage earners tend to be lower in relation to median incomes than for childless singles. But patterns differ across countries both in quantitative and qualitative terms. For instance, whereas support for families with children is often structured in such a way as to make it easier for them to escape poverty than it is for their childless counterparts (e.g., Australia, Ireland, New Zealand, and the United Kingdom), the reverse appears to be true in a few other countries (e.g., Spain, the United States).

Benefit Levels Relative to Unemployment Benefits

Minimum-income benefits form an integral part of the redistribution system. In setting entitlements, policy makers need to consider not only poverty thresholds and the income position of low-wage workers, but also the levels of other, higher-tier benefit payments. Where minimum-income programs act as fallback benefits for people not (or no longer) entitled to unemployment compensation, their generosity has important implications for the functioning of unemployment benefits.

For instance, as a measure to facilitate effective job searches, unemployment benefit recipients are typically confronted with declining benefit payments or expiring entitlement once they have been out of work for a specified period. Such "threat points" reinforce job-search incentives and have been shown to improve job-finding rates, even before benefits are reduced.[13] But whether these measures have their intended effect depends in part on the existence and generosity of minimum-income benefits that may top up unemployment compensation or substitute for it entirely. Such interactions may or may not be intended. On the one hand, substitution can be a concern as the required contact intensity with case workers is typically lower, and job-search requirements less demanding, for social assistance claimants than for those claiming unemployment benefits.

On the other hand, the balance of the two main objectives of unemployment compensation (facilitating a job search and providing a degree of income security) may change depending on the labor market situation. For instance, as job vacancies dry up during a recession, and demand-side restrictions become more binding, job-search incentives may be less effective and concerns about the adequacy of income support for the growing number of longer-term unemployed may be more pressing. In this case, the existence and availability of minimum-income benefits may provide a welcome mechanism that provides additional protection for job searchers and their families.

Table 9.4 shows income levels of minimum-income for recipients relative to those provided by unemployment benefits. Where unemployment benefits are paid at

Table 9.4 Minimum-Income Benefit Levels Relative to Unemployment Benefits 2007, as a Percentage, for Two Different Levels of Previous Earnings and at Different Points during an Unemployment Spell

| | Point during Unemployment Spell (months)[a] | Below-average Earner (67 Percent of AW) No Children | | Below-average Earner (67 Percent of AW) 2 Children (Ages 4 and 6) | | Average Earner (100 Percent of AW) No Children | | Average Earner (100 Percent of AW) 2 Children (Ages 4 and 6) | |
		Single Person	1-earner Couple	Lone Parent	1-earner Couple	Single Person	1-earner Parent	Lone Parent	1-earner Couple
Australia	1+	100	100	100	100	100	100	100	100
Austria	1–9	91	114	97	113	66	84	79	92
	10+	99	124	103	119	72	91	84	97
Belgium	1–12	61	81	91	87	61	81	91	87
	13+	73	81	89	85	73	81	89	85
Canada	1–8	49	75	80	85	36	55	64	68
Czech Republic	1–6	92	120	98	122	76	100	88	106
Denmark	1–48[b]	97	89	94	103	97	89	94	103
Finland	1–23[b]	92	107	79	110	87	98	74	104
	24+	122	140	94	141	122	140	94	142
France	1–23	70	91	86	97	51	65	71	80
	24+	105	121	111	125	105	121	111	125
Germany	1–12	79	99	107	106	58	76	92	90
	1–3	42	73	75	89	39	68	72	85
Hungary	4–9	70	127	107	127	70	127	107	127
	10–12	102	185	130	156	102	185	130	156

Country	Age								
Iceland	1–4	81	113	85	108	70	93	78	94
	5–36	92	135	90	118	92	135	90	118
Ireland	1–15	100	100	100	100	100	100	100	100
Japan	1–9	64	92	107	134	54	78	103	115
Korea	1–7	45	73	97	119	34	55	75	89
Luxembourg	1–12	70	97	79	100	50	67	58	73
Netherlands	1–2	103	106	90	101	73	89	79	88
	3–22	108	109	92	102	78	94	83	92
New Zealand	1+	100	100	100	100	100	100	100	100
Norway	1–24	80	111	92	134	60	85	83	106
	24+	80	111	92	134	60	85	83	106
Poland	1–12	54	76	77	97	54	76	77	97
	1–18c								
Portugal	1–28	30	60	65	92	20	40	45	65
	29–42	56	89	91	129	56	89	91	129
Slovak Republic	1–6	46	76	77	93	31	51	54	65
Spain	1–6	43	54	64	72	38	46	47	51
	7–24	49	63	75	84	38	46	54	60
Sweden	1–9b	84	105	71	105	84	105	71	105
	10–28	93	115	74	111	84	105	71	105

(Continued)

Table 9.4 *Table 9.4* Minimum-Income Benefit Levels Relative to Unemployment Benefits 2007, as a Percentage, for Two Different Levels of Previous Earnings and at Different Points during an Unemployment Spell (*Cont'd*)

	Point During Unemployment Spell (Months)[a]	Below-average Earner (67 Percent of AW)				Average Earner (100 Percent of AW)			
		No Children		2 Children (Ages 4 and 6)		No Children		2 Children (Ages 4 and 6)	
		Single Person	1-earner Couple	Lone Parent	1-earner Couple	Single Person	1-earner Parent	Lone Parent	1-earner Couple
Switzerland	1–18	87	110	97	109	68	84	69	78
United Kingdom	1–6	100	100	100	100	100	100	100	100
United States	1–6[d]	14	25	73	90	11	19	57	71

NOTES: Housing-related support is included in the net incomes of both the unemployment and minimum-income recipients (using housing-cost assumptions as explained in the notes to Figure 9.2). Greece, Italy, Mexico, and Turkey are not shown as they do not operate broad minimum-income cash-benefit programs (nor, in the case of Mexico, a generally available unemployment benefit system).

[a] The period indicates the maximum duration of unemployment benefits for a 40-year-old worker with a "long" employment and contribution record. Separate periods are shown for each successive benefit program (e.g., insurance and assistance benefits) or if benefit levels in a given program decline during the entitlement period.

[b] Membership in the unemployment insurance fund is voluntary.

[c] Unemployment benefit durations are longer for families with children.

[d] Unemployment benefit durations are longer in states where the unemployment rate exceeds a specified level.

AW is average wage of a full-time worker in industry sectors C–K (ISIC Revision 3.1).

SOURCE: OECD tax-benefit models (www.oecd.org/els/social/workincentives).

different rates depending on the duration of unemployment, separate lines are shown for each possible benefit level. Unsurprisingly, ratios between minimum-income and unemployment benefits tend to be higher for those experiencing declining unemployment benefits during a longer unemployment spell, notably in countries operating both unemployment insurance and assistance benefits (see Table 9.2). In most cases, however, initial unemployment benefits provide incomes that are significantly above minimum-income levels. The gap between the two is greatest in Hungary and Poland, Japan and Korea, Portugal and Spain, as well as Canada and the United States—especially for unemployed individuals living alone. However, for those with below average previous earnings, some earnings-related unemployment insurance benefits can be quite close to, or even below, the level of social assistance or other minimum-income benefits. This is the case for one-earner couples in a number of continental and all northern European countries, as well as in the Czech Republic.

In countries where minimum-income benefits are also the main out-of-work benefit, the ratios are 100 percent (Australia, New Zealand). The same is true for Ireland and the United Kingdom, where eligible job seekers are entitled to a flat-rate insurance benefit during an initial period of unemployment and the follow-up assistance benefit is paid at the same level as long as the family has no other incomes.

A ratio of minimum-income to unemployment benefit levels above 100 percent provides an indication of the potential importance of minimum-income payments as top-up benefits for those with low unemployment benefit entitlements.[14] This can provide useful contextual information for understanding the characteristics of benefit recipients. For instance, for most family types, the net incomes provided by the Finnish Basic Allowance and Labour Market Support benefits (paid to job seekers who are not—or are no longer—entitled to earnings-related unemployment insurance payments) tend to be below social assistance levels. As a result, about 40 percent of social assistance recipients are receiving these unemployment benefits at the same time (STAKES 2008). Because they are already registered as job seekers and have access to relevant support from the Public Employment Service, this has important implications for the scope of reintegration services to be provided by the social assistance administration.

Related Support Measures: Health Care

In addition to cash support, countries operate a number of further programs to address the needs of social assistance clients. This includes "near-cash" or in-kind support, which may provide help with basic consumption items on a regular or case-by-case basis (such as for food, clothing, housing, or transport), as well as assistance that seeks to promote reintegration and self-sufficiency (such as education, training, or rehabilitation measures).

Access to health care is one type of support that is especially important for the current and future well-being of benefit clients and their families. Where employment barriers are health-related, it is also an essential component of reintegration and rehabilitation strategies. Because of the high cost of health-related services and products, support in this area can make a big difference to the living standards and the work incentives of benefit recipients.

A working paper version of this chapter presents a summary of responses to a recent questionnaire on health-related support that was sent to responsible government departments in OECD member countries (Immervoll 2009). This questionnaire collected information on basic health care coverage of benefit recipients and low-income groups, including those in irregular or low-paid work. It covered support for meeting the cost of health coverage, as well as help with out-of-pocket payments, such as deductibles or co-payments. This latter category is important because out-of-pocket expenses for hospitalization, doctor visits, or items such as eye glasses or dental products can be high relative to the budgets of low-income families, even if these families are covered under the basic health care scheme.

Where basic health care is financed out of general tax revenues, coverage is universal with citizenship or residence being the only condition for access (Australia, Canada, Denmark, Iceland, New Zealand, Norway, Portugal, Spain, Sweden, the United Kingdom). As a result, benefit recipients, as well as other low-income groups, are automatically covered and help with paying for coverage is not. However, most of these countries provide help with meeting out-of-pocket expenditures for low-income groups (Australia, Denmark, Iceland) or benefit recipients.

Where health care is insurance-based, membership in public or private programs may be mandatory so that coverage can also be de facto universal (Czech Republic, Finland, Japan, Korea, the Netherlands, Switzerland). Where this is not the case, uninsured family members, such as those without work, can be covered alongside an insured person at no additional cost (Belgium, France, Germany, Greece, Luxembourg, Poland). Yet, in a number of countries, those with low or irregular employment incomes may not be covered on a mandatory basis, although they generally have the option of contributing (Austria, Belgium, Germany, Luxembourg, Poland). In the United States, a large proportion of workers is not covered by employment-based insurance and often have income too high to be eligible for state-supported programs.

In almost all OECD countries, benefit recipients are normally covered automatically at no or reduced cost. Such concessions are often lost when moving to a low-wage job (e.g., France, Germany, Hungary, Japan), although contributions in most countries are a percentage of earnings and, therefore, are lower for low-paid workers. In about one-third of the countries surveyed, benefit recipients (as well as low-income groups) are also entitled to lower out-of-pocket payments for medical goods or services. In the United States, there is no automatic health coverage for benefit recipients (Medicaid, the main public program for low-income working-age individuals, covered about 40 percent of those below the official poverty line in 2007).

In a number of countries, health-related support for benefit recipients is financed directly by the relevant benefit agency. Funding arrangements that oblige benefit-paying institutions to bear the cost of these support measures can reinforce incentives for these institutions to seek to reduce benefit dependency.

RECIPIENTS

Data on the number of people covered by minimum-income benefits in OECD countries are not currently available on a comprehensive basis.[15] One source that does show recipient numbers for noncategorical social assistance, as well as lone-parent benefits for a subset of OECD countries, is Carcillo and Grubb (2006), who compiled information from a range of available administrative data sources (OECD [2003a] contains further data and a detailed discussion of methods and concepts). For the purpose of that study, it was necessary to avoid double counting benefit recipients who receive multiple benefits at the same time (or at different times during the same year). Therefore, it made sense to categorize recipients according to the *main* out-of-work benefit they received. As a result, those receiving both social assistance and unemployment benefits would normally not show up in the social assistance recipient totals. Perhaps more importantly, the administrative data relate to claimants whereas minimum-income benefits are targeted toward families. For the purpose of analyzing the redistributive scope of minimum-income benefits, one would typically be less interested in claimant counts and more interested in the number of individuals who live in a beneficiary household.

With these limitations in mind, the data provided by Carcillo and Grubb (2006) show that the share of working-age individuals receiving benefits of last resort are modest, mostly between 2 and 4 percent, but below 2 percent in a few countries. The policy significance of these benefits is, however, greater than these figures suggest. As has been highlighted, the statistics only count one adult per family as a recipient; the number of individuals whose families are supported by minimum-income benefits is higher. More importantly, behavioral requirements and other barriers (such as the perceived burden of filing an application) in effect exclude some of those who would otherwise be entitled. Studies on benefit take-up regularly find very high non-take-up rates for means-tested benefits, on the order of 40 percent or more, indicating that the deterrent effect of the various barriers combined is indeed significant (Hernanz, Malherbet, and Pellizzari 2004; Bargain, Immervoll, and Viitamäki forthcoming). Finally, because out-of-work benefits affect both income levels and work incentives, their generosity and structure has implications for both recipients and nonrecipients. For instance, to the extent that they achieve their objectives, work-related requirements reduce benefit dependency by strengthening labor market attachment.

Considering these effects in combination, one can expect low-income groups *potentially* targeted by social assistance benefits to be much more sizable than indicated by the preceding recipiency statistics. This is confirmed by calculations combining survey data with a detailed representation of benefit entitlement rules. For instance, in the late 1990s, 8 percent of working-age adults in the United States lived in households whose income position would have made them eligible for social assistance–type cash transfers at some point during the year (i.e., without counting near-cash benefits such as Food Stamps). In Germany, the corresponding figure is as high as 14 percent.[16] Over a longer period, the proportion of individuals who experience at least one spell where family incomes fall below minimum-income thresholds will be even higher.

In view of the poverty alleviation objectives of minimum-income benefits, and the findings of high non-take-up rates, an important perspective of recipiency statistics is the fraction of poor people that these benefits reach. As an illustration of orders of magnitude, Figure 9.4 combines administrative data on benefit recipients for two Nordic countries with survey-based totals of the number of income-poor households. The resulting proportions are "pseudocoverage rates" in the sense that they express the relative sizes of two groups that may only be partially overlapping (a number of nonpoor households may receive minimum-income benefits). Two observations stand out. First, it is clear that a large number of income-poor households do not receive minimum-income support even in countries where benefit levels are relatively generous. Because benefit levels (see Figure 9.2) are close to the poverty cutoff in both countries, the principal driving factors are likely to be

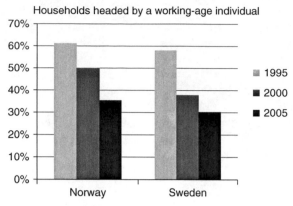

Figure 9.4 Number of Households Receiving Minimum-Income Benefits Relative to Income-Poor Households.
SOURCES: Calculations based on the following sources. Benefit recipiency data: update of the data series described in Carcillo and Grubb (2006). Number of poor households: OECD income distribution database.

non-take-up as well as nonincome characteristics that may make some of the income-poor households ineligible (notably assets or noncompliance with job-search or other activity requirements).

A second striking pattern of the pseudocoverage rates is their variability over time. Given uncommonly high unemployment rates in Nordic countries during the mid-1990s, this illustrates the countercyclical role of minimum-income safety nets even in countries where unemployment-benefit generosity and durations are above average. It also suggests that the demand for minimum-income support will grow significantly following the recent economic crisis and that the safety net will be severely tested, especially once entitlements to first-tier out-of-work benefits expire. But the downward trend also highlights the important role of "mutual obligations" policies and other measures aiming to reduce dependency on last-resort benefits: While labor markets weakened between 2000 and 2005 in both Norway and Sweden, the number of minimum-income benefit claimants continued to decline (both in absolute terms and as a proportion of poor households).

RESPONSIBILITIES OF BENEFIT RECIPIENTS

Why "Rights and Responsibilities"?

The large numbers of individuals potentially entitled to receiving minimum-income benefits highlight the importance of an appropriate balance between encouraging self-sufficiency and providing assistance for those who cannot support themselves. A simple income guarantee with no conditions attached could result in very high rates of benefit dependency and, if benefits are means-tested, the possibility of a downward spiral of weak work incentives and declining employability. Depending on the generosity of support, it could also be very costly for public finances. Budgetary pressures are certainly one reason why governments have increasingly considered a more work-oriented approach to minimum-income benefits. A welfare-to-work approach may also make income support for low-income groups politically more acceptable.

Another reason is that, in most countries, last-resort benefit payments alone simply do not provide enough income to ensure effective protection from income poverty. Where more generous benefit payments are economically or politically infeasible, there is a strong case for structuring financial support in a way that enables and encourages benefit recipients to seek income from employment. There is convincing evidence that welfare-to-work policies *can* be effective at increasing employment levels among the groups most likely to draw on minimum-income benefits. Several initiatives that have targeted safety-net benefit recipients show that substantial shares of them do respond to these measures: If the conditions are right, they *will* work and reduce their reliance on public support.

However, the large numbers of individuals "potentially entitled" to minimum-income benefits could also indicate that many may simply be unable to earn incomes above the levels that these benefits provide. Therefore, there is a real danger that severe behavioral requirements, strictly enforced, would lead to much higher poverty risks. For instance, there is evidence for the United States that, while many lone parents have left welfare and found work, as many as 25 percent of them are neither employed nor receiving welfare benefits.[17] Even if strict eligibility conditions are successful at increasing employment and reducing poverty rates overall, families excluded from the benefit can face much deeper poverty, which is a concern in itself and can also lead to political backlash. In addition to the direct income effect, overly strict eligibility conditions and rigorous gatekeeping can also have negative consequences for the effectiveness of employment-oriented policies: Those excluded from benefit payments may have no or incomplete access to job-search assistance and other counseling or reintegration measures. By dropping out of the system, they are then no longer "reachable." Finally, there have been concerns about the appropriateness of an indiscriminate pursuance of the self-sufficiency objective itself. This issue is central to the question of whether, and for how long, lone parents should be exempt from activity requirements and whether such requirements are appropriate for individuals facing severe social difficulties. It is possible that "families who are in turmoil or who cannot organize their lives sufficiently to comply with the rules are the same ones who are forced off welfare, and are likely to be worse off as a result" (Moffitt 2008, 22).

Compared with unemployment benefit recipients, those entitled to lower-tier income support face greater employment difficulties on average. Training, public sector job creation programs and other active labor market programs can help address some of these difficulties. But existing research shows that targeting is key and that overall success rates might be low especially for those facing substantial or multiple employment barriers. In terms of beneficiaries' responsibilities, the notion that public support ought to be linked to behavioral requirements is more controversial when applied to individuals who are faced with multiple or particularly serious challenges to finding paid work, or whose earnings capacity is such that they see little gain from substituting earnings for state transfers.

In spite of these challenges, minimum safety-net benefits are of particular significance in this debate. First, because there is generally little other public support to fall back on, too strict an application of behavioral eligibility conditions could result in extremely low incomes for those excluded from benefit payments. Concerns about

those potentially "falling through the cracks" become more acute if potential beneficiaries fail to live up to their responsibilities, not because they are unwilling but
because they are unable to comply.

Second, there are important links between benefits of last resort and other, higher-
tier, support systems. As entitlements to primary out-of-work benefits such as unemployment insurance payments are tied more visibly to job-search and availability
criteria, lower-tier assistance benefits are likely to play a stronger role as a fallback
option. Whether or not such benefit substitution is intended, there is a clear need to
coordinate activation and reintegration policies between the different benefit layers.

Finally, the group of low-income individuals relying on benefits of last resort is
very heterogeneous. It includes those with low-paid, irregular, or undeclared employment; the long-term unemployed; individuals who have never worked; those with
disabilities, health problems, or substance abuse issues; those requiring support
because of difficult family or social circumstances (including lone parents, migrants,
and victims of family violence); homeless people; those released from a penal institution; and those facing any combination of these criteria. Any strategy to encourage
self-sufficiency among such a diverse client group is likely to be both complex and
demanding. The challenge is to channel the right type of support to the right people
while responding to a broad range of different circumstances and needs.

Targeting: The Right Mix of Rights and Responsibilities, for the Right People, at the Right Time

In essence, the attraction of a "rights and responsibilities" approach is that it potentially increases employment while improving the targeting of minimum safety nets.
By imposing more demanding behavioral conditions for benefit receipt, it makes
work relatively more attractive and limits opportunities for benefit claims that might
be considered "undeserving" (e.g., those with incomes from undeclared employment
or a strong preference for leisure). At the same time, work-related behavioral requirements seek to improve employability. Both effects would in theory reduce the number
of beneficiaries, and this effect can be further strengthened by providing job-search
assistance and other employment-oriented support. With a reduced number of beneficiaries and stronger work incentives, more adequate support is feasible for those
who need it most.

But a second concern of targeting efficiency is that those unable to achieve self-
sufficiency should not be left without sufficient support. As discussed, the downside
of stringent requirements is that they can make support inaccessible for some.
Sanctioning those unable to comply reduces benefit expenditures but clearly makes
little sense from a redistributive point of view. Policy makers would likely be concerned if sanctions for failing to comply with work requirements are frequently
applied to individuals who are in fact not ready for work. Evidence suggesting such
a pattern in the United States shows that this is a real danger. For instance, decisions
about sanctions can be affected by administrative error with potentially grave consequences for sanctioned families. In this context, a transparent and efficient appeals
process, though costly to operate, is an important element of effective benefit administration. By providing some evidence on the frequency of unjustified sanctions, it
can also help uncover structural problems, such as insufficient resources to properly

account for clients' circumstances. Children, who are directly affected by benefit cuts but can do little to avoid them, are a group of particular concern. Many countries implicitly recognize this by protecting child-related benefit amounts from sanctions, but this does not protect children from deteriorating living standards caused by cuts in non-child-related benefit components.

In principle, these issues can be tackled from two sides. First, behavioral obligations, and the sanctions that back them up, should take account of individual circumstances. Second, those who are not job-ready can be given an opportunity to participate in programs aiming to overcome employment barriers. Participation in these support programs can be made mandatory. Complementing these programs, other work-related support measures can seek to address barriers that are not primarily related to the employability of the individual (e.g., child care for parents).

Targeting is key and in view of the wide heterogeneity of the group of minimum-income benefit recipients, implementing effective targeting mechanisms presents a major challenge. Providing customized packages of client support and obligations requires detailed information and adequate staff and other resources. Statistical profiling approaches can help exploit available information, but they are no substitute for intensive and face-to-face contact with claimants, especially in the more difficult cases where clients face severe or multiple barriers to social or economic participation. This type of interaction requires a significant commitment of staff resources and, hence, public expenditures to provide the necessary service capacity. One way to make service delivery potentially more responsive to claimants' circumstances is to decentralize service delivery, and possibly also administrative responsibilities, for social assistance benefit payments. The funding mechanisms can also have a direct effect on how support is targeted in practice. For instance, a rights-based entitlement to financial support is likely to put less pressure on case workers to deny benefit payments than would a "queuing" system whereby support is subject to availability of funds (as was the case in Poland prior to a 2004 reform, and is the case for those claiming Temporary Assistance for Needy Families [TANF] support in the United States).

Beyond matching claimants with appropriate interventions, targeting also has an important time dimension. Clearly, job-search assistance, labor market reintegration programs, and work requirements are most effective when suitably sequenced. This may mean employing different types of requirements and support measures at the same time. For instance, one would expect synergies of combining job-search obligations with employment counseling. However, mandating certain activities can be counterproductive if they compromise the individual's own initiative to escape benefit dependency. For instance, job training or counseling may leave too little time for formal and informal job searches (the so-called lock-in effect of mandatory participation in active labor market programs). At the same time, an overly aggressive push for work that does not allow for sufficiently careful job search may reduce the quality of job matches and result in less stable employment.

Some of these timing issues have received considerable attention in the debate on activating recipients of first-tier unemployment benefits but have been shown to be of less practical relevance for the more disadvantaged recipients of social assistance. A likely reason is that the nature of the employment barriers facing the latter group is such that they are on average less likely to succeed at independent job-search activities. But due to the heterogeneity of the group of welfare recipients, timing issues can be expected to be significant nonetheless for some subgroups. For young welfare recipients, the existing evidence suggests that work requirements should start at a very early stage as lacking work experience seems to be the main barrier to employment (Martin and Grubb 2001). As noted, there are also important, and controversial, timing issues for lone parents as compulsory work or participation in labor market programs means that they can spend less time with their (possibly young) children.

WHAT WORKS? BENEFIT DEPENDENCY, EMPLOYMENT, POVERTY

Several OECD countries have introduced active labor market programs for welfare benefit clients and tightened requirements to cooperate with work-oriented reintegration measures.[18] However, experience with these types of measures is much more extensive in the case of first-tier out-of-work benefits. As a result, most of the available evidence on "what works" relates to unemployment benefits (Heckman, LaLonde, and Smith 1999; Martin and Grubb 2001; OECD 2005; Carcillo and Grubb 2006; Kluve 2006). Broadly, the key messages from this literature are as follows:[19]

- *Job-search assistance and job-search requirements:* Most empirical studies indicate that job-search assistance and counseling have positive employment effects at relatively low cost, especially when combined with job-search requirements that are backed up with moderate benefit sanctions. These measures work best for individuals with relatively good labor market prospects. However, some doubts remain on the effects on job quality, as measured in terms of earnings and job duration.

- *Training:* Training and education programs typically represent the most sizable component of total expenditures on activation measures. Evidence, as well as theory, suggests opposing effects during and after the training programs. During participation, less time is available for a job search, which can reduce search-intensity and job-finding rates (the lock-in effect mentioned before). However, once training is completed, employment outcomes are mainly positive and mostly outweigh short-run losses. Outcomes differ significantly between groups, however, with larger employment gains found for adult women and little impact for prime-aged men. Individuals with relatively good labor market prospects appear to benefit significantly, whereas the negative lock-in effect is found to dominate for young job seekers. The effectiveness of human-capital development measures also vary by type of program, with more positive employment effects of on-the-job training and less favorable results in the case of classroom training. Whereas employment effects of training measures can be positive, the empirical evidence typically shows no or very little impact on hourly wages.

- *Work requirements and employment programs:* Private-sector employment programs can be effective at increasing employment probabilities of participants. In contrast, job-creation schemes in the public sector have been shown to be generally unsuccessful at integrating benefit recipients into the regular labor market. Such programs might, however, still be justified on other grounds. They can serve as availability tests for individuals who are perceived to lack the motivation for a job search. Also, they might aim at promoting work habits (a form of on-the-job training) and social inclusion of participants, who may already have been out of work for some time. However, there is little concrete evidence on the merits of public-sector employment programs in terms of promoting such nonemployment outcomes.

These insights provide a useful background when considering the appropriate balance of rights and responsibilities for those relying on minimum-income benefits. However, the nature of these recipients' labor market difficulties is likely to be substantially different than the difficulties of those receiving unemployment benefits. Therefore, these findings, which already indicate some degree of effect heterogeneity, are unlikely to apply equally to these different groups. In addition, most of the preceding results focus entirely on the effects of activation measures in terms of employment and beneficiary status. Although these are clearly important, concerns about the high poverty risks facing those on benefits of last resort suggest that a broader set of outcome measures, including the effects of "activating" policy measures on the incomes of different groups, is desirable.

Policy packages

There are only a limited number of comprehensive evaluations of broader welfare-to-work packages targeted at recipients of social assistance and similar benefits.[20] Strikingly, and although income consequences are of crucial importance when considering reforms of income safety nets, most evaluations do not analyze effects on poverty rates and related indicators but instead are limited to employment outcomes and recipient numbers (often referred to as "caseloads"). The well-studied US welfare reform implemented in 1996 is one major exception, and therefore, it is useful to consider the main evaluation results in some detail.[21] For a number of reasons, the findings cannot be expected to apply directly in other policy settings (for instance, the US reform was essentially confined to lone parents). They do, however, give some indication of the trade-offs that characterize different policy choices.

A number of studies in the United States have paid particular attention to the effect of welfare-to-work measures on the number of recipients of TANF. Recipiency statistics are a very incomplete measure of success as they say nothing about the well-being of individuals who successfully found employment, of those remaining on benefits, or of those with neither work nor received benefits. But lower benefit dependency does represent a positive outcome if other indicators show no deterioration (and if other benefits do not substitute for the one in question).

In any case, bringing down the number of benefit recipients has been a major objective associated with reforming welfare benefits in a considerable number of US states—and one that has been reinforced by the formula used for allocating federal TANF contributions to states, which rewards caseload reductions. This objective is, for instance, reflected in the use of so-called *diversion payments* (lump-sum payments on the condition that people do not apply for the regular benefit during a specified period), as used in more than half of the states. There are also reports that a range of "hassle techniques" may be used systematically to discourage benefit applications (Midgley 2008). Terminating benefits and ending participation is in these cases likely to be the principal reason for applying strict benefit sanctions. In other states, sanctions are instead partial and used mainly as a motivational device to provide incentives for behavior that is deemed beneficial or to restore compliance with relevant eligibility conditions. Clearly, the direct impact of such partial sanctions on recipiency numbers will be less strong.

Most US studies suggest that, overall, the number of people receiving TANF (or its predecessor Aid to Families with Dependent Children) declined by 60 percent between 1994 and the early 2000s, with about one-third of this impact directly attributed to the introduction of "work-first" measures (Besharov 2006). However, cuts in spending on a particular benefit do not necessarily translate into lower overall spending. Despite a significant decline in TANF expenditures, per capita spending on *total* means-tested support (including the Earned Income Tax Credit) almost doubled between 1990 and 2004, suggesting that substitution effects might be important and that work-support measures, such as the Earned Income Tax Credit as well as extended availability of public support for child care and health insurance, are essential ingredients of packages aiming to reduce reliance on out-of-work benefits (Moffitt 2008, Figure 1).[22]

There is evidence that *earnings and employment* of low-income lone parents (the principal target group of the US reform) increased as a result of stepping up welfare-to-work measures. But, unsurprisingly, the more rigorous eligibility requirements, and the resulting narrowing of the group entitled to benefits, meant that average household *incomes* rose by less or not at all (Cancian et al. 2003). About one-third of women leaving TANF were not in employment (at a time when benefit time limits were not yet binding: Acs and Loprest 2004). In fact, even for those finding employment, the effect on earnings was not much bigger than the loss in benefit incomes. For instance, in his review article, Moffitt (2008, 24) notes that "if 'making work pay' means ensuring that earnings of a woman are greater off welfare than her welfare benefits on welfare, the evidence does not indicate a very strong effect of that kind, if any." Importantly, several studies have shown that benefit losses were often compensated by higher earnings of household members *other* than the benefit recipient (Bavier 2001). A point rarely mentioned in the US debate is that, because TANF is almost exclusively received by lone parents, these "other" household members could be children or young adults, which can be a cause for concern.

Another set of studies shows that incomes rose and poverty fell but mainly among those who *did not enter* welfare rather than among leavers (Grogger and Karoly 2005). This is again indicative of an important role for work-support measures. Because of the way federal funding is allocated to states, some of the positive employment effects can be attributed to a virtuous cycle of declining beneficiary numbers, lower spending on out-of-work benefits, and a resulting increase in funds available for work-related support.[23] This has facilitated continued employment for working lone parents as well as transitions into work. But because this mechanism is essentially procyclical, and works in the opposite direction during extended downturns, many commentators in the United States emphasize the importance of a strong economy for making welfare-to-work measures effective (e.g., Blank 2003). A second main conclusion emerging from the US experience is that work-first measures are good at increasing employment and reducing benefit dependency, but they do little to improve family incomes. Work-support measures, in turn, have a small effect on employment but are effective at boosting incomes and reducing poverty. In combination, these measures strengthen employment and improve the income position of those finding employment. But concerns remain for those who do not.

Individual policy measures

The US evidence demonstrates that the effectiveness of welfare-to-work policies depends on a large number of factors. Therefore, it can be difficult to draw conclusions about the effects of individual isolated measures. In fact, because different policy elements interact, evaluations of entire packages are arguably more useful. It is, however, interesting to ask whether individual measures can nevertheless be effective even without being necessarily embedded in a broader reform package and what design features are associated with positive or negative outcomes.

Job-search requirements backed up by moderate *sanctions* have generally been shown to work well as an instrument to promote transitions from social assistance into work.[24] Measures to intensify job searches and to develop search skills are relatively cost-effective and the "threat" effects of even small sanctions appear to be sizable. For instance, an evaluation of introducing temporary and partial sanctions (up to 20 percent) in the Dutch city of Rotterdam resulted in a doubling of transition rates from welfare to work (van den Berg, van der Klaauw, and van Ours 2004). There is also evidence that the lock-in effect is of much less relevance for those welfare recipients who are unlikely to succeed at finding a job on their own. In the Rotterdam study, applying sanctions at an earlier stage during the benefit spell was associated with lower long-term unemployment. Mandating participation in time-intensive counseling sessions for social assistance recipients in Aarhus, Denmark, has lead to significant lock-in effects for those who are essentially job-ready but not for groups facing more substantial employment barriers (Bolvig, Jensen, and Rosholm 2001, cited in Ochel 2004). Similar results have been reported for Norway (Røed and Raaum 2006). However, if introduced without intensive counseling and other job-search assistance, tightening requirements mainly increases employment among individuals with comparatively good labor market prospects.[25] Moreover, with overly demanding requirements, there is a risk that individuals with weaker job prospects would leave the benefit rolls without work and face much-reduced access to job-search assistance and other employment-related support measures.

Small lock-in effects are also reported for *employment programs* and strictly enforced *work requirements*. A study of a workfare program recently introduced in Germany, the so-called one-euro jobs, finds little negative impact on transition rates into work for participants *during* the program (Hohmeyer and Wolff 2007). Strictly enforced work requirements and participation in employment programs also do not appear to lead to lower-quality job matches. OECD (2005) reports on empirical studies that suggest work-first strategies may have little effect on employment stability and can even improve it. However, the German study suggests that the hoped-for positive longer-term impact of workfare measures on employment probabilities is also very limited (the "post-program effect" is insignificant for men and small for women). Findings in other countries are more positive and suggest that work requirements can be especially effective when employment is in the private sector. For instance, this has been shown for the UK New Deal for Young People (Dorsett 2001). The workfare measures introduced by Danish municipalities as part of the Active Social Policy program were found to be particularly effective, boosting welfare-to-work transition rates by some 300 percent (Bolvig, Jensen, and Rosholm 2003).

One disappointing result of work-first strategies is the frequent lack of discernible positive effects on wage growth (e.g., Card, Michalopoulos, and Robins 2001). But compared with work-first strategies, human-capital investment approaches are less effective at increasing employment in the short term. It is also not clear that they perform better in terms of job stability or earnings progression, and they are expensive to operate. Employment gains are, however, possibly greater in the long term (Bloom and Michaelopoulos 2001; Hotz, Imbens, and Klerman 2006). The small number of studies that do follow participants of *training and education* programs over a longer period suggest that benefits in terms of employment or earnings take two or more years to emerge (Dyke et al. 2005; OECD 2005). Whether or not training and education improves labor market prospects depends very much on the circumstances of the benefit recipient. Carcillo and Grubb (2006) cite evidence that less job-ready individuals benefit more from vocational training. Yet this is also the group whose employment probability increases strongly as a result of participation in workfare and employment programs. On the basis of available evidence, therefore, it is difficult to conclude whether a lack of work experience or insufficient skills are the main barrier to employment for social assistance clients.

A number of US studies (such as evaluations of the Portland Job Opportunities and Basic Skills program) found that the most successful programs employed a mixed strategy combining a strong work focus for job-ready clients and targeted educational and training programs for those with very low education levels (Blank 2003). Favorable results of a combination of work-first and qualification programs are also reported for Norway (Dahl and Lorentzen 2005). As might be expected, the outcome of comparing employment effects between work-first and human-capital strategies depends strongly on the specific types of measure being compared. For instance, the study of the effects of the UK New Deal for Young People showed that subsidized private-sector employment has a much larger positive impact on employment outcomes than full-time training or education. But the outcomes for those in the training and education program were no worse when compared with voluntary work or community service (Dorsett 2001).

CONCLUDING COMMENTS: CURRENT AND FUTURE CHALLENGES

The recent economic downturn has been putting pressures on governments to strengthen income support measures (OECD 2009b). Although buoyant labor markets in many OECD countries have helped to restrain recipiency numbers since the mid-to-late 1990s, a rapid decline in economic activity can be expected to be a powerful driver of the demand for minimum safety-net benefits.

In addition to the expected lengthening of average unemployment spells, and the resulting rising number of people running out of unemployment benefit entitlements, those with temporary jobs or other forms of nonstandard employment are often not entitled to unemployment benefits in the first place. For these individuals, employment durations are shorter, transitions into and out of work more frequent, and coverage by social insurance benefits can be less universal as a result. They are also typically more easily shed from the workforce. With increasing shares of nonstandard workers in a number of OECD countries,[26] this may cause social assistance benefit rolls to react more strongly to labor market conditions (i.e., become more countercyclical) than was the case in the past. In the medium term, some of these challenges point to the need for a debate on the relative roles of insurance and assistance benefits. For instance, should coverage of insurance benefits be extended to nonstandard workers or should lower-tier assistance benefits be strengthened?

More urgently, there is a need to consider how an activation and reintegration focus can be maintained when labor demand is weak and competition for existing job vacancies intense. But even in a labor market recovery, minimum-income recipients tend to face significantly less promising employment prospects than recipients of unemployment benefits with more recent work experience. Yet, in most countries, the group of minimum-income beneficiaries is very heterogeneous and includes, for instance, those with recent but intermittent employment records and other recent job losers who do not qualify for insurance benefits. Increasing numbers of benefit recipients are likely to test the capacity of welfare agencies and public employment services to administer high-quality activation programs and job-search assistance to everybody. This will further add to the challenge of targeting activation and support measures in a way that keeps benefit spell durations short for the most employable, while preventing less employable clients from becoming permanently benefit-dependent.

Arguably the most immediate priority, however, is to prevent support seekers from going without effective minimum safety nets at a time when they are most needed. Preventing steep increases in the extent and severity of poverty is likely to present a particularly difficult short-term challenge for those countries that are not currently operating broad minimum-income programs. As existing minimum-income programs see new clients added at increasing rates in the wake of the global downturn, they will only be able to continue meeting their objectives of poverty alleviation and activation if they are equipped with the financial and operational capacity to deal with the inflow of new claimants and an increasing stock of recipients.

Notes

1. Much more comprehensive earlier reviews of social assistance policies in different countries include Eardley et al. (1996), OECD (1998a, 1998b, 1999) as well as Adema, Gray, and Kahl (2003). In-depth information on and analyses of policies in individual countries are available in the OECD's *Benefits and Wages* series, which includes information on policy institutions and parameters, as well as indicators on income adequacy and work incentives (www.oecd.org/els/ social/workincentives). Activation policies are the subject of ongoing OECD policy reviews and other analytical work (see www.oecd.org/els/employment/ almp).

2. Depending on the structure of support for individuals with health problems as well as for (early) retirees, these groups may fall into the scope of broadly defined minimum-income programs. At the same time, very large numbers of recipients of disability or early retirement benefits in several OECD countries illustrate that these benefits can end up being used for contingencies for which they were not designed (such as long-term unemployment). The particular issues that are pertinent for these two groups are outside the scope of this chapter but are discussed specifically in the OECD series *Sickness, Disability and Work* (see www.oecd.org/els/disability) and *Pensions at a Glance* (www. oecd.org/els/social/pensions). The 2009 issue in this series contains a chapter on poverty among old-age individuals (OECD 2009a). See also www.oecd.org/

olderworkersforum for in-depth country reviews of the situation of older workers.

3. For instance, the distinction between cash, near-cash, and in-kind benefits can be problematic and certain components may not be properly recorded (e.g., special payments in exceptional circumstances or other discretionary payments, such as reemployment support). Also, the decentralized delivery of minimum-income benefits can lead to incomplete reporting, or nonreporting, of spending by local authorities to the central government. Importantly, noncategorical social assistance, which is the main last-resort benefit in most countries, is recorded under the "other social policy areas" heading, which may lead some countries to treat it a residual category when reporting these data.

4. Further details on eligibility and entitlement conditions for each program are given on www.oecd.org/els/social/workincentives (using the link "tables summarizing tax-benefit policy features").

5. For instance, unlike unemployment benefit recipients in most countries, social assistance recipients often do not enjoy any legal job or status protection in the form of "suitable-job" criteria. Formally, they would therefore have to accept any available job although the extent to which this is enforced in practice is difficult to establish. Reasons for deviating from strict formal availability criteria may, for instance, be related to employers' concerns that pushing referrals of overqualified benefit claimants could damage their motivation for the job (see, e.g., Box 3 in Tergeist and Grubb 2006).

6. In addition, several countries operate parental-leave benefits that are not means-tested (see www.oecd.org/els/social/family/database).

7. A recent summary of countries' experience with "make-work-pay" programs is given in Immervoll and Pearson (2009).

8. In Ireland, unemployment assistance (Jobseekers' Allowance) is much more important than the general social assistance benefit (Supplementary Allowance).

9. The Domestic Purposes Benefit in New Zealand also provides support for some other groups, such as those caring for family members at home.

10. The assumption of 20 percent of average wage is motivated by an attempt to capture differences between countries that operate explicit "reasonable rent" ceilings and those that do not (or where there is a large discretionary element involved in making such decisions). To show this, it is necessary to choose a rent level that is sufficiently high so that relevant limits become applicable.

11. Benefit phaseouts can lead to substantial "leaky bucket"–type efficiency losses and, hence, very high marginal costs of redistributing extra amounts to the poor by raising minimum-income benefits. For instance, calculations for 15 European Union countries reported in Immervoll et al. (2007) show that in countries with relatively generous existing welfare provisions, it typically costs €2.5 or more to redistribute an extra euro in this way. However, the same calculations also indicate considerable scope for improving safety nets where they are currently less developed. This is notably the case in some Southern European countries, where costs of strengthening minimum-income provisions are much lower.

12. OECD (8007b) analyzes the tax treatment of minimum wages on both the employee and employer sides.

13. This effect has been documented in numerous studies in the United States (Card and Levine 2000; Katz and Meyer 1990), as well as in Europe (Røed and

Zhang 2003; Lalive et al. 2006). However, more recently, a few authors have questioned whether this phenomenon is as economically significant as the earlier studies appear to indicate (Card et al. 2007; Boon and van Ours 2009).

14. In combination with the income levels of minimum-income recipients relative to the poverty line in Figure 9.2, it also indicates the extent to which unemployment benefit claimants are likely to be affected by income poverty.

15. Jointly with the European Commission, the OECD Secretariat has recently initiated a project that collects benefit recipient data for a broad range of working-age benefits. A first set of comparable results is expected for 2012.

16. The OECD Secretariat has commissioned these calculations as part of a project titled "Welfare Implications of Social Protection." See Dang et al. (2006). They are based on the assumptions of 100 percent benefit take-up and full compliance with activity requirements and related eligibility conditions.

17. See Blank (2007).

18. In a longer working paper version of this chapter (Immervoll 2009), I summarize the main behavioral requirements that are in place for minimum-income benefit claimants, as well as the sanctions that may be used to enforce them. In general, however, information on the tightness of benefit sanction regimes is difficult to compare across countries based on formal rules that provide little indication of how they are applied in practice.

19. "Positive" effects here mean that those directly concerned by the measures are doing better. Studies almost never implement a fuller cost-benefit framework that would also account for the costs of implementing the respective programs or for the consequences of higher off-flow from unemployment for existing workers (substitution or displacement effects). In addition, the majority of studies adopt a short-term perspective and, therefore, do not capture any longer-term impact of activation measures.

20. Even in countries where evaluations of activation measures have focused on means-tested benefits (e.g., New Start Allowance in Australia, TANF in the United States), few or no such studies exist for other benefits that may still be available to those not complying with relevant behavioral requirements (Special Benefit in Australia; Food Stamps in the United States).

21. The main element of this reform was replacing the Assistance for Families with Dependent Children with the TANF, which is time-limited and subject to more stringent behavioral requirements (in practice, time limits and eligibility conditions, as well as benefit levels, vary enormously across states). Midgley (2008) provides an excellent overview of the academic and political debate leading to this reform.

22. Acs and Loprest (2004) find that Food Stamps were received by up to 70 percent of former TANF recipient families and that 20 percent of TANF leavers were in receipt of Supplemental Security Income (a disability-related transfer for low-income households).

23. The amount of baseline funding from the federal budget to states is fixed over a number of years (so-called block grants) although actual federal contributions depend on a number of "success" indicators (e.g., caseload, share of benefit recipients in work or employment-related activities). In addition, states have a considerable degree of discretion over how funds are used, so reduced spending on basic benefit payments created more room for extending other types of support, notably for child care.

24. *Voluntary* job-search assistance programs, such as the New Deal for Lone Parents introduced in the UK in the late 1990s, are also effective for those who participate, but take-up rates are very low.

25. Findings in a recent study of the introduction of a job search diary in Australia are typical in this respect (Borland and Tseng 2007).

26. Although trends are far from uniform across OECD countries, the share of temporary employment in EU-15 countries has increased by about 20 percent during the past decade (to 14.8 percent in 2007). Temporary work accounts for more than 20 percent of total employment in Poland and Portugal, whereas almost every third employment contract in Spain is nonpermanent. Outside of Europe, Japan has seen a particularly strong expansion of nonstandard forms of employment.

References

Acs, G., and P. Loprest. 2004. *Leaving Welfare*. Kalamazoo, MI: Upjohn Institute.

Adema W., D. Gray, and S. Kahl. 2003. *Social Assistance in Germany*. Labour Market and Social Policy Occasional Papers 58. Paris: Organization for Economic Co-operation and Development.

Bargain, O., H. Immervoll, and H. Viitamäki. forthcoming "No Claim, No Pain. Measuring the Non-Take-up of Social Assistance using Register Data." *Journal of Economic Inequality*. http://dx.doi.org/10.1007/s10888-010-9158-8.

Besharov, D. 2006. *Two Cheers for Welfare Reform*. Washington DC: American Enterprise Institute.

Blank, R. M. 2003. "U.S. Welfare Reform: What's Relevant for Europe?" *CESifo Economic Studies* 49(1): 49–74.

——. 2007. "Improving the Safety Net for Single Mothers Who Face Serious Barriers To Work." *Future of Children* 17(2): 183–197.

Bavier, R. 2001. "Welfare Reform Data from the Survey of Income and Program Participation." *Monthly Labor Review* 124(7): 13–24.

Bloom, D., and C. Michalopoulos. 2001. *How Welfare and Work Policies Affect Employment and Income: A Synthesis of Research*. New York: Manpower Demonstration Research Corporation.

Bolvig, I., P. Jensen, and M. Rosholm. 2001. *Effekter af aktiveringsindsatsen i Århus Kommune*. Aarhus, Denmark: Aarhus University.

——.2003. *The Employment Effects of Active Social Policy*. IZA Discussion Paper 736. Bonn : Institute for the Study of Labor.

Borland, J., and Y. P. Tseng. 2007. "Does a Minimum Job Search Requirement Reduce Time on Unemployment Payments? Evidence from the Job Seeker Diary in Australia." *Industrial and Labour Relations Review* 60(3): 357–78.

Cancian, M., R. Haveman, D. R. Meyer, and B. Wolfe. 2003. *The Employment, Earnings, and Income of Single Mothers in Wisconsin Who Left Cash Assistance: Comparisons among Three Cohorts*. Special Report 85. Madison, WI: Institute for Research on Poverty.

Carcillo, S., and D. Grubb. 2006. "From Inactivity to Work: The Role of Active Labour Market Policies." OECD Social, Employment and Migration Working Papers 36, Organization for Economic Co-operation and Development, Paris. www.oecd.org/els/workingpapers.

Card, D., and P. B. Levine. 2000. "Extended Benefits and the Duration of UI Spells: Evidence from the New Jersey Extended Benefit Program." *Journal of Public Economics* 78: 107–138.

Card, D., C. Michalopoulos, and P. Robins. 2001. "The Limits to Wage Growth: Measuring the Growth Rate of Wages for Recent Welfare Leavers." NBER Working Paper 8444, National Bureau of Economic Research, Cambridge, MA.

Dahl, E., and T. Lorentzen. 2005. "What Works for Whom? An Analysis of Active Labour Market Programmes in Norway." *International Journal of Social Welfare* 14 (2): 86–98.

Dang, T. T., H. Immervoll, D. Mantovani, K. Orsini, and H. Sutherland, 2006. "An Age Perspective on Economic Well-Being and Social Protection in Nine OECD Countries." OECD Social, Employment and Migration Working Paper 34, Organization for Economic Co-Operation and Development, Paris.

Dorsett, R. 2001. "The New Deal for Young People: Relative Effectiveness of the Options in Reducing Male Unemployment." PSI discussion paper, Policy Studies Institute, London.

Dyke, A., C. J. Heinrich, P. R. Mueser, and K. R. Troske. 2005. The Effects of Welfare-to-Work Program Activities on Labor Market Outcomes. IZA Discussion Paper 1520. Bonn: Institute for the Study of Labor.

Eardley, T, J. Bradshaw, J. Ditch, I. Gough, and P. Whiteford. 1996. *Social Assistance in OECD Countries: Synthesis Report*. Paris: Organization for Economic Co-operation and Development; London: Department of Social Security, Her Majesty's Stationery Office.

Grogger, J., and L. Karoly. 2005. *Welfare Reform: Effects of a Decade of Change*. Cambridge, MA: Harvard University Press.

Heckman, J. J., R. J. LaLonde, and J. A. Smith. 1999. "The Economics and Econometrics of Active Labor Market Programs." In *Handbook of Labor Economics*. Edited by O. Ashenfelter and D. Card, 1865–2097. New York: Elsevier.

Hernanz, V., F. Malherbet, and M. Pellizzari. 2004. "Take-Up of Welfare Benefits in OECD Countries: A Review of the Evidence." OECD Social Employment and Migration Working Paper 17, Organization for Economic Co-operation and Development, Paris. www.oecd.org/els/workingpapers.

Hohmeyer, K., and J. Wolff. 2007. *A Fistful of Euros: Does One-Euro-Job Participation Lead Means-Tested Benefit Recipients into Regular Jobs and out of Unemployment Benefit II Receipt?* IAB Discussion Paper 3207. Nuremberg: Institute for Employment Research.

Hotz, V. J., G. Imbens, and J. Klerman. 2006. "Evaluating the Differential Effects of Alternative Welfare-to-Work Training Components: A Reanalysis of the California GAIN Program." *Journal of Labor Economics* 24: 521–566.

Immervoll, H. 2009. "Minimum-Income Benefits in OECD Countries: Policies and Challenges." OECD Social, Employment and Migration Working Paper 100, Organization for Economic Co-operation and Development, Paris. www.oecd.org/els/workingpapers.

Immervoll, H., and M. Pearson. 2009. "A Good Time for Making Work Pay? Taking Stock of In-Work Benefits and Related Measures across the OECD." OECD Social, Employment and Migration Working Paper 81 and IZA Policy Paper 3. Paris: Organization for Economic Co-operation and Development; Bonn: IZA. www.iza.org/en/webcontent/publications/policypapers.

Immervoll, H., H. J. Kleven, C. T. Kreiner, and E. Saez. 2007. "Welfare Reform in European Countries: A Micro-simulation Analysis." *Economic Journal* 117 (517): 1–44.

Kluve, J. 2006. *The Effectiveness of European Active Labor Market Policy*. IZA Discussion Paper 2018. Bonn: Institute for the Study of Labor.

Martin, J. P., and D. Grubb. 2001. "What Works and for Whom: A Review of OECD Countries' Experiences with Active Labour Market Policies." IFAU Working Paper 2001:14, Office of Labour Market Policy Evaluation (IFAU), Uppsala, Sweden.

Lalive, R., J. C. van Ours, and J. Zweimüller. 2006. "How Changes in Financial Incentives Affect the Duration of Unemployment." *Review of Economic Studies* 73(4): 1009–1038.

Midgley, J. 2008. *Welfare Reform in the United States: Implications for British Social Policy (with Commentaries by Kitty Stewart, David Piachaud and Howard Glennerster)*. LSE STICERD Research Paper. CASE131. London: London School of Economics.

Moffitt, R. 2008. "Welfare Reform: The U.S. Experience." *Swedish Economic Policy Review* 14 (2): 49–54.

OECD. 1980–2007. OECD Social Expenditure Database (SOCX). www.oecd.org/els/ social/expenditure.

———. 1998a. *The Battle against Exclusion, Social Assistance in Australia, Finland, Sweden and the United Kingdom*. Vol. 1. Paris: Organization for Economic Co-operation and Development.

———. 1998b. *The Battle against Exclusion, Social Assistance in Belgium, the Czech Republic, the Netherlands and Norway*. Vol. 2. Paris: Organization for Economic Co-operation and Development.

———. 1999. *The Battle against Exclusion, Social Assistance in Canada and Switzerland*. Vol. 3. Paris: Organization for Economic Co-operation and Development.

———. 2003a. "Benefits and Employment, Friend or Foe? Interactions Between Passive and Active Social Programmes." In *Employment Outlook*. Paris: Organization for Economic Co-operation and Development.

———. 2003b. *Managing Decentralisation. A New Role for Labour Market Policy*. Paris: Organization for Economic Co-operation and Development.

———. 2005. "Labour Market Programmes and Activation Strategies: Evaluating the Impacts." In *Employment Outlook*. 173–208. Paris: Organization for Economic Co-operation and Development.

———. 2007a. "Can Parents Afford To Work? Childcare Costs, Tax-Benefit Policies and Work Incentives." In *Benefits and Wages. OECD Indicators*. 119–166. Paris: Organization for Economic Co-operation and Development.

———. 2007b. "Special Feature: The Tax Treatment of Minimum Wages." In *Taxing Wages*. 22–34. Paris: Organization for Economic Co-operation and Development.

———. 2008. *Growing Unequal? Income Distribution and Poverty in OECD Countries*. Paris: Organization for Economic Co-operation and Development.

———. 2009a. "Incomes and Poverty of Older People." In *Pensions at a Glance. Retirement-income Systems in OECD Countries*. 55–84. Paris: Organization for Economic Co-operation and Development.

———. 2009b. "The Jobs Crisis: What Are the Implications for Employment and Social Policy?" In *OECD Employment Outlook: Tackling the Jobs Crisis*. 17–116. Paris: Organization for Economic Co-operation and Development.

Ochel, W. 2004. "Welfare-to-Work Experiences with Specific Work-First Programmes in Selected Countries." CESifo Working Paper 1153, CESifo, Munich.

Røed, K., and O. Raaum. 2006. "Do Labour Market Programmes Speed Up the Return to Work?" *Oxford Bulletin of Economics and Statistics* 68 (5): 541–568.

Røed, K., and T. Zhang. 2003. "Does Unemployment Compensation Affect Unemployment Duration?" *Economic Journal* 113: 190–206.

STAKES. 2008. "Social Assistance 2007." Statistical Summary 37/2008, National Research and Development Centre for Welfare and Health; Helsinki.

Tergeist, P., and D. Grubb. 2006. "Activation Strategies and the Performance of Employment Services in Germany, the Netherlands and the United Kingdom." OECD Social, Employment and Migration Working Paper 42, Organization for Economic Co-operation and Development, Paris. www.oecd.org/els/workingpapers.

Van den Berg, G., B. van der Klaauw, and J. van Ours. 2004. "Punitive Sanctions and the Transition Rate from Welfare to Work." *Journal of Labor Economics* 22(1): 211–241.

10

Social Assistance Schemes in Developing Countries

MARGARET GROSH, CARLO DEL NINNO, AND EMIL TESLIUC ■

There are a wide variety of social assistance[1] programs in the developing world. They include cash transfers, in-kind transfers, workfare programs, fee waivers, and price subsidies. Many have analogues in the European or US histories of social assistance. All meet the conceptual definition of being noncontributory transfer programs. Each provides income or lowers the cost of essential goods or services, thereby increasing the ability of recipient households to obtain a minimum standard of living. The programs also differ in important ways and may have different secondary objectives or impacts. They also differ with respect to administrative requirements, political economy, and the like, which is why there are so many different kinds and variants of programs. In their diversity, they can fit into more niches, and when used in sensible combinations, they provide a comprehensive and realistic social assistance strategy.

This chapter reviews the most prevalent types of social assistance programs found in developing countries, drawing from a recent book by Grosh et al. (2008). There we provide a vision of effective safety nets that focus on seven characteristics. They should be equitable, adequate, cost-effective, incentive compatible, sustainable, dynamic, and fit appropriately to the country context. In the interests of keeping the treatise here to a chapter, we focus on the first two aspects of this vision—targeting and benefit level. If a program goes wrong on these, then it is unlikely to be effective in reducing poverty and the other traits will have lesser importance.

The first section of the chapter provides a brief overview of patterns of social assistance expenditures. The second section is on targeting, starting with a brief introduction of the available methods, then taking a more detailed look at the variety of social assistance programs in developing countries and discussing the types of targeting methods used, finally concluding with a brief synopsis of outcomes. The third section of the chapter looks at benefit levels, reviewing theory and practice. The fourth section concludes.

SOCIAL PROTECTION AND SOCIAL ASSISTANCE SPENDING IN DEVELOPING COUNTRIES

Across world regions, there is large variation in *social protection spending*—the sum of social assistance and social insurance spending driven primarily by differences in social insurance spending. As expected, higher-income regions spend more on social protection. Social protection spending is highest in the Organization for Economic Co-operation and Development (OECD) and second highest in Eastern Europe and Central Asia region.

Social assistance spending in developing countries is not large, and average spending does not vary much across regions or countries (see Figure 10.1). In 87 developing countries surveyed by Weigand and Grosh (2008),[2] average spending on safety nets is 1.9 percent of gross domestic product (GDP) and median spending is 1.4 percent of GDP. For about half of the countries, spending falls between 1 and 2 percent of GDP. The top social assistance spender is the Middle East and North Africa (with 2.2 percent of GDP on average), notably because the spending mix is burdened by costly, regressive consumer subsidies. The Eastern Europe and Central Asia region spends about 1.8 percent of GDP on social assistance programs, complementing a social insurance system with reasonably high coverage and moderate replacement rates. Latin America and the Caribbean follow, with expenditures of 1.3 percent of GDP, including conditional cash transfer programs costing on average one-third to one-half of a percent of GDP. Social assistance spending is among the lowest in Asia, where demand for redistributive policies has been and remains low. The smaller number of observations makes the averages less robust for Sub-Saharan Africa.[3]

Targeting and Eligibility Criteria

All social safety net programs offer cash or in-kind transfers to a specific target group. To separate the target group of the program from the rest of the population, different

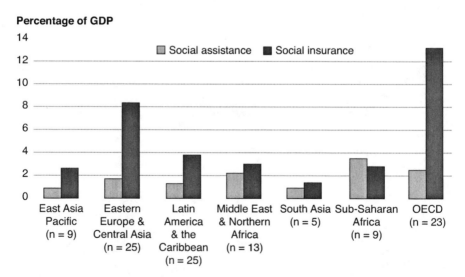

Percentage of GDP

Figure 10.1 Social Assistance and Social Insurance as a Percentage of GDP by Region, Selected Years.
NOTE: Not all the reports Weigand and Grosh (2008) use offer data on all categories of spending. For the OECD (2004), we used 23 countries, as such countries as Mexico and Poland are already accounted for in the regional averages.
SOURCES: Weigand and Grosh (2008); OECD (2004).

targeting methods, reviewed in Table 10.1, can be used either individually or in combination. The means test is the conceptual gold standard and the method used in most OECD countries for poverty-targeted programs. However, it is information-intensive and less likely to be accurate where required information is scarce or unrecorded and where administrative capacities are low, conditions that are prevalent in many developing countries. Thus, programs in developing countries use a much wider range of targeting methods.

For each type of safety net program operating in developing countries, we will present the most typical targeting methods used and provide examples of how eligibility criteria are crafted. We first present four classes of programs that provide direct increases in income—food transfers, cash transfers, conditional cash transfers, and

Table 10.1 TARGETING METHODS

Type of needs Assessment	Targeting Method	Description
Individual or household assessment	Means-test	A government employee directly assesses, household by household or individual by individual, whether the means of the applicant fall below a threshold and, hence, is eligible for the program. The means being tested typically include incomes and assets. Programs differ substantially with respect to the comprehensiveness of the means taken into account and the verification of their means.
	Proxy means-test	Proxy means-tests use a relatively small number of household characteristics to calculate a score that indicates (is correlated with) the household's economic welfare. The score is derived using a multivariate regression of consumption or income on a few household characteristics. Applicant households are eligible when their score falls below the program threshold.
	Community targeting	A community leader or group of community members whose principal function in the community are not related to the transfer program decide who in the community should receive benefits.
Categorical targeting	Geographical targeting	Eligibility for benefits is determined, at least partly, by location of residence. This method uses existing information such as surveys of basic needs or poverty maps.
	Demographic targeting	Eligibility is determined by age, gender, disability status, or some other demographic characteristic.

(*Continued*)

Table 10.1 TARGETING METHODS (*CONT'D*)

Type of needs Assessment	Targeting Method	Description
Self-targeting		A good or service that is open to all but designed in such a way that take-up for it will be much higher among the poor than the nonpoor.
	Workfare	Use of low wages on public works schemes so that only those with a low opportunity cost of time due to low wages or limited hours of employment will requests jobs.
	Inferior commodities	Transfer of free or subsidized commodities with "inferior" characteristics (e.g., such as low-quality wheat).
	Location of point-of-sale	Location of point-of-sale or point-of-service units (e.g., ration stores, participating clinics, or schools) in areas where the poor are highly concentrated so that the nonpoor have higher (private and social) cost of travel.

income from labor-intensive public works. Then, we consider fee waivers and price subsidies that reduce the cost of achieving a minimum standard of living. There is much more that could be said about how to implement each, and their overall role in social assistance policy, but we leave that to other literature and focus here on the targeting methods.

Food-Based Programs

Food-based programs were a staple of social assistance in decades past when international food aid was large and in kind and when local market stabilization schemes implied that the government was holding and rotating large food stocks. They are now somewhat less common as these factors are reduced and as the recognition that households use cash resources well grows. Nonetheless, they still serve as the base social assistance program in a number of countries and as an important component in others.

Food-based programs can serve a mix of objectives. Income support is often a driving force, albeit sometimes not a well-articulated one. Food-based programs may also have more or less explicit nutritional goals, usually related to caloric sufficiency but sometimes to adequate micronutrient intake. There are a variety of food-based programs: rations, supplementary feeding programs, school feeding programs, and emergency food distribution programs.

FOOD RATIONS
Typically, beneficiaries collect rations at designated public or private distribution centers either for free or at a reduced price. In India, for example, consumers,

who have been certified as having a (proxy means-tested) income below the poverty line can purchase wheat and other commodities at reduced prices through the public distribution system. Take-home rations are a special case in which rationed quantities of food are delivered directly to beneficiary households. Such programs are less common than in years past, but India, Egypt, and Iraq all operate substantial programs. A smaller take-home rationing program can also be found in Bangladesh and Indonesia. Several food-ration programs have their genesis in reforms of prior price subsidy programs. In Indonesia, for example, the National Food Logistics Agency used to run a market price stabilization intervention. That program became more limited over time, but the National Food Logistics Agency now runs a reduced price rice ration scheme for the poor.

Food-based transfer programs use the full gamut of targeting mechanisms including means and proxy means tests; self-targeting methods through the use of inferior commodities; and methods based on nutritional risk criteria such as age or pregnancy. Targeted households usually receive a ration card that entitles them to a certain amount of food at a subsidized price as in the Arab Republic of Egypt and in India's targeted public distribution system. The progressiveness of transfers depends on how well they are targeted, as well as the impact of waiting time and possible stigma on participation by poor and nonpoor households (self-targeting).

SCHOOL FEEDING PROGRAMS

School feeding programs provide meals for children at school to encourage their enrollment, to improve their micronutrient intake, and/or their ability to pay attention in class. They can vary from the provision of breakfast, lunch as in the Thailand School Lunch Project, or a midmorning snack as in Bangladesh (Ahmed 2004), to a combination of these as in Colombia, Costa Rica, Guatemala, and Peru. School feeding programs are often integrated with other interventions, such as health and nutrition education, parasite treatment, health screening, and provision of water and sanitation. In many cases, dry rations are provided for students to take home, in which case they operate largely as implicit income transfers.

Targeting in school feeding programs is generally limited to the selection of schools, such as those in poorer areas, or schools of lower status or grade level. Targeting children within schools is generally thought to be stigmatizing and avoided. Gender targeting can also be used to provide take-home rations if female enrollment and attendance are particularly low. Geographic targeting can be sharply progressive if program coverage is low and schools selectively serve poor students. As coverage increases, targeting becomes less precise.

SUPPLEMENTARY FEEDING PROGRAMS

Supplementary feeding programs provide food to mothers and young children. The food may be prepared and eaten on site—for example, as at child feeding centers in Bangladesh, Indonesia, Peru, and Thailand—or provided as a so-called dry ration to take home as in Chile, where food supplements are distributed on a monthly basis through the primary health care system. Bolivia, Colombia, the Republic of Congo, Guatemala, Indonesia, Jamaica, Senegal, and Thailand also have run supplementary feeding programs (Gillespie 1999).

The typical target groups for supplemental feeding programs are pregnant and lactating women and children under the age of three or five years (categorical targeting).

Many programs give more benefits to those who are malnourished (underweight or stunted) or those failing to grow according to norms.

EMERGENCY DISTRIBUTION OF FOOD

Emergency distribution of food includes direct provision during crises, emergencies, and situations in which people are displaced. Emergency food programs provide a safety net of last resort whose objective is to save lives by preventing starvation, malnutrition, morbidity, and possible death when public and private institutions fail to provide basic needs. Targeting is typically based on location—areas facing drought, to camps for refugees, or for internally displaced populations. In emergency settings, food transfers may be the only resources households receive.

Cash Transfer Programs

There are four main types of cash transfer programs in developing countries: last-resort or need-based social assistance; family allowances; social pensions; and Food Stamps. All will be familiar to students of OECD social assistance policy. Collectively, their use is growing in the developing world. Whereas cash transfer programs used to be relatively uncommon outside of Eastern Europe and the former Soviet Union, they are now increasingly common in all regions of the world, sometimes providing the main basis for social assistance, sometimes still on a small and tentative footing.

NEEDS-BASED SOCIAL ASSISTANCE PROGRAMS

Needs-based social assistance programs provide a monthly cash transfer to the poorest households, which are usually identified based on a means or proxy means test. These programs are common in Eastern Europe and former Soviet Union countries. Albania, Bulgaria, Kyrgyz Republic, Lithuania, Romania, and the Ukraine, for example, operate guaranteed minimum-income programs covering between 3 and 10 percent of the population. In combination with other programs, such as unemployment insurance, a social pension or disability benefits, they succeed in covering almost entirely the poorest 20 percent of the population. Armenia and Georgia operate larger last resort programs where beneficiaries are identified using a proxy means test. Some last resort programs are also found elsewhere in poor countries, for instance, in Mozambique and Zambia in Sub-Saharan Africa (Devereux et al. 2005; Schubert 2005) and in Pakistan in South Asia (ADB 2006) although usually at a much smaller scale.

As a general rule, the design of these programs tends to be simpler in low-income, low-capacity settings and get more complicated in programs operating in middle-income countries. One example is benefit formulas. Most low-income countries operate flat benefits that are the same for all recipients as in the Kalomo District Pilot Social Cash Transfer Scheme in Zambia or that are differentiated by household size as in Mozambique, where transfers range from US$3 to US$6 per month depending on the number of children (Devereux et al. 2005). In many upper-middle-income countries, benefit levels vary depending on household resources as in the case of guaranteed minimum income programs operating in Bulgaria, Lithuania, or Romania.

Beneficiaries of needs-based transfers are targeted using a variety of household-specific methods. Proxy means tests predominate in Latin America. Means tests predominate in Eastern Europe and Central Asia as in Bulgaria, Hungary, and Romania. Mozambique uses health status indicators such as being chronically sick or malnourished (Devereux et al. 2005). Either the central government can set the selection criteria, which are then applied locally, or they can be decided at the local level so as to take local conditions, preferences, and priorities into account. In Uzbekistan, the communes use local information to achieve better poverty targeting than could be expected on the basis of proxy indicators alone (Alderman 2001, 2002).

NONCONTRIBUTORY PENSIONS
Many countries provide noncontributory pensions for some or all of those who do not fall under the country's contributory pension scheme and, in some cases, all those above a fixed age. Under these noncontributory schemes, benefits are paid without regard to past participation in the labor market. Noncontributory (or "social") pensions can be universal for those who reach a certain age, as for Bolivia's and Lesotho's programs. Or age may be coupled with a poverty-targeting criterion such as a means test, as in South Africa; a proxy means test, as in Chile; or a community-based needs assessment, as in Bangladesh.

FAMILY ALLOWANCE PROGRAMS
Family allowance programs are common in Eastern Europe and the former Soviet Union. Benefits are often small—a few US dollars a month, representing a fraction of the cost of the food basket—although in some middle-income transition states, including the Czech Republic and Hungary, they provide a more substantial contribution to the cost of raising a child. Family allowances can take various forms including means-tested child benefits as used in the Czech Republic, Poland, and South Africa; birth grants or categorical transfers for all children under a fixed age as in Hungary or Romania; and programs for the children of public sector or formal sector employees, which are popular in some middle-income countries such as Argentina or Uruguay (Lindert, Skoufias, and Shapiro 2006).

FOOD STAMPS, VOUCHERS, AND COUPONS
Food stamps, vouchers, and coupons are near-cash instruments targeted to poor households (Castañeda 1998; Grosh 1992; Hoddinott 1999; Rogers and Coates 2002) that they can use to purchase food at authorized retail locations. Retailers who accept these instruments can redeem them for cash through the banking system. The value of the food stamp is backed by the government's commitment to pay. Such programs have been implemented in Colombia, Honduras, Jamaica, Mexico, Sri Lanka, the United States, and a few other countries. The amount of the transfer is often based on the gap between the amount of resources spent on food and that needed to acquire a minimum basket of commodities. In practice, the benefits are often worth only a few US dollars and represent a small share of the cost of the food basket. For example, in Jamaica, the value of food stamps was only 12 percent of the food budget of the lowest quintile of the population, compared with the United States, where food stamps are worth 56 to 70 percent of households' mean food expenditures (Castañeda 1998). Some programs restrict households to buying only a few specific items whereas

others allow them to purchase any foods they wish. The foods authorized for purchase in the Jamaican Food Stamp Program included rice, cornmeal, skim milk, and wheat flour, which were commodities previously covered by general price subsidies (Ezemenari and Subbarao 1999; Grosh 1992).

Food stamp programs are typically targeted using means- or proxy means-testing. They can include self-targeting elements. In Honduras, the Bono Escolar (Food Stamps for Schoolchildren) benefit was distributed through primary schools in selected areas and the Bono Materno Infantil (Food Stamps for Mothers and Young Children) benefit was distributed at health centers in poor areas; thus, targeting was achieved through school attendance by children or the use of health clinics by mothers.

Conditional Cash Transfer Programs

Conditional cash transfers (CCTs) provide money to poor families contingent on them making investments in human capital such as keeping their children in school or taking them to health centers on a regular basis. The CCT programs have two explicit goals: to reduce the current level of poverty, and to promote investments in the human capital of the poor to reduce their level of future poverty. The balance between these goals varies somewhat among programs and affects some of their design features. The union of them has dramatically increased the political acceptability of social assistance in many countries and, hence, the budget for social assistance. Throughout Latin America, and now in several other countries around the world, CCT programs are the backbone of social assistance programming.

The classic CCT programs, with Mexico's Oportunidades (formerly known as PROGRESA) as the iconic example, emphasize the short-run poverty relief and social assistance goal by covering children from birth to some point in the teen years. Conditions cover enrollment and minimum attendance at primary and at least junior secondary grades. The program also has conditions for the use of a basic package of preventive health care services, at least for children from birth to age five or six years. Because the programs cover all poor families with children in a wide age range, they serve as a broad social assistance program as well as a demand-side subsidy for health and education services.

Most CCT programs use a combination of targeting methods to select their beneficiaries. For example, areas of concentrated poverty may be selected using geographic targeting. Poor households can then be selected using proxy means tests (Brazil's Bolsa Familia uses an income test) or community targeting.

Workfare or Public Works Programs

Labor-intensive public works programs have two main objectives when done as part of safety nets. First, they provide a source of income to poor workers, and second, they help build and rehabilitate public infrastructure. In the safety-net literature, the shorthand term *public works* is often used for such programs. Public works programs are often a good choice in postcrisis countries when they function in lieu of unemployment insurance (for those not covered), as in Korea following the 1997 economic crisis and Argentina following the peso crises that began in 1999. They are also valuable when infrastructure reconstruction and employment generation are priorities after a natural disaster, as in Sri Lanka following the 2005 tsunami. In countries where formal unemployment insurance is infeasible or unaffordable, public works programs that guarantee employment serve an insurance function, though so far only India provides such a guarantee. Theoretically, public works programs can provide on-the-job training and thus help integrate people who are outside the mainstream labor market because they lack the necessary skills, though many programs stop short of these goals and organizational requirements. In general, labor-intensive public works schemes are used more in low-income settings where their self-targeting feature is especially attractive and where infrastructure development is still needed.

Public works programs differ in relation to the type of activity involved, the type of job provided, and the level of labor intensity. The selection of activities to be carried out determines the types of jobs to be performed and the labor intensity. Traditionally, public works programs have involved activities such as road construction and maintenance, which require a high level of labor intensity. Other common activities include the maintenance of public spaces and buildings and soil conservation. Malawi, South Africa, and Zimbabwe, for example, have used innovative methods to include weaker populations by providing lighter tasks that involve service provision, such as child care (Oxfam 2002; Southern African Labour and Development and Research Unit 2005).

Targeting in public works programs is a three- or four-step process. The *first* step is to select areas where public works programs will be located. Locating programs in poor areas and communities that have a high unemployment level will increase the amount of direct (in terms of transfers) and indirect benefits (in terms of the physical assets that the program creates or maintains) that go to the poor. This can be achieved by allocating budgets for public works programs to local governments in proportion to the level of poverty in their jurisdictions, as occurred in Argentina and Indonesia (Sumarto, Suryahadi, and Pritchett 2000; Ravallion 2002). The *second* step is to select projects, opting for those with the highest possible labor intensity while achieving cost-effectiveness. The *third*, and crucial, step is to determine the wage rates. For workers to self-select themselves into the program wages should be somewhat lower than the locally prevailing market wage for unskilled labor. On the other hand, a lower wage rate will reduce the level of total transfers to the poor. When the wage rate cannot be set below the market wage because of minimum wage legislation, or when the size of the program is small relative to demand, additional targeting methods are required. For example, Bulgaria's From Assistance to Employment program uses means-testing, Colombia's Empleo en Acción (Employment in Action) program uses proxy means-testing, and Malawi uses community-based targeting. Programs also typically ration demand by capping the total number of days of work to be provided to individual workers. In Argentina's Trabajar workfare program, for example, the wage payment was set slightly below the legal minimum wage. As the economic crisis that began in Argentina in 1991 became more severe, unemployment and wages worsened and program wages were adjusted downward. Participation was capped at 90 days per worker.

Fee Waivers, Exemptions, and Scholarships

Unlike the other programs discussed so far, fee waivers, exemptions, and scholarships do not directly increase income but rather decrease the requirement for expenditures for services society deems essential. The two main types of programs discussed here are fee waivers and exemptions for health care and fee waivers and scholarships for schooling.

Fee waivers and exemptions for health care are programs that enable the poor to obtain free health care even when fees are charged. The waivers may include the cost of health care services and/or drugs for which significant charges apply. Exemptions are granted to everyone for defined services and enable people to receive those services for free. Such services usually have aspects of public goods or alternatively provide early interventions that should reduce the need for subsequent, more expensive treatment. Frequently exempted services include treatment for tuberculosis, immunization, and prenatal care. Additionally, care in primary health care clinics or a subset of primary health care clinics in rural areas might also be covered.

Fee waivers are granted to individuals, households, or groups based on their poverty or vulnerability. Three main methods are used to select individual beneficiaries of health waivers, given here in approximate order of frequency. The first is a rough means-test based on interviews at health facilities by social workers, clerks, or medical staff, as in Cambodia. The second is certification by a ministry of welfare that is often associated with establishing eligibility for other programs, as in Armenia, Chile, and Jamaica. The third method of selection involves a community group or a committee of users of health services. In Thailand, for example, village headmen can allocate medical care cards to the poor (Giedion 2002). Most countries have experienced problems related to their eligibility criteria, and the lack of clear identification criteria seems to be a major problem.

Fee waivers and scholarships for schooling include a number of forms of assistance to households to meet the costs of schooling, such as stipends, education vouchers, targeted bursaries, and interventions related to tuition and textbooks. The level of benefits ranges from covering some or all of the direct costs of schooling such as fees (as in Zimbabwe and several other African countries), uniforms (India), books (Indonesia), or transport (Colombia) to compensation for a significant share of the opportunity costs of students' time. Some programs are specifically targeted at girls in an attempt to improve their educational achievement; for example, Bangladesh, Guatemala, and Pakistan have a stipend programs for girls (Braun-Munzinger 2005). In some cases (Pakistan), programs are complemented by grants to schools to ensure that the quality of education offered is sufficient. Others (Kenya and Malawi) have eliminated direct fees for primary education for all students (Wilson 2006; World Bank 2007a).

The selection of beneficiaries of school waivers is usually done in two or more steps beginning with geographic targeting to focus budget resources on areas or schools with more poor students. In programs with low benefit levels, the second step is often a school- or community-based committee that determines which children will benefit, as is done by Indonesia's scholarship program. In several countries, including Indonesia, an explicit quota of scholarships may be set for girls. In programs involving significant cash transfers, a social welfare office will typically be involved in conducting a proxy means test.

General Price Subsidies

General price subsidies offer goods or services below market prices to any consumer, either in unlimited quantities or subject to a quota. The commodities covered by these programs range from staple food commodities such as rice, wheat, and maize (corn-meal) to lighting and cooking fuel and gasoline for transport. The stated objective of consumer subsidies is to guarantee access to food and other essential commodities at prices that consumers can afford. Controlling the prices of staple commodities is crucial not only for poor, food-insecure households, but it also responds to the political need to prevent prices from becoming too high. Reforms to remove existing subsidies are usually difficult to implement and are often marred by general discontent, political opposition, and sometimes riots. Examples include the food riots that followed a selective increase of commodity prices in Egypt in 1977, and, more recently, the food riots that occurred in the wake of currency devaluation and subsequent increases in the costs of traded commodities in Indonesia and Zimbabwe in 1997.

Given the nature of general subsidy programs, beneficiaries are not selected directly, and only indirect methods can be used to ensure that the poor benefit more than the rich. The selection of (economically) inferior commodities is crucial for achieving some form of self-targeting. Tunisia in the early 1990s provides an example of one of the most successful attempts to shift general subsidies to self-targeted goods (Tuck and Lindert 1996). Geographic targeting can be used to increase the share of benefits accruing to the poor by restricting access to a fixed ration of food sold at subsidized prices in public shops located in areas identified as food-deficit zones or in areas that have higher prices or larger numbers of vulnerable households.

Other targeting methods include opening stores at inconvenient times and lengthy queuing times, based on the argument that even though access is, in principle, universal, nonpoor households have higher opportunity costs of time. However, as retailers only collect cash and not the value of the time costs, this results in an excessive burden and an economic loss (often referred to as deadweight loss in economic terms) to society in general. The poor may not benefit from rationing by waiting because market access and cash constraints may limit the amount purchased while better-off consumers might find the time to line up. This was observed in Egypt (Alderman and von Braun 1984) and with a rice subsidy in urban Burkina Faso (Delgado and Reardon 1988) when poor households did not have the cash to buy the amount needed for the whole month. The need to make small purchases might also influence the market selected and force the poor to pay relatively high prices in unsubsidized markets (Rao 2000).

Price discrimination for energy products is possible when all consumers have access to the same commodity. For example, where connections to the grid are available, subsidies on electricity use can be rationed by guaranteeing a minimum lifeline consumption level, with prices increasing as the amount of electricity used increases, as is done in Jordan. Note, however, that in this case, meters need to be available to facilitate the implementation of step pricing.

A Summary of Targeting Practice

A few methods of targeting and types of programs go hand-in-hand, for example, self-selection and commodity price subsidies or workfare programs. However, several different methods can often be used for a particular type of program. For instance, cash and food transfers can be targeted by means-tests, proxy means-tests, nutritional status or risk factors, geographic area, demographic characteristics, or self-selection. Often, programs use a number of methods: combining methods usually yields better targeting than a single one.

The complexity of eligibility and recertification procedures and of the targeting methods employed go hand-in-hand with the level of economic development and institutional capacity of the country. Many middle-income countries have developed sophisticated and effective individual- or household-level targeting instruments using means-tests or proxy means-tests. In low-income countries, programs tend to employ simpler targeting methods based on demographical or geographical criteria or community targeting.

Targeting success is highly variable. A number of programs, especially in upper-middle-income countries, have errors of inclusion as low as those found in the United States, but many programs are less progressively targeted. Coady, Grosh, and Hoddinott (2004) find that median performance in 122 programs in 48 countries was moderately progressive, but in one-quarter of the programs, outcomes were actually regressive. Means-tests and proxy means-tests have the highest administrative cost per beneficiary, but they tend to produce the lowest errors of inclusion and are often good investments. Self-selection via a low wage rate and geographic targeting are also powerful and proven targeting tools. However, the pattern of outcome by targeting method is weak, with a great deal of variation in outcome between the best and worst of a single method. For every method save self-targeting based on a work requirement, the sample of programs included at least one example of a regressive program. Given that good incidence is achievable in many settings and that poor performance is also found in many, where poor performance is found, it may not be inherent, but can be improved on.

Errors of exclusion are much more difficult to assess because targeting assessments in developing countries are not usually done as a recalculation of eligibility for benefits based on program application data. Rather, they are based on observing program participation rates from household surveys. Analyses of this type combine the effects of any lack of offer by the government (many programs are rationed by budget and serve only the first to apply), self-selection due to lack of information, high opportunity costs of application, or stigma and the results of an erroneous targeting decision. That said, participation rates are highly variable and, on average, rather low. Lindert, Skoufias and Shapiro (2006) examine 40 programs in 8 countries from Latin America and show mean coverage rates for the lowest quintile of 19 percent. Tesliuc et al. (forthcoming) compile evidence for 74 programs in 26 countries and show coverage rates for the lowest quintile of 42 percent.

DETERMINING BENEFIT LEVELS IN THEORY AND PRACTICE

The level of benefits is an important element of the design of a social assistance program that contributes to the effectiveness of the program. This section looks at the theory concerning the size of transfers, discusses the criteria for adjusting benefit levels to household circumstances, and reviews the evidence on the generosity of safety-net programs in practice.

Considerations for Determining the Size of the Transfers

A basic question in any safety-net program is how generous the program should be, that is, how much to pay. No clear-cut answer to this question is available. Ultimately, the level of the benefit is one of the products of the iterative process of designing a program. Program designers select a benefit level such that the overall program will fit within its budgetary, administrative, and political constraints, while maximizing its outcomes for beneficiaries. However, this summary is too general to be a useful guide for practitioners. We will try to break down these decisions and highlight the key elements and trade-offs that occur when selecting a program's benefit level.

First and foremost, the benefit level depends on the objective of the program. The benefit level should be consistent with program theory, that is, the stylized model of how policy makers think the program's output will affect the outcomes they are trying to influence. A benefit level compatible with program theory will be the smallest transfer necessary to achieve the desired impact on intended outcomes (consumption, income, earnings, school enrollment, or use of health services).

Last-resort programs aim to reduce poverty; hence, the benefit level is set as a fraction of the income gap of expected beneficiaries. This is the case for programs such as the Family Poverty Benefit in Armenia and Targeted Social Assistance in Georgia. A number of variations on this principle are possible. In low-income countries, benefits are often set relative to the costs of an "adequate" food basket or the food poverty line. For example, the cash transfer program from the Kalomo District in Zambia pays US$10 per month to beneficiary households, equivalent to the cost of a 50-kilogram bag of maize, which enables them to have a second meal per day. In guaranteed minimum income programs, which are common in Europe and Central Asia and in countries of the OECD, the level of benefit is the difference between the eligibility threshold and the income of each family. Programs that compensate poor consumers for one element of expenditure, so-called *gap formulas,* are used, for example, for family allowances that cover a portion of the cost of raising a child, heating allowances that cover the seasonal increase in heating costs during the winter, and food stamps that cover only the food poverty gap.

The CCT programs encourage poor beneficiaries to invest in children's human capital by conditioning the benefit on the use of school, nutrition, and/or health services. The level of benefit will thus reflect two objectives: reducing current poverty among beneficiaries, and providing incentives for human-capital accumulation. The principles for the first objective are similar to those for last-resort programs. For the second objective, the level of benefits is set to compensate households for the direct and part or all of the indirect costs of using the services. The total benefit to a household may include more than one component. An education grant might compensate households for the opportunity cost of the time children spend in school and not working, plus for the direct costs of schooling. A health and/or nutrition grant could additionally compensate families for the cost of the time spent taking their children for health checks and/or attending nutritional education events. Some programs, such as the Programa de Asignación Familiar II (Family Allowance Program) in Honduras and the Red de Protección Social (Social Protection Network) in Nicaragua, alternatively offer a supply grant to the service providers—schools and health posts—to cover the cost of improved service. A few CCT programs offer grants to poor households without children in the target age group. This assistance may be unconditional or conditioned on the use of preventive care by adults with the benefit level set at a level congruent with desired outcomes on the health side of the program. (See Table 10.1.)

In workfare programs, the gross benefit level is the wage rate, but because workers would rarely be entirely idle in the absence of the program (they might engage in street vending, odd jobs, or labor on their own farms), they often forego some earnings; thus, the true benefit is the gross wage net of such foregone earnings. The level of net wage is influenced both by the gross wage and by how the work is arranged: In rural areas, work during the agricultural slack season will have lower opportunity costs, and in urban areas, labor is often performed quite early in the day, and sometimes for six rather than eight hours, leaving time for some other activities in the remainder of the day. In Ethiopia's Productive Safety Net Program, the labor market is so thin in some of the very poor rural areas where the program is concentrated that fixing a wage rate that is both below the prevailing wage and that delivers sufficient value is difficult. Thus, the total benefit package is designed to fill the food gap during the three months of the hungry season. In this case, the wage may be too high to induce adequate self-targeting, so the number of days of work allowed is capped at five days per family member per month and the community selects which families are the poorest and allowed to participate.

In-kind transfers have diverse objectives. If the program's objective is to provide a feeding supplement to schoolchildren, then the benefit level will be the cost of the food bundle. If the in-kind transfer is a vehicle for transferring income to poor households, then the same principles in determining the appropriate size of the transfer apply as for a cash transfer, though with some complications. If the in-kind transfer provides less of an item than the household would normally consume (is inframarginal), economic theory suggests that the subsidy is equivalent to a cash transfer of equivalent size, albeit with administrative costs that may be substantially higher. If the in-kind transfer is larger than what the household would normally consume, then the household may raise its consumption of the target good and/or may sell some portion of it, often at a discount, which will lower the real value of the transfer.

A second element that is taken into account in setting the level of benefits is the program's overall budget constraints. As an example, consider a transfer program whose objective is to reduce poverty. The process will likely start with an assessment of the poverty level in the country and the selection of a subgroup of poor households that the program will serve. Based on the group to serve and the program logic as described previously, with allowance for administrative costs, policy makers can estimate an initial budget requirement for the program. Such an estimate is rarely the end of the story. Often this initial estimate is larger than the budget available for the program. Dealing with this imbalance will typically involve an iterative process as illustrated in Figure 10.2.

One option is to reconsider a program's generosity. Few safety-net programs attempt to top up the consumption of their beneficiaries to the poverty line. Many programs provide benefits to bring beneficiaries up to a fraction of the poverty line or to some arbitrary level lower than the poverty line, but the utility of this approach is limited. Extremely low benefits do not protect beneficiaries from poverty—that is, they are not cost-effective—and may not justify their administrative costs—that is, they are inefficient. Peru used such a model in 2004, covering a large fraction of the

Table 10.2 Household Characteristics Included in the Benefit Formula in a Number of CCT Programs

| Country/Program | Benefits Varies by | | | | | | | | |
| | HH Structure | | | | Age of Children | Gender | Duration in Program | Payee | Frequency of Payments |
	HH Income	No. of Children	Cap	Other HH Members					
Kenya CT for OVC			Max=3						Bimonthly
Cambodia JFPR								Parent/guardian	Quarterly
Turkey SRMP								Mothers	Bimonthly
Brazil Bolsa Familia	■		Max=3					Mother	Monthly
Chile Solidario							■	Head of household	Monthly
Colombia Families en Accion					■			Mother	Bimonthly
Dominican Republic Solidaridad				■				Head of household	Bimonthly
Ecuador BDH								Women	Monthly
Honduras PRAF II					■			Mother	Quarterly
Jamaica PATH								Family representative	Bimonthly
Mexico Oportunidades							■	Mother	Bimonthly
West Bank Gaza			■	■					
Bangladesh FSSAP								Female student	Twice a year

NOTE: CT = cash transfers; OVC = orphans and vulnerable children; JFRP = Japan Fund for Poverty Reduction; SRMP = Social Risk Mitigation Project; BDH = Bono de Desarollo Humano; PRAF = Programa de Asignacion Familiar; PATH = Program of Advancement through Health and Education; FSSAP = Female Secondary School Assistance Program

SOURCE: Fiszbein and Shady (2009).

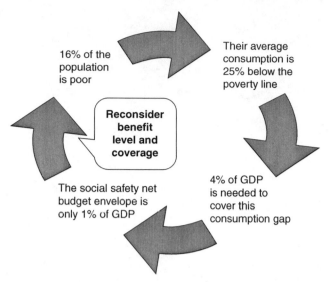

Figure 10.2 Reconciling Needs with Budget Constraints.

population with a food-based transfer with low transfers per beneficiary unit. Lindert, Skoufias, and Shapiro (2006, 26), in their review of the redistributive power of social protection programs in Latin America, characterized the Peruvian safety-net model as "giving peanuts to the masses." Not surprisingly, country-specific studies summarized in World Bank (2007b) find that such programs have had almost no impact on extreme poverty or nutritional status.

Another option is to restrict coverage of the program or eligibility for the program. If program designers choose to restrict coverage, they may attempt to cover as many of the poorest beneficiaries that can be reached with an adequate level of the benefit, given the budget constraint. If only 1 percent of GDP can be allocated for such a program, then the program may target only a quarter of the poor, that is, the poorest 4 percent of the population. Economic theory suggests that under the circumstances, directing the available resources toward the poorest is the best welfare-enhancing solution, as the marginal value of a monetary unit is higher for the poorest. A variant of this rationing process is to focus on specific vulnerable groups, or on households deprived in a number of areas, for example, poor and living in substandard housing. If program designers choose to restrict eligibility, they may choose to restrict it to a subset of the poor considered to be deserving. The notion of *deserving poor* varies from society to society, but the most common definition is households or individuals who cannot support themselves through work. Thus, some programs may restrict eligibility to families with more than three children and/or elderly people, who together represent about 50 percent of the poor in many countries. Many programs would combine these two options, restricting both the generosity and the coverage of the program typically to the poorest and most destitute.

In the end, defining the appropriate benefit level is a balancing act: finding a level that is neither too high to generate dependency nor too low to lack impact. If the benefit is too small, the program fails to achieve its objective. If the program is too generous, it may have adverse consequences, such as reducing work incentives or crowding out private transfers, which would diminish or even outweigh its positive impact. Worldwide, programs with benefits that are too low occur more frequently than programs with benefits that are too high.

Other Elements of Benefit Formulas

In addition to determining the average size of the benefit, program designers need to decide whether they would like to tailor the benefit level to the characteristics of the household, that is, to use a benefit formula. Benefit formulas may be flat—that is, all beneficiaries receive the same benefit—or they may vary according to the characteristics of the beneficiary household in a number of ways. Box 10.1 illustrates some of the household characteristics used for the determination of the benefit level in a number of CCT programs. Some of the main variations include the following:

- Benefits vary by family poverty level, with larger benefits for poorer families.
- Benefits vary by family size or composition, with benefits determined by the total number of family members or of the number of family members not expected to work.
- Benefits vary by the age of family members, for example, benefits tied to education may be larger for older children in recognition of the higher opportunity costs of their time or to cover the greater number of inputs they need such as textbooks.
- Benefits vary by gender, for example, benefits tied to education may be higher for girls in countries with a marked gender gap in schooling.
- Benefits vary over time, being higher during the hungry season or the heating season or at the beginning of the school year to cover enrollment fees, uniforms, and shoes.
- Benefits vary by region to reflect differences in the cost of living in different areas.
- Benefits vary with longevity in the program, tapering down after a certain period as a way to encourage families to leave the program.
- Benefits differ in ways that promote certain behaviors even beyond a program's basic conditions. For instance, a CCT program might require school attendance all year to receive the base benefit, but provide a small bonus for good test scores at the end of the year.

In general, variable benefit formulas will make a program more efficient, that is better able to deliver the level of transfer needed to raise most families toward the poverty line and/or induce the desired behavioral changes at minimum transfer cost. However, differentiating implies both obvious administrative costs and some less obvious costs because of the complexity involved. Much more effort will be needed to explain the formulas to client families, to the public, and to program monitors and additional effort will be devoted to quality control procedures around the level of benefit determination. Private costs for applicants may also rise.

Box 10.1

THE VALUE OF A CCT PROGRAM'S EDUCATION GRANT: FROM THEORY TO PRACTICE

The Programa de Asignación Familiar II was a CCT program in Honduras that offers an education grant to poor children conditional on school attendance. To determine the value of the grant, the technical advice provided to the government by its consultant, the International Food Policy Research Institute, was based on both economic theory and microeconomic evidence.

Economic theory suggests that each family demands a certain level of services, such as education, up to the point where the actual value of future educational benefits from sending a child to school is equal to the marginal cost of sending the child to school. The expected value of future benefits depends on, among other factors, the family's expectations about the child's future income and the relationship between education and income. The marginal costs of sending the child to school include the direct costs incurred when the child is sent to school, as well as the opportunity cost of dedicating the child's time to learning instead of using it to generate income. Based on these expected costs and benefits, each family demands that level of service that will allow it to maximize its welfare over time. This maximization process leads to a demand curve that reflects the relationship between levels of service demand and price, assuming that consumers' preferences and incomes and the prices of other products remain constant. The sum of all services sought by each family produces an aggregate demand curve that can be interpreted as the relationship between service price and the number of families willing to pay this price for its use.

The designers of the Honduran CCT program used household survey data to estimate that children provided about 3 percent of labor hours and 2 percent of household income, or about L 326 (about US$22) per year per child (about nine days of work during coffee harvest time). The direct costs of schooling were estimated to be L 6 (about US$0.40) per year for matriculation and fees; L 241 (about US$16) per year for books, uniforms, and supplies; and L 25.5 (about US$1.70) per month for 10 months for lunch and transportation money. Thus, the total cost (adding up the lost income per child plus the direct costs of schooling) is about L 828 (about US$56) per child per year.

Source: IFPRI (2000).

Determining the Recipient of the Benefits

Most programs around the world and over time have paid either the head of household or whichever member of the household carried out the transactions associated with registering for a program. Recently, however, program designers are putting much more thought into who within a household should receive payments. This reflects the growing recognition in the economics literature that households contain members with different needs, preferences, and power and that various members may allocate the funds received differently. The literature generally concurs that women will spend at least as much as men on children's welfare, in many cases more, and are less likely to favor boys over girls in doing so. The strength of this effect varies from place to place and study to study (Haddad, Hoddinott, and Alderman 1997; Quisumbing and Maluccio 2000), but the policy implication is that transfers placed in the hands of women will help children's welfare at least as much as, and sometimes much more than, transfers placed in the hands of men.

Based on these findings, many new programs, especially CCT programs, explicitly deliver the benefit into the hands of the mother or a proxy for her. This is done in the belief that women are more likely to invest additional monies in the well-being of their children than men are and the recognition that, on average, in most countries and households, women will be the ones bearing the implicit time costs of obtaining the required health and education services and likely shouldering a large share of the household chores children would have done had they not been attending school. A smaller number of programs, most often scholarship programs, transfer money directly to students. This is done to help motivate the students to study and ensure that they have as much influence over the money as if they had earned it themselves.

Handling Inflation

Benefits in cash need to be increased from time to time to protect households from inflation. Many programs only do this in an ad hoc manner every few years and require special legislation or a decree each time. In such cases, the real value of the benefits and the program's impact usually plummet for a time before recovering. A more desirable procedure is to have a regular, perhaps annual, review of benefit levels as part of the budget cycle, or even an automatic indexing of benefits. In either case, program managers should consider both how price levels (especially those pertinent to the poor) have changed, and how wages in low-skill occupations have changed, because these will affect incentives to work and the positioning of assistance recipients vis-à-vis workers.

Benefit Levels in Practice

The question of how generous safety-net programs are in practice can be answered in many ways, and probably because of this, little comparative evidence is available. Some of the most common ways to express the generosity of a program are as follows:

- By reporting the level of the benefit in local currency. This is not always simple, however, as programs often offer different benefits to individuals or households in different circumstances. In such cases, information about the levels of benefits can be presented as a table as shown in Box 10.1.
- By reporting the level of the benefit in comparable purchasing power (in purchasing parity power dollars, for instance). The intent is to facilitate comparisons across countries, but such information is difficult to compare, because the same type of benefit may be assigned to different assistance units (individuals, families, households) in different countries. Moreover,

the adjustments for differences in purchasing power may be insufficient to characterize a benefit as generous or not across countries, as generosity is a relative concept. For instance, in the United States, a benefit of US$10 per person per month would be considered ungenerous, but in a poor country where a large fraction of the population lives on less than US$1 per day, it may be considered quite generous.

• By reporting the level of the benefit as a share of the poverty line or other type of indicator, such as the minimum wage, the average wage, the minimum pension, the social pension, or the level of unemployment benefits. For example, in the OECD, the generosity of safety-net programs is expressed as a share of the wage of the average production worker in the manufacturing sector. Such comparisons are useful for comparing a program's generosity with the generosity of other programs or types of earnings within a country, for instance, to ascertain whether the benefit level is likely to create disincentives for work. It is less useful for cross-country comparisons.

Our preference for comparing generosity is the ratio of benefits to the total consumption of beneficiary households. This measure can be estimated using household surveys that collect information on household consumption and the value of safety-net benefits received during a certain period. This measure is preferable, as it takes into account many of the complexities of the provision of safety-net benefits and transforms them into a single index comparable across households and countries: Benefits are implicitly aggregated at the household level, the unit where they are shared and used to finance consumption. This measure, however, does not adjust for one element of program generosity, the duration for which benefits are provided to eligible applicants.

We used household-level information for 55 cash transfer programs from 27 middle-income countries to illustrate how the generosity of these programs varies by program type. Figure 10.3 shows key values of the distribution of generosity statistics as well as maximum and minimum values. The median value of benefits as a share of the consumption of recipient households for the programs in Europe and Central Asia is 13.0 percent for family allowances, 13.5 percent for last-resort programs, 9.0 percent for CCT programs, and 19.5 percent for social pensions. Whereas the generosity of family allowance and CCT programs is concentrated in a narrow interval, the values are more dispersed for other types of programs. The higher generosity of social pensions is not surprising: These are the programs meant to sustain households that are not expected to work.

We found that even in middle-income countries, the generosity of most safety-net programs is modest or moderate. For a majority of programs, including income replacement programs such as social pensions or last-resort programs, it ranges between 5 percent and 20 percent of the pretransfer consumption of beneficiary households.

REFLECTIONS

This chapter examines two design features that contribute to the success of safety-net programs, the ability to correctly identify the right beneficiaries (the target group) and

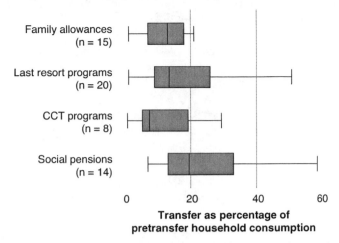

Figure 10.3 Generosity of Selected Safety-Net Programs, Europe and Central Asia and Latin America and the Caribbean, Selected Years, 2001–2004.

NOTE: *n* = number of programs. The median value is the line inside the shaded rectangle, the 25th percentile is the lower value of the shaded rectangle, and the 75th percentile is the upper value of the shaded rectangle. Programs whose generosity is 1.5 times more than, or less than, the median were excluded.

SOURCES: Tesliuc et al. (forthcoming); Grosh et al. (2008).

to provide them with enough resources to alleviate the social conditions for which the programs have been put in place. An important point underscored here and in Grosh et al. (2008) is that successful safety-net programs can be designed and implemented in all country settings, including low-income countries. In low-income countries, the design of the program—including the choice of targeting method and benefit formula—should be simplified in line with the often lower administrative capacity.

For a wide range of safety net programs, the chapter reviews the typical targeting methods used to select beneficiaries. Diversity is a hallmark—in methods available and used, and in outcomes. A few methods of targeting and types of programs go hand-in-hand, for example, self-selection and commodity price subsidies or workfare programs. However, several different methods can often be used for a particular type of program; for instance, cash and food transfers can be targeted by means-tests, proxy means-tests, nutritional status or risk factors, geographic area, demographic characteristic, or self-selection. Often, programs use a number of methods: Combining more targeting methods usually yields better targeting than using a single method does.

The complexity of the eligibility and recertification procedures, and of the targeting methods employed, go hand-in-hand with the level of economic development and institutional capacity of the country. Many middle-income countries have developed sophisticated and effective individual- or household-level targeting instruments, using means-tests or proxy means-tests. In low-income countries, programs tend to employ simpler targeting methods based on demographical or geographical criteria or community targeting.

To achieve its intended outcomes, a program's benefit level should be consistent with its objectives. However, budget constraints often make for hard trade-offs between coverage and benefit level. Programs with benefits that are too small will have little impact on beneficiaries and administrative costs will be high relative to the level of benefits. Programs with high benefits will have a larger impact on recipient households, but they will have a higher fiscal burden, require more care in relation to design and targeting, and may induce greater work disincentives. In general, in developing countries, programs with benefits that are too low are more frequent than programs with benefits that are too high. We found that even in middle-income countries, the generosity of most safety-net programs is modest or moderate, in the range of 5 to 20 percent of the pretransfer consumption of beneficiary households, substantially lower than in developed countries, which implies that labor disincentives could be less of a concern than in more generous European programs.

Throughout the discussion an implicit theme is that although good programs are based in sound empirics, the links between poverty measurement and program benefits are not direct. Program eligibility is very often not linked to direct monetary measures of poverty; benefit levels are often not sufficient to fill the poverty gap; and benefit formulae are rarely customized to exact income levels. The approximations and limitations that reign in social assistance policy in developing countries, thus, provide a degree of insulation from both the politics of social policy and the debates that can rage around poverty measurement.

Notes

1. In the United States, the terms *welfare* or *income support* may be used rather than *social assistance*. In the term *social, safety-net programs* or sometimes *social transfers* are often used. We use these terms interchangeably throughout this chapter.
2. To fill the gap in knowledge about safety-net spending in developing countries, we use the information provided by Weigand and Grosh (2008) that more closely follows the conceptual definition of safety nets used in this chapter. Weigand and Grosh (2008) compile data from World Bank public expenditure reviews and other similar analytical work, covering one year per country between 1996 and 2006. These studies, performed as one-time or periodic reviews of social policy, try to sort through countries' budgets and programmatic structures to assemble comprehensive numbers, an exercise inherently different from that usually carried out for a given country as part of its annual budgetary process. Some of the limitations of this data set are its incomplete coverage (covers 87 of 180 developing countries), regional bias (coverage is very limited for Sub-Saharan Africa, with only 9 of 47 countries representing only 18 percent of total population), and limited comparability (not all studies reporting safety-net spending have used the same conceptual definition).
3. For instance, the average of 3.5 percent for Sub-Saharan Africa is based on only six observations and includes external financing; it excludes many countries with little or no spending on social assistance.

References

ADB. 2006. *Social Protection Index for Committed Poverty Reduction*. Manila: Asian Development Bank.

Ahmed, Akhter U. 2004. "Assessing the Performance of Conditional Cash Transfer Programs for Girls and Boys in Primary and Secondary Schools in Bangladesh." Project report prepared for the World Bank, Washington, DC, by International Food Policy Research Institute.

Alderman, Harold C. 2001. "Multi-Tier Targeting of Social Assistance: The Role of Intergovernmental Transfers." *World Bank Economic Review* 15 (1): 33–53.

———. 2002. "Do Local Officials Know Something We Don't? Decentralization of Targeted Transfers in Albania." *Journal of Public Economics* 83 (3): 375–404.

Alderman, Harold, and Joachim von Braun. 1984. *The Effect of the Egyptian Food Ration and Subsidy System on Income Distribution and Consumption.* Report 45. Washington, DC: International Food Policy Research Institute Research.

Braun-Munzinger, Corinna. 2005. "Education Vouchers: An International Comparison." Working paper, Centre for Civil Society, New Delhi.

Castañeda, Tarcisio. 1998. *The Design, Implementation and Impact of Food Stamp Programs in Developing Countries.* Washington, DC: World Bank.

Coady, David, Margaret Grosh, and John Hoddinott. 2004. *Targeting of Transfers in Developing Countries: Review of Lessons and Experience.* Regional and Sectoral Studies. Washington, DC: World Bank.

Delgado, Christopher, and Thomas Reardon. 1988. "Why the Urban Poor Pay More for Their Grain: Transaction Derived Cereal Prices in Burkina Faso." Paper presented at the American Association of Agricultural Economics Annual Meeting, July 1988, Honolulu, Hawaii..

Devereux, Stephen, Jenni Marshall, Jane MacAskill, and Larissa Pelham. 2005. *Making Cash Count: Lessons from Cash Transfer Schemes in East and Southern Africa for Supporting the Most Vulnerable Children and Households.* Report for the United Nations Children's Fund. London and Brighton: Save the Children, HelpAge International, and Institute of Development Studies.

Ezemenari, Kene, and Kalanidhi Subbarao. 1999. "Jamaica's Food Stamp Program: Impacts on Poverty and Welfare." Policy Research Working Paper 2207, World Bank, Washington, DC.

Fiszbien, Ariel, and Norbert Schady. 2009. *Conditional Cash Transfers: Reducing Present and Future Poverty.* Washington, DC: World Bank.

Giedion, Ursula. 2002. "The Case of Thailand." Presentation at the World Bank seminar on Protecting the Poor: User Fees for Health Services, Washington, DC, June 26, 2002.

Gillespie, Stuart. 1999. *Supplementary Feeding for Women and Young Children.* Washington, DC: World Bank, Human Development Network.

Grosh, Margaret, Carlo del Ninno, Emil Tesliuc, and Azediune Ouerghi. 2008. *For Protection and Promotion: The Design and Implementation of Effective Safety Nets.* Washington, DC: World Bank.

Grosh, Margaret. 1992. "The Jamaican Food Stamps Programme: A Case Study in Targeting." *Food Policy* 17 (1): 23–40.

Haddad, Lawrence, John Hoddinott, and Harold Alderman. 1997. *Intrahousehold Resource Allocation in Developing Countries: Models, Methods, and Policy.* Baltimore: Johns Hopkins University Press.

Hoddinott, John. 1999. *Principles and Practice in the Design of Food-Based Targeted Assistance.* Washington, DC: World Bank.

IFPRI. 2000. *Second Report—Implementation Proposal for the PRAF/ IDB Project: Phase II.* Washington, DC: International Food Policy Research Institute.

Lindert, Kathy, Emmanuel Skoufias, and Joseph Shapiro. 2006. *Redistributing Income to the Poor and the Rich: Public Transfers in Latin America and the Caribbean.* Social Protection Discussion Paper 605. Washington, DC: World Bank.

OECD. 2004. *Benefits and Wages: OECD Indicators.* Paris: Organization for Economic Co-operation and Development.

Oxfam. 2002. *Cash for Work Programming. A Practical Guide.* Nairobi: Oxfam GB Kenya Programme.

Quisumbing, Agnes R., and John A. Maluccio. 2000. *Intrahousehold Allocation and Gender Relations: New Empirical Evidence from Four Developing Countries.* Food Consumption and Nutrition Division Discussion Paper 84. Washington, DC: International Food Policy Research Institute.

Rao, Vijayendra. 2000. "Price Heterogeneity and 'Real' Inequality: A Case Study of Poverty and Prices in Rural South India." *Review of Income and Wealth* 46 (2): 201–211.

Ravallion, Martin. 2002. "Are the Poor Protected from Budget Cuts? Evidence for Argentina." *Journal of Applied Economics* 5 (1): 95–121.

Rogers, Beatrice Lorge, and Jennifer Coates. 2002. *Food-Based Safety Nets and Related Programs.* Social Safety Net Primer Series 0225. Washington, DC: World Bank.

Schubert, Bernd. 2005. *Social Cash Transfers. Reaching the Poorest: Health, Education and Social Protection Sector Project: Systems of Social Protection. A Contribution to the International Debate Based on Experience in Zambia.* Eschborn, Germany: German Agency for Technical Cooperation.

Southern African Labour and Development and Research Unit. 2005. *Addressing Social Protection Challenges in the Context of HIV and AIDS: A Role for PWPs in East and Southern Africa?* Cape Town: University of Cape Town.

Sumarto, Sudarno, Asep Suryahadi, and Lant Pritchett. 2000. "Safety Nets and Safety Ropes: Who Benefited from Two Indonesian Crisis Programs: The 'Poor' or the 'Shocked?'" Policy Research Working Paper 2436, World Bank, Washington, DC.

Tuck, Laura, and Kathy Lindert. 1996. *From Universal Food Subsidies to a Self-Targeted Program: A Case Study of Tunisian Reform.* Discussion Paper 351. Washington, DC: World Bank.

Weigand, Christine, and Margaret Grosh. 2008. *Levels and Patterns of Safety Net Spending in Developing and Transition Countries.* Social Protection Discussion Paper. Washington, DC: World Bank.

Wilson, Michael. 2006. *Moving Toward Free Basic Education: Policy Issues and Implementation Challenges.* Washington, DC: United Nations Educational, Scientific, and Cultural Organization and the World Bank.

World Bank. 2007a. *Implementing Free Primary Education: Achievements and Challenges.* Washington, DC: World Bank, Education Sector, Human Development Network.

———. 2007b. *Peru: Social Safety Nets in Peru.* Report 42093-Pe. Washington, DC: World Bank.

11

Europe's Other Poverty Measures

Absolute Thresholds Underlying Social Assistance

RICHARD BAVIER ■

The first thing many of us learn about international poverty measurement is that European nations apply a "relative" poverty threshold, typically 50 (Organization for Economic Co-operation and Development [OECD]) or 60 (European Union "at-risk" measure) percent of median income, that is higher than ours, and that they also do a better job of reducing poverty. Unlike the European model, the "absolute" US poverty threshold does not increase in real value when the nation's standard of living rises, even though it is obvious that what we think of as living in poverty today, such as having no electricity or indoor plumbing, would not have been a sign of poverty a century ago. The 1995 National Academy of Sciences report advised the United States to emulate Europe and adopt a relative, or at least a "quasi-relative," threshold, indexed each year by changes in spending on food, clothing, and shelter between the 30th and 35th percentiles of couples with two children (Citro and Michael 1995). Couples in this range have incomes above US$50,000 and most own their own homes. So indexing a poverty threshold to their spending on basics would tend to reflect economic gains among families who are well above what most people regard as poverty.

Is this the lesson about poverty measurement that the United States should learn from Europe?

STANDARD BUDGETS IN SUPPORT OF EUROPEAN SOCIAL ASSISTANCE

Another lesson, not typically featured at conferences on international poverty measurement, is that "absolute" measures of need frequently underlie the social assistance schemes that help Western European nations measure up well against "relative" poverty thresholds.[1] At the Joint OECD/University of Maryland International Conference on Measuring Poverty, Income Inequality, and Social Exclusion: Lessons from Europe, Grosh, del Ninno, and Tesliuc (2012, Chapter 10) summarized material from their comprehensive World Bank handbook of social assistance program design (Grosh, del Ninno, Tesliuc, and Ouerghi 2008). Even though the paper thoroughly schematized and illustrated the design of transfer and tax policies from both developed and developing nations by delivery mode (cash and noncash transfers, tax expenditures, services), targeting methods, behavioral requirements, and adjustments for budget constraints, there is little attention, in that paper or in other conference papers, devoted to the needs standards underlying the social assistance programs or how they relate conceptually to the measure of poverty.

In fact, in some nations, maximum social assistance levels may be simply a product of political expediency. However, with many OECD members, benefits reflect the influence of standard budgets, defined by Gordon Fisher as, "a list of goods and services that a family of a specified size and composition would need to live at a designated level of well-being, together with the costs of those goods and services" (Fisher 2007). Standard budgets have been classified as *descriptive*, based on information about actual spending of a typical family of a specific type, or *prescriptive*, a normative budget based on expert opinion about the cost of a nutritionally adequate diet, housing of appropriate size and quality, clothing allowance, and so on (Johnson, Rogers, and Tan 2001). A recent variation in the United Kingdom and Ireland has supplemented expert judgment with experiential and evaluative advice by ordinary citizens about what constitutes normal consumption (Bradshaw et al. 2008; Vincentian Partnership for Justice 2006).

Although the methods and purposes of standard budgets have varied widely, they often have been employed to support improvements in wages and government assistance levels by application of empirical evidence and independent professional judgment. This progressive thread is rarely visible in characterizations of standard budgets as "arbitrary" (Förster and Mira d'Ercole 2012, Chapter 2; Citro and Michael 1995; citations in Fisher 2007; Förster 1994) and even "paternalistic" (Citro and Michael 1995).

Sweden's National Board of Consumer Affairs maintains a budget representing a "reasonable" standard of living, reflecting "neither minimal nor superfluous consumption," that is used by the National Board of Health and Welfare to advise local authorities on setting social assistance (*Socialbidrag*) levels (Eardly et al. 1996; Fisher 2007; Salonen 2002; Veit-Wilson 1998). Eardly et al. (1996, 358) explain, "The standard rate is meant to cover the cost of food, clothing and shoes, sport and leisure, consumable goods, furniture, household utensils, newspapers, telephone rental and television license fees, household electricity and home insurance costs, along with smaller medical treatments and dental care." The central German government provides the federated Lander with boundaries for social assistance benefit levels (*Sozialhilfe*) that conform to "human dignity" and were based initially on a budget of basic goods (Eardly et al. 1996; Fisher 2007; Förster 1994; Nelson 2004). In the Netherlands, social assistance benefits are keyed to statutory minimum wages that are themselves grounded historically in standard budgets (Eardly et al. 1996; Fisher 2007; Veit-Wilson 1998). The Swiss Conference of Public Assistance Institutions establishes budgets used by cantons in setting social assistance levels. Eardly et al. (1996, 374) note that amounts are included for "maintenance, 'free share' (*Sakgeld* or pocket money), rent, clothes, electricity, radio, television and telephone fees, and transport." Provinces in Canada establish their own social assistance rates under the Canada Social Transfer program. Typically, assistance reflects either a "preadded budget" amount for all nonshelter needs supplemented by a separate shelter component, or an itemized budget amount for specific needs categories, or a flat amount varied by household structure (Eardly et al. 1996; Federal–Provincial–Territorial Directors of Income Support, 2006).

In other OECD nations, standard budgets are not used to set assistance levels directly, but to influence wage setting or the planning of social assistance spending. The Family Budget Unit, an educational charity in the United Kingdom, produces two budget levels, a low cost but acceptable budget it characterizes as a poverty line, and a modest but adequate level. Budgets specific to geographic area and demographic group have been used in wage negotiations and by the United Kingdom's poverty advocacy groups to assess the adequacy of social assistance benefits. Recently, the Joseph Rowntree Foundation combined the approaches of expert standard budgets with input from ordinary citizens to produce a new minimum income standard that it commends for the same sort of uses (Bradshaw et al. 2008). In Ireland, a nongovernmental agency, Combat Poverty, received a statutory charge to advise government on all aspects of public policy pertaining to poverty (Combat Poverty Agency 2008). Its annual budget advice to the government uses minimum essential budgets developed by the Vincentian Partnership for Justice (2006), employing a combination of focus groups of ordinary citizens and advice by experts. *Minimum essential budgets* include amounts for food, clothing, personal care, household goods, household services, social inclusion and participation, educational costs, household fuel, and savings and contingency costs.

Standard budgets were employed in Australia already early in the twentieth century in a landmark wage judgment (Saunders 1998). The Social Policy Research Center has taken the lead in developing contemporary indicative budget standards for a range of Australian household types. The standards are intended to inform debate about adequate income levels and have been instrumental in a recent round of minimum wage decisions (Saunders 2004). At the request of federal and territorial officials, Statistics Canada has produced a market-basket measure to be used in assessing social assistance adequacy (Hatfield 2002). France's guaranteed minimum wage (*Salaire Minimum Interprofessionnel de Croissance*) was based on a compromise among subsistence budgets and, over the years, has been updated by a variety of price and wage changes. It is a benchmark in debates over social assistance levels (Veit-Wilson 1998). In short, whereas international comparisons featured at the OECD/University of Maryland conference employ relative poverty thresholds, expressed as a point on the income distribution (Förster and Mira d'Ercole 2012, Chapter 2; Immervoll 2012, Chapter 9; Maquet and Stanton 2012, Chapter 3; Grosh, del Ninno, and Tesliuc 2012, Chapter 10), individual member nations often use standard budgets to support wage and social assistance levels.

US STANDARDS OF NEED

Standard budgets have a long history in the United States for similar reasons (Fisher 2007; Johnson, Rogers, and Tan 2001). During the Progressive Era, standard budgets were often used in advocating for improvements in the living conditions of industrial workers and their families. The US Bureau of Labor Statistics began its involvement with standard budgets during World War I in support of wage determinations for the flood of new government workers into the District of Columbia. Subsequent Bureau of Labor Statistics budgets have had both statistical and administrative uses, including the current Lower Living Standard Income Level.

Currently, the US functional equivalent of European standard budgets used in setting social assistance levels are standards of need for specific budget categories, such as food or housing, underlying federal means-tested noncash assistance programs. The most familiar is the Thrifty Food Plan, maintained by the Department of Agriculture and the descendent of the economy and low-cost food plans employed by Mollie Orshansky in developing the threshold adopted as the official US measure of poverty in 1969. The Thrifty Food Plan is said to represent "the cost of a nutritionally adequate diet," reflecting "up-to-date dietary recommendations, food composition data, food habits, and food price information" (Carlson et al. 2007).

Program-based needs standards underlying US noncash assistance are not as "absolute" as the official poverty threshold is said to be. Section 8 rental assistance prescribes that families need a dwelling that meets a range of quality and safety standards and has the appropriate number of bedrooms. The program subsidizes units that meet this standard generally up to the 40th percentile of such rents, termed Fair Market Rent. As rents increase with the average size and quality of the rental stock, this ceiling on rental subsidies increases in real dollars as well.

Medicaid reimburses states for a share of expenditures on behalf of eligible persons for inpatient hospital services, laboratory and x-ray services, and physician services, among others. As the professional standard of medically necessary care expands, so does the scope of reimbursable services.

The largest federal child care assistance program, the Child Care and Development Fund, requires states to perform market rate surveys at least every two years and document that their maximum benefits are reasonably sufficient (National Child Care Information Center 2006). Real increases in the quality of available child care services tend to be captured in maximum benefit levels that the Department of Health and Human Services suggests states set at the 75th percentile of surveyed providers.

In theory, even the value of the Thrifty Food Plan would increase in real terms if one of the occasional studies by the Center for Nutrition Policy and Promotion showed that the current Thrifty Food Plan amount would no longer purchase a nutritionally adequate diet based on current nutrition standards, food consumption patterns, and prices (Carlson, Lino, and Fungwe 2007).

LESSONS FOR POLICY

One factor explaining the prevalence of empirically arguable needs standards supporting social assistance is the audience, not a conference of poverty experts but representatives of elected governments and, ultimately, their electorates. These needs standards operate in the context of public choice about social assistance spending. They are successful to the extent that they gain and maintain the consent of the governed and their representatives. By comparison, relative thresholds, such as 50 or 60 percent of median income, are useful for international comparisons precisely *because* they do not reflect what each separate nation's public and government understand as the level of basic needs (Förster and Mira d'Ercole 2012, Chapter 2; Förster 1994). For the purposes of researchers, a strong empirical defense of the poverty line is unnecessary. Any marker of economic status, even one that is arbitrary in the sense that it has no convincing intrinsic justification, can serve the purposes of economists well as long as it performs its function of measuring variation accurately near the bottom of the distribution.

The prevalence of concrete needs standards in governmental proceedings and of relative thresholds at conferences devoted to international statistics no doubt is due partly to the relative comfort levels of legislators and voters, on the one hand, and poverty experts, on the other, when it comes to abstract thinking. However, it also is true that the expert poverty literature's dismissal of standard budgets as "subjective" and "arbitrary" is a loose and unhelpful usage of language (Citro and Michael 1995; Förster 1994; Ruggles 1990). Drawing the poverty line is not self-referential. It is subjective neither in the sense of a private experience, like pain, nor like a taste for spinach. Psychologically, we may each have a different tolerance for observing deprivation before we are discomforted, but when people argue that the poverty line is too high or too low, they do not support their opinions by referring to their own internal states. Neither is the poverty line arbitrary, if by that we mean that generally accepted standards of reason and evidence are irrelevant. If that were the way the threshold was understood, we would not find experts offering objective evidence and argument that their proposals for revision are reasonable but the current threshold is not.

Poverty thresholds may be arbitrary within the narrow concept of rationality found in neoclassical economic theory, where reasoning is strictly instrumental and evaluations, such as about what people *need*, reflect tastes or preferences that are arbitrary in the sense that we do not reason or argue about them—*de gustibus non est disputandum*. But the question of what people need *est disputandum* when we develop and modify assistance programs. In these contexts, valuations are not just the givens that tell instrumental reason what to maximize, but rather are what reasoning and persuasion are intended to inform and influence.

We reason about the adequacy of the Thrifty Food Plan by comparing it to prices and, every decade or so, to nutrition standards and food consumption patterns. We reason about the Fair Market Rent ceilings by testing the "success rates" of voucher holders—the rate at which they can actually find standard quality units available under the Fair Market Rent. We reason about whether a couple with a teenaged son and daughter need an apartment with two bedrooms or three. We argue about whether state Medicaid programs must cover Viagra for its medically accepted indications. Evidence and argument are presented, and minds can change. Intellectual assent can be earned. Still, it is true that the outcome of this reasoning and argument cannot compel assent, in the manner of a scientific experiment or a mathematical deduction. However, to the extent that the process is characterized by openness and transparency, participatory rather than strategic communication, appropriate opportunities for informed participation by all affected parties or their representatives, and reviewable in the electoral process, the outcomes represent how a democracy rationally aggregates and resolves issues about inherently evaluative matters. The outcomes are due consent, at least until the next election.

The poverty literature warns that government's determination of how much people need may be dominated by a desire not to pay very much—not that official needs standards are arbitrary but that they are determined by unspoken and invalid criteria (Fisher 2007; Veit-Wilson 1998; Citro and Michael 1995; Ruggles 1990). In other words, government is apt to confuse two distinct kinds of questions about social assistance: (1) What do we as a nation regard as the minimum that it is indecent for people to be without? (Or, more progressively, what do we as a nation regard as necessary for full participation in society?) (2) How much will we pay? Standard budgets bring empirical evidence and independent expert judgment to bear on the first question, which can help insulate it from preferences about the second. Nutritional science and price surveys, for example, cannot draw a food poverty line, but they can make one more rational by reducing the risk that invalid assumptions will go unexamined and unchallenged.

Someone willing to grant the point that empirically argued standards of need may be more suited than a random point on the income distribution for convincing voters and their representatives to spend tax revenues may yet remain skeptical about the effectiveness of these needs standards. Although we have seen that European social assistance levels often are grounded in standard budgets, international comparisons of government efforts to reduce relative poverty typically rate the United States toward the bottom (Förster & Mira d'Ercole 2012, Chapter 2; OECD 2008). However, to infer from benefit levels that needs standards are inadequate is to confuse government's answer to the first kind of question with its answer to the second kind. When researchers develop alternate US poverty thresholds starting with standards of need underlying federal noncash assistance programs, they consistently come out well above the current official poverty threshold (Bavier 2009; Bernstein, Brocht, and Spade-Aguilar 2000; Renwick and Bergmann 1993; Ruggles 1990; Schwarz and Volgy 1992; Weinberg and Lamas 1993). The federal government's *programmatic* standards for food, shelter, health care, and other basic needs imply a higher poverty threshold than the federal government's current *statistical* measure of what people need. As we think about adopting a quasi-relative poverty threshold, we should bear in mind these lessons from Europe and the United States, suggesting that an empirically arguable threshold would be more useful in the context of public choice about assistance spending.

Notes

1. When comparing nations with very large differences in median incomes, relative thresholds set at 50 or 60 percent of median income can produce nonsensical results. This is one of the reasons that the United Nations supports absolute poverty thresholds for statistical purposes, although comparing its daily $1.25 per person threshold to the official US absolute threshold reinforces the view that poverty is, in some fundamental sense, relative (Commission on Sustainable Development 2001).

References

Bavier, Richard. 2009. "A Legislatively-Based Poverty Threshold." Retrieved from: http://www.irp.wisc.edu/research/povmeas/pdfs/LegislativelyBasedThresholds.pdf.
Bernstein, Jared, Chauna Brocht, and Maggie Spade-Aguilar. 2000. *How Much Is Enough? Basic Family Budgets for Working Families.* Washington, DC: Economic Policy Institute.

Bradshaw, Jonathan, Sue Middleton, Abigail Davis, Nina Oldfield, Noel Smith, Linda Cusworth, and Julie Williams. 2008. *A Minimum Income Standard for Britain: What People Think*. York, UK: Joseph Rowntree Foundation. http://www.jrf.org.uk/publications/minimum-income-standard-britain-what-people-think.

Carlson, A., M. Lino, and T. Fungwe. 2007. *The Low-Cost, Moderate-Cost, and Liberal Food Plans, 2007*. CNPP-20. Washington, DC: US Department of Agriculture, Center for Nutrition Policy and Promotion.

Carlson, Andrea, Mark Lino, Wen Yen Juan, Kenneth Hanson, and Peter Basiotis. 2007. *Thrifty Food Plan, 2006*. CNPP-19. Washington, DC: US Department of Agriculture, Center for Nutrition Policy and Promotion. http://www.cnpp.usda.gov/Publications/FoodPlans/MiscPubs/TFP2006Report.pdf.

Citro, Constance, and Robert T. Michael, eds. 1995. *Measuring Poverty: A New Approach*. Washington, DC: National Academy Press.

Combat Poverty Agency. 2008. "Advice to Government Budget 2009." Policy submission, Combat Poverty Agency, Dublin, Ireland. http://www.cpa.ie/publications/submissions/2008_Sub_PBS2009.pdf.

Commission on Sustainable Development. 2001. "Combating Poverty." Report of the Secretary-General, United Nations Department of Economic and Social Affairs, New York. http://www.un.org/esa/dsd/susdevtopics/sdt_pove_documents.shtml.

Eardly, Tony, Jonathan Bradshaw, John Ditch, Ian Gough, and Peter Whiteford. 1996. *Social Assistance in OECD Countries, Volume II: Country Reports*. London: Department for Work and Pensions. http://www.dwp.gov.uk/asd/asd5/rrep047.pdf.

Federal–Provincial–Territorial Directors of Income Support. 2006. *Social Assistance Statistical Report: 2005*. Ottowa, Ontario: Human Resources and Skills Development Canada.

Fisher, Gordon. 2007. "An Overview of Recent Work on Standard Budgets in the United States and other Anglophone Countries." Working paper, US Department of Health and Human Services, Washington, DC. http://aspe.hhs.gov/poverty/papers/std-budgets/.

Förster, Michael F. 1994. *Measurement of Low Incomes and Poverty in a Perspective of International Comparisons*. OECD Labor Market and Social Policy Occasional Papers 14. Paris: Organization for Economic Co-operation and Development. http://www.oecd.org/dataoecd/45/58/1895548.pdf.

Förster, Michael F., and Marco Mira d'Ercole. 2012. "The OECD Approach to Measuring Income Distribution and Poverty." In *Counting the Poor: New Thinking about European Poverty Measures and Lessons for the United States*. Edited by Douglas J. Besharov and Kenneth A. Couch, 25–58. New York: Oxford University Press.

Grosh, Margaret, Carlo del Ninno, and Emil Tesliuc. 2012. "Social Assistance Schemes in Developing Countries." In *Counting the Poor: New Thinking about European Poverty Measures and Lessons for the United States*. Edited by Douglas J. Besharov and Kenneth A. Couch, 211–234. New York: Oxford University Press.

Grosh, Margaret, Carlo del Ninno, Emil Tesliuc, and Azedine Ouerghi. 2008. *For Protection and Promotion, the Design and Implementation of Effective Safety Nets*. Washington, DC: The World Bank.

Hatfield, Michael. 2002. *Constructing the Revised Market Basket Measure*. Hull, Quebec: Human Resources and Skills Development Canada. http://dsp-psd.pwgsc.gc.ca/Collection/MP32-30-01-1E.pdf.

Immervoll, Herwig. 2012. "Minimum-Income Benefits in OECD Countries." In *Counting the Poor: New Thinking about European Poverty Measures and Lessons for the United States.* Edited by Douglas J. Besharov and Kenneth A. Couch, 169–210. New York: Oxford University Press.

Johnson, David S., John M. Rogers, and Lucillia Tan. 2001. "A Century of Family Budgets in the United States." *Monthly Labor Review* 124(5): 28–45. http://www.bls.gov/opub/mlr/2001/05/art3full.pdf.

Maquet, Isabelle, and David Stanton. 2012. "Income Indicators for the EU's Social Inclusion Strategy." In *Counting the Poor: New Thinking about European Poverty Measures and Lessons for the United States.* Edited by Douglas J. Besharov and Kenneth A. Couch, 59–78. New York: Oxford University Press.

National Child Care Information Center. 2006. *Child Care and Development Fund Report of State and Territory Plans FY 2006–2007.* Fairfax, VA: National Child Care Information Center. http://nccic.acf.hhs.gov/pubs/stateplan/stateplan-intro.html.

Nelson, Kenneth. 2004. "The Formation of Minimum Income Protection." Luxembourg Income Study Working Paper 373, Luxembourg Income Study, Luxembourg. http://www.lisproject.org/publications/liswps/373.pdf.

OECD. 2008. *Growing Unequal? Income Distribution and Poverty in OECD Countries.* Paris: Organization for Economic Co-operation and Development. http://masetto.sourceoecd.org/vl=3979219/cl=26/nw=1/rpsv/ij/oecdthemes/99980142/v2008n9/s1/p1l.

Renwick, Trudi, and Barbara Bergmann. 1993. "A Budget-Based Definition of Poverty, with an Application to Single-Parent Families." *Journal of Human Resources* 28 (1): 1–24.

Ruggles, Patricia. 1990. *Drawing the Line—Alternative Poverty Measures and Their Implications for Public Policy.* Washington, DC: Urban Institute Press.

Salonen, Tapio. 2002. *Child Poverty in Sweden—2000.* Stockholm: Save the Children Sweden. http://www.crin.org/docs/resources/publications/RB-childpoverty.pdf.

Saunders, Peter. 1998. *Using Budget Standards To Assess the Well-Being of Families.* Social Policy Research Center Discussion Paper 93. Sydney: Social Policy Research Centre. http://www.sprc.unsw.edu.au/media/File/dp093.pdf.

———. 2004. *Budget Standards Alive and Well.* Social Policy Research Center Newsletter 87. Sydney: Social Policy Research Centre. http://www.sprc.unsw.edu.au/media/File/NL87.pdf.

Schwarz, John E., and Thomas J. Volgy. 1992. *The Forgotten Americans.* New York: W.W. Norton and Company.

Veit-Wilson, John. 1998. *Setting Adequacy Standards: How Governments Define Minimum Incomes.* Bristol: The Policy Press. http://www.staff.ncl.ac.uk/j.veit-wilson/documents/sas.pdf.

Vincentian Partnership for Social Justice. 2006. *Minimum Essential Budget Standard for Six Household Types.* Dublin: Vincentian Partnership for Social Justice. http://www.budgeting.ie/images/stories/Publications/2006MinimumBudgetFullReport.pdf.

Weinberg, Daniel H., and Enrique J. Lamas. (1993). "Some Experimental Results on Alternate Poverty Measures." In *Proceedings of the Social Statistics Section.* 549–555. Alexandria, VA: American Statistical Association.

PART FOUR

Nonincome Monetary Measures

12

Asset-Based Measurement of Poverty

ANDREA BRANDOLINI, SILVIA MAGRI, AND
TIMOTHY M. SMEEDING ∎

INTRODUCTION

Income insufficiency, relative to some socially acceptable minimal level of income need, is still the most common criterion to define poverty in rich countries, despite different measurement choices on the adjustment for household size, the exact definition of income, and the absolute/relative characterization of the poverty line (US Census Bureau 2008; European Commission 2008). The role of assets is absent, except as reflected in reported income. Yet assets and lack thereof are important for measuring material well-being and social exclusion as well as for program eligibility and take-up (e.g., Smeeding 2002; Yates and Bradbury 2009).

The role of wealth in poverty definition may be seen from two different perspectives. First, wealth affects current well-being. Consumer units with total earnings below the poverty threshold have different standards of living depending on the value of their net assets. A sudden income drop need not result in lower living conditions if the unit can decrease accumulated wealth, or if it can borrow. On the other hand, income can be above the poverty threshold, yet a family can feel vulnerable because it lacks the financial resources to face an adverse income shock. Assets and liabilities are fundamental to smoothing out consumption when income is volatile. Their insurance role is intertwined with the existence of and access to private or public insurance mechanisms. Second, the possession of tangible and intangible assets is a major determinant of the longer-term prospects of households. The chances in one's life depend on the set of opportunities open to an individual, which are, in turn, a function of her or his intellectual and material endowments. In the presence of capital market imperfections, individuals with low endowments may be stuck in a poverty trap. Whenever the policy objective is to level the playing field, wealth redistribution may be an effective alternative to income redistribution, particularly if a minimum endowment reinforces the sense of responsibility of individuals and their attitude to pursue more efficient behaviors (Bowles and Gintis 1998).

Even though the two perspectives clearly overlap, we consider here only the first one. We focus on how net worth affects households' current economic well-being, with the purpose of developing statistical measures to monitor the social situation of a community. The chapter is organized as follows. In the next section, we outline a conceptual framework for including wealth into poverty analysis and review the income–net worth and asset–poverty measures. In the third section, we consider in greater detail the application of the income–net worth approach. We briefly describe the data at our disposal in the fourth section, and present comparative results from applying the two approaches in the fifth section. In the final section, we provide an assessment of these alternative approaches and draw some conclusions.

DEFINING ASSET-BASED MEASURES OF POVERTY

In poverty analysis, income is generally defined to include all labor incomes; private transfers; pensions and other social insurance benefits; cash public social assistance; and cash rent, interests, dividends and other returns on financial assets, possibly net of interest paid on mortgages and other household debts. Income can be taken before (like in the United States) or after (like in the European Union) direct taxes and social security contributions. More comprehensive definitions might include non-cash imputed rent for owner-occupied dwellings, but they are uncommon.

These definitions do account for (net) household wealth, but only through the (net) income flow it generates in the current year. They ignore the possibility that a consumer unit decreases accumulated savings to meet its current needs. This simple consideration suggests that the concept of available resources can be broadened by adding to current income from labor, pensions, and other transfers a function of wealth holdings more general than its annual return. On the other hand, we could refrain from integrating income and net worth into a single measure of economic resources and maintain the distinction between these two dimensions in poverty analysis. A simple formalization may help us to distinguish these two alternatives.

Let us suppose that an individual receives income Y_t from labor, pensions, and other transfers (henceforth, *labor income*, for simplicity) in year t, and that at the beginning of the period, he holds net worth NW_{t-1}. In the standard income insufficiency approach, total current income CY_t is defined as the sum of labor income Y_t and property income $r_t NW_{t-1}$, where r_t is the (weighted) average rate of return on assets:[1]

$$CY_t = Y_t + r_t NW_{t-1}. \tag{12.1}$$

Poverty occurs whenever CY_t falls short of a prefixed threshold Z_t, which represents the minimum acceptable level of command over resources.

As they share the same currency metrics, income and wealth are perfectly fungible and one unit of wealth can be straightforwardly substituted for one unit of income.[2] This implies that the total available financial resources FR_t are given by the sum of income and net worth:

$$FR_t = Y_t + (1 + r_t) NW_{t-1}. \tag{12.2}$$

With definition (12.2), an individual would be classified as poor if total financial resources FR_t were less than Z_t.

This suggestion of taking into account all net worth to identify poverty status is extreme, but the comparison of (12.1) and (12.2) helps to define the boundaries of the financial poverty region in the labor income and net worth space. This is shown in Figure 12.1. According to the standard approach, individuals are poor if their current income CY_t is less than the poverty line Z_t, that is if $Y_t < Z_t - r_t NW_{t-1}$. The poverty region is the union of the dotted and gridded areas below the "standard poverty frontier." When all net worth is used to identify the poor, the poverty region shrinks to the gridded area only, as an individual is now classified as poor if their financial resources FR_t are less than the poverty line Z_t, or $Y_t < Z_t - (1+r_t)NW_{t-1}$.

It may be excessive to impose a condition that all wealth should be suddenly decreased to sustain current living standards. On the other hand, people save to transfer resources over all their future life, and it is then sensible to suppose that part of the accumulated savings is used for current spending, especially when adverse circumstances make it necessary. This means identifying, in Figure 12.1, a poverty frontier that lies between the standard frontier and the one assuming full use of all available financial resources. A possible solution is to use the "annuity value of net worth," as proposed by Weisbrod and Hansen (1968). Weisbrod and Hansen's "income–net worth" concept is an augmented income definition where the yield on net worth in year t is replaced with the n-year annuity value of net worth:

$$AY_t = Y_t + \left[\frac{\rho}{1-(1+\rho)^{-n}}\right]NW_{t-1}, \qquad (12.3)$$

with n and ρ being the length and the interest rate of the annuity. In (12.3) net worth is converted into a constant flow of income, discounted at the rate ρ, over a period of n years. If n goes to infinity, the annuity consists entirely of interest, and (12.3) would coincide with (12.1) for ρ equal to r_t. At the other extreme, if the time horizon is one year, AY_t is simply the sum of current labor income and $(1+\rho)$ times net worth, which would coincide with (12.2) for ρ equal to r_t. Hence, as shown in Figure 12.1,

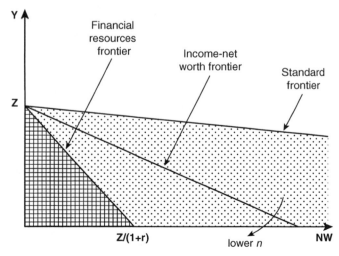

Figure 12.1 Poverty in the Labor Income and Net Worth Space: Income–Net Worth.
NOTE: See text for further explanation.

the poverty frontier for the income–net worth concept lies between the frontiers for (12.1) and (12.2).

The critical parameter in (12.3) is the length of the annuity n. The lower n, the steeper is the income–net worth frontier and the smaller is the poverty region. By shortening the period over which individuals are supposed to spread evenly their wealth, the fraction of personal wealth included into the assessment of the poverty status would be larger and the number of people classified as poor would ceteris paribus be smaller. How can n be chosen? Weisbrod and Hansen (1968) proposed to equate it with the person's life expectancy, under the assumption that no wealth is left at death, even though the formula could easily allow for a bequest.

The income–net worth measure is an elegant way of combining income and net worth, but requires several assumptions, such as the choice of the values for ρ and n, which are discussed in greater detail in the next section. We might be reluctant to impose so much structure on the measurement, especially when we take into account the profound implications that such a measure has for the age structure of poverty. Accumulated assets at older ages with a shorter annuity horizon increase the income–net worth of the elderly as compared to younger persons with longer time horizons and fewer accumulated assets. An alternative approach is to maintain the analysis in the bidimensional space of income and net worth and to supplement the income-based notion of poverty with an asset-based measure.

In order to construct a second, separate measure of asset poverty, we need to clarify its meaning and how its threshold can be set. Consistent with our focus on statistical measures for monitoring current living conditions, we see *asset poverty* as capturing the exposure to the risk that a minimally acceptable living standard cannot be maintained should income suddenly fall; whereas, *income poverty* refers to the static condition where income alone is insufficient to maintain this standard. Following this distinction, an asset-based measure can be understood as referring to "vulnerability" more than "poverty" (World Bank 2001, 139).

A simple way to translate these ideas into practice is to consider a consumer unit as asset-poor whenever its wealth holdings are not sufficient to secure it the socially determined minimum standard of living for a given period of time. With this definition, the asset-poverty line is straightforwardly defined as the income-poverty line multiplied by a factor related to the length of the reference period. Figure 12.2 shows the asset- and income-poverty regions in the labor income and net worth space. The asset-poverty line is set at a fraction ζ of the income-poverty line Z_t, so that an individual is asset-poor if $NW_{t-1} < \zeta Z_t$; income-poverty occurs, as before, if $Y_t < Z_t - r_t NW_{t-1}$. Accounting for wealth allows us to separate the income-poor who would have sufficient wealth to keep them at the poverty line for a period of at least $\zeta \times 12$ months (dotted area) from those who lack this buffer (gridded area). Both groups experience low incomes, but the latter is clearly worse off than the former. Moreover, a third group comprises individuals who currently have sufficient income to achieve the minimally acceptable standard of living, but do not have enough assets to protect them from a sudden drop of their earnings (striped area). Exploring the concept of asset poverty enriches our analysis by identifying income-poor individuals who are in a particularly critical situation as well as those nonpoor who are vulnerable to an adverse income shock.

In empirical estimates of the asset-poverty incidence, one needs to choose the length of the reference period and the wealth aggregate. Haveman and Wolff (2004)

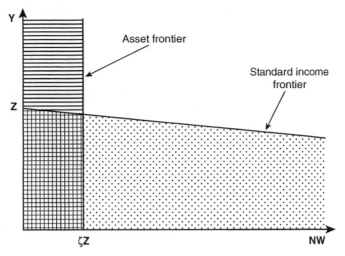

Figure 12.2 Poverty in the Labor Income and Net Worth Space: Asset- and Income-Poverty Measures.
NOTE: See text for further explanation.

take the period to be three months, and consequently set the asset-poverty threshold at one-fourth of the expenditure-based absolute poverty line proposed by the US National Academy of Sciences report. They use two different wealth concepts: *net worth,* which includes all marketable assets net of all debts, which is seen as an indicator of "the long-run economic security of families"; and *liquid assets,* which include only financial assets that can be easily monetized and are an indicator of "emergency fund availability" (Haveman and Wolff 2004, 151). Short and Ruggles (2005) also use the three-month reference period, whereas Gornick, Sierminska, and Smeeding (2009) take a six-month reference period in their cross-national examination of older women's poverty.[3]

The indicated value of ζ, one-fourth, and one-half, look sensible, but are arbitrarily chosen. Given our interpretation of asset poverty, a promising way to pin down the value of ζ could be to rely on results of studies of precautionary savings. For instance, Carroll, Dynan, and Krane (2003) estimate from a sample of US workers that an increase in the probability of suffering a job loss by one percentage point leads to an increase in total wealth of about two months of annual income. Barceló and Villanueva (2009) calculate that Spanish temporary employees hold an average buffer of liquid wealth of four to five months of earnings. Using the 1995 and 1998 waves of the US Survey of Consumer Finance, Kennickell and Lusardi (2005) find that the median value of the ratio of desired precautionary saving over permanent or normal income is around 10 percent. This ratio, however, rises for households more vulnerable to negative shocks, as the median goes up to 35 percent of normal income among the elderly households and to 16 percent among business households. These values can be read as suggesting an amount of precautionary savings ranging between one and three months of the normal income. Even though these estimates provide no confirmation of the values used for ζ, it is interesting to note that their order of magnitude is similar across very dissimilar contexts and nations.

APPLICATIONS OF THE INCOME–NET WORTH MEASURE

Weisbrod and Hansen (1968, 1316–1317) made clear that the income–net worth indicator must be seen as a conceptually consistent way of combining current income and net worth independently of its practical feasibility. In particular, it does not imply "either that people generally do purchase annuities with any or all of their net worth, that they necessarily *should* do so, or that they *can* do so." Yet, the assumption that a family seeks to spread evenly all its wealth over its lifetime is essentially arbitrary, as pointed out by Projector and Weiss (1969) and Atkinson (1975, 66). Moreover, expression (12.3) may ignore the life-cycle patterns of saving and fail to account for the higher saving potential of young units. More generally, the application of Weisbrod and Hansen's approach requires many measurement choices: the annuitization formula, the length of the annuity and its interest rate, the wealth aggregate that is annuitized, the treatment of couples, the population subgroups whose wealth is annuitized, the allowances for bequests and for precautionary saving.[4]

Possibly because of the number of necessary measurement choices, possibly as a result of the lack of suitable databases, Weisbrod and Hansen's approach has not been extensively followed in the poverty literature. Almost all applications relate to the United States and often use life expectancy of the family head or of the head and the spouse as a measure of the length of the annuity. More heterogeneity can be found in the choice of the annuity interest rate. Overall, the impact of including a measure of net worth in the calculation is not negligible as seen in Appendix 12.A. Whatever the precise formulation, the income–net worth approach results in the elderly looking much better, on average, than they would be viewed using income alone. This is shown in Figure 12.3, which reports, separately for males and females, the annuity rate at different ages obtained by applying the expression in (12.3) to the life tables for Italy in 2002 for two values of the interest rate (2 percent and 6 percent). The annuity rate is always higher than the interest rate, as it implies that some fraction of wealth is run down even at young ages. The annuity rate rises rapidly with age: With a 2 percent interest rate, it goes from 4.5 percent for women and 5.1 percent for men at age 55 to 8.9 percent and 11.0 percent, respectively, at age 75 years. Thus, annuitization with zero bequests increases income–net worth as a person ages, almost in a monotonic fashion, and especially when net worth does not decline in old age.

DATA AND MEASUREMENT ISSUES

In the next section, we present cross-country comparative results on asset-based measures of poverty based on the Luxembourg Wealth Study (LWS) database. The LWS database provides microdata on household income and wealth for 10 rich countries. Data were made comparable by a thorough process of ex post harmonization, but important differences in definitions, valuation criteria, and survey quality are nonetheless still reflected to some extent in the underlying data (see Niskanen 2007). Moreover, the degree to which LWS-based estimates match aggregate figures varies across surveys. These caveats have to be borne in mind when reading the results discussed in the following.[5]

We use three wealth variables: total financial assets, total debt, and net worth. *Net worth* does not include business equity, as that information is only available in some

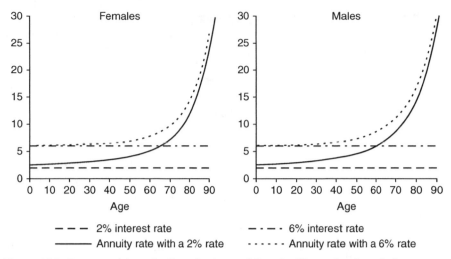

Figure 12.3 Percentage Annuity Rates by Age and Sex: An Illustration from Italy.
SOURCE: Based on the life tables for Italy in 2002. See text for further explanation.

countries; moreover, we do not consider this variable for Norway and Sweden, as the valuation of real property on a taxable basis makes the results for these two countries less comparable to those of the others. *Disposable income* is the sum of wages and salaries, self-employment income, capital income (interest, rent, dividends, private pensions), and cash and near-cash public income transfers including social insurance benefits, net of direct taxes, and social security contributions. The imputed rent on owner-occupied houses is not included, nor are subtracted interest paid on mortgages or consumer loans.

We equivalize both income and wealth with the *square root equivalence scale,* whereby the number of equivalent adults is given by the square root of the household size. Whether wealth should be equivalized is still an unsettled issue, but it is a natural choice in our context where we focus on the capacity of wealth to contribute to the achievement of a minimally acceptable standard of living. For each country, we define two types of income poverty thresholds: The first is a standard relative poverty line set at 50 percent of the national median of equivalized disposable income. These are called the "National lines" in Tables 12.2 to 12.4. The second line is called the "US-PSID (Panel Study of Income Dynamics) poverty line" and allows us to compare the situation across countries in absolute terms. It is constructed by taking the value of one-half of the median income poverty line in the PSID and converting this dollar amount to other currencies by using the OECD (2008) purchasing power parity indices for gross domestic product.[6] In our empirical application, we maintain these income-based poverty thresholds as reference points also for the asset-based measures. This choice is natural for asset poverty, where we set the threshold at one-fourth of the annual income-based poverty line, which suggests the notion that individuals have wealth sufficient to keep them at the poverty line for at least three months. However, this choice is more controversial for the income–net worth indicator. Here, we use the same poverty thresholds that we use for income. It may also be appropriate to set the thresholds at 50 percent of the national median of equivalized income–net worth. The latter solution is probably more consistent with a fully relative approach, but it implies that the change in poverty incidence would reflect both the use of the different indicator and the shift of the poverty line. In order to focus on the first effect, we have chosen not to recompute the poverty threshold as we change the indicator.

INTEGRATING WEALTH INTO POVERTY ANALYSIS: COMPARATIVE RESULTS FROM THE LWS

Table 12.1 reports the available per capita values of income, total financial assets, and net worth. The impact of different survey characteristics is well illustrated by the comparison between the two US sources: Total financial assets are about 50 percent higher in the Survey of Consumer Finances (SCF) than in the PSID, thanks to the specific focus on wealth and the oversampling of the rich in the former. However, mean net worth, which includes the value of real estate and debt, is higher in the SCF, by 33 percent, whereas the median is instead almost a tenth higher in the PSID, suggesting that the latter may perhaps better cover middle- and lower-class wealth holding. These problems aside, Table 12.1 reveals how constructing a measure that combines income and wealth is likely to significantly affect country comparisons. The Finnish and Italian mean incomes are relatively close, and are lower than the German one by 14 percent and 20 percent, respectively. But the evidence on mean net worth is strikingly different: The wealth of the Italians is twice as much as that of the Finns and almost 1.4 times that of the Germans. The mean Italian even looks wealthier than the mean US person on the basis of the PSID data. Differentials are further amplified by considering the medians.

For Finland, Germany, Italy, and the United States, Table 12.2 shows how income-based poverty measures change as income is replaced by the income–net worth indicator. (All income and asset variables are equivalized.) With the relative income-based national poverty lines, the largest share of income poor is found in the United States, the more so if the SCF is used instead of the PSID. These results are consistent with the Current Population Survey-based Luxembourg Income Study results for the United States.[7] Germany and Italy follow, preceding Finland. If we take the US relative poverty line as in the PSID as the standard, the US-PSID poverty rates for income are identical by construction. But now the incidence of poverty looks considerably higher in all three European countries, which have much lower median real incomes than the United States does. Note that a perceptible increase in the head count also occurs for the SCF, owing to its much lower median income relative to the PSID.[8]

In all countries, replacing the actual annual yield of net worth in the income definition with its annuity value brings about a sizeable reduction of poverty rates. Figures in Table 12.2 are computed by applying definition (12.3) using either net worth or total financial assets (top and bottom panels, respectively) for two values of the annuity interest rate, 2 percent and 10 percent. Following other applications in the literature, we use the income–net worth concept only for older households. More precisely, when the household head is older than 54 years, we replace cash property income with a zero-bequest annuity whose length is given by the remaining years of life of the household head, as indicated in the country's life table by sex and age for the year of the survey. When the head is 54 years old or younger, we do not make this replacement. By substituting for income alone with income–net worth, with the

Table 12.1 PER CAPITA DISPOSABLE INCOME, TOTAL FINANCIAL ASSETS, AND NET WORTH

Country	Disposable Income		Total Financial Assets		Net Worth		Net Worth to Disposable Income Ratio
	US Dollars	Index: US-PSID = 100	US Dollars	Index: US-PSID = 100	US Dollars	Index: US-PSID = 100	
Canada (1999)	14,215	68.9	10,962	39.1	36,475	55.3	2.6
Finland (1998)	11,277	54.7	6,547	23.3	33,968	51.5	3.0
Germany (2002)	13,146	63.7	8,448	30.1	51,492	78.1	3.9
Italy (2002)	10,546	51.1	10,800	38.5	70,342	106.6	6.7
Norway (2002)	17,168	83.2	17,819	63.5	—	—	—
Sweden (2002)	12,776	61.9	12,441	44.3	—	—	—
UK (2000)	12,892	62.5	12,011	42.8	57,051	86.5	4.4
US-PSID (2001)	20,629	100.0	28,061	100.0	65,957	100.0	3.2
US-SCF (2001)	18,325	88.8	42,155	150.2	87,437	132.6	4.8
Canada (1999)	11,938	77.8	863	64.8	13,020	91.7	1.1
Finland (1998)	9,603	62.6	1,301	97.6	18,545	130.6	1.9
Germany (2002)	10,879	70.9	0	0.0	12,914	90.9	1.2
Italy (2002)	8,868	57.8	2,817	211.4	42,268	297.7	4.8
Norway (2002)	14,569	94.9	3,754	281.6	—	—	—
Sweden (2002)	11,256	73.3	2,461	184.6	—	—	—
UK (2000)	10,907	71.1	1,544	115.8	26,071	183.6	2.4
US-PSID (2001)	15,349	100.0	1,333	100.0	14,200	100.0	0.9
US-SCF (2001)	12,459	81.2	1,950	146.3	13,000	91.5	1.0

NOTE: All values are in US dollars at purchasing power parities.

SOURCE: Authors' elaborations on LWS data (as of February 27, 2009).

Table 12.2 SHARE OF INCOME-POOR AND INCOME–NET WORTH–POOR HOUSEHOLDS, ALL HOUSEHOLDS

Country	National Lines			US-PSID Line		
	Income–net Worth Poor	Income Poor	Difference	Income–net Worth Poor	Income Poor	Difference
	Net Worth					
Annuity interest rate: 2 percent						
Finland (1998)	8.4	10.6	-2.2	30.8	39.8	-9.0
Germany (2002)	11.3	12.9	-1.6	25.8	30.6	-4.8
Italy (2002)	9.2	12.5	-3.3	29.8	42.3	-12.5
US-PSID (2001)	14.5	17.4	-2.9	14.5	17.4	-2.9
US-SCF (2001)	16.6	19.5	-2.9	23.7	27.5	-3.8
Annuity interest rate: 10 percent						
Finland (1998)	8.4	10.6	-2.2	28.5	39.8	-11.3
Germany (2002)	11.2	12.9	-1.7	24.9	30.6	-5.7
Italy (2002)	8.9	12.5	-3.6	27.8	42.3	-14.5
US-PSID (2001)	14.5	17.4	-2.9	14.5	17.4	-2.9
US-SCF (2001)	15.9	19.5	-3.6	22.9	27.5	-4.6

Total Financial Assets

Annuity interest rate: 2 percent

Finland (1998)	10.2	10.6	-0.4	39.6	39.8	-0.2
Germany (2002)	13.4	12.9	0.5	30.5	30.6	-0.1
Italy (2002)	12.3	12.5	-0.2	40.5	42.3	-1.8
US-PSID (2001)	16.3	17.4	-1.1	16.3	17.4	-1.1
US-SCF (2001)	19.0	19.5	-0.5	26.6	27.5	-0.9

Annuity interest rate: 10 percent

Finland (1998)	10.0	10.6	-0.6	38.6	39.8	-1.2
Germany (2002)	13.1	12.9	0.2	29.6	30.6	-1.0
Italy (2002)	12.1	12.5	-0.4	39.7	42.3	-2.6
US-PSID (2001)	16.3	17.4	-1.1	16.3	17.4	-1.1
US-SCF (2001)	18.5	19.5	-1.0	26.2	27.5	-1.3

SOURCE: Authors' elaborations on LWS data (as of February 27, 2009). All values are in US dollars at purchasing power parities and are equivalized by the square root equivalence scale.

national poverty lines, the portion who are poor falls by around three percentage points in the United States and Italy in the top left quarter of Table 12.2, and a little less in Finland and Germany. The impact is far larger with the common US-PSID threshold, especially for Italy. The change of the annuity interest rate from 2 percent to 10 percent makes some difference only when the common real US-PSID line is used. The country ranking does not vary, but the higher net worth holdings of Italian households produce the biggest reductions in measured poverty.

The comparison based on net worth is somewhat biased because it includes home equity, whereas income does not include the rental value of owner-occupied housing. On the other hand, home ownership provides not only a store of value but also a direct benefit by allowing people to satisfy the basic need of being sheltered (Fisher et al. 2007, 2009). This means that the house may not be a perfectly fungible asset, even if new financial instruments allow households to cash in part of housing equity by means of home equity loans. Another possibility is to narrow the wealth concept that is annuitized. By considering total financial assets, the reduction in measured poverty turns out to be fairly modest, at most one percentage point with the national lines, and less than three points using the fixed US-PSID line (bottom panel of Table 12.2).

In summary, poverty incidence varies according to both the poverty measure and the concept of income–net worth. The biggest variations across nations in income–net worth poverty are not due to the annuity rates assumed, but rather, to whether total net worth including housing is considered or whether we restrict the analysis to financial assets alone.

The results just discussed refer to the whole population and consider jointly the unadjusted incomes of younger households with the income–net worth of older households. Table 12.3 presents the same statistics for the latter group, households whose head is aged 55 years and over, alone. Income poverty is higher for this sub-group than for the whole population in Finland and the United States, whereas it is lower in Italy and Germany (compare Tables 12.2 and 12.3). The adoption of the income–net worth indicator understandably has a much larger impact on this sub-group because owner-occupied housing with no remaining mortgage payments is common for the age 55-years-and-over population in these nations. Germany is a partial exception to this pattern, as shown by Chiuri and Jappelli (2010), and indeed it exhibits the lowest poverty reduction in the top left quarter of Table 12.3.

More interestingly, there is a pronounced narrowing of the relative national line poverty differential between the United States and the European countries, indicating that the North American elderly are relatively richer once income–net worth is used as the measure of well-being (see top half of Table 12.3). Italy, on the other hand, exhibits the lowest incidence of (relative) poverty among households with heads aged 55 years or more. This result is driven by the fact that home ownership in Italy is very high and outstanding mortgage debt is very low. These factors together explain the large effects on poverty using income–net worth in the top half of Table 12.3 as compared to those for income–net worth using only financial assets in the bottom half, which are under four percentage points regardless of country or annuity rate.[9]

Next, we consider evidence for the second measure we employ in the study, which isolates the role of assets in buffering households from unexpected shocks. Table 12.4 contains information on asset-poverty incidence in eight LWS countries, the four already considered plus Canada, Norway, Sweden, and the United Kingdom. This

Table 12.3 Share of Income-Poor and Income–Net Worth–Poor Households, Households with Head Aged 55 Years and Over

Net Worth

Country	National Lines			US-PSID Line		
	Income–net Worth Poor	Income Poor	Difference	Income–net Worth Poor	Income Poor	Difference
Annuity interest rate: 2 percent						
Finland (1998)	6.7	13.3	−6.6	26.9	52.8	−25.9
Germany (2002)	7.8	11.4	−3.6	22.5	33.3	−10.8
Italy (2002)	5.2	11.9	−6.7	22.1	47.2	−25.1
US-PSID (2001)	8.9	18.0	−9.1	8.9	18.0	−9.1
US-SCF (2001)	13.5	21.9	−8.4	18.3	29.5	−11.2
Annuity interest rate: 10 percent						
Finland (1998)	6.5	13.3	−6.8	20.6	52.8	−32.2
Germany (2002)	7.4	11.4	−4.0	20.2	33.3	−13.1
Italy (2002)	4.5	11.9	−7.4	18.0	47.2	−29.2
US-PSID (2001)	8.9	18.0	−9.1	8.9	18.0	−9.1
US-SCF (2001)	11.6	21.9	−10.3	15.9	29.5	−13.6

Table 12.3 SHARE OF INCOME-POOR AND INCOME–NET WORTH–POOR HOUSEHOLDS, HOUSEHOLDS WITH HEAD AGED 55 YEARS AND OVER (*CONT'D*)

Country	National Lines			US-PSID Line		
	Income–net Worth Poor	Income Poor	Difference	Income–net Worth Poor	Income Poor	Difference
			Total Financial Assets			
Annuity interest rate: 2 percent						
Finland (1998)	12.2	13.3	-1.1	52.3	52.8	-0.5
Germany (2002)	12.6	11.4	1.2	33.0	33.3	-0.3
Italy (2002)	11.4	11.9	-0.5	43.7	47.2	-3.5
US-PSID (2001)	14.6	18.0	-3.4	14.6	18.0	-3.4
US-SCF (2001)	20.5	21.9	-1.4	26.8	29.5	-2.7
Annuity interest rate: 10 percent						
Finland (1998)	11.6	13.3	-1.7	49.5	52.8	-3.3
Germany (2002)	11.8	11.4	0.4	31.1	33.3	-2.2
Italy (2002)	10.9	11.9	-1.0	41.9	47.2	-5.3
US-PSID (2001)	14.6	18.0	-3.4	14.6	18.0	-3.4
US-SCF (2001)	19.1	21.9	-2.8	25.6	29.5	-3.9

SOURCE: Authors' elaborations on LWS data (as of February 27, 2009). All values are in US dollars at purchasing power parities and are equivalized by the square root equivalence scale.

concept of asset poverty tries to capture whether a consumer unit could maintain a standard of living above the poverty line for a certain period if it had no income, nor any financial resources or borrowing ability other than accumulated wealth. The figures in Table 12.4 take the period over which a household would attempt to meet their expenses from these resources to be three months; that is, the asset-poverty line is set at one-fourth of the annual income-based poverty line. As before, we use two wealth aggregates: financial assets and net worth.

The figures for income poverty, using national or US-PSID lines, are the same as in Table 12.2. Given the available data, we are now able to examine a larger number of nations, and we find Sweden at the bottom of the poverty ranking together with

Table 12.4 SHARE OF INCOME-POOR AND ASSET-POOR HOUSEHOLDS,
SELECTED COUNTRIES

Country	Income Poverty Line	Income Poor	Net Worth Poor	Income and Net Worth Poor	Financial Asset Poor	Income and Financial Asset Poor
National lines						
Canada (1999)	10,327	16.5	33.8	11.3	56.5	13.4
Finland (1998)	7,956	10.6	28.3	5.7	49.0	7.7
Germany (2002)	8,736	12.9	38.0	8.4	52.3	10.4
Italy (2002)	7,591	12.5	14.3	4.4	31.7	9.2
Norway (2002)	12,123	12.0	—	—	36.1	6.8
Sweden (2002)	8,934	10.2	—	—	42.8	6.0
UK (2000)	8,979	14.6	24.7	5.4	46.0	9.7
US-PSID (2001)	12,989	17.4	33.2	11.0	52.6	14.7
US-SCF (2001)	10,562	19.5	31.7	11.2	44.6	15.1
US-PSID line						
Canada (1999)	12,989	26.8	18.4	16.5	60.1	21.0
Finland (1998)	12,989	39.8	11.3	19.1	57.9	29.0
Germany (2002)	12,989	30.6	20.9	18.8	55.8	23.6
Italy (2002)	12,989	42.3	5.2	11.1	40.3	26.8
Norway (2002)	12,989	14.8	—	—	37.5	8.2
Sweden (2002)	12,989	32.3	—	—	47.4	19.6
UK (2000)	12,989	31.8	13.2	12.6	50.4	21.3
US-PSID (2001)	12,989	17.4	22.2	11.0	52.6	14.7
US-SCF (2001)	12,989	27.5	17.0	15.4	47.2	21.1

SOURCE: Authors' elaborations on LWS data (as of February 27, 2009). All values are in US dollars at purchasing power parities and are equivalized by the square root equivalence scale. The asset poverty line is set at one-fourth of the income poverty line.

Finland; Norway in the middle with Italy and Germany; and the United Kingdom and Canada close to the top. Using the national poverty lines, the United States still has the highest income poverty rates. Changing to the "real" US-PSID poverty line at the bottom, Norway is least poor based on income alone, followed by the United States.[10]

The rate of net worth poverty is two to three times that of income poverty in most nations, owing to those who have very low or no assets, both in terms of overall net worth and liquid assets. Of course, it would be difficult to liquidate housing wealth if income flows were zero, but the availability of home equity loans and second mortgages makes this possible in most nations (see Fisher et al. 2007, for US estimates).

Most interestingly, the fraction of units that are both income- *and* financial asset-poor are only a few points less than those who are income-poor (second vs. last column in Table 12.4). When we take the asset nonpoor from the income poor, poverty falls by about two to three percentage points in all countries using the national lines, except in Norway, the United Kingdom, and Sweden, where the drops are larger, in the four to five points range. Using the US-PSID poverty line and the extant purchasing power parities, we find that poverty drops are even larger, with Norway again being the least poor country. In most nations, 20 percent to 30 percent of the populations are both income- and asset-poor.

Regardless of whether the poverty threshold is set nationally or at the US level, the application of our asset-poverty measures highlights the fact that a large proportion of nonpoor households in all countries are "vulnerable" in the sense that they do not have enough financial assets to maintain them at the poverty line for at least three months (compare the last two columns of Table 12.4). This proportion is probably not independent of the development of the welfare state, and indeed the lowest proportion is found for Italy, where social assistance measures are relatively less generous than in other European countries. The link between asset poverty (or nonpoverty) and the development of the welfare state is an interesting subject for future research.

CONCLUSIONS

The integration of wealth into the analysis of poverty poses both empirical and conceptual problems. On the empirical side, in many countries there are household-level data that can help us to shed light on cross-national differences in household finances. Thanks to the meticulous work done to construct and document the LWS database, we now have some broadly comparable national wealth data sets, but we are also aware that many problems remain. Comparative results must be taken with caution. The challenge is to begin a much needed process of ex ante standardization of methods and definitions, which involves wealth data producers. The LWS database provides a starting point, and the launch of the new Eurosystem Household Finance and Consumption Survey will give further impetus to this process (Eurosystem Household Finance and Consumption Network 2009).

The availability of good data, however, does not suffice. The development of analytical tools for the integration of wealth into the measurement of poverty has lagged behind in the poverty research agenda. There are notable exceptions, as our concise review has shown. In this chapter, we have sketched a conceptual framework for asset-based measures of poverty. It is a first attempt to systematize the field, providing a unified way to look at existing research. Our empirical comparative results, however tentative because of the data problems, suggest that asset-related measures of poverty have additional informational value with respect to income-based statistics and others such as material hardship. The pools of asset poor and income poor and the way in which they overlap differ across countries. The concept of asset poverty has wide policy interest, as many countries, including the United States, are emphasizing the accumulation of financial assets by lower income families as an antipoverty strategy (see Blank and Barr 2008), even while the asset tests in many income transfer programs reduce access and eligibility (Bansak and Raphael 2007; Smeeding 2002). We need to better understand the properties of these alternative indicators and assess their sensitivity to different assumptions, especially in the case of the income–net worth measure.

ACKNOWLEDGMENTS

We thank Tony Atkinson, Kenneth Couch, and Maureen Pirog for very useful comments, and Deborah Johnson and Dawn Duren for manuscript preparation. We also thank participants in the joint OECD/University of Maryland conference "Measuring Poverty, Income Inequality, and Social Exclusion. Lessons from Europe" (Paris, March 16–17, 2009); the Third Meeting of the Society for the Study of Economic Inequality (Buenos Aires, July 21–23, 2009); the Third OECD World Forum on "Statistics, Knowledge and Policy" (Busan, October 27–30, 2009); the Association for Public Policy Analysis and Management special preconference workshop "European Measures of Income, Poverty, and Social Exclusion: Recent Developments and Lessons for U.S. Poverty Measurement" (Washington, DC, November 4, 2009); and in seminars at the University of Rome Sapienza and University of Modena. The views expressed here are solely ours; in particular, they do not necessarily reflect those of the Bank of Italy or the Institute for Research on Poverty.

Notes

1. Should we apply Hicks's well-known definition that "a person's income is what he can consume during the week and still expect to be as well off at the end of the week as he was at the beginning" (1946, 176), we should subtract from CY_t the loss in purchasing power caused by inflation on nonindexed nominal assets such as bank deposits or treasury bills; that is, we should replace the nominal rate of return r_t with the real rate of return $(r_t - \pi)$, where π is the inflation rate. We ignore this correction, as it has never been applied in the literature.
2. Not all assets can be sold immediately at their market value. For our purposes, an asset may be valued on a *realization* basis, net of the costs that have to be incurred in the case of immediate sale, or "the value obtained in a sale on the open market at the date in question" (Atkinson and Harrison 1978, 5).
3. In an investigation of the distribution of income and wealth among old Europeans based on data from the Survey of Health, Ageing and Retirement in Europe, Christelis et al. (2009) define *financial fragility* as a situation where a

household's financial wealth does not exceed three months of the household gross income.

4. Rendall and Speare (1993) proposed a more general annuitization formula, allowing for different life expectancies for the partners in a couple.

5. For a description of the LWS database, see http://www.lisdatacenter.org/ and Sierminska, Brandolini, and Smeeding (2008). The list of the original surveys used in this chapter, the agency producing them, and some summary characteristics are reported in Appendix 12.B.

6. The half median poverty line in the PSID in Table 12.1 is much higher than the official US absolute poverty line used annually by the Census Bureau to measure US poverty. The US poverty line is now 26 percent of Current Population Survey median income, whereas our fixed poverty line is 50 percent of PSID median income (Smeeding 2006).

7. Found at http://www.lisdatacenter.org/data-access/key-figures/.

8. In 2000, the official US poverty rate using the US cash-only before-tax income definition produced a poverty rate of 11.3 percent as compared to the 17.4 percent and 19.5 percent rates in Table 12.4 (US Census Bureau 2008, Table B-1, 46). Apart from many differences in methods and definitions, it should be borne in mind that the former figure is based on an absolute poverty line, whereas the latter two figures are based on relative poverty lines.

9. These differences do not reflect demographic factors across these nations, especially at older ages. Instead the differences are due to types of wealth holding and the relative values of each type of wealth, for instance housing wealth in Italy (see Table 12.1).

10. Using SCF data, Haveman and Wolff (2004) find a lower incidence than we do of income, net worth, and liquid asset poverty in the United States in 2001 (13.2 percent, 24.5 percent, and 37.5 percent, respectively). These different results reflect differences in definitions as well as the use of the absolute poverty line proposed by the US National Academy of Sciences report (Citro and Michael 1995).

References

Atkinson, Anthony B. 1975. *The Economics of Inequality.* 1st ed. Oxford: Clarendon Press.

Atkinson, Anthony B., and Anthony J. Harrison. 1978. *Distribution of Personal Wealth in Britain.* Cambridge: Cambridge University Press.

Bansak, Cynthia, and Steven Raphael. 2007. "The Effects of State Policy Design Features on Take-Up and Crowd-Out Rates for the State Children's Health Insurance Program." *Journal of Policy Analysis and Management* 26 (1): 149–175.

Barceló, Cristina, and Ernesto Villanueva. 2009. "The Response of Household Wealth to the Risk of Losing the Job: Evidence from Differences in Firing Costs." Mimeo, Banco de España, Madrid.

Blank, Rebecca M., and Michael Barr. 2008. *Insufficient Funds: Savings, Assets, Credit, and Banking among Low-Income Households.* New York: Russell Sage Foundation Press.

Bowles, Samuel, and Herbert Gintis. 1998. "Efficient Redistribution: New Rules for Markets, States and Communities." In *Recasting Egalitarianism: New Rules for Communities, States and Markets.* Edited by Erik Olin Wright, 3–71. London: Verso.

Burkhauser, Richard V., J. S. Butler, and James T. Wilkinson. 1985. "Estimating Changes in Well-Being across Life: A Realized versus Comprehensive Income Approach." In *Horizontal Equity, Uncertainty, and Economic Well-Being*. Edited by David Martin and Timothy M. Smeeding, 69–90. Chicago: University of Chicago Press.

Burkhauser, Richard V., and James T. Wilkinson. 1982. "The Effect of Retirement on Income Distribution: A Comprehensive Income Approach." *Review of Economics and Statistics* 65 (4): 653–658.

Carlin, Thomas A., and Edward I. Reinsel. 1973. "Combining Income and Wealth: An Analysis of Farm Family 'Well-Being.'" *American Journal of Agricultural Economics* 55 (1): 38–44.

Carroll, Christopher D., Karen E. Dynan, and Spencer D. Krane. 2003. "Unemployment Risk and Precautionary Wealth: Evidence from Households' Balance Sheets." *Review of Economics and Statistics* 85 (3): 586–604.

Citro, Constance F., and Robert T. Michael, eds. 1995. *Measuring Poverty: A New Approach*. Washington, DC: National Academy Press.

Chiuri, Maria C., and Tullio Jappelli. 2010. "Do the Elderly Reduce Housing Equity? An International Comparison." *Journal of Population Economics* 23 (2): 643–663.

Christelis, Dimitris, Tullio Jappelli, Omar Paccagnella, and Guglielmo Weber. 2009. "Income, Wealth and Financial Fragility in Europe." *Journal of European Social Policy* 19 (4): 359–376.

Crystal, Stephen and Dennis Shea. 1990. "The Economic Well-Being of the Elderly." *Review of Income and Wealth* 36 (3): 227–247.

El Osta, Hisham S., Ashok K. Mishra, and Mitchell J. Morehart. 2007. "Determinants of Economic Well-Being among U.S. Farm Operator Households." *Agricultural Economics* 36 (3): 291–304.

European Commission. 2008. *The Social Situation in the European Union 2007: Social Cohesion through Equal Opportunities*. Luxembourg: Office for Official Publications of the European Communities.

Eurosystem Household Finance and Consumption Network. 2009. *Survey Data on Household Finance and Consumption. Research Summary and Policy Use*. European Central Bank Occasional Paper 100. Frankfurt am Main: European Central Bank.

Fisher, Jonathan, David Johnson, Joseph T. Marchand, Timothy M. Smeeding, and Barbara Boyle Torrey. 2007. "No Place like Home: Older Adults, Housing, and the Life-Cycle." *Journal of Gerontology: Social Sciences* 62B (2): 8120–8128.

———. 2009. "Identifying the Poorest Older Americans." *Journal of Gerontology: Social Sciences* 64B (6): 758–766.

Gornick, Janet C., Eva Sierminska, and Timothy M. Smeeding. 2009. "The Income and Wealth Packages of Older Women in Cross-National Perspective." *Journal of Gerontology: Social Sciences* 64B (3): 402–414.

Haveman, Robert, and Edward N. Wolff. 2004. "The Concept and Measurement of Asset Poverty: Levels, Trends and Composition for the U.S., 1983–2001." *Journal of Economic Inequality* 2 (2): 145–169.

Hicks, John R. 1946. *Value and Capital*. 2nd ed. Oxford: Clarendon Press.

Irvine, Ian. 1980. "The Distribution of Income and Wealth in Canada in a Lifecycle Framework." *Canadian Economic Association* 13 (3): 455–474.

Kennickell, Arthur B., and Annamaria Lusardi. 2005. "Disentangling the Importance of the Precautionary Saving Motive." Mimeo, Federal Reserve Board of Governors, Washington, DC.

Moon, Marilyn L. 1976. "The Economic Welfare of the Aged and Income Security Programs." Review *of Income and Wealth* 22 (3): 253–269.

Niskanen, Emilia. 2007. *The Luxembourg Wealth Study: Technical Report on LWS Income Variables*. Luxembourg Income Study, Technical Paper No. 2, Luxembourg. http://www.lisdatacenter.org/wp-content/uploads/2011/02/technical-report-on-income-variables-2011-03.pdf.

OECD. 2008. "Rates of Conversion." In *OECD Factbook 2008: Economic, Environmental and Social Statistics*. Paris: Organization for Economic Co-operation and Development. http://titania.sourceoecd.org/vl=945493/cl=11/nw=1/rpsv/factbook/040201.htm.

Projector, Dorothy, and Gertrude Weiss. 1969. "Income–Net Worth Measures of Economic Welfare." *Social Security Bulletin* 32 (11): 14–17.

Radner, Daniel B. 1990. "Assessing the Economic Status of the Aged and Nonaged Using Alternative Income-Wealth Measures." *Social Security Bulletin* 53 (3): 2–14.

Rendall, Michael S., and Alden Speare. 1993. "Comparing Economic Well-Being among Elderly Americans." *Review of Income and Wealth* 39 (1): 1–21.

———. 1995. "Elderly Poverty Alleviation through Living with Family." *Journal of Population Economics* 8 (4): 383–405.

Sierminska, Eva, Andrea Brandolini, and Timothy M. Smeeding. 2008. "Comparing Wealth Distribution across Rich Countries: First Results from the Luxembourg Wealth Study." In *Banca d'Italia: Household wealth in Italy. Papers presented at the conference held in Perugia, 16–17 October 2007*. 167–190. Rome: Banca d'Italia.

Short, Kathleen, and Patricia Ruggles. 2005. "Experimental Measures of Poverty and Net Worth: 1996." *Journal of Income Distribution* 13 (3–4): 8–21.

Smeeding, Timothy M. 2002. "The EITC and USAs/IDAs: Maybe a Marriage Made in Heaven?" *Georgetown Public Policy Review* 8 (1): 7–27.

———.2006. "Poor People in Rich Nations: The United States in Comparative Perspective." *Journal of Economic Perspectives* 20 (1): 69–90.

Taussig, Michael K. 1973. *Alternative Measures of the Distribution of Economic Welfare*. Princeton: Princeton University, Industrial Relations Section.

US Census Bureau. 2008. *Income, Poverty, and Health Insurance Coverage in the United States: 2007*. Prepared by Carmen DeNavas-Walt, Bernadette D. Proctor, and Jessica C. Smith. Current Population Reports P60–235. Washington, DC: US Government Printing Office.

Weisbrod, Burton A., and W. Lee Hansen. 1968. "An Income–Net Worth Approach to Measuring Economic Welfare." *American Economic Review* 58 (5): 1315–1329.

Wolff, Edward N., and Ajit Zacharias. 2007. "The Levy Institute Measure of Economic Well-Being in the United States, 1989–2001." *Eastern Economic Journal* 33 (4): 443–470.

World Bank. 2001. *World Development Report 2000/2001: Attacking Poverty*. Oxford: Oxford University Press.

Yates, Judith, and Bruce Bradbury. 2009. "Home Ownership as a (Crumbling) Fourth Pillar of Social Insurance in Australia." Mimeo, Social Policy Research Center, University of New South Wales, New South Wales, Australia.

Some Applications of the Income–Net Worth Measure to Microdata

Authors	Country	Year	Source	Reference Population	Length of Annuity (n)	Annuity Interest Rate (ρ) (%)
Carlin and Reinsel (1973)	US	1966	Pesticide and General Farm Survey	All farm families	Life expectancy of wife assumed two years younger than spouse	6
Taussig (1973)	US	1967	Survey of Economic Opportunity	—	—	6
Moon (1976)	US	1967	Survey of Economic Opportunity	All families with a person aged 65 years and over	Average life expectancy of aged family member and spouse	4
Irvine (1980)	Canada	1972	Statistics Canada and Survey of Consumer Finance	All households	Stochastic process to retrieve mortality rates	5.5
Burkhauser and Wilkinson (1982)	US	1969–1975	Retirement History Study	Subsample of married men aged 58 through 63 years who worked in 1969 but had retired in 1975	Life expectancy at the average age of the sample in 1969 and 1975	5
Burkhauser, Butler, and Wilkinson (1985)	US	1969–1979	Retirement History Study	Household aged 55–64 years		5
Crystal and Shea (1990)	US	1983–1984	Survey of Income and Program Participation	All persons	Individual life expectancy	2

Wealth Concept	Impact on Mean		Poverty Line	Head Count Ratio (%)		Other Adjustments
	Income[a]	Income–net Worth		Income[a]	Income–net Worth	
Net worth	$5,300 $4,200[b]	$7,600 $6,100[b]	$2,500	32	15	—
—	—	—	—	—	—	—
Net worth	$2,427[b]	$3,743[b]	$2,000	40.4	25.2	Downward adjustment of home equity
Net worth	$8,359	$12,160.5	—	—	—	Also estimates of future earnings and discounted value of lifetime earnings
Net worth	—	—	Census Bureau poverty line $3,257 in 1975	—	—	—
Net worth	1969: $20,179 1979: $11,207	1969: $35,076 1979: $19,875	—	—	—	—
Total assets	0–64: $22,780 65+: $23,109	0–64: $23,410 65+: $28,637	—	—	—	70 percent of home equity as fungible; adjustment for underreporting

(*Continued*)

Authors	Country	Year	Source	Reference Population	Length of Annuity (n)	Annuity Interest Rate (ρ) (%)
Radner (1990)	US	1984	Survey of Income and Program Participation	All households	Expected remaining lifetime of the unit	2
Rendall and Speare (1993)	US	1984	Survey of Income and Program Participation	All households with a person aged 65 years and over	Life expectancies of family head and spouse; infinite horizon for nonelderly.	−0.41.6
Rendall and Speare (1995)	US	1984	Survey of Income and Program Participation	All households with a person aged 65 years and over	Life expectancies of family head and spouse; infinite horizon for nonelderly.	−0.42
Short and Ruggles (2005)	US	1996	Survey of Income and Program Participation	All persons	Life expectancy of family head	2 4 2/6
El Osta, Mishra, and Morehart (2007)	US	2001	Agricultural and Resource Management Survey	Farm households	Life expectancy of the unit	4
Wolff and Zacharias (2007)	US	1989 1995 2001	Survey of Consumer Finance	All persons	Maximum life expectancy between head and spouse	Weighted average of historic real rates

[a] The income concept varies across studies.
[b] Median.
[c] Impact when one-third of financial assets are included.
[d] Ratio of the median to the poverty line.
NOTE: SSA is Social Security Administration.

Wealth Concept	Impact on Mean		Poverty Line	Head Count Ratio (%)		Other Adjustments
	Income[a]	Income–net Worth		Income[a]	Income–net Worth	
Financial assets (because of the higher liquidity)	$14,600[b]	$14,600[b] $16,600[c]	—	—	—	—
Total assets	1.77[d] 1.97[d]	2.42[d] 2.57[d]	1.25 × SSA line	15.1 12.0	8.9 8.2	Correction for: remaining work lifetime; death of partner
Total assets	—	—	1.25 × SSA line	—	—	They also consider results under a model with bequests. The elderly switch from finite to infinite horizon.
Total assets Net worth Total assets/ debt	—	—	Official	13.3	11.3 11.0 12.6	—
Net worth	—	—	—	—	—	—
Net worth less gross value of owner-occupied housing	$42,198[b]	$45,392[b]	—	—	—	Income adjusted by household production and public services

APPENDIX 12.B

LWS Household Wealth Surveys

Country	Name	Agency	Wealth Year[a]	Income Year	Type of Source	Oversampling of the Wealthy	Sample Size	No. of Nonmissing Net Worth	Number of Wealth Items
Canada	Survey of Financial Security (SFS)	Statistics Canada	1999	1998	Sample survey	Yes	15,933	15,933	17
Finland	Household Wealth Survey (HWS)	Statistics Finland	End of 1998	1998	Sample survey	No	3,893	3,893	23
Germany	Socio-Economic Panel (SOEP)	Deutsches Institut Für Wirtschafts-forschung (DIW) Berlin	2002	2001	Sample panel survey	Yes	12,692	12,129	9
Italy	Survey of Household Income and Wealth (SHIW)	Bank of Italy	End of 2002	2002	Sample survey (panel section)	No	8,011	8,010	34
Norway	Income Distribution Survey (IDS)	Statistics Norway	End of 2002	2002	Sample survey plus administrative records	No	22,870	22,870	35
Sweden	Wealth Survey (HINK)	Statistics Sweden	End of 2002	2002	Sample survey plus administrative records	No	17,954	17,954	26

(Continued)

Country	Name	Agency	Wealth Year[a]	Income Year	Type of Source	Oversampling of the Wealthy	Sample Size	No. of Nonmissing Net Worth	Number of Wealth Items
United Kingdom	British Household Panel Survey (BHPS)	ESRC	2000	2000	Sample panel survey	No	4,867[b]	4,185	7
United States	Panel Study of Income Dynamics (PSID)	Survey Research Center of the University of Michigan	2001	2000	Sample panel survey	No	7,406	7,071	14
	Survey of Consumer Finances (SCF)	Federal Reserve Board and US Department of Treasury	2001	2000	Sample survey	Yes	4,442[c]	4,442[c]	30

[a] Values refer to the time of the interview unless otherwise indicated.

[b] Original survey sample. Sample size can rise to 8,761 when weights are not used.

[c] Data are stored as five successive replicates of each record that should not be used separately; thus, actual sample size for users is 22,210. The special sample of the wealthy includes 1,532 households.

SOURCE: Sierminska, Brandolini, and Smeeding (2008), Table 1.

13

Consumption-Based Measures in Developing Nations

Lessons from Brazil

PETER LANJOUW ■

INTRODUCTION

The analysis of poverty and inequality is a well-established field of research that serves as an important input into policy making. Even though the very meaning of poverty and inequality remains the subject of debate, and differences of opinion persist in how to best study such themes, certain basic steps in the empirical analysis of household welfare have become reasonably standard.

Whereas the ultimate shape and scope of the analysis can vary dramatically, a nearly universal requirement for any empirical study of well-being is that individuals (or households) must be ranked on the basis of one or more indicators of living standards—usually income or consumption expenditures (but sometimes other indicators such as nutritional status, access to basic services, or even a composite measure). The choice and definition of an appropriate indicator might seem a fairly straightforward task. However, a person embarking on such an exercise is quickly confronted by a whole range of issues, many of which will require some kind of decision making and on which guidance, in the form of best-practice conventions or theoretically derived results, is still rather scarce. As the basic welfare indicator serves as the foundation on which most of the subsequent, detailed, analysis of welfare is based, it is important to select an indicator that can command broad endorsement and that will hopefully not require substantive revision.

In this chapter, we are concerned with deriving a welfare indicator for households that captures the economic dimensions of well-being. We focus specifically on a developing country setting, Brazil, and illustrate how, in this setting, we construct a welfare indicator based on consumption expenditures. There are both conceptual and pragmatic reasons why consumption expenditures available from household surveys might be preferred for the purpose of poverty and inequality analysis to an indicator such as household income. It is argued, for example, that *consumption* represents the *achievement* of a particular welfare level, whereas *income* reflects *opportunity* to achieve a certain level. A focus on achievement in certain cases may be of particular interest to policy makers or researchers, particularly in developing country circumstances where extreme destitution may be directly associated with actual physical survival. Consumption expenditures reflect not only what a household is able to command based on its current income, but also whether that household can access credit markets or household savings, or can tap into intrafamilial or intracommunity transfers of resources, at times when current incomes are low or even negative (due perhaps to seasonal variation or a harvest failure). For this reason, there may be a significant wedge between current consumption and current income levels, with consumption providing a better picture of a household's longer run standard of living than a measure of current income. Further, in a developing country setting, measuring consumption expenditures is often easier than tabulating household incomes, particularly for the poor. While poor households are probably purchasing and consuming only a relatively narrow range of goods and services, their total income may derive from multiple different activities with strong seasonal variation and with associated costs that are not always easily assigned. Getting an accurate net income figure for such households can be frustratingly difficult. Where consumption information is collected, an additional advantage is that not only are consumption expenditures available, but an absolute poverty line can often be derived from the same survey, thereby strengthening the link between the welfare indicator used in the analysis and the threshold determined to separate the poor from the nonpoor.

This chapter examines the construction of a consumption measure for the specific case of Brazil, providing an illustration of the conceptual approach and practical implementation of this procedure. The setting is quite specific, and it is unlikely that precisely the same issues would be confronted in another context. But the goal is to convey a flavor of the kind of issues that may be encountered. In Brazil, detailed information on household consumption expenditures have been collected in the most recent *Pesquisa de Orçamentos Familiares* (POF) of 2002/2003 fielded by the Instituto Brasileiro de Geografia e Estatística (IBGE). We consider how best to construct a consumption aggregate from these data for the purpose of analyzing poverty and inequality. The discussion first considers the available building blocks for producing a consumption aggregate in the POF and reviews some of the principles and issues that can guide decisions as to whether, and provides a flavor of the details involved in deciding how, specific items should be included in the aggregate. The development of the argument points toward a few limitations in the way certain components of consumption are collected and raises some concerns with respect to the observed presence of extreme values in the data set. Such outliers can have a very strong impact on poverty and inequality measures, and to the extent that one might have doubts that the outliers are actually conveying accurate information, there are arguments in favor of trimming these extreme observations from the data. Some of these issues are explored via simple sensitivity analysis. The conclusion is drawn that as details of the consumption aggregation procedure can have a significant bearing on measured welfare, analysts working with such data should be familiar with these details and should beware of the intimate link between methodological considerations and conclusions.

THE BRAZIL POF SURVEY AND SOME BASIC PRINCIPLES

Brazil's POF is a nationally representative expenditure survey that was fielded by IBGE in 2002/2003. Previous waves of the POF, in 1987/1988 and 1995/1996, had been fielded only in nine metropolitan areas (plus Goiânia and Distrito Federal), but in 2002/2003, IBGE extended the sample to the country as a whole. It is representative at the state level for urban and all-state totals: for rural areas, the sample is designed be representative at the regional level only. The broad spatial coverage of the 2002/2003 POF is extremely valuable for the purpose of welfare analysis, because it marks the first time in several decades that a nationally representative survey yielding consumption information is available in Brazil. The overall sample size of the POF 2002/2003 is just under 50,000 households.

Historically, the principal objective of the POF surveys had been to provide detailed information on household expenditures required to produce cost of living indices such as the Consumer Price Index. In recent years, there has also been a growing interest in the collection of data that are better suited to the measurement of economic well-being. Analysis of well-being in Brazil has tended to employ income data from the *Pesquisa Nacional por Amostro de Domicilios* (PNAD). Ferreira, Lanjouw, and Neri (2003) suggest that the PNAD might not be suitable for at least some aspects of welfare analysis in Brazil. This appears to be especially the case for analyzing rural welfare, where it is unclear that the PNAD survey collects reliable information on farming activities (see also Elbers et al. 2001). One other survey fielded by IBGE in recent years has included consumption information—the *Pesquisa Sobre Padroes de Vida* of 1996. However, this survey had a relatively abbreviated consumption questionnaire, was fairly small in sample size (about 5,000 households), and covered only the northeast and southeast of the country (see Ferreira, Lanjouw, and Neri 2003, for further discussion).

The process of creating a consumption aggregate is guided by a number of considerations. Here we provide an overview of some of the issues that arise and the principles that can be applied. Our treatment is informal and far from exhaustive. A more complete reference document on this whole topic can be found in Deaton and Zaidi (2002). An important initial consideration is that, as our measure is supposed to proxy welfare, there is an interest in having as *comprehensive* a measure of consumption as possible. This is because a consumption measure that is narrowly defined would imply, when comparing welfare levels of households or individuals, that omitted components do not contribute in any way to welfare. Or alternatively, that while certain consumption components are omitted and are important to welfare, they would be distributed across members of the population in such a way that they would not affect rankings were they to be included. The extent to which these implicit assumptions seem reasonable varies with the specific components of consumption in question, but as a general rule, one would want to include as many components of consumption as is feasible.

However, it is often not possible to include all components of consumption in an equally straightforward manner. For several components it becomes necessary to introduce additional assumptions in order to be able to add these to the consumption aggregate. This can quickly add to the complexity of the exercise and can threaten the *transparency* of the process.

Some additional complexity need not in and of itself justify abandoning the exercise, except insofar as the *credibility* of the entire undertaking is thrown into doubt. The value of the entire enterprise of welfare analysis rests crucially on the degree to which the conclusions can receive broad endorsement. As subsequent strategies aimed at income redistribution or poverty alleviation all rest on the credibility of the underlying consumption aggregate, it is vitally important not to sacrifice credibility in the process of adding some particularly tricky consumption component to the aggregate.

In deriving a "preferred" consumption measure for Brazil on the basis of the POF data, the multiple objectives of comprehensiveness, transparency, and credibility received central focus. The exercise was approached in a series of tentative steps, with care being taken to not force disparate consumption components into the final aggregate at the cost of unacceptably speculative assumptions or convoluted argumentation.

Constructing the POF Consumption Aggregate

The POF survey collects information on household acquisitions of goods (purchased for own use or for other households, received as gift, and self-produced) in the previous periods of 7, 30, and 90 days, and 12 months. Different recall periods for different consumption items are commonly introduced in survey questionnaires in accordance with the frequency with which the items are typically purchased. The ultimate goal is to derive an overall aggregate consumption measure over a certain period of time, say, one year. In this case, multiplying the "typical" week's consumption of those goods that are usually purchased on a weekly basis by 52 weeks is likely to be more accurate than to ask households to report their annual spending on such frequently purchased goods. At the same time, asking about purchases over the past year of infrequently acquired goods such as large consumer durables, would seem quite reasonable. In the POF survey, the seven-days recall module refers to acquisitions of food, both inside and outside the home, and transport expenses. A 30-day recall period was applied to a range of nonfood consumption goods, such as pharmaceutical products, and also leisure and entertainment. The 90-day reference period includes clothing and a variety of services, among other items. The expenses made throughout the 12-month period comprise the acquisition of durable goods (e.g., houses, cars, and electronic appliances). The overall POF-based consumption measure for Brazil comprises 10 broad categories of items: Food consumption (including consumption inside and outside the home); Housing; Health; Schooling/Education; Transport; Clothes; Culture/Leisure; Personal Services; Hygiene and personal care; and Others.

Although the process of constructing a consumption aggregate would seem to imply that the exercise is simply one of assembling all the subcomponents of consumption from the various categories into a broad aggregate, in fact there is a need to consider each component in turn as there are certain types of goods that cannot be so readily incorporated into the aggregate. In general, special consideration must be given to: (1) "lumpy" items purchased sporadically; (2) items that serve as inputs into production or investments; (3) items with low elasticity with respect to total expenditure; and (4) items acquired for other households. In certain circumstances, such items may not end up being included in the final consumption aggregate. We discuss briefly the criteria for not including these items in a consumption aggregate that is intended for welfare analysis.

"LUMPY" AND INFREQUENT ACQUISITIONS
Consumer durable purchases are typically large expenditures that occur very infrequently. A classic example is the purchase of a car or motorcycle. A particular

household is likely to purchase a car only once every number of years. With a 12-month recall period, there will be a certain subset of households in the data who do indeed report purchasing a car. They will report spending a considerable sum of money for this item. Other households in the data set will, in fact, own a car but will have purchased it in some preceding period and will thus report zero expenditure in purchasing a car during the past year. Attributing a consumption value of zero to households that own but did not purchase a car in the specific recall period will understate their welfare because they will in fact be consuming the services of a car. Attributing the purchase value to those households in the data that happened to buy a car during the reference period will overstate their welfare because they will not be consuming all of the services provided by it in this one-year reference period. The car's services will be consumed over a period of several years. The attributes of this type of consumer durable imply that it is unappealing to simply add expenditures over the reference period directly to the consumption aggregate. Where possible, a flow of consumption from consumer durables can be added to the consumption aggregate, imputed from the available information on ownership, age, and replacement value of consumer durables. Deaton and Zaidi (2002) provide a good discussion of the available methods. However, in the POF, although there is a section on the inventory of durable stocks for households owning goods over a longer time span, the questionnaire does not include information on value (either at the time of the original purchase or in terms of the current replacement value), so it is not possible to calculate the flow of services from durables. Rather than including purchases on large, infrequent, durables in the consumption aggregate, it is preferable to drop such expenditures from the aggregate.

ITEMS THAT SERVE AS INPUTS INTO PRODUCTION OR INVESTMENTS

One key concern throughout the process must be to avoid treating spending for production or investment purposes as consumption. If one includes expenditures on inputs into household production, and the income from household production is in turn devoted (at least in part) to consumption expenditure, then double counting occurs, and the consumption aggregate is overstating the actual welfare levels achieved by the household. In most circumstances, the distinction between productive inputs and consumption is rather obvious. For example, it is clear that fertilizer expenditures should not be reflected in the consumption aggregate for farming households. However, in some cases, the distinction is less clear. In developing countries such as Brazil, where incomes derive to a considerable extent from home enterprise activities (e.g., farming or small-scale commercial activities), expenditures on productive activities are often a large fraction of total spending. Great care must be taken to not treat these as consumption expenditures.

AMBIGUOUS CONSUMPTION ITEMS WITH LOW ELASTICITY
WITH RESPECT TO TOTAL EXPENDITURE

In some cases, it is difficult to determine the effect on welfare of certain expenditures. Spending on health products and services are a good example. It is difficult to measure the extent to which health expenditures increase welfare because it is not possible to measure the loss of welfare from illness and the increase in welfare from its alleviation. Similarly, it is not obvious that in the case of two households with identical expenditures except that one is also spending for health care, that this latter household has higher welfare than the former. Mechanically including such expenditures is unappealing, but at the same time, excluding health expenditures altogether could mean that one may miss important welfare differences between two people, both of whom are sick, but only one of whom is paying for treatment. The question then arises whether dropping from the analysis such expenditures is likely to significantly affect welfare comparisons across households. Deaton and Zaidi (2002) recommend confronting this question by analyzing the elasticity of expenditure on health items and services with respect to total expenditure. The higher the elasticity, the stronger the case for inclusion. This is because failure to include these expenditures could result in a significant reranking of households in terms of total expenditures. When the elasticity is low, dropping health expenditures from the analysis is less risky: Household rankings in terms of final expenditures are not so dependent on this decision. We will analyze the elasticity of health and education expenditures in POF data when explaining the components of the consumption aggregate.

ITEMS ACQUIRED FOR OTHER HOUSEHOLDS

Goods acquired for gifts to other households should be excluded from the consumption aggregate, because their inclusion would involve double-counting if, as one would expect, the transfers show up in the consumption of other households. Therefore, it is recommended to include only the goods acquired as a gift from others, which increase the well-being of that household, but not the expenses made in that household for increasing consumption of other households.

Food Consumption

We turn now to a brief discussion of the broad subcategories of spending in the POF and how each was treated in the development of an overall consumption aggregate. Where specific issues arise, they are highlighted, and the particular course of action taken to address them is described.

The food consumption module in the POF comprises a diary left with each household for a period of seven days. Households are requested to provide a detailed description for each day of the week, of all items of food that are purchased or otherwise acquired—including acquisition through home production in the case of households involved in farming, livestock rearing, and so on. The questionnaire requires the household's key informant to note each specific food item acquired, the quantity obtained (including specifying the unit of measurement in which the quantity is recorded), and also the value, location, and the form of the acquisition (e.g., purchased, received as gift, produced by the household itself). In this way, very detailed information is collected from each household about its food purchases during a period of seven days.

The food component of the consumption aggregate comprises the value of spending on, and acquisition out of home production of, food items for consumption both inside and outside the home. Aggregating across all items, over the whole week, yields a measure of household weekly food consumption. Multiplying this by the number of weeks in a month or in a year yields a measure of monthly or annual food consumption. Although it may not be strictly the case that all food acquired in a

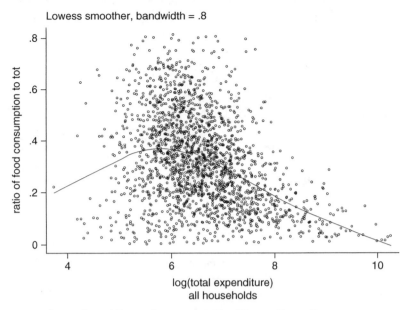

Figure 13.1 Share of Food Expenditure versus Total Expenditure: Ceara.

given week is consumed that week, the general assumption is that at the monthly or annual level, total food expenditures indicate the value of total food consumed by the household. This procedure provides the first component of the overall POF-based household consumption aggregate.

Figure 13.1 relates household-level food shares in one state, Ceara, to total consumption expenditures (based on the total expenditure figure that has been produced by IBGE to accompany the POF data). A nonparametric regression curve traces out the Engel curve summarizing the relationship, on average, between total household consumption and the value of food consumption. Contrary to Engel's law, which states that the food share declines with total consumption, there is clear evidence here that the Engel curve in Ceara first rises before it starts to decline.[1] Why is this happening? Consider a simple example. Suppose that most households in Brazil actually purchase food on a fortnightly basis (with households uniformly spread across weeks) but that the recording period in the POF is one week. Let F = average weekly food consumption expenditure and Y = average weekly total consumption expenditure. Suppose further that nonfood expenditure = $(Y - F)$ is correctly measured due to a longer recording period. If n households are sampled from a group with identical $\{F,Y\}$, $n/2$ will have food purchases of $f = 2F$, with $y = Y + F$, and $n/2$ will have $f = 0$, with $y = Y - F$. The mean food expenditure is correctly estimated as $(1/2)\times2F + (1/2)\times0 = F$. However, the distribution of consumption and income, and hence the Engel curve, are incorrectly estimated. The true food share is F/Y, whereas the empirical food shares are zero, with probability of one-half, and $2F/(Y + F)$ with probability of one-half. The food share is increasing in y.

From Figure 13.1, it appears that one of the reasons why the Engel curve first rises is due to the presence of a number of very low food shares among households with low total expenditures. Indeed, in the raw data of the POF 2002/2003, there are 1,636 households (3.4 percent of the total) with no reports on food consumption whatsoever.

It is difficult to imagine that those observations provide an accurate depiction of consumption patterns—that the very poor should be devoting all, or the bulk, of their budget to nonfood items. Our conjecture here is that for those households, food expenditures may simply have been inaccurately collected due to an inappropriate reference period in the consumption questionnaire.[2]

It is not clear what should be done about this. The presence of noise in the food consumption measure need not affect our calculation of average food consumption in the state as a whole. However, given that welfare analysis focusing on poverty or inequality is particularly interested in the tails of the consumption distribution, the discussion here suggests that at least some of those who would be counted as the poor might be measured with error. To the extent that this problem occurs only with respect to food consumption, one might hope that for those households with significant nonfood expenditures, their overall ranking in the welfare distribution may not be affected too badly by this problem. As a result, this issue may be of less concern when trying to identify the rich (in an analysis of inequality, for example). However, among those with low incomes, for whom food expenditures are typically particularly important, the presence of noise in the food consumption data is likely to lead to an overestimate of overall poverty and to make less sharp the distinction between the *poor* and the *nonpoor* in terms of household and individual characteristics.[3]

To address this problem in the process of constructing the POF-based consumption aggregate, the following procedure was implemented. Food expenditure of the households with missing reports was predicted, based on a model for food expenditure as a function of a set of households' housing and demographic characteristics and area of residence, estimated on the subset of households with nonzero food expenditures. The parameters estimates derived from this model were used to impute food expenditures for all households that recorded zero food spending (except for 97 households with per capita income below the political indigence line of R$50, who were expected to have no reports on food consumption because of real difficulties, rather than because of the short recall period).[4] Testing for the sensitivity of poverty and inequality measures to this imputation in the final consumption aggregate revealed that measures showed little sensitivity to the imputation in food expenditure.

HOUSING

In building up to a final consumption aggregate, a next broad category of consumption items that can be added to food consumption relates to the consumption of housing services. In the POF survey, the housing component of the consumption aggregate comprises rents, basic services, small-scale home renovations, furniture and household items, appliances and appliance repairs, and cleaning materials. For those households that are renting their homes, monthly rental payments can be straightforwardly included as a measure of the consumption of services that derive from housing. Households owning their dwellings do not pay rent, but are clearly consuming housing services, and so it is important to also include an expenditure figure for such households. In the POF, owner occupiers are asked to provide an estimate of the rental value of their home. In a setting where there is an active rental market, owner occupiers are likely to be well informed about the value of their home and the kind of rent they would have to pay for a home with similar quality and location attributes. On close examination and comparison also against predicted rental payments, it was found that household responses to such hypothetical questions in the POF were generally quite satisfactory and could be used in the consumption aggregate. In other settings, it is sometimes necessary to consider imputation models (as applied with Food in the earlier discussion) in order to include housing consumption in the overall aggregate.

Expenditures on basic services (e.g., water, sewage) were included in the POF consumption aggregate. This is not an uncontroversial decision. Although such expenditures represent a large share of total expenditure for only a few households, Deaton and Zaidi (2002) generally recommend against the incorporation of expenditures on publicly provided services in the consumption aggregate. This is because finding the proper set of prices with which to value these goods is difficult. Including expenditures on networked water and sanitation, for example, while not being able to properly take account of the fact that some households are not connected to a water network at all, that some households do not receive bills although they are connected, and that some households receive only sporadic supply of water and supplement their publicly provided water with purchases from private vendors, could introduce important biases in rankings of households.[5] If there is any reason to think that expenditures on networked water, electricity, and gas are only weakly linked to the welfare that is associated with the actual consumption of those services, the general recommendation would be to exclude these expenditures from the consumption aggregate. Other services, such as Internet access, telephone expenditures, and television subscriptions, are more straightforwardly added to the consumption aggregate.

Expenditures on home renovations in the consumption aggregate include the more frequent expenditures on housing maintenance, such as upkeep, gardening, and home repairs. These were collected as expenditures within the 90-day reference period. The POF survey also collected expenditures on renovations over the 12-month reference period. In this case, the renovations are less frequent and lumpy because they include spending on construction activities. These last expenditures were not included as part of the consumption aggregate. As commented in point (1), this type of occasional and high expenditure can introduce a wedge between the welfare levels of households that incurred this type of expenditure in the reference period and the households who had the same type of purchase in a previous period. The same issue is relevant for the inclusion of durable items as furniture and appliances (fridge, televisions), as well as repair of these appliances. Each item was scrutinized in turn to decide if the purchase of a given durable good was to be considered an occasional and lumpy expenditure. Only those items that were considered as frequent and less lumpy were included in the POF consumption aggregate. Ideally, one would like to try to value the consumption of services from large, long-lived, durable goods such as washing machines or televisions even though direct inclusion of expenditures on such items would not be appropriate. When ancillary information on, say, the original purchase price of the durable good, the age of the good, and its current replacement value is available, then one can construct models to calculate the value of the stream of services derived from these items over the course of a year or a month (see Deaton and Zaidi 2002). In the POF survey, however, such ancillary information was not available, and it was not possible to apply such methods.

Health and Education

As previously described, if one wished to include expenditures on health, then one should also take into consideration the implicit loss of welfare due to illness. Otherwise, two people with the same total expenditure levels but different expenditures on health would be judged to enjoy the same welfare level. However, valuing the loss of welfare due to illness is very difficult to do. Of course, certain health expenditures related to prevention and care can be considered as more discretionary and welfare-enhancing. These can more reasonably be included in the consumption aggregate. Deaton and Zaidi (2002) suggest that the decision to include or exclude health expenditures can be informed by an analysis of the income elasticity of the health expenditures. If the income elasticity is high, then overall rankings of households may change depending on whether such expenditures are included. When the elasticity is low, rankings are likely to be more robust, and the consequence of not including health spending in the consumption aggregate may be relatively innocuous. Deaton and Zaidi (2002) show that in developing countries, this elasticity is typically quite low (varying between 0.74 and 0.86), which suggests that noninclusion in the consumption aggregate has some justification.

Elasticities for education can be computed in a similar way. Here, too, there can be reasons to be concerned about inclusion. On the one hand, education directly adds to welfare. On the other, education is an investment. Inclusion of education expenditures can clearly introduce a wedge in welfare levels between households without children going to school and those with children at school. Again, the higher the elasticity, the stronger the case for inclusion in the consumption aggregate.

The results presented in Tables 13.1, 13.2, and 13.3 compare the elasticity of health and education with respect to total expenditures and to family income for Brazil using the POF. Table 13.1 indicates that the elasticity of education expenditures is larger than the elasticity of health expenditures, providing some justification to the inclusion of all of the education expenditures, but not of health. The elasticity of health is 0.97, which is lower than the elasticity of education expenditures, but greater to a considerable extent than the elasticity found in the countries analyzed by Deaton and Zaidi (2002). The elasticity of the health and education expenditures was also estimated by income deciles (Tables 13.2 and 13.3). We can see that the elasticities are always higher for education expenditures than they are for health expenditures, but not by much. In the case of health, the elasticity is highest in deciles four and six. For the bottom deciles, the elasticity is lower.

The results in Tables 13.1 to 13.3 for Brazil are thus somewhat mixed. Elasticities were on the high side for health expenditures, but even higher for education expenditures. In the end, the following procedure was adopted. Expenditures in health and dental insurance plans were included to the consumption aggregate. Insurance expenditures are discretionary and preventative and, thus, can be related to a higher level of welfare. Such expenses also represent a fairly sizeable component of total expenditures incurred by Brazilian families.[6] Other types of health expenditures, such as the purchase of pharmaceutical products and medical attention, were not included, however, because in this case it is not possible to capture the welfare loss from the diseases they are supposed to alleviate. Expenditures in education were included, because expenditures in private school fees can be directly related to a higher level of welfare of households paying for educational services. Although education

Table 13.1 ELASTICITIES OF HEALTH AND EDUCATION EXPENDITURES

Variable	Elasticity	Standard Deviation	t	p Value
Health × income	0.81	0.0136	59.64	<0.0001
Health × expenditure	0.97	0.0100	69.80	<0.0001
Education × income	1.13	0.0200	54.88	<0.0001
Education × expenditure	1.30	0.0200	62.59	<0.0001

NOTE: The sample design of the survey was considered for the calculation.
SOURCE: 2002–2003 POF.

Table 13.2 ELASTICITIES OF HEALTH EXPENDITURES BY DECILES OF INCOME DISTRIBUTION

Income Decile	Elasticity	Standard Deviation	t	p Value	Observations
1	0.037	0.061	0.60	0.548	2,762
2	0.567	0.222	2.56	0.011	3,116
3	0.550	0.276	2.00	0.046	3,421
4	**1.589**	0.324	4.91	0.000	3,655
5	0.572	0.316	1.81	0.071	3,782
6	**1.214**	0.289	4.20	0.000	3,968
7	0.953	0.248	3.85	0.000	4,122
8	0.921	0.190	4.86	0.000	4,338
9	0.964	0.123	7,.86	0.000	4,502
10	0.655	0.033	19.64	0.000	4,633

NOTE: The sample design of the survey was considered for the calculation.
SOURCE: 2002–2003 POF.

Table 13.3 ELASTICITIES OF EDUCATION EXPENDITURES BY DECILES OF INCOME DISTRIBUTION

Income Decile	Elasticity	Standard Deviation	t	p Value	Observations
1°	0.027	0.076	0.36	0.718	2,067
2°	0.830	0.278	2.98	0.003	2,190
3°	0.730	0.357	2.05	0.041	2,397
4°	1.018	0.454	2.24	0.025	2,491
5°	1.053	0.424	2.49	0.013	2,755
6°	0.907	0.395	2.29	0.022	2,852
7°	1.688	0.355	4.75	0.000	3,070

(Continued)

Table 13.3 ELASTICITIES OF EDUCATION EXPENDITURES BY DECILES
OF INCOME DISTRIBUTION (*CONT'D*)

Income Decile	Elasticity	Standard Deviation	t	p Value	Observations
8°	1.567	0.289	5.43	0.000	3,283
9°	1.382	0.190	7.29	0.000	3,619
10°	0.835	0.053	15.79	0.000	3,954

NOTE: The sample design of the survey was considered for the calculation.

SOURCE: 2002–2003 POF.

can also be considered an investment instead of consumption, the inclusion of education expenditures in the consumption aggregate is unlikely to lead to double counting as the returns from this particular investment will probably not be reflected in current consumption levels. It is not uncommon to treat education as a consumption item, but the decision is obviously a matter of judgment.

Transport Services

Expenses in transport services were included as part of the consumption aggregate. Although some of these expenditures can also be considered as "regrettable necessities" for getting to the work place, it was not possible to distinguish them from transportation expenses for other purposes.

Clothing, Culture and Leisure, Personal Services, and Personal Hygiene and Care

These components of the consumption aggregate comprise all types of expenditures on clothing, leisure (e.g., tickets to cinema), personal services (e.g., haircuts, beauty) and personal care. Each is likely to increase welfare of the households without introducing biases in the comparability of households' welfare levels. Notwithstanding the fact that expenditures in clothing and shoes can be considered infrequent purchases, the value of these purchases is rather modest, so they were included in the aggregate.

Considerations for Other Expenditures

The remaining components of the consumption aggregate comprise professional services (such as notaries, lawyers); expenditures in ceremonies, celebrations, and anniversaries (that are collected for the 12-month reference period); and expenses related to taxes, contributions, banking fees, among others. The procedure followed was to include all such items except for occasional expenditures (such as occasional ceremonies). As with consumer durables, these are infrequent expenditures that can become very costly and ideally we would like to have some smoothed value rather than actual, total expenditure on the event. The sole exception was made with respect to birthday parties and wedding anniversaries—events that occur on an annual basis. For such items, the 12-month reference period is the appropriate one and one could thus justify including these items in the consumption aggregate.

Following Deaton and Zaidi (2002), expenditures on taxes, contributions, and levies are not part of consumption, but a deduction from income, and should therefore not be included in the consumption aggregate. Consequently, the POF consumption aggregate does not include such payments. Deaton and Zaidi (2002) recommend including property taxes only when there is evidence that they could be linked to the provision of a specific service to the households. In the Brazil case, there were no clear grounds for relating property taxes (Imposto sobre a Propriedade Predial e Territorial Urbana and Imposto Territorial Rural) to specific services and a better level of well-being. However, payments that could be linked to service provisions such as insurance payments were included. Taxes related to the acquisition of goods already excluded (e.g., purchases of cars) were omitted as well. Expenses related to financial transactions, such as the paying off of debts, were not included as part of the aggregate.

As recommended by Deaton and Zaidi (2002), expenditures on gifts and transfers were excluded from the aggregate. Including them would involve double-counting if the transfers show up in the consumption of other households. Large expenditures that may be considered investments, such as the purchase of real estate, gold bars, and such, were excluded from the consumption aggregate. They can also introduce bias in the comparison with households already owning these assets.

TRIMMING OF OVERALL CONSUMPTION

Our examination of the components of the POF questionnaire has led us to suggest that the consumption data may suffer from certain types of measurement error. In the case of food expenditures, we have suggested that there may be grounds for concern associated with an inappropriate recall period of one week, which resulted in a large percentage of zero, or very low, expenditures in the data. Further, we have noted that we are unable to impute a stream of consumption services from the very long list of consumer durables included in the data set. We are compelled in this case to include actual expenditures on such items (abstracting away from those highly infrequent and costly items that we suggest should be excluded altogether). This means that, once again, there will be many households that record zero expenditures on specific items and other households that record expenditures that are probably in excess of the value of the stream of consumption that they derive from the item during the reference period. The overall effect, again, is the same as if we had measurement error in the data.

Measurement error is a concern in all data sets of this nature. Our examination of the POF has highlighted a few specific issues that arise there. Similar, if not identical, issues are likely to plague other consumption surveys. Nor are income surveys immune from concerns with measurement error. The effect of measurement error in the analysis of welfare can be quite significant. As has been shown by Ravallion (1988), Lanjouw and Lanjouw (2001) and Deaton and Zaidi (2002), measured poverty is likely to be higher than it should be in the presence of measurement error. Similarly, measured inequality will be biased upward.

These considerations often lead to the suggestion that some protocol for trimming extreme values from the consumption aggregate be considered prior to utilization of the consumption aggregate in applied welfare analysis. To highlight the most pronounced potential impact of trimming, we conduct sensitivity analyses, not with reference to the recommended consumption aggregate outlined, but rather to the most naïve possible aggregate that simply brings together all of the consumption components. Table 13.4 shows that sensitivity of measured inequality at the level of each Brazilian state is indeed quite significant. At the level of Brazil as a whole, untrimmed per capita consumption inequality yields a Gini coefficient of 0.559.[7] When half of a percentage point of all observations is dropped from both the bottom and from the top of the per capita consumption distribution, the Gini declines to 0.531. A trimming protocol, similar to the common practice in the use of the Current Population Study data for the United states when studying income inequality, where we cut 2.5 percentage points from both ends of the distribution yields a Gini of 0.507.

At the all-Brazil level, our measure of inequality is likely to be overstated due to the fact that spatial price differences have not been accommodated.[8] However, Table 13.4 indicates that high inequality also occurs at the level of each state, but that, again, measured inequality is quite sensitive to the question of whether extreme value observations are to be trimmed or not. In Ceara, for example, measured inequality is even more sensitive to trimming than at the all-Brazil level. The Gini coefficient in Ceara declines from 0.577 to 0.505 when 2.5 percentage points of observations are dropped from both tails of the income distribution.

What specific trimming protocol to adopt cannot be easily answered. It is likely that a consumption aggregate constructed following the recommendations of the previous sections would be less sensitive to trimming than Table 13.4 suggests. After all, the consumption aggregate prescribed incorporates imputed food consumption for some households and excludes some of the larger durable good expenditures and this would presumably remove some of the extreme values at the top end of the consumption distribution. Clearly, as the demonstration provided in Table 13.4 illustrates, measured inequality, and to some extent poverty, will be quite sensitive to decisions regarding the definition of the consumption aggregate, to the adoption of trimming protocols, as well as to other adjustments such as those for spatial price variation.

CONCLUSION AND RECOMMENDATIONS FOR THE FUTURE

We have briefly scrutinized the Brazil POF 2002/2003 questionnaire and data set with a view toward identifying and discussing some of the principles and issues associated with construction of a consumption aggregate. We have emphasized that a consumption aggregate compiled for the purpose of welfare analysis (poverty and inequality, for example) may require different treatment than one compiled for some other purpose. We have emphasized that the objective here is to be able to produce reliable and credible comparisons of welfare across households and individuals. We have suggested that such a measure of consumption would exclude expenditures that are better seen as investments or inputs into production. Moreover, we have described the desirability of capturing not simply expenditure levels, but rather a monetary value of the stream of services that is enjoyed by an individual or household from the consumption of a particular good or service. We have underscored that there can be a tension between the level of comprehensiveness of a consumption aggregate on the one hand (in principle, the more comprehensive the better) and the transparency and interpretation of the aggregate, on the other.

Our examination has led to various suggestions for treatment of specific consumption items. We have also indicated that there may be reasons to worry about measurement error in the final consumption aggregate that cannot be avoided. At least some of that measurement error may be associated with certain design features of the POF questionnaire, and in that light we can conclude with two principal recommendations for revision of the questionnaire for future reference.

1. Recall period for food expenditures: We noted that the POF data appears to include a relatively large proportion of households that report zero, or very low, spending on food based on the recall period of one week in the questionnaire. It is unlikely that such households are, in fact, not consuming food. Rather it seems possible that many households in Brazil purchase food on a fortnightly, or even monthly, basis. Future experimentation with the design of the POF consumption questionnaire may wish to consider alternative recall periods to the one-week recall. Experiments along such lines could reveal whether this conjecture has any basis in fact. In general, care should be taken to ensure that recall periods applied in a consumption survey accord closely with existing consumption patterns. Careful pretesting of the questionnaire prior to full-fledged fielding of the household survey can be very helpful in this regard but, as was seen in the case of the POF, may not guarantee that problems will not arise.

2. Consumer durables consumption: We have noted that the POF consumption questionnaire includes a very exhaustive listing of expenditures on a variety of infrequently purchased goods and services, most notably consumer durables. However, information on stocks of durables owned is far less exhaustive. Moreover, there is no information collected on households' estimation of the current value of the durables that they own. The absence of such information makes it very difficult to include in the consumption aggregate a calculation of the stream of services consumed by households of all durables that they own. In general, the design of a survey aimed at constructing a consumption aggregate for purposes of welfare analysis should review carefully the methodologies that can be drawn on in order to yield the most comprehensive measure of consumption possible. In a relatively rich country such as Brazil, where the ownership of consumer durables is likely to be quite widespread, there is an urgent need to ensure that the information that underpins imputation methodologies for consumer durable expenditures is duly collected.

In sum, the construction of a consumption aggregate is part science, part art. In most practical settings, there will be many issues and difficulties encountered during the process of producing a consumption aggregate. Many of these cannot be resolved conclusively and to everyone's complete satisfaction. Judgment calls are required, and it is likely that not everyone will agree to the choices made. Therefore, it is very

Table 13.4 SENSITIVITY OF MEASURED INEQUALITY TO TRIMMING OF TOP AND BOTTOM EXTREME VALUES

State	Untrimmed	Trimmed (Both Sides)		
	Gini	0.5 percent	2.5 percent	5.0 percent
Rondonia	0.513	0.476	0.455	0.428
Acre	0.568	0.537	0.518	0.489
Amazonas	0.550	0.509	0.481	0.450
Roraima	0.499	0.474	0.454	0.430
Para	0.471	0.445	0.425	0.402
Amapa	0.481	0.464	0.450	0.432
Tocantins	0.555	0.504	0.478	0.450
Maranhao	0.477	0.456	0.433	0.405
Piaui	0.534	0.498	0.470	0.438
Ceara	0.577	0.535	0.505	0.467
Rio Grande do Norte	0.567	0.528	0.497	0.461
Paraiba	0.548	0.518	0.491	0.451
Pernambuco	0.533	0.504	0.480	0.449
Alagoas	0.591	0.553	0.520	0.481
Sergipe	0.550	0.527	0.506	0.475
Bahia	0.557	0.520	0.498	0.468
Minas Gerais	0.528	0.503	0.479	0.451
Espiritu Santo	0.552	0.529	0.507	0.481
Rio de Janeiro	0.572	0.550	0.528	0.500
Sao Paulo	0.501	0.476	0.454	0.432
Parana	0.527	0.501	0.481	0.452
Santa Caterina	0.480	0.455	0.436	0.408
Rio Grande do Sul	0.522	0.490	0.468	0.440
Mato Grosso do Sul	0.519	0.491	0.466	0.436
Mato Grosso	0.523	0.490	0.461	0.428
Goias	0.504	0.474	0.453	0.427
Distrito Federal	0.572	0.541	0.521	0.497
All Brazil	0.559	0.531	0.507	0.480

important that the exercise be approached systematically and that there is clear documentation of how each step in the process has occurred. Welfare analyses that build on the consumption aggregate can have far-reaching implications for policy debate and design. Therefore, sensitivity analyses that gauge the degree to which conclusions are robust to alternative definitions of the consumption aggregate should be undertaken and reported. Comparisons across countries, time periods, and settings, in which it has not been possible to ascertain that the definition of consumption is identical should be aware of the lessons demonstrated by the sensitivity analyses conduced here: At least part, and perhaps a great deal of observed differences observed may be driven by noncomparability of the underlying welfare definitions.

ACKNOWLEDGMENT

This chapter was prepared as a paper for the OECD/University of Maryland Conference "Measuring Poverty, Income Inequality and Social Exclusion: Lessons from Europe," Paris, March 16–17, 2009. I am grateful to Fang Lai, Phillippe Leite, and Emmanuel Skoufias for their many contributions to this project, and to Kathleen Beegle, Gero Carletto, Francisco Ferreira, Jed Friedman, Jesko Hentschel, and Kinnon Scott, for helpful discussions. The views in this chapter are my own and should not be taken to reflect those of the World Bank or affiliated institutions. All errors are my own.

Notes

1. This relationship is observed not only in Ceara. A similar graph produced at the all-Brazil level reveals a similar pattern. Thomas (1986) documents this phenomenon in many different data sets. It should be noted, however, that the range over which the Engel curve is rising in these data is higher than one normally sees.
2. Anecdotal evidence suggests that indeed, in Brazil, it is not uncommon for households to purchase many of their food items in bulk. Such behavior is understandable in a setting where historically, high rates of inflation provided households with a real incentive to immediately convert their monthly salary into purchases of real goods and services.
3. Ravallion (1988) and Deaton and Zaidi (2002) discuss issues surrounding poverty measurement in the presence of noisy data in greater detail. See also Lanjouw and Lanjouw (2001).
4. We also tried this procedure with propensity score matching and found very similar results for the imputation.
5. Hentschel and Lanjouw (1996) discuss these issues in some detail.
6. The decision to include insurance expenditures, while possibly preserving rankings of households in terms of welfare, quite possibly leads to some overstatement of overall inequality of consumption spending. This is because low-income households probably do not have insurance and are more likely to make direct expenditures. As such expenditures are not included in the consumption

aggregate, the effect is to widen the gap between those with high- and those with low-consumption levels.

7. This compares with a Gini of 0.507 reported in World Bank (2006) based on the consumption aggregate definition outlined herein.

8. World Bank (2006) analyzes poverty and inequality in Brazil on the basis of the POF survey and includes as well a correction for spatial price variation. The overall Gini reported in World Bank (2006) following adjustment for spatial price variation is 0.479–0.481, depending on the specific price index used.

References

Deaton, Angus, and Salman Zaidi. 2002. "Guidelines for Constructing Consumption Aggregates for Welfare Analysis." Living Standards Measurement Survey Working Paper 135, World Bank, Washington, DC.

Elbers, Chris, Jean Lanjouw, Peter Lanjouw, and Phillippe G. Leite. 2001. "Poverty and Inequality in Brazil: New Estimates from Combined PPV-PNAD Data." Mimeo, Development Research Group, World Bank, Washington, DC.

Ferreira, Francisco H.G., Peter Lanjouw, and Marcelo C. Neri. 2003. "A New Poverty Profile for Brazil Using PPV, PNAD and Census Data." *Revista Brasileira de Economia* 57 (1): 59–92.

Hentschel, Jesco, and Peter Lanjouw. 1996. "Constructing an Indicator of Consumption for the Analysis of Poverty: Principles and Illustrations with Reference to Ecuador." Living Standard Measurement Survey Working Paper 124, World Bank, Washington, DC.

Instituto Brasileiro de Geografia e Estatística. 2002. *Pesquisa de Orçamentos Familiares of 2002/2003*. Rio de Janiero: Instituto Brasileiro de Geografia e Estatística. http://www.ibge.gov.br/home/estatistica/populacao/condicaodevida/pof/2002/.

Lanjouw, Jean O., and Peter Lanjouw. 2001. "How To Compare Apples and Oranges: Poverty Measurement Based on Different Definitions of Consumption." *Review of Income and Wealth* 47 (1): 25–42.

Ravallion, Martin. 1998. "Expected Poverty Under Risk-Induced Welfare Variability." *Economic Journal* 98: 1171–1182.

Thomas, Duncan. 1986. "The Food Share as a Welfare Measure." PhD diss., Princeton University.

World Bank. 2006. *Brazil: Measuring Poverty Using Household Consumption*. Report 36358-BR. Washington, DC: World Bank.

14

Alternatives to Income-Based Measures of Poverty

KENNETH A. COUCH ■

In developed countries, the use of income as the basic indicator of economic well-being has become commonplace although it is agreed by most analysts that if we could do a good job of measuring consumption, it would be preferable. In this volume, Chapter 12 by Brandolini, Magri, and Smeeding and Chapter 13 by Lanjouw interject some real-world considerations into deliberations on which measure might be better in practice. The work of Brandolini et al. pushes the frontier of income-based measures, adding annuity values of a broad measure of wealth and a more narrow one of financial assets in order to expand the measure of resources available to families to reflect their ability to access stocks of wealth available to them. The work of Lanjouw provides a look at the development of a consumption-based survey for measuring economic well-being. In a theoretical world, it might be preferable to use consumption as a direct measure of current well-being because it measures purchases of goods and services (and related flows from existing stocks of durables) rather than potential use as income does. But it is clear that serious attempts to construct complete measures of available resources beginning from either income or consumption surveys quickly confront many of the same measurement issues. Ultimately, analysts must decide which construct most closely matches the concept they would ideally like to measure and weigh that against practical difficulties of implementation.

Brandolini, Magri, and Smeeding use the Luxembourg Wealth Study in their work to examine the impact that placing a value on wealth and financial assets has on measured poverty rates. As they note in their introduction, when family resources are measured, most often sources of cash income are collected whether they originate from private employers or the government. In both the current official US poverty measure and those employed in the European Union and Organization for Economic Co-operation and Development, earnings and cash transfers comprise the bulk of income available to individuals for their consumption.

It is notable that a literature is beginning to emerge in the academic community regarding the reliability of reports of components of cash income in surveys relative to administrative sources against which they may be benchmarked. Further, there is considerable discussion of whether one data source or another is more or less reliable in use for policy evaluations.[1] Although analysts often take it for granted that the components of cash income are measured reliably, researchers continue to work toward refinement of these measures.

An additional complication that arises when building a measure of family resources from survey-based data on cash income is that this does not reflect taxation. As discussed elsewhere in this volume (see Chapter 1 by Besharov and Couch), the European Union and Organization for Economic Co-operation and Development already adjust cash income for taxes and levies, which finance social insurance programs. The United States does not currently use a disposable income concept for poverty measurement but would under the National Academy of Sciences recommendations (see Chapter 1 by Besharov and Couch or Chapter 8 by Johnson). Again, a significant effort has been made in the United States to provide computer programs that adjust gross income for appropriate federal taxes based on the location and family circumstances of the individual.

Even though analysts seek to adjust survey-based measures of income for the tax system, it is not always possible using the information available to directly simulate the relevant tax codes. The types of questions asked on surveys do not necessarily align exactly with the information used within a country's revenue system in a manner that allows accurate simulation of the tax-filing process. At a basic level, the orientation of the survey is often at the level of who lives within a physical structure. Tax filings typically reference individuals or married couples. Thus, there can be a basic mismatch between survey structures and the concept that researchers might like to simulate. When these simulations extend to tax credits that may be provided as rebates to low-income individuals, inaccurate assumptions may be required regarding filing for the benefit.[2]

Also, in the recommendations of the National Academy of Sciences for amendment of the US poverty measure, components of major in-kind transfers would be valued. The conceptual questions regarding the value of public benefits to individuals are well-known. However, whether the correct conceptual approach is to value benefits at their cost, as the amount a low-income family would freely spend on them, or in some other way is a decision based on professional judgment.

Thus, the adjustments necessary to obtain a measure of the combined income and near-income resources available to families are not inconsequential or trivial, although they are conceptually desirable. Families do spend after-tax cash income. They also receive consumption value from in-kind benefits so they should be incorporated into a measure of available resources.

The work of Brandolini, Magri, and Smeeding begins with this as a starting point but notes that income is only indirectly related to what we would ideally like to measure: consumption. Even though questions about consumption are not asked in most surveys aimed at collecting information about income and benefits over time, other information is routinely collected that might allow analysts to better gauge resources beyond income and in-kind assistance that families might access to augment their consumption.[3] In particular, many surveys contain questions that allow measurement of components of wealth as well as other more liquid financial assets.

Those who hold assets, whether financial or real, can use them to smooth out consumption by immediately spending down the most liquid assets or by selling or taking loans against others. So, considering some individuals to be poor or at risk of poverty based on disposable income alone (even if augmented with valuations of in-kind benefits and the full impact of the system of taxation) may be inappropriate when they have significant asset holdings.

To examine this issue, Brandolini et al. construct annuity values for liquid and illiquid financial assets. As they explain, there are different methods by which annuity values might be assigned to individuals based on their asset holdings, but a key issue is at what point individuals are assumed to consume from their assets and how one might reasonably think about the rate at which they would be willing to liquidate them. One could clearly consume from liquid assets at any point in time when the individual or their household was facing duress, or one might alternatively assume (as they do) that only older individuals would be willing to view their assets as an annuity to be spent. Similarly, assumptions have to be made regarding the horizon over which individuals would consume the assets. As they point out, an infinite horizon suggests individuals would only spend income earned from the assets, but they employ an assumption that older individuals spend the entire stock of wealth over their lifetimes. Similarly, an interest rate for payments from the assets also needs to be assumed. What Brandolini et al. assume in their analysis is reasonable but nonetheless reflects multiple choices that must be made by the researcher.

From a practical perspective, Brandolini et al. use the Luxembourg Wealth Study data to examine four countries and find that when annuity values are placed on wealth, this results in large decreases in poverty particularly relative to an absolute standard. They further show that because those with significant home equity tend to be older, assigning to them an annuity value for wealth has a dramatic impact in reducing poverty against either a relative or absolute standard.

Brandolini, Magri, and Smeeding also construct a measure of financial vulnerability by identifying families with either a level of wealth or financial assets less than three times the relevant poverty threshold. The proportion of families without three months of liquid financial assets available to help them smooth consumption during a period with an unexpected loss of income is quite high, more than 30 percent in each of the eight countries they examine in this particular part of their analysis. Thus, many families have limited potential to smooth consumption over time using the most liquid measure of financial assets they consider.

As the discussion has emphasized, judgment decisions and potential sources of inaccuracy are contained in the process of measuring resources available to families and households beginning with cash income. The process of moving forward to disposable income, which requires the valuation of the use of housing when it is owner occupied, the valuation of in-kind benefits received from the government, adjustments for federal tax receipts and credits, and the like, certainly highlight the fact that measuring resources available to households even in highly developed countries is not a simple process. These measures are imperfect; however, in developed economies, many think they are the best available starting point for the analysis of economic well-being because the dominant resource available to most individuals is the money they earn and this is the primary resource they have available for consumption.[4]

The second chapter in this section on alternatives to income-based measures provides a detailed discussion of the fielding of a recent consumption survey in a major and rapidly emerging economy, Brazil. Peter Lanjouw explains that similar measurement issues arise in the context of measuring consumption that others are more familiar with from approaches that focus on measuring income. He discusses these issues in the context of the survey structure and responses to the *Pesquisa de*

Orçamentos Familiares of 2002/2003, a consumption survey fielded by the Instituto Brasileiro de Geografia e Estatística. The survey collects systematic information on expenditures by trying to match the segments of its questionnaire to the frequency with which different goods are likely to be purchased.

In contrast to the standard treatment of poverty measurement in the United States and Europe, Lanjouw first provides a compelling argument regarding the case of examining consumption as a measure of well-being. Many individuals have access to government-provided services, possess individually owned assets, and receive transfers from families and friends. These resources enable individuals to consume beyond their current income. So, while we have good reason to believe that current period earnings and cash (or in-kind) transfers from the government or friends would correlate highly with total consumption expenditures, the extent to which this is true is an empirical issue surrounded by complex measurement difficulties.

Lanjouw discusses important measurement issues that must be addressed to provide a measure of consumption. The principal issues are (1) how to deal with lumpy purchases of consumer durables, (2) items with low elasticity with respect to total income, (3) appropriate treatment of items used as production inputs, and (4) exclusion of items purchased for other households.

Perhaps the most challenging of these measurement issues are the first two. When consumers purchase durables that are used over many years, but data regarding them are obtained in an essentially cross-sectional survey, the tempos of purchases and the data are inconsistent. Different approaches and recommendations to resolving this type of inconsistency is an important part of the discussion provided by Lanjouw. Some of the technical issues involved are similar to those encountered in an income-based approach such as that of Brandolini et al., which requires valuation of different components of wealth.

If one thinks of some of the information collected in familiar surveys that is used as the basis for imputing an annuity value of housing (a commonly owned asset) to owner occupiers, similar information must be collected regarding durables in a consumption survey to impute a reasonable value of consumption to the owners of the assets. This would consist, at minimum, of the date of purchase, the price paid, and money owed on it. Beyond this, there are many available methods of valuing durable assets and analysts must make a choice of how to impute the value to add to current consumption (as discussed in Chapter 6 by Frick and Grabka).

Whether to include purchases that are basically nondiscretionary is similarly important. As an example, if a person has an acute health problem that reduces welfare, does the expenditure really increase welfare? Generally, if expenditures have a low elasticity with respect to income, they are seen as being unlikely to contribute to net welfare and it is generally recommended that they be excluded from consumption-based measures of well-being. For example, if health expenditures are in response to an acute event, they are likely offsetting a health episode that has reduced well-being, and it has been argued that purchases of this type should not be included in constructing a consumption-based measure of well-being. The work contained in Chapter 5 of this volume by Sutherland, and Tsakoglou on obtaining a value of medical insurance to add to disposable income runs into a similar conceptual problem. There, they grapple with whether the value placed on medical care should be the money actually spent on an individual's health care or the average cost of care for someone in their group.

After discussing the major measurement issues confronted in taking the data from the *Pesquisa de Orçamentos Familiares* and constructing a distribution of consumption expenditures, Lanjouw uses data from the survey to demonstrate the sensitivity of measures of inequality to analytical choices involved in their construction. Overall, if measurement issues regarding the elements of consumption expenditures are ignored, estimates of inequality are typically 25 percent higher than if systematic efforts are made to address them. Sensitivity to estimation methods of this magnitude are common in many of the chapters found in this volume that are based on an income approach. For example, in the Brandolini et al.'s chapter, imputing an annuitized value of wealth to individuals ages 55 years and older in the countries they examine typically has the impact of reducing the poverty rate among that group by 10 to 20 percent.

CONCLUSION

In developed countries where most goods consumed are purchased in markets, it seems sensible that the usual approach to measuring resources available for consumption begins with cash income and transfers. As that measurement process extends to include in-kind transfers, economies of scale, and adjustments for taxation, numerous judgments must be made regarding the methods to be used. Further, assessing the ability of individuals to smooth out their consumption during periods of low income requires the adoption of a specific method of valuing assets. These different methods of valuation involve professional judgments that ultimately have a large impact on measured inequality and poverty. In the analysis of Brandolini, Magri, and Smeeding, assigning individuals an annuitized value of their housing and financial net worth as an additional source of income results in large reductions in the rate of poverty particularly against an absolute standard.

Rather than engaging with the extensive technical issues involved in measuring cash income and then valuing in-kind benefits, the impact of taxation, influences of family structure, and potential flows from assets, it is natural to wonder if measuring consumption directly might provide a less technical solution while providing more useful information about people's behavior. Lanjouw provides an interesting explanation of the conceptual difficulties involved in measuring consumption, as well as the practical problems that arise in designing and fielding a consumption survey. Beyond market transactions, individuals still consume part of residences they may own as well as other durables. The same problems that arise in analyses such as that of Brandolini et al. in imputing the value of those assets to individuals will also appear in a consumption-based approach.

Given the relatively scarce information available regarding consumption patterns in the United States, more attention should be paid to this type of analysis. Focusing more attention on consumption patterns of low-income families would be useful in helping us understand the extent to which individuals can buy the things they need, even in periods of low income. However, the analysis by Lanjouw aptly demonstrates that a consumption-based approach is likely to encounter many of the same analytical issues as one that begins with cash income as its basis.

Notes

1. See work by Couch and Placzek (2010) and Kornfield and Bloom (1999) on this point.
2. See Burkhauser, Couch, and Glenn(1996) for an applied simulation of the US tax system including a benefit-incidence analysis of Earned Income Tax Credits.
3. Chapter 17 by Headey, Krause, and Wagner discusses the use of consumption questions within one panel study: Household, Income, and Labour Dynamics in Australia.
4. It is often pointed out by US analysts that it might be better to directly measure consumption. The closing chapter of this volume by Smeeding discusses the data currently available in the United States that measures consumption patterns, and it is clear that generating a consumption-based measure in the United States would require additional data collection efforts.

References

Burkhauser, Richard V., Kenneth A. Couch, and Andrew J. Glenn. 1996. "Public Policies for The Working Poor: The Earned Income Tax Credit Versus Minimum Wage Legislation." In *Research in Labor Economics*. Vol. 15. Edited by Sol W. Polachek, 65–109. Brighton and Hove, Sussex: Emerald Publishing.

Couch, Kenneth A., and Dana W. Placzek. 2010. "Earnings Losses of Displaced Workers Revisited." *American Economic Review* 100 (1): 572–589.

Kornfield, R., and H. S. Bloom. 1999. "Measuring Program Impacts on Earnings and Employment: Do Unemployment Insurance Wage Reports from Employers Agree with Surveys of Individuals?" *Journal of Labor Economics* 17 (1): 168–197.

PART FIVE

Multidimensional Measures

15

Developing and Learning from EU Measures of Social Inclusion

ERIC MARLIER, BEA CANTILLON, BRIAN NOLAN,
KAREL VAN DEN BOSCH, AND TIM VAN RIE ■

This chapter describes the main concepts and broader measures of social inclusion used by the European Commission and European Union (EU) countries in the context of the social open method of coordination (OMC). The main aim of the discussion is to bring out the value of going beyond purely income-based measures of poverty to include other dimensions, which is what the indicators adopted for monitoring the social OMC are intended to achieve. For this purpose, we draw on the EU Statistics on Income and Living Conditions (EU-SILC) and the EU Labor Force Surveys (LFS), which provide data on most of these indicators on a comparable basis across EU member states. Some general lessons, unresolved issues, and priority areas for development are also explored or highlighted. It is of particular relevance to US debates that these unresolved issues include the balance to be struck between using standards that are fixed versus standards that vary across time or countries. The core message, though, is that a multidimensional set of indicators can do justice to the complexity of the concepts involved in a much better way than can be achieved by considering only income-based measures.

SETTING THE SCENE

Since 2000, EU countries and the European Commission have cooperated in the field of social policy on the basis of the so-called OMC. The OMC has significantly developed over time and now covers EU cooperation in three main policy areas or "strands": social inclusion (formally launched at the March 2000 Lisbon European Council),[1] pensions (since 2001), and health care and long-term care (since 2004). It also includes information exchanges in the field of *making work pay*. Since 2006, the three social "processes" that were progressively implemented under the OMC (one process for each main strand) have been *streamlined* into one integrated "social OMC" built around 12 commonly agreed EU objectives (3 for each main strand, as well as 3 overarching objectives that address horizontal issues that cut across them).[2]

Concerns about poverty and social exclusion in the EU are far from new. Back in 1975, the European Communities adopted the first European Action Program to combat poverty.[3] Under Jacques Delors, the social dimension received more attention, based on a foundation of scientific research on poverty. The Final Report on the Second Program, taking expenditure rather than income as the indicator of resources, included the estimate for 1985 of 50 million poor people in the 12 member states (see O'Higgins and Jenkins 1990), based on the study carried out by Hagenaars, de Vos, and Zaidi (1994).

At the same time, the underlying concepts were increasingly debated (see, for example, Room 1995; Silver 1995; Nolan and Whelan 1996). What is the meaning of the phrase *poverty and social exclusion* now widely used throughout the EU? In what sense is "social inclusion" the opposite of "social exclusion"? Do we mean "poverty" or "risk of poverty"? These issues go to the heart of societal objectives and are not yet fully resolved. Moreover, the debate has been widened by the 2004 and 2007 EU enlargements.[4] To what extent, for example, are notions like "social inclusion" and "social cohesion" differently interpreted in "new" EU countries that previously had communist regimes? We cannot provide here an extensive discussion, but there are certain essential elements that form the historical conceptual context in which the indicators adopted by the EU for monitoring the social OMC (hereafter: commonly agreed indicators) have been developed:

- The long-standing *social inclusion* objective of the EU is concerned that all EU citizens participate in the benefits of economic integration and economic growth. The EU cannot be successful if significant groups are left behind as prosperity increases.
- The definition of *poverty* has therefore been based on the notion of *participation*. The EU Council of Ministers in 1975 defined the poor as "individuals or families whose resources are so small as to exclude them from the minimum acceptable way of life of the Member State in which they live", with "resources" being defined as "goods, cash income plus services from public and private sources" (EU Council of Ministers, 1975, 34). In this sense, it is a *relative* definition, and the primary frame of reference is the country in which one lives—a point that is highly significant when we come to the indicators adopted.
- The move to *poverty and social exclusion* reflected a growing acceptance that *deprivation* is a multidimensional concept, and that, while financial poverty remains a major preoccupation, our concerns have to be broader. The European Commission, in its 1992 submission on "Intensifying the Fight against Social Exclusion," argued that the term *social exclusion* is more encompassing than the term *poverty* is. It suggested that social exclusion captures more adequately the "multi-dimensional nature of the mechanisms whereby individuals and groups are excluded from taking part in the social exchanges, from the component practices and rights of social integration" (European Commission 1992, 8).
- With this broader focus came an emphasis on *dynamics*. People are excluded not just because they are currently without a job or income, but also because they have few prospects for the future or for their children's future. "When poverty predominantly occurs in long spells [. . .] the poor

have virtually no chance of escaping from poverty and, therefore, little allegiance to the wider community" (Walker 1995, 103). Just as poorer member states aspire to converge to the EU average, poorer EU citizens aspire to better individual prospects.

- The concept of exclusion introduces the element of *agency*.[5] When René Lenoir coined the phrase *les exclus* in 1974, he was concerned with those who were excluded from the French welfare state. In all countries, the design of social protection and the way in which it is administered exclude certain citizens. The state is a major actor, but it is not the only actor.

- Recognition of the limitations of an income measure has led to the EU adopting in 2001 the phrase *at risk of poverty* to denote people living in households with incomes below a specified threshold, indicating that persons living in households with incomes below the poverty line are not necessarily living "in poverty."

We briefly describe in the next section, the set of indicators adopted to monitor progress in the social OMC, in particular those aimed at capturing the multidimensionality of social inclusion. Drawing on the most recent data from EU-SILC and EU LFS (the two EU statistical sources for most of the indicators used by the EU for monitoring the social OMC; see Appendix 15.A), the third and fourth sections then bring out the value of an analysis of the social situation that draws on various dimensions covered by these commonly agreed upon indicators, compared with one that would only look at income-based measures of poverty and inequality. In the third section, our focus is on the overlaps and complementarities of individual indicators, whereas in the fourth section, we consider the portfolio of commonly agreed upon indicators as a whole (i.e., the relationships between them).

PORTFOLIO OF INDICATORS ADOPTED BY THE EU FOR MONITORING THE SOCIAL OMC: MAJOR PROGRESS MADE IN MULTIDIMENSIONAL COVERAGE OF SOCIAL INCLUSION

Social indicators are used for a variety of purposes at the national and international level, but in the social OMC, they have to serve the specific function of facilitating the comparison of actual performances achieved by EU countries through their national (and subnational) social policies and, hence, of improving mutual learning and exchange of good practice across member states. As emphasized by Atkinson, Cantillon, Marlier and Nolan (2002) in their independent study on EU indicators for social inclusion commissioned by Belgium during its presidency of the EU in 2001, for indicators to be fit for their intended purpose, their construction needs to follow a *principle-based approach*. A specific *methodological framework*, therefore, is required for developing the indicators that are needed for the social OMC. The "Report on Indicators in the Field of Poverty and Social Exclusion" (Social Protection Committee 2001), prepared by the Indicators Sub-Group of the Social Protection Committee[6] and adopted by the Laeken European Council in December 2001, set out methodological principles for the construction of the commonly agreed social inclusion indicators, and proposed the so-called *Laeken indicators*.[7] The approach

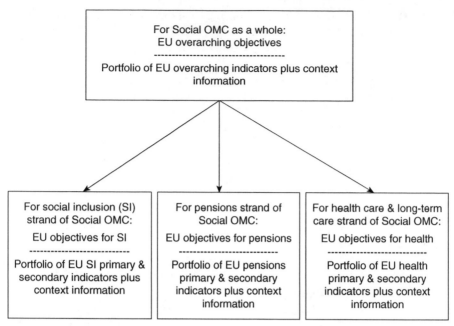

Figure 15.1 Social OMC Framework.

followed since the adoption in 2006 of an integrated monitoring framework for the social OMC is very close to the one endorsed in 2001.

The commonly agreed indicators are now organized according to the structure of the common objectives for the social OMC: one set of indicators and "context information" appropriate to the overarching objectives agreed for the social OMC as a whole, and one appropriate to each of the three social strands covered by the social OMC (see Figure 15.1), that is, four portfolios in total.[8] The focus is for the most part on social outcomes rather than the means by which they are achieved, but to facilitate mutual learning, these are supplemented with information (input indicators and context information) that allows a linkage between policies and social outcomes.

The methodological framework for the selection of commonly agreed indicators adopted in 2006 specifies that:

- Individual indicators should (1) have a clear accepted normative interpretation; (2) be robust and statistically validated; (3) be measurable in a sufficiently comparable way across EU countries; (4) be timely and susceptible to revision; and (5) be responsive to policy interventions but not subject to manipulation. (It should be mentioned that the 2006 framework allows for the adoption of "commonly agreed *national* indicators." These are based on commonly agreed definitions and assumptions but, contrary to the "commonly agreed *EU* indicators," they do not satisfactorily fulfill all the criteria for the selection of EU indicators [especially the comparability and/ or normative value requirements]. This flexibility has allowed some indicators to be included that were seen as covering important social dimensions but for which no "robust" EU indicators could be built, for instance, because of lack of comparable data, diverging concepts used in the different member states, etc.)

- Each of the four portfolios should be comprehensive and cover all key dimensions of the common objectives, should be balanced across the different dimensions, and should enable a synthetic and transparent assessment of a country's situation in relation to the common objectives. A direct consequence of this is that the EU portfolio of social inclusion indicators should cover not only income but also all the other important dimensions of social exclusion.

As shown in Tables 15.1a and 15.1b, the social inclusion portfolio now comprises 12 *primary indicators*, six *secondary indicators* and 13 *context information* statistics:

1. The *primary indicators* (see Table 15.1a) provide a "synthetic set of lead indicators" covering all key dimensions of the commonly agreed EU objectives and/or highlighting the social situation of key subpopulations. In the social inclusion area, they encompass income poverty *risk* (indicators P1–P3), unemployment and joblessness (P4 and P5), low educational qualifications (P6), employment situation of migrants (P7), material deprivation (P8), and access to healthcare (P10). They also include indicators that are currently being developed, relating to housing and child well-being (P9[9] and P11, respectively). A gender breakdown of each of the primary indicators for social inclusion and a breakdown of most by broad age groups are provided. For some indicators, other breakdowns are also given.
2. The *secondary indicators* (see Table 15.1b) support the lead indicators by describing in greater detail the nature of the problem or by describing other important dimensions of the phenomena. In the case of social inclusion, they provide the following: poverty risk by different breakdowns and for alternative thresholds (S1), persons with low educational attainment and low reading literacy performance of pupils (S2 and S3), depth of deprivation (S4), and housing (S5 and S6).
3. In addition, a further set of 12 statistics has been specified for the social inclusion portfolio as providing *context information* (see Table 15.1b) to help in interpreting the primary and secondary indicators: income inequality, regional cohesion, life expectancy, income poverty, population in jobless households, in-work poverty risk, making work pay (traps), adequacy of social assistance, health, and housing.

The choice of indicators is necessarily constrained by the availability of reliable and comparable data, and it was unsurprising that the original set of social inclusion indicators adopted in 2001 relied heavily on information about income and labor force status, where comparative data were already relatively well developed. The set of indicators that is now being employed covers more dimensions, and when the indicators still under development are complete, the portfolio will be truly multidimensional in scope.

As a result of both the availability of EU-SILC data and the growing urgency of addressing key issues in view of the economic and financial crisis, significant progress was made in 2009 on commonly agreed indicators on material deprivation and on housing (see Tables 15.1a and 15.1b). There have also been significant advances in the area of child well-being with the adoption of the EU Report on "Child Poverty and Well-Being in the EU" in January 2008 by the European Commission and all 27 member states.[10] However, the slot foreseen in Table 15.1a for one or more "child well-being" indicator(s) still needs to be filled in.

Despite the important progress made recently, significant challenges remain in improving the EU monitoring framework of the social OMC, as we briefly discuss in our concluding section. We now move on to an examination of how some of the currently available indicators can be used to investigate some key relationships between various income and nonincome dimensions of social inclusion.

Table 15.1a EU Social Inclusion Portfolio—Commonly Agreed
Primary Indicators

Income poverty:	P1. At-risk-of-poverty rate, which is calculated with a threshold set at 60 percent of the national equivalized median income and which has to be analyzed together with the actual value of the threshold in PPS for two illustrative household types (a single-person household and a household consisting of two adults and two children)
	P2. Persistent at-risk-of-poverty rate (indicator not yet available for all EU countries)
	P3. Relative median poverty risk gap
Unemployment and Joblessness:	P4. Long-term unemployment rate (at least 12 months of unemployment on the International Labor Organization definition)
	P5. Population living in jobless households (distinguishing between adults aged 18–59 years and children under 18)
Low educational qualifications:	P6. Early school leavers not in education or training (aged 18–24 years)
Employment situation of immigrants:	P7. Employment gap of immigrants (to be supplemented with relevant national data covering other key aspects of the social inclusion of immigrants)
Material deprivation:	P8. Population living in materially deprived households
Housing:	*P9. Indicator(s) to be developed; work in progress*
Access to health care:	P10. Self-reported unmet need for medical care (to be analyzed together with health care utilization)
Child well-being:	*P11. Indicator(s) to be developed; work in progress*

NOTE: Indicators P7 and P10 are commonly agreed *national* indicators (see text). Without the option of agreeing national rather than EU indicators, the only measure covering the situation of migrants and the only measure addressing the issue of access to health care could not have been included in the EU framework.

Table 15.1b EU SOCIAL INCLUSION PORTFOLIO—COMMONLY AGREED
SECONDARY INDICATORS AND CONTEXT INFORMATION

Commonly agreed secondary indicators

Income poverty:	S1. Poverty risk by different breakdowns (household types, work intensity of household, most frequent activity status, accommodation tenure status) and poverty risk according to different at-risk-of-poverty thresholds (40, 50, and 70 percent of the national equivalized median income)
Low educational attainment:	S2. Persons with low educational attainment S3. Low reading literacy performance of pupils aged 15 years
Material deprivation:	S4. Depth of material deprivation
Housing:	S5. Persons in households with high housing costs (more than 40 percent of their total disposable household income) S6. Persons living in overcrowded households

Commonly agreed context information

Income inequality:	Income quintile ratio (S80/S20) and Gini coefficient
Regional cohesion:	Dispersion of regional employment rates
Life expectancy:	Healthy life expectancy and life expectancy at birth and at 65 years (by socioeconomic status when available)
Income poverty:	At-risk-of-poverty rate anchored at a moment in time and at-risk-of-poverty rate before social cash transfers (other than pensions)
Jobless households:	Persons living in jobless households (by main household types)
In-work poverty risk:	In-work poverty risk (for full-time/part-time workers)
Making work pay:	Unemployment trap, inactivity trap, low-wage trap
Adequacy of social assistance:	Net income of social assistance recipients as a percentage of the at-risk-of-poverty threshold for three jobless household types
Health:	Self-reported limitations in daily activities (by income quintiles, sex, and age)
Housing:	Population living in households facing housing deprivation (i.e., poor housing conditions) and housing costs share (median share of housing costs in total disposable household income for both total population and population at risk of poverty)

THE EU SOCIAL INCLUSION PORTFOLIO OF INDICATORS IN PRACTICE: OVERLAPS AND COMPLEMENTARITIES

In this section, we examine the various dimensions covered in the EU social inclusion portfolio of indicators and try to assess, in particular, how much they differ with regard to the relative performance of different EU countries. Do the same countries perform well on all indicators, or do they all have their own special domain(s) where they stand out? Here the country is generally the unit of analysis (sole exceptions are Figure 15.6c and Table 15.3) rather than the individual person or household, which has some important implications as we shall see. We consider the indicators in pairs and explore how they can be used to "tell a story" about differences across member states, about the impact of enlargement, and about the relation between different dimensions of poverty and social exclusion. Clearly, a comprehensive account and understanding of the complex phenomena at stake would require a differentiated examination of the causes of poverty and social exclusion, based on a detailed and multidimensional analysis of the underlying microdata on households and individuals, and drawing on a variety of sources and the extensive research literature available for individual countries. Such a (very valuable) enterprise is well beyond the scope of the present chapter. Instead, by deliberately limiting our analysis to these aggregate indicators (which are available from the Internet at the time of writing this chapter; see Appendix 15.A), our aim is to bring out the potential of these indicators and also the limits to such an analysis. The expectation is certainly not that countries would rely solely on these indicators in monitoring, analyzing, and reporting on poverty and social exclusion; rather, it is that the national indicators they develop and use for these purposes, together with in-depth multidimensional analysis of the underlying microdata, should be *linked back* to the common indicators as far as possible in order to facilitate mutual learning between the different member states. So, what we want to show through a number of examples is the value of considering not only income-based measures but also indicators covering other dimensions of social exclusion.

Our main focus is on the EU set of primary indicators with two important exceptions. For housing, we use the two EU-agreed secondary indicators (S5 and S6 in Table 15.1b) because housing is an important dimension of social inclusion and is (currently) not covered in the primary set. In our analysis of the primary indicator on material deprivation, we also look at indicator S4 to address the depth of deprivation.

Income Poverty

The portfolio of indicators contains three primary indicators on income poverty: the at-risk-of-poverty rate (the headcount; see definition in Table 15.1a), the persistent at-risk-of-poverty rate (the proportion of persons being at risk of poverty in the current year, and also in at least two of the three previous years), and the relative median poverty risk gap (which measures how far the median at-risk-of-poverty person is below the poverty risk threshold). Unfortunately, results for the persistent poverty risk are not yet available from EU-SILC for most member states as they require four years of observations; therefore, they are not analyzed here. Crucially, the income poverty threshold employed is explicitly, and intentionally, relative to median income

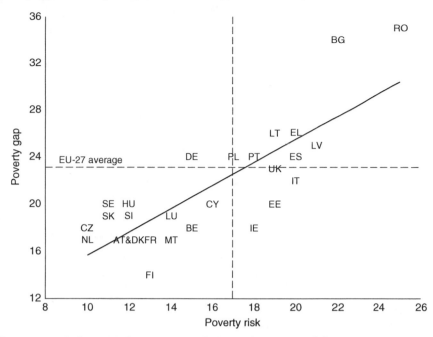

Figure 15.2a Relative Median Poverty Risk Gap and Poverty Risk for EU Countries, 2007.
NOTE: Data are presented as percentages. EU-27 averages are population-weighted averages of the 27 national rates (see Table 15.A) The regression line is fitted by ordinary least squares to EU-27 countries. For poverty gap, data are provisional for PT.
SOURCE: EU-SILC (2007).

in the country in question, not in the EU as a whole. This is consistent with the core definition of poverty adopted by the Council, and already quoted above, which refers to the minimum acceptable way of life in one's own country.

In Figure 15.2a, we plot the at-risk-of-poverty rate against the relative median poverty risk gap. These two indicators are clearly related (explored later in Table 15.6), but there are some interesting outliers. For example, Ireland combines a relatively high poverty-risk headcount with a fairly low median poverty-risk gap, whereas the reverse is true for Germany. Romania and Bulgaria combine the highest poverty risks with the highest poverty gaps. Moreover, their poverty gaps are much larger than what could be predicted by a regression line. By contrast, another striking outlier is Finland, where the poverty-risk gap is much smaller than in any other EU country and the poverty risk is significantly lower than the EU average but not among the lowest ones (eight member states have lower at-risk-of-poverty rates). It is likely that the level of the poverty-risk threshold with respect to minimum social benefits, as well as the coverage of these benefits, is part of the explanation for these outliers.[11]

The variation of the at-risk-of-poverty rates across countries merits closer attention. It is interesting to observe that the 2004 enlargement has not appreciably increased the range of rates of poverty risk, which vary between 10 percent (for the Czech Republic and the Netherlands) and 20 to 21 percent (Italy, Greece, Spain, and Latvia). By contrast, the most recent EU enlargement (in 2007) did broaden the

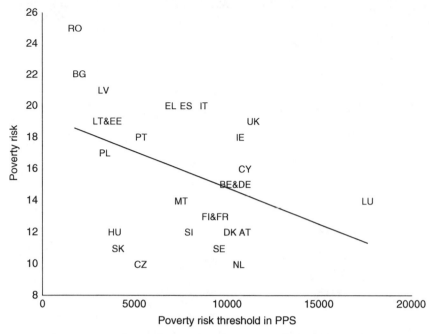

Figure 15.2b Poverty Risk Rate (Percent) and Poverty Risk Threshold (in PPS) for EU
Countries, 2007.
NOTE: The regression line is fitted by ordinary least squares to EU-27 countries. The
national thresholds presented are annual amounts and apply to one-person households.
SOURCE: EU-SILC (2007).

range significantly: The poverty risk in Bulgaria is 22 percent and in Romania
25 percent.

Figure 15.2b plots the poverty-risk rates against the poverty-risk thresholds,[12]
which are the national reference incomes below which one is considered at risk of
poverty and which are determined by the overall living standards in the country
(being a proportion of national median incomes). It is clear from this figure that
there is a tendency for the poverty risk to fall as we move from poorer countries to
richer countries. However, there is substantial dispersion around the linear regression line fitted to predict poverty risk for the EU-27 member states as a function of
their national poverty-risk threshold (and the R^2 is only 0.17).[13] All but 1 of the 12
EU countries lying below the regression line are among those with the most equal
income distributions. Indeed, according to the 2007 EU-SILC data, 10 of these countries have Gini coefficients between 23 and 26 percent and 1 (the Netherlands) has a
Gini of 28 percent; only Poland has a Gini just above the EU-27 average (32 percent
vs. 31 percent). The only other countries with a Gini coefficient below 30 percent are
Belgium (26 percent) and Luxembourg (27 percent); Belgium lies almost on the line,
whereas Luxembourg is clearly an outlier. Bulgaria and Romania are distinctive in
having very low thresholds and very high at-risk-of-poverty rates compared with
other EU countries; they are also distinctive in having a very high Gini coefficients
(35 percent for Bulgaria and 38 percent for Romania).

Thus, whereas the 2004 enlargement did not really increase the difference in the at-risk-of-poverty rates between the best performers and the worst (2 to 1 for EU-15 vs. 2.1 to 1 for EU-25), the 2007 enlargement did increase this difference (to 2.5 to 1). The at-risk-of-poverty rates clearly have to be interpreted in the light of the thresholds in each country; these are intended to capture exclusion vis-à-vis what is viewed as acceptable in the country, but the differences between them also help to convey the differences in real living standards involved. (See also the section on material deprivation.)

Long-Term Unemployment and Joblessness

The concern about long-term unemployment, defined as the proportion of people unemployed (International Labor Organization definition)for at least 12 months in the total active population aged 15 years or more, is not a recent one and has been further exacerbated by the global financial and economic crisis. A second very important EU indicator of possible labor market exclusion is provided by the proportion of adults aged between 18 and 59 years who live in *jobless households,* that is, in households where all members aged 18–59 years are either economically inactive or unemployed.[14] Living in jobless households is seen as particularly problematic, not only because of the generally precarious income situation of those households, but also because children growing up in that context may find it more difficult to find their own place in the labor market in later life.

Figure 15.3 shows that the link between long-term unemployment and the proportion of adults in jobless households is positive but not very pronounced. One observes a (rather mixed) group of countries where the rates of both long-term unemployment and jobless households are low (with Cyprus in the extreme bottom left corner), and a group where both are high. The latter group includes some countries with Bismarckian welfare states (Belgium, France, and Germany), and also some Eastern European countries (Bulgaria, Hungary, Poland, and Romania). Portugal suffers from fairly high rates of long-term unemployment, but these do not result in many adults living in jobless households. Conversely, in the United Kingdom, many adults live in jobless households, though long-term unemployment is low. Slovakia combines a very high long-term unemployment rate (8.3 percent as opposed to 3 percent for the EU-27 average) with a just below average level of joblessness (8.9 percent vs. 9.3 percent).

Three reasons are likely to account for the lack of a clear picture from the data. First, persons may be out of work for other reasons than unemployment (e.g., caring responsibilities, disability). Second, and more importantly, the extent to which unemployment is translated into joblessness at the household level depends on who the unemployed are and also on how unemployment is spread/polarized among households (and is possibly related to household formation). In many Southern European countries, unemployed young adults often continue to live with their parents. Conversely, for single persons and single parents, unemployment by definition means living in a jobless household, so if there is a large proportion of such persons in a country, the proportion of persons living in jobless households is more likely to be elevated.

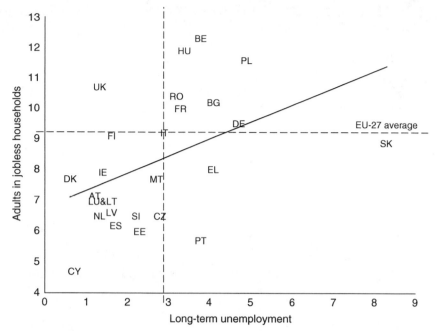

Figure 15.3 Long-Term Unemployment and Adults in Jobless Households for EU Countries, 2007.

NOTE: Data are presented as percentages.

"Jobless households": 2006 data for DK, data missing for SE. The regression line is fitted by ordinary least squares to EU-27 countries. AT and LU are clustered.

SOURCE: LFS (2007).

Early School Leaving

The *early school leavers* indicator, that is, the share of persons aged 18–24 years who have only lower secondary education and have not received education or training in the previous four weeks, receives considerable attention at the EU level both in the social OMC and in the European Employment Strategy. It does not only include dropouts but also persons who have finished lower secondary education with a proper diploma and who may have then entered the labor market; the upper age limit of compulsory schooling, therefore, can be one of the determinants of the differences across countries.[15] Figure 15.4 shows that the three best-performing countries on this indicator are in Eastern Europe (Poland, Czech Republic, Slovakia) and Finland; it is in Malta, Portugal, and Spain that the poorest outcomes are registered.

If we disregard the three outliers in Figure 15.4 (Malta, Portugal, and Spain), we see a tendency for countries with higher poverty-risk rates to also have higher levels of early school leaving.[16] Moreover, for similar poverty-risk rates, "old" member states tend to have higher rates of early school leaving (for instance, the Czech Republic compared to the Netherlands or Lithuania and Estonia compared to the United Kingdom).

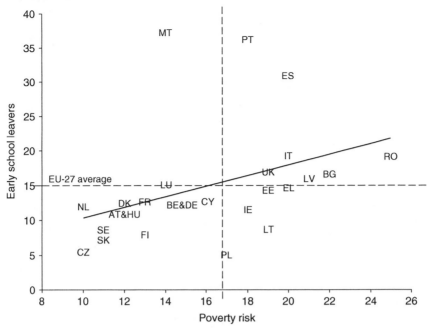

Figure 15.4 Early School Leavers (LFS) and Poverty Risk (EU-SILC) for EU Countries, 2007.

NOTE: Data are presented as percentages. "Early school leavers": 2006 for Czech Republic; missing ("uncertain/unreliable") data for SI. The regression line is fitted by ordinary least squares to EU-27 countries.

SOURCES: LFS (2007); EU-SILC (2007).

Employment Gap of Immigrants

The employment gap of immigrants measures the difference between the employment rate of immigrants and that of the nonimmigrant population, where immigrants are defined as persons born abroad.[17] Figure 15.5 reveals first of all that the employment gap is negative in many countries (negative values are located in Eastern and Southern Europe and also in Luxembourg), indicating that immigrants are in fact more likely than nonimmigrants to be employed. Clearly, the composition of the immigrant population in terms of age, country of origin, and year of immigration is an important factor here. Although employment is a crucial aspect of people's income and living conditions, the description of this indicator rightly notes that it needs to be supplemented by relevant national data covering other key aspects of the social inclusion of migrants (European Commission 2009b, 20).

One might expect that in countries where long-term unemployment is high, the immigrant employment gap is higher because unemployment might then hit the more vulnerable group of immigrants more strongly than it will affect the nonimmigrants. Figure 15.5 suggests that such a tendency is indeed present, and we can point to Poland, Germany, and Belgium as clear examples. But there are also important exceptions—in particular Denmark, Sweden, and the Netherlands. On top of very low long-term unemployment rates, these latter countries have the

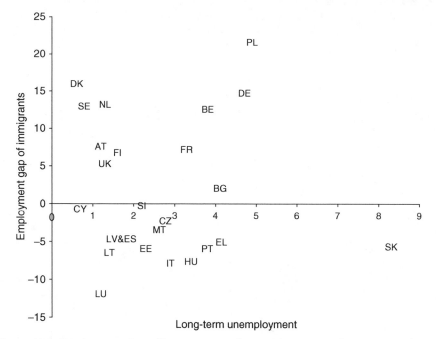

Figure 15.5 Employment Gap of Immigrants and Long-Term Unemployment Rate for
EU Countries, 2007.
NOTE: Data are presented as percentages. Data related to employment gap of immigrants
are missing for IE and RO; the EU-27 average for the gap is 2.6 and for long-term
unemployment 3 percent.
SOURCE: LFS (2007).

highest overall levels of employment among EU member states (74.2–77.1 percent in
2007), but these very good performances of the labor market do not extend to the
immigrant population. In fact, in these countries, the employment rate among nonimmigrants is very high, but the employment rate among immigrants is not necessarily lower than it is in countries that score better on the immigrant employment
gap (for interesting comparative EU figures on employment and unemployment gap
by country of birth and by nationality, see European Commission 2009a).[18]

The specific situation of Slovakia needs to be highlighted, as this country combines the highest rate of long-term unemployment with very good performance on
the indicator measuring the employment gap of immigrants.

Material Deprivation

The measurement of material deprivation has been regularly on the EU agenda since
2004 but it is only since the second half of 2009 that two indicators have been formally agreed upon and added to the EU set of commonly agreed indicators for social
inclusion (see previous discussion: indicators P8 in Table 15.1a and S4 in Table
15.1b). Originally proposed by Guio (Guio 2009), these indicators significantly
improve the multidimensional coverage of the EU portfolio for social inclusion.

Based on the limited information available from the EU-SILC data set, they focus on the proportion of people living in households who cannot afford at least three of the following nine items: (1) coping with unexpected expenses; (2) one week annual holiday away from home; (3) avoiding arrears (in mortgage or rent, utility bills, or hire purchase installments); (4) a meal with meat, chicken, or fish every second day; (5) keeping the home adequately warm; (6) a washing machine; (7) a color television; (8) a telephone; (9) a car. So, these measures aggregate information focused on some key aspects of *material* living conditions; they do not aim at covering all the dimensions of social exclusion (e.g., health, employment, education, social participation). This approach, in terms of "enforced lack," makes the suggested indices more comparable with inter alia income poverty (see below).

When using these indicators of material deprivation in a comparative context, two important points need to be highlighted. First, as emphasized by Marlier et al. (2007): "the essential interest here is not so much in individual items per se as in the underlying situation of more generalized deprivation that they can help to capture" (177). Indeed, "a useful analogy may be the way a battery of different survey responses can be used to categorize respondents by, say, personality type: any one response item may not be a reliable indicator, but taken together a set of responses can provide a very much more reliable basis for categorization" (194). The second important point is that whatever the common set of items used throughout the EU for measuring material deprivation, one needs to ensure that these items correctly capture living patterns and expectations of the society; and, therefore, they should be tested regularly to reflect possible societal changes. As indicated in Dickes, Fusco, and Marlier (2010), "the recent global economic and financial turmoil is, for instance, likely to affect the national perceptions of social needs."[19] Therefore, in 2011, when the data from the special 2009 EU-SILC module on material deprivation with a broader set of variables become available, it will be particularly important to come back to these measures in order to refine them.

We see from Table 15.2a that the range across countries in terms of the percentage (materially) deprived is wide—from 3 percent in Luxembourg and 6 percent in Sweden and the Netherlands up to as high as 53 percent in Romania and 72 percent in Bulgaria. This variation is much wider than the range in poverty-risk rates, which is only from 10 percent to 25 percent (see Figure 15.2a). This reflects the fact that differences in average living standards across countries as well as the distribution within them now come into play.

As shown in Figure 15.6a, the most striking examples in this respect are Hungary and Slovakia (which have high levels of deprivation but low income poverty rates) as well as, though to a lesser extent, the Czech Republic (lowest poverty risk in EU, together with the Netherlands, but intermediate performance on deprivation). Conversely, Spain has a high poverty risk (fourth highest in EU, *ex aequo* with Greece and Italy), whereas it has a relatively low level of material deprivation (sixth best performance, *ex aequo* with Austria, Ireland, and the United Kingdom). If we look more closely at the impact of the two most recent EU enlargements, we see that among the 15 old member states the link between poverty risk and material deprivation is strong (R^2: 0.39). The 2004 enlargement from 15 to 25 countries (notably Hungary, Slovakia, and the Czech Republic; see earlier discussion) has significantly weakened this link (R^2: 0.10). Finally, the 2007 enlargement has significantly increased the relationship between these two indicators (R^2: 0.30); this is due to the fact that the

Table 15.2a MATERIAL DEPRIVATION AND POVERTY-RISK THRESHOLD
FOR EU COUNTRIES, 2007

Country	Percentage of Persons Deprived for at Least 3 of 9 Items	Mean Number of Items Lacked Among Deprived Population	Poverty-risk Threshold (PPS)
Luxembourg (LU)	3	3.4	17,575
Netherlands (NL)	6	3.4	10,631
Sweden (SE)	6	3.5	9,581
Denmark (DK)	7	3.8	10,175
Finland (FI)	9	3.5	9,223
Austria (AT)	10	3.5	10,880
Spain (ES)	10	3.4	7,807
Ireland (IE)	10	3.6	10,706
United Kingdom (UK)	10	3.5	11,366
Belgium (BE)	12	3.7	10,035
Germany (DE)	12	3.6	10,403
France (FR)	12	3.6	9,363
Malta (MT)	13	3.4	7,543
Slovenia (SI)	14	3.5	7,979
Estonia (EE)	15	3.6	4,059
Italy (IT)	15	3.7	8,748
Czech Republic (CZ)	16	3.7	5,348
Greece (EL)	22	3.9	6,946
Portugal (PT)	22	3.7	5,360
Lithuania (LT)	30	4.0	3,512
Slovakia (SK)	30	3.7	4,133
Cyprus (CY)	31	3.6	10,938
Hungary (HU)	37	3.9	3,979
Poland (PL)	38	3.9	3,422
Latvia (LV)	45	4.0	3,356
Romania (RO)	53	4.5	1,765
Bulgaria (BG)	72	4.5	2,006
EU-27 average	18	3.8	—

NOTE: Countries ranked in ascending order based on national percentages of people deprived for three or more items. Poverty risk thresholds are annual amounts (in PPS) calculated for one-person households. Interpretation: In Luxembourg, 3 percent of the population is "deprived" on the material deprivation indicator, that is, lack at least three of the nine items considered; and, on average, the deprived population lacks 3.4 of these nine items. The national poverty risk threshold is 17,575 PPS.

SOURCE: EU-SILC (2007).

two new member states (Bulgaria and Romania) combine both the highest poverty-risk rates and the highest proportions of materially deprived persons.

Unfortunately, data that would allow the evolution over time of material deprivation to be tracked only cover the period from 2005 to 2007; and for Bulgaria and Romania, data are only available for 2007. Using the little information available to date, Figure 15.6b shows that in the EU-15 countries both poverty-risk and material deprivation rates have remained stable, whereas, in the 10 new member states that joined the EU in 2004 (NMS-10), material deprivation rates have declined significantly (by 5 points between 2005 and 2006 and by 5 more points between 2006 and 2007) and poverty rates have declined very slightly.

Table 15.2a also allows us to look at the relationship between deprivation and the national relative income thresholds, which in turn reflect median income levels in each country. We see that the extent of material deprivation is generally much higher in the countries with lower poverty-risk thresholds (the R^2 between the proportions of materially deprived persons and these thresholds is 0.58 for EU-27). Out of the eight countries with the highest levels of material deprivation (Bulgaria, Romania, Latvia, Poland, Hungary, Cyprus, Slovakia, and Lithuania: proportions between 30 and 72 percent), seven (exception: Cyprus) are among the eight countries with the lowest thresholds (all below 4,200 purchasing power standards [PPS]). Cyprus, on

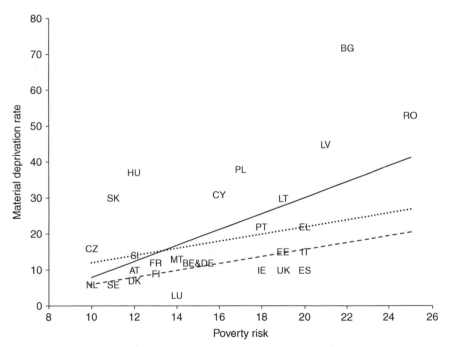

Figure 15.6a Link between Material Deprivation and Income Poverty: Material Deprivation and Poverty Risk for EU Countries, 2007.
NOTE: Data are presented as percentages. The thick regression line is fitted by ordinary least squares to EU-27 countries, the thin line to EU-25 countries, and the dotted line to EU-15 countries.
SOURCE: EU-SILC (2007).

the other hand, has a high level of deprivation but also a very high income threshold, whereas Estonia has a below EU-27 average deprivation rate but a low threshold.

The level of deprivation is clearly influenced by both the level of median income and how many fall well below it, which is what the at-risk-of-poverty rate captures. Countries such as Denmark, Finland, and Sweden have lower proportions of materially deprived persons than their level of threshold/median income would suggest, reflecting (at least in part) the fact that income is relatively equally distributed so the proportion falling below the threshold is low. A country such as Italy has a higher level of deprivation than its threshold/median income might suggest, consistent with the above-average at-risk-of-poverty rate. Romania and Bulgaria, though, have both the lowest thresholds and the highest at-risk-of-poverty rates in the EU, and it is no surprise that they also have the highest proportion of their populations deprived. Thus, placing the measures of material deprivation alongside the at-risk-of-poverty rates helps to bring out in a direct and concrete way the fact that different living standards underpin those poverty rates.

This is also the case when we look in Table 15.2a at the depth of deprivation (mean number of items lacked) among those above the deprivation cutoff, in other words, living in deprivation. Although this does not vary much across countries, it tends to be highest in the countries with the highest proportion deprived. Within countries, Figure 15.6c shows that the depth of deprivation is everywhere a good deal higher for those below the poverty-risk threshold than above it (though the gap is

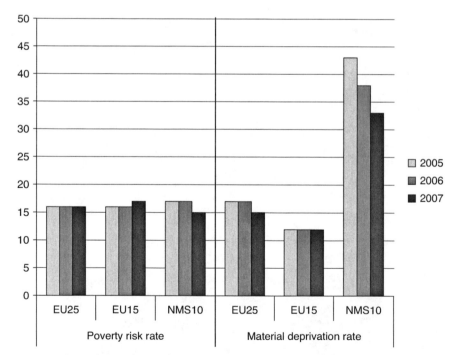

Figure 15.6b Evolution over Time of Material Deprivation and Income Poverty for EU Countries, 2005–2007.
NOTE: Data are presented as percentages.
SOURCE: EU-SILC (2005, 2006, 2007).

considerably wider in some countries than in others). It also shows that deprivation depth for those at risk of poverty in some of the richer countries is lower than the corresponding figures for those *not at risk* in the poorest countries.[20] This does not invalidate the poverty measures for the rich countries, because they relate (supposedly) to norms of acceptability in those countries, but it does help reinforce the long-standing importance assigned by the EU to seeking convergence in average income/living standards across its member states. (On the latter issue, Marlier et al. [2007] suggest that the EU portfolio of indicators on social inclusion should be complemented with a "background statistic" based on a common income threshold set at 60 percent of the EU-wide median. The suggested use of this statistic, which could be calculated from pooled EU-SILC data, "is intended to address the key issue of social cohesion/convergence across the Union rather than capturing *absolute* poverty" [155].)

The various results presented in the preceding discussion bring out the value of complementing the indicators based on the relative EU at-risk-of-poverty measure with indicators of material deprivation, particularly in the enlarged EU. It is also interesting to mention that the association between the material deprivation rate and the median poverty-risk gap (i.e., the difference between the income poverty threshold and the median equivalized income of income-poor persons, expressed as a percentage of the income poverty threshold) is stronger (R^2 is 0.59 at EU-27 level; see Table 15.6) than that with the income poverty rate. This brings out that the proportion deprived is influenced not just by the level of the income threshold vis-à-vis other countries and how many are below it, but also how far they fall below the threshold.

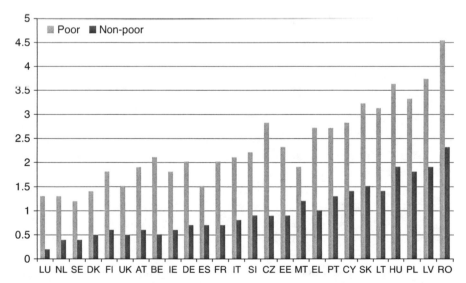

Figure 15.6c Overlap between Material Deprivation and Income Poverty: Mean Number of "Lacked" Items among Income-Poor and Non-Income-Poor Population for EU Countries, 2007.
NOTE: In Luxembourg, on average those above the 60 percent of median income poverty risk threshold lack 0.2 item out of these nine items, whereas those below the threshold lack 1.3 items. Data not available for BG.
SOURCE: EU-SILC (2007).

Finally, the material deprivation indicators are very valuable in the insights they provide into the extent and nature of deprivation being experienced by different groups and household types within countries. For example, comparing the deprivation rates of the elderly and the nonelderly shows that older persons fare better within their societies in northern "old" member states than in most "new" member states or old southern countries (see Table 15.2b). This may provide a rather different picture to that given by comparisons of income poverty rates within countries, because deprivation indicators will capture not only income differences between groups but also the differential impact of various forms of state provision of services, of assets such as home ownership, and of other factors affecting living standards. This type of analysis provides an important perspective in understanding the needs of different household types and framing policy to respond. (See Dewilde [2009] and Jehoel-Gijsbers and Vrooman [2008].) The EU indicators also allow one to compare deprivation levels across different groups below the income poverty threshold within countries, and at the national level, some countries have focused particular attention on those who are both below that threshold and experiencing serious deprivation—sometimes labeled the "consistently poor" (see Nolan and Whelan 2010). In the light of the well-recognized weaknesses of looking only at income for comprehensively capturing living standards, this provides a way of prioritizing the most vulnerable within countries (though it would be less suitable for making comparisons across countries with very different levels of relative income poverty and/or deprivation as in the case of the EU).

Unmet Need for Medical Care

Self-reported unmet need for medical care is defined in the EU portfolio of primary indicators for social inclusion as the proportion of persons reporting that they did not obtain medical care they needed for one of the following three reasons: financial barriers, too long waiting times, or facility too far to travel. Figure 15.7 shows that unmet medical need is a nearly non-existing problem in several of the rich EU countries with highly developed welfare states in North-Western Europe as well as in the Czech Republic, Hungary, Malta, Slovakia, and Slovenia. Much larger proportions of persons reporting unmet medical need are observed in the Baltic States, Romania, Poland, and Portugal as well as, though to a lesser extent, Greece and Italy (there are no data available for Bulgaria to date).[21]

The relationship of unmet medical needs with poverty risk has an interesting triangular shape. Whereas some countries with relatively high poverty risks manage to keep unmet medical need very low (Ireland, United Kingdom, Spain), there are no countries with low poverty risks and high levels of unmet need. One interpretation of this finding could be that a low poverty risk (as measured by the EU indicator, i.e., in relative terms) can only be sustained by countries with a system of generous social transfers with broad coverage, and that welfare states that achieve that, also provide accessible health care.[22]

Housing Indicators

Since the beginning of the social OMC, the EU had singled out housing as one of the areas that should be regularly monitored at the national and EU levels on the basis of

Table 15.2b MATERIAL DEPRIVATION AND POVERTY RISK FOR EU COUNTRIES, NATIONAL PERCENTAGES AMONG POPULATION AGED 18–64 YEARS AND POPULATION AGED 65 AND OVER, 2007

Country	Material Deprivation		Poverty Risk	
	18–64 Years	65+ Years	18–64 Years	65+ Years
Austria (AT)	10	10	11	14
Belgium (BE)	11	10	13	23
Bulgaria (BG)	69	81	19	23
Cyprus (CY)	29	44	10	51
Czech Republic (CZ)	15	17	8	5
Denmark (DK)	7	4	11	18
Estonia (EE)	14	20	16	33
Finland (FI)	10	8	11	22
France (FR)	12	8	12	13
Germany (DE)	13	7	15	17
Greece (EL)	21	29	19	23
Hungary (HU)	36	35	12	6
Ireland (IE)	10	4	15	29
Italy (IT)	14	14	18	22
Latvia (LV)	42	59	18	33
Lithuania (LT)	28	39	16	30
Luxembourg (LU)	3	1	13	7
Malta (MT)	12	12	12	21
Netherlands (NL)	6	3	9	10
Poland (PL)	38	41	17	8
Portugal (PT)	21	27	15	26
Romania (RO)	49	66	21	31
Slovakia (SK)	28	42	9	8
Slovenia (SI)	14	18	10	19
Spain (ES)	9	11	16	28
Sweden (SE)	6	3	10	11
United Kingdom (UK)	10	5	15	30
NMS-10 average	32	36	14	11
EU-27 average	18	16	15	20

SOURCE: EU-SILC (2007).

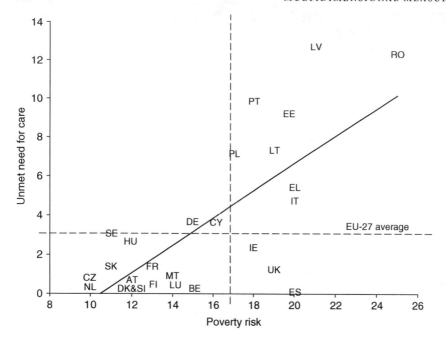

Figure 15.7 Unmet Need for Medical Care and Poverty Risk for EU Countries, 2007.
NOTE: Data presented as percentages. Unmet need for care: data missing for BG; "Waiting list" information not available for DK; "Too far to travel" information not available for SI and FI. The regression line is fitted by ordinary least squares to the EU-27 countries.
SOURCE: EU-SILC (2007).

commonly agreed indicators (see Social Protection Committee 2001). But it is only since the second half of 2009 that housing is covered in the EU portfolio of indicators for social inclusion. Despite this major step forward, some important dimensions of housing are not yet covered and further progress will be needed. The EU has not yet adopted any primary indicator in the field of housing, so this section focuses on the two secondary indicators now included in the EU portfolio (see Table 15.1b): indicators S5 (households with high housing costs) and S6 (overcrowding).

The "burdened by housing costs" indicator measures the percentage of the population living in a household where the total housing costs (net of housing allowances) represent more than 40 percent of total disposable household income (net of housing allowances). The "overcrowding rate" represents the percentage of people living in a household where at least one of the following criteria is not fulfilled: one room for the household, one room for each couple, one room for each single person aged 18 years or older, one room for two single people of the same sex between 12 and 17 years of age, one room for each single person of different sex between 12 and 17 years of age, and one room for two people under 12 years of age. The values reported here are for all households, including one-person households.[23]

It is worth noting that there is very little association between the two housing indicators that indeed shed light on very different aspects of housing. A relatively large group of countries perform quite well on both indicators, whereas Bulgaria, Romania, and Slovakia perform poorly on both. A number of old EU member states with relatively high median incomes (Germany, Denmark, the Netherlands, and the United Kingdom) combine low overcrowding rates and relatively high levels of housing costs burden. By contrast, a set of countries have low proportions of people burdened by housing costs but high rates of overcrowding; all of these are new member states. Cyprus and Malta are exceptions, as on both indicators they have the best results in the whole EU-27.

At the macro-level, there is no clear link between the at-risk-of-poverty rate and the two EU indicators on housing. For the EU-27 countries, the R^2 between poverty risk and overcrowding is 0.15 and between poverty risk and housing cost burden, it is even lower (0.06). If we now change the unit of analysis and move from country to people and households, that is, from the macro- to the micro-level, then the picture becomes different as can be seen from Table 15.3. For the EU-27, the proportion of persons living in overcrowded households is almost two times higher in the income-poor population than in the non-income-poor population (27 percent vs. 15 percent). For the indicator on housing cost burden, the difference is even more striking: 39 percent as opposed to 8 percent, that is, a ratio close to 5.

If we move back to our main unit of analysis (i.e., individual countries) and consider the macro-level link between overcrowding and material deprivation (rather than poverty risk), the association between these two EU indicators is quite strong with an R^2 of 0.58 for the EU-27. The link is much weaker between material deprivation and housing cost burden, where the R^2 is 0.28 for EU-27.

THE PORTFOLIO OF INDICATORS AS A WHOLE

Building on the results presented in the preceding section, we now look more closely at the value added of a multidimensional portfolio of indicators for monitoring the social OMC. First, we look at the way countries are ranked on the basis of each individual primary indicator. In doing this, we disregard indicators P7 and P10 (i.e., "employment gap of immigrants" and "self-reported unmet need for medical care"; see Table 15.1a) as these are labeled "national," meaning, as previously discussed, that they do not meet all the methodological criteria required for "EU" indicators proper. In particular, this means that they should not be used for direct cross-country comparisons (such as international rankings) without being properly contextualized. So, in the first subsection, we focus only on the six EU primary indicators for social inclusion available to date. To explore the relationship between indicators, an alternative to rankings is to calculate the correlations of the indicators' values. This is what we do in the second subsection, where we look at the extent to which the primary indicators are correlated at the *macro-level*. Here, we consider all eight primary indicators available, that is, the six "EU" measures and the two "national" measures. Finally, in the third subsection, we briefly discuss whether composite indicators might provide useful tools in an EU comparative context.

Interrelation Between Indicators: Rankings

From our discussion of the different indicators in the third section (on the overlaps and complementarities of individual indicators), it is clear that the various indicators

Table 15.3 Overlap between Housing and Income Poverty: Overcrowded Households and Housing Cost Burden among Income-Poor and Non-Income-Poor Population for EU Countries, 2007

Country	Overcrowding			Burdened by Housing Costs		
	Non-poor	Poor	Total	Non-poor	Poor	Total
Austria (AT)	12	33	15	2	32	5
Belgium (BE)	2	10	4	5	39	10
Bulgaria (BG)	47	62	50	32	70	40
Cyprus (CY)	1	4	1	1	8	2
Czech Republic (CZ)	29	63	32	7	39	10
Denmark (DK)	5	22	7	8	58	13
Estonia (EE)	42	47	43	2	19	5
Finland (FI)	4	18	6	3	18	5
France (FR)	7	22	9	4	19	6
Germany (DE)	2	8	3	16	68	23
Greece (GR)	26	35	28	3	66	16
Hungary (HU)	44	63	46	4	32	7
Ireland (IE)	3	5	4	1	12	3
Italy (IT)	20	37	24	3	27	8
Latvia (LV)	60	57	59	4	31	10
Lithuania (LT)	50	57	52	1	20	5
Luxembourg (LU)	5	26	7	1	23	4
Malta (MT)	4	3	4	1	11	3
Netherlands (NL)	1	6	2	14	61	19
Poland (PL)	48	68	52	6	33	11
Portugal (PT)	14	21	15	4	22	7
Romania (RO)	53	59	54	10	43	18
Slovakia (SK)	39	56	41	15	53	19
Slovenia (SI)	38	48	39	3	22	5
Spain (ES)	3	7	4	3	22	7
Sweden (SE)	7	28	9	3	46	8
United Kingdom (UK)	4	11	6	10	47	17
EU-27 average	15	27	17	8	39	13

NOTE: Data are presented as percentages.

SOURCE: EU-SILC (2007).

for social inclusion agreed upon by the EU do indeed tell a different story about the relative social performances of EU member states. They also tell different stories in terms of policy evaluation.

As an illustration, we first focus on the six "EU" indicators included in the social inclusion portfolio and explore their interaction more explicitly: the at-risk-of-poverty rate, relative median poverty-risk gap, long-term unemployment, adults living in jobless households, early school leavers, and material deprivation. Table 15.4 shows the rankings, from 1st position (best performance, i.e., in view of the nature of the indicators considered, lowest percentage) to 27th position (poorest performance), of the EU-27 countries on each of these indicators. There is considerable movement up and down the ranking as we move from one indicator to another. When the common indicators were first mooted, there was general agreement that they should be multidimensional. This view was held largely on a priori grounds: that it was right in principle. Now that we have the experience of values being given to the indicators, enriched by enlargement, we can see that the multidimensional approach is indeed crucial. The best performers on poverty risk have a strong tendency to be ranked lower on long-term unemployment and/or on the proportion of adults living in jobless households. Fourteen countries (eight "old" and six "new" member states) are among the top three countries for at least one of the six indicators. Thus, just over half of the EU countries can claim to be in the "top three."

Another way of conveying the same type of message is to look at the same six primary indicators and, for each of them, to divide countries into quartiles taking the median across countries as the "benchmark." This is what we do in Table 15.5. As for all six indicators, a low value represents a good performance, countries in the first quartile are marked "++," in the second quartile "+," in the third "-," and in the fourth "—." (In interpreting the results, it should be borne in mind that the various dimensions of poverty and social exclusion covered by the indicators are represented by differing numbers of indicators.)

The second to last column in Table 15.5 provides the number of EU primary indicators on which each country performs poorly relative to the median (scores "-" or "—"). It shows a much denser concentration of poor performances (at least 5 of 6) for Bulgaria, Estonia, Greece, Italy, Poland, Portugal, and Romania. Conversely, some countries stand out for the small number (maximum 1) of poor performances; these include various rich countries with extensive welfare states (Austria, Denmark, Finland, Luxembourg, the Netherlands, and Sweden) as well as Slovenia. In order to better identify good performance, the last column in Table 15.5 indicates the number of EU primary indicators on which each country performs in the top quarter ("++"), which may be helpful in seeking to spot possible good practices. All except eight countries (Belgium, Bulgaria, Germany, Greece, Ireland, Italy, Latvia, and Romania) are in the top quarter for at least one of the six indicators considered. The subset of best-performing countries (3 or more "++") is close though not identical to the one identified earlier. It consists of Austria, Denmark, Finland, the Netherlands, and Sweden (as above), and also of the Czech Republic (new); Luxembourg and Slovenia are no longer part of the list.

The fact that 19 countries of 27 are in the top quarter for at least one indicator illustrates the diversity in national situations and policies. It also serves to bring out the importance for countries and the European Commission of making full use of the whole EU portfolio of indicators rather than solely concentrating on a few lead indicators.

Table 15.4 Ranking of EU Countries for Six Primary Indicators of Social Inclusion, 2007

Country	Poverty Risk	Median Poverty Risk Gap	Long-term Unemployment	Adults in Jobless Households	Early School Leavers	Material Deprivation
Czech Republic (CZ)	1	7	16	5	2	17
Netherlands (NL)	1	2	6	5	10	2
Sweden (SE)	3	13	3	NA	5	2
Slovakia (SK)	3	10	27	16	3	20
Austria (AT)	5	2	4	11	7	6
Denmark (DK)	5	2	1	12	12	4
Hungary (HU)	5	13	20	25	7	23
Slovenia (SI)	5	10	13	5	NA	14
Finland (FI)	9	1	10	17	4	5
France (FR)	9	2	19	20	14	10
Luxembourg (LU)	11	10	4	9	18	1
Malta (MT)	11	2	15	12	26	13
Belgium (BE)	13	7	21	26	11	10
Germany (DE)	13	19	25	19	14	10
Cyprus (CY)	15	13	2	1	13	22
Poland (PL)	16	19	26	24	1	24
Ireland (IE)	17	7	8	14	9	6
Portugal (PT)	17	19	21	2	25	18

Country						
Estonia (EE)	19	13	14	3	16	15
Lithuania (LT)	19	24	8	9	6	20
United Kingdom (UK)	19	18	6	23	21	6
Spain (ES)	22	19	12	4	24	6
Greece (EL)	22	24	23	15	17	18
Italy (IT)	22	17	17	18	23	15
Latvia (LV)	25	23	10	8	19	25
Bulgaria (BG)	26	26	23	21	20	27
Romania (RO)	27	27	18	22	22	26

NOTE: Poverty gap: provisional data for PT. Jobless households: 2006 data for DK and data not available (NA) for Sweden. Early school leavers: provisional data for LV and PT; 2006 data for CZ; unreliable/uncertain data for SI. For each indicator, the first position is given to the country that has the "best" performance (i.e., respectively: lowest poverty-risk rate, lowest long-term unemployment rate, lowest proportion of adults in jobless households, lowest percentage of early school leavers, and lowest materially deprived population), the second to the country that has the second "best" performance, etc. Countries with equal rates are assigned equal rankings. The order of countries in the table reflects the ranking on the poverty-risk indicator.

SOURCES: EU-SILC (2007) and LFS (2007).

Table 15.5 Quartile Scores of EU Countries for Six Primary Indicators of Social Inclusion, 2007

Country	Poverty Risk	Poverty Gap	Long-term Unemployment	Adults in Jobless Households	Early School Leavers	Material Deprivation	Poorest Performance (- or —)	Best Performance (++)
Austria	++	++	++	+	+	+	0	3
Belgium	+	+	−	−	+	+	2	0
Bulgaria	−	−	−	−	−	−	6	0
Cyprus	−	−	++	++	+	−	3	2
Czech Republic	++	+	−	++	++	−	2	3
Denmark	++	++	++	+	+	++	0	4
Estonia	−	−	−	++	−	−	5	1
Finland	+	++	+	−	++	++	1	3
France	+	++	−	−	−	+	3	1
Germany	+	−	−	−	−	+	4	0
Greece	−	−	−	−	−	−	6	0
Hungary	++	−	−	−	+	−	4	1
Ireland	−	+	+	−	+	+	2	0
Italy	−	−	−	−	−	−	6	0
Latvia	−	−	+	+	−	−	4	0
Lithuania	−	−	+	+	++	−	3	1

Luxembourg	+	+	++	+	-	++	1	2
Malta	+	++	-	+	—	+	2	1
Netherlands	++	++	++	++	+	++	0	5
Poland	-	-	—	—	++	—	5	1
Portugal	-	-	—	++	—	-	5	1
Romania	—	—	-	—	—	—	6	0
Slovakia	++	+	—	-	++	-	3	2
Slovenia	++	+	+	++	NA	-	1	2
Spain	—	-	+	++	—	+	3	1
Sweden	++	-	++	NA	++	++	1	4
United Kingdom	-	-	++	—	—	+	4	1

NOTE: For all indicators considered, a high value represents a poor national performance. Country figures are being compared with the EU median for each indicator. ++indicates that the country's performance is in the first quartile, + in the second; - in the third, and — in the fourth quartile. NA refers to nonavailable data.

SOURCES: EU-SILC (2007), and LFS (2007).

Interrelation Between Indicators: Correlations

Rankings may be misleading, because, where observations are bunched, a country may lose several places on account of a tiny difference. An alternative is provided by the correlations of the indicator values (though these are more easily affected than rankings by outliers). If the different indicators are highly correlated across countries, then this suggests that there is little value added from considering additional dimensions in determining *stricto sensu* their relative performance. It should be reemphasized that we are considering here countries as the unit of analysis. We learn nothing from these correlations about the extent to which risks are correlated at the individual level within any country. The at-risk-of-poverty rate may be much higher in countries with high rates of early school leavers, but this does not automatically imply that individual early school leavers in country A are at higher risk of poverty. In order to explore the latter correlation, we would have to go back to the microdata, that is, the observations on individual persons and households, which is not the purpose of our discussion here.

Table 15.6 shows the correlations between the primary indicators for which data are available at the time of writing this chapter. If we first look at the poverty risk rate (which is clearly the lead indicator in the primary list), we see that it correlates very strongly with the relative median poverty-risk gap (0.81) and unmet need for medical care (0.72), as well as, quite strongly, with material deprivation (0.55). As to the poverty gap, it correlates very strongly with unmet need for medical care (0.75) and also, as already highlighted, with material deprivation (0.77, i.e., a much higher correlation than for the poverty risk).

The correlations of poverty risk and poverty-risk gap with the indicators of labor market exclusion are very low (we will come back to this). By contrast, the association between long-term unemployment and material deprivation is limited (0.38) but yet significant at the 0.05 level.

Among the other indicators, we can see a number of significant correlations among the indicators of labor market exclusion, even if they are not very high. This is the case between jobless households and employment gap of immigrants (0.40) and also, as previously emphasized, long-term unemployment and adults living in jobless households (0.45). Otherwise, the only significant, and in fact very strong, correlation is observed between deprivation and unmet need for medical care (0.73).

Why are the correlations among most of the indicators very small or even insignificant? First of all, and most obviously, some indicators refer to quite different domains and, therefore, low correlations are not particularly surprising. There is a priori no particular reason why countries that perform well on dealing with early school leavers should also be successful in satisfactorily meeting the medical needs of their population, and in fact we observe no correlation between these indicators. But there are also instances where low correlations are unexpected. An instructive example is the nearly zero correlation between the joblessness measure and the poverty-risk rate. If one looks within nearly all EU countries, one finds a very strong association at the household level between joblessness and poverty risk, as can be seen from the examination of the EU poverty-risk indicator broken down by the "work intensity" of the household. Therefore, one might expect that countries where there are many jobless households would also have higher poverty-risk rates. This would certainly be correct, but for the fact that other variables intervene.

Table 15.6 Correlations among the Primary Indicators across EU-27 Countries, 2007

	Poverty Risk	Poverty Risk Gap	Long-term Unemployment	Adults in Jobless Households	Early School Leavers	Employment Gap of Immigrants	Material Deprivation	Unmet Need for Care
Poverty risk	1.00	0,81**	0.03	0.09	0.38	−0.32	0.55**	0.72**
Poverty gap	0.81**	1.00	0.25	0.19	0.21	−0.18	0.77**	0.75**
Long-term unemployment	0.03	0.25	1.00	0.45*	−0.05	−0.04	0.38*	0.13
Adults in jobless households	0.09	0.19	0.45*	1.00	−0.26	0.40*	0.27	−0.06
Early school leavers	0.38	0.21	−0.05	−0.26	1.00	−0.37	−0.02	0.15
Employment gap of immigrants	−0.32	−0.18	−0.04	0.40*	−0.37	1.00	−0.18	−0.25
Material deprivation	0.55**	0.77**	0.38*	0.27	−0.02	−0.18	1.00	0.73**
Unmet need for care	0.72**	0.75**	0.13	−0.06	0.15	−0.25	0.73**	1.00

NOTE: Correlations calculated pairwise (pairwise exclusion of missing values); **indicates that the correlation is significant at the 0.01 level (two-tailed) and *that it is significant at the 0.05 level (two-tailed).

SOURCES: EU-SILC (2007) and LFS (2007).

In fact, an important intervening variable is the extent of income protection. It is well known that there is a strong negative correlation between the extent of social income protection and the poverty-risk rate. It has more rarely been observed that there is in fact a *positive* relation between the degree of income protection and the proportion of jobless households. That there is such a relation makes perfect sense: in the absence of social protection, living in a jobless household is often not a viable option, and people either have to find work, or become part of another household. The fact that both poverty risk and joblessness are correlated with the degree of income protection, but with opposite signs, explains why we find little correlation across countries between the first two variables.

The example of poverty risk, joblessness, and income protection contains a more general point, which is relevant to the policy lessons that can be derived from such indicators: Sometimes there is a trade-off between different policy objectives, where increasing the effectiveness of a particular policy instrument as regards one objective may in fact exacerbate other problems. Governments often have to define priorities—investing in schools or in hospitals—because of budget constraints. Moreover, societies can make different democratic choices. These are important reasons why one should not rely on one or two indicators, but should use the entire portfolio.

A Composite Indicator?

An issue that inevitably arises when dealing with a multidimensional set of indicators is whether it is helpful to add up indicators for different fields to arrive at a total score, to which we refer here as a *composite* indicator.[24] The popularity of such an approach has been demonstrated inter alia by the United Nations Development Program Human Development Index, which is a composite of three basic components: longevity, education, and standard of living. Certainly, for the general public, composite indicators can serve a "headline" function, and newspapers are keen to report the resulting rankings of countries. In this way, the attention of the public can be drawn to issues in which they otherwise might show little interest. There are, however, a number of technical and political reasons why we do not feel that composite measures can play a useful monitoring role as part of the social OMC or in other international policy frameworks.

The design of any such index requires us to make social judgments about the weights to be placed on the different dimensions and the way in which they are combined. The weights are a matter for value judgments, and the adoption of a specific composite index may conceal the resolution of what is at heart a political problem. It ignores the advice that "weighing together different welfare components should be avoided to the very last so as not to conceal dissensions in a 'scientific' model" (Erikson 1974, 279).

The aim of policy should be to improve overall performance and, ideally, bring all countries to a high level, with countries encouraged to pursue a balanced approach to different dimensions of deprivation rather than "bang bang" policies concentrating on a single objective. This is best achieved by focusing on a portfolio of indicators rather than a single measure that seeks to summarize performance across them.[25]

CONCLUSIONS AND MOVING FORWARD

In this chapter, we have seen that the EU portfolio of commonly agreed indicators serves to bring out the diversity and multidimensionality of poverty and social exclusion and also of national situations and policies. This we regard as the key message from the EU experience that might usefully be injected into US debates, which have tended to focus on how best to improve the measure of income poverty rather than broaden the range of information employed. The EU has adopted indicators that meet its specific needs as a union of member states, so that measures that adopt a national rather than EU-wide frame of reference in assessing what constitutes an acceptable minimum standard of living have a major role. Nonetheless, the enlargement of the EU to include a much broader range of countries in terms of average income has also reinforced the long-standing commitment to working toward convergence in living standards across countries.

It is important to reemphasize that no country scores consistently better than the cross-country median on all indicators, and that most countries excel (are in the top quartile) on at least one indicator. Across countries, there is remarkably little correlation between different indicators, reflecting different social, demographic, and economic situations, but also different (implicit) policy priorities and trade-offs. Even where indicators are quite strongly correlated across countries, there are always countries that do not conform to the general pattern and these cases may contain valuable policy lessons (e.g., the poverty rate and unmet medical need). The case for a comprehensive portfolio of indicators, covering all key dimensions of the common EU objectives and balanced across the different dimensions, seems thus well established.

Some remaining gaps in the current EU portfolio of social inclusion indicators may be noted. The need for primary indicators on housing and child well-being is explicitly flagged for development and insertion in the EU set (see Table 15.1a). The Indicators Sub-Group of the EU Social Protection Committee and Eurostat have already devoted considerable effort to discussion and analysis of the options in these areas, and in the space available, we simply highlight some suggestions in other fields without being able to tease out the arguments in detail.[26]

An important priority might now be given to the development of a measure of premature mortality or life expectancy by socioeconomic circumstances, to be produced on a regular but not necessarily annual basis. Another area meriting attention is mental health and disability, where problems in definition and data loom large. Some of the existing EU indicators should also be refined—for example, an EU indicator of literacy for the working-age population would be a useful complement to the existing one for second-level school pupils, regional breakdowns for existing indicators where possible would be a valuable addition, and it would be highly valuable to complement the "working poor" EU indicator with a measure of the extent of low pay. The highly complex issue of intra-household allocation of resources (the topic for the 2010 EU-SILC module) will have to be further explored. Progress would also be needed in the understanding of the dynamics of income, poverty, and social exclusion at the micro-level, based on panel data, and the factors/processes associated with it (including the intergenerational transmission of disadvantage).

People living in institutions, migrants and ethnic minorities, other vulnerable groups including the homeless,[27] people with disabilities, those with addiction problems, and such are generally undercounted or missed by household surveys, and these require special attention. In view of the importance attached to learning about what does and does not work elsewhere, the EU institutions should also consider, in collaboration with the Organization for Economic Cooperation and Development (OECD), the extension of (some of) the commonly agreed social indicators to cover, for example, the United States, Australia, Canada, Japan, and New Zealand. This would clearly also be of considerable value to countries such as the United States in facilitating investigation of the factors underlying differences in performance—on the indicators they decide to focus on—between them and elsewhere.

It will also be important to enhance understanding of what the at-risk-of-poverty rates in the different member states, which are at the core of the set of indicators, actually mean in concrete terms. Providing the value of the national thresholds expressed in PPS is obviously valuable contextual information, but one ought to go further by investigating what these thresholds imply in terms of actual standard of living in each member state. What can a household on 60 percent of the median income, adjusted for its size and composition, in each country actually consume? A comparison with budget standard studies, which have been carried out in various countries, would be very useful in this regard (even when these standards are not fully comparable). Information on the actual expenditures of households around the poverty line could also help. A next step would be to use this information to investigate how much the appropriate purchasing power parities adjustment varies across the income distribution in the different member states. If the price relativities were moving against the poor, then this would become apparent from the implied budgets.[28] Such an analysis could valuably be supplemented by qualitative information on how people "at risk" actually live. This approach would make more meaningful the otherwise arcane statistical procedures on which the poverty-risk indicator is based. It would also be a good way to engage those experiencing poverty and social exclusion, including the organizations representing them, and other bodies. The extent of deprivation being experienced by those below the income thresholds, and which types of household are most likely to be both on low income and materially deprived, is also important information in this context. This approach may once again have considerable relevance for the United States, as it considers how to reframe its official poverty measurement, providing a way of identifying and prioritizing the most vulnerable.

Finally, it will be important to investigate in a systematic way the relationship between the level of the relative income thresholds and the minimum income provided or implied in most EU countries' national social security systems. The EU and OECD have already started looking into this. It is often not a straightforward matter because the minimum guaranteed income can be complex to define, with support coming from a variety of schemes and varying not only with household size and composition, but also with tenure and housing costs and perhaps other features of the household's situation. However, it would be very useful both in providing a benchmark against which the level of the relative income thresholds in different countries can be framed, and indeed understanding the varying proportions falling below those thresholds. This can be seen as one example of the broader issue of linking what is happening in terms of social protection and social inclusion with developments in the broader economy, including employment and incomes, which has become even more important with the economic and financial crisis. Though their institutional contexts and priorities may be quite different, the EU and the United States share the recognized need to tackle poverty and social exclusion more effectively in the face of that crisis. The EU's broad-ranging approach to monitoring progress toward social inclusion has developed very rapidly over the last decade and in doing so has had to deal with many of the issues that underpin US debates. It illustrates that while seeking to refine the measure of income poverty is important, incorporating indicators relating to other dimensions provides a more comprehensive basis for assessing progress and designing policy responses.

POSTSCRIPT

This chapter was finalized in December 2009. In June 2010, the 27 EU Heads of State and Government adopted the "Europe 2020 Strategy" on smart, sustainable, and inclusive growth, with five "headline targets" to be achieved by 2020. These include a social inclusion target: to lift at least 20 million people out of the risk of poverty and social exclusion in the EU.[29] The president of the European Commission at that point noted, "The Europe 2020 agenda, in setting a social inclusion target, has highlighted three dimensions of poverty and exclusion. It is also essential, however, that Member States—and the EU as a whole—continue to monitor performance according to the full set of commonly agreed social indicators underpinning EU coordination and cooperation in the social field" (Barroso 2010). For a thorough discussion of the Europe 2020 Strategy and social inclusion target, see Marlier and Natali (2010).

ACKNOWLEDGMENTS

Eric Marlier is from the CEPS/INSTEAD Research Institute (Luxembourg); Bea Cantillon, Karel Van den Bosch, and Tim Van Ric from the Herman Deleeck Centre for Social Policy (Belgium); and Brian Nolan from University College Dublin (Ireland). We would like to thank Tony Atkinson with whom some of the authors of this chapter have previously investigated in more depth several of the issues that could only be briefly addressed here (see in particular Atkinson et al. [2002] and Marlier et al. [2007]). Thanks also to Alessio Fusco, Anne-Catherine Guio, Peter Lelie, David Stanton, and Don Williams for helpful comments. These persons should not, however, be held responsible in any way for the present contents.

Notes

1. The European Council, which brings together the EU heads of state and government and the president of the European Commission, defines the general political direction and priorities of the EU. The decisions taken at the European Council meetings (or summits) are summarized in "Presidency Conclusions" available from the Web site of the EU Council of Ministers: http://www.european-council.europa.eu/council-meetings/conclusions?lang=en. All presidency Web sites can also be found at this address. Since the March 2000 Lisbon Summit, every spring, the European Council holds a meeting that is

more particularly devoted to economic and social questions—the Spring European Council.

2. The 12 EU objectives for the streamlined social OMC were adopted by the EU in March 2006. See http://ec.europa.eu/social/main.jsp?catId=755&langId=en. The "overarching objectives" of the social OMC provide linkage across the three social policy strands as well as between the EU social, economic, and employment strategies. For instance, the third overarching objective is "to promote good governance, transparency and the involvement of stakeholders in the design, implementation and monitoring of policy."

3. See inter alia Marlier et al. (2007) for a short review of the EU poverty programs.

4. As a result of the 2004 enlargement, the EU grew from 15 to 25 member states. The 10 new EU countries were Cyprus, the Czech Republic, Estonia, Hungary, Latvia, Lithuania, Malta, Poland, Slovenia, and Slovakia. In 2007 (the most recent enlargement), Bulgaria and Romania joined. For a list of all 27 EU member states as well as their official abbreviations, see Appendix 15.A.

5. The notion of agency has been examined by Sen (1985, 1992) in his work on social justice.

6. The Social Protection Committee is comprised of high-level officials from the relevant ministries in each member state and reports to the EU ministers in charge of social policy.

7. The methodological principles adopted in Laeken were consistent with those put forward in the aforementioned study by Atkinson et al. carried out on behalf of the EU Belgian presidency, where they were originally proposed. Readers interested in a detailed discussion of these principles and, more broadly, of comparative EU indicators for social inclusion can refer to this study, which was subsequently published (see Atkinson et al. 2002).

8. The most recent list of indicators that have been commonly agreed upon by the EU for monitoring the social OMC was adopted by the EU Social Protection Committee in the second half of 2009. This list includes four portfolios of indicators and context information: one for the social OMC as a whole (overarching portfolio) and one for each of the three social strands (social inclusion, pensions, and health portfolios). For each indicator, it provides the agreed definition and sociodemographics breakdowns. See European Commission (2009b).

9. The current EU social inclusion portfolio (as agreed by the EU in the second half of 2009) includes two secondary indicators and two "context information" statistics. Further methodological work as well as further improvement of the data will be needed before one or more primary indicator(s) can be added to the portfolio.

10. See http://ec.europa.eu/social/main.jsp?catId=751&langId=en&pubId=74&type=2&furtherPubs=yes.

11. Countries' abbreviations are provided in Appendix 15.A. For a detailed description of the data sources used for the figures and tables presented in the chapter, see the Appendix.

12. National thresholds are expressed in Purchasing Power Standards (PPS), which—on the basis of purchasing power parities—convert amounts expressed in a national currency to an artificial common currency that equalizes the purchasing power of different national currencies (including those countries that share a common currency). The national thresholds in Figure 15.1b are for a

one-person household (see also Table 15.2a). For other types of households, the corresponding thresholds can easily be obtained by multiplying the thresholds provided by the "equivalized size" (see Appendix 15.A) of the household. In Denmark, for instance, the threshold for a one-person household is 10,175 PPS; it is then $(2.1 \times 10,175) = 21,367$ for a household consisting of two adults and two children aged under 14 years.

13. $R2$ provides the share of the variance predicted by the "model" in the total variance and thus gives an indication of how well the model performs in predicting the observed outcomes. In the case of a simple linear regression (as presented in this chapter), $R2$ is the square of the Pearson correlation coefficient. In view of the small number of observations, this measure of "goodness of fit" should be interpreted cautiously. Table 15.6 presents the correlations between various indicators reviewed in this chapter—for instance, for poverty risk by poverty gap, the correlation is as high as 0.81.

14. Households consisting solely of students are excluded from this indicator.

15. See, for instance, the "Joint Employment Report 2008/2009" and the "Joint Report on Social Protection and Social Inclusion 2009" (EU Council of Ministers 2009a, 2009b).

16. If we disregard Malta, Portugal, and Spain, the link between early school leaving and poverty risk is quite strong: $R2$ is equal to 0.45.

17. It is up to each country to decide whether or not they include nationals born abroad, as appropriate.

18. This points to a general problem with indicators that are defined in terms of the difference as regards a certain outcome between a disadvantaged group and an advantaged group. Although there are important theoretical reasons for adopting this kind of indicator, these indicators have the drawback that a positive change can be the result of an improvement among the disadvantaged group and/or a decline among the advantaged group. Mutatis mutandis, the same applies to comparisons between countries. This makes it difficult to interpret changes over time and differences between countries.

19. Dickes et al. (2010) analyze the data of a Eurobarometer survey on "poverty and exclusion" conducted in 2007 on behalf of the European Commission in all 27 member states. They investigate whether deprivation can be measured on the basis of a same set of items in all EU member states, and their analysis, primarily based on multidimensional scaling, clearly points to "a high level of agreement among countries about what constitutes necessities of life."

20. In Spain and the United Kingdom, for example, the deprivation depth for those at risk of poverty is 1.5, whereas in Latvia and Hungary, the corresponding figure for those *not* at risk of poverty is 1.9; in Romania, it is 2.3 (this figure is not available to date for Bulgaria).

21. As mentioned in Table 15.1a, it would be useful to analyze these figures inter alia in the light of the actual health care utilization in the different EU countries.

22. But the opposite is not true. There are countries with low unmet needs that have high poverty risks.

23. Given the definition adopted, one-person households are considered overcrowded if they live in a studio with a bedroom not separated from the living room. An indicator excluding one-person households has also been agreed upon at EU level.

24. It is important to highlight that our focus here is not on aggregate indices such as the one discussed in the section on material deprivation. Instead of first aggregating across fields for an individual and then across individuals (as in the deprivation measure), in what we call here *composite indicator,* the aggregation is made first across people and then across fields. A composite indicator is thus a combination of aggregate indicators.

25. For a detailed discussion on composite indicators, see Marlier et al. (2007, 182–185).

26. For a detailed discussion see Marlier et al. (2007), Chapter 5. See also Marlier (2008).

27. On the measurement of homelessness, see inter alia the Web site of the EU-funded project on "Mutual Progress on Homelessness through Advancing Strengthening Information Systems (MPHASIS)": http://www.trp.dundee.ac.uk/research/mphasis/.

28. As has been emphasized in research on the monitoring of the Millennium Development Goals, the relevant adjustment is one that relates to consumption, not national product in total, and one that is relevant to households at risk of poverty. As it is put by Deaton, "the consumption bundles of the poor are not the same as the average consumption bundle, and price movements in the latter can be different from price movements in the former, for example if the relative price of food increases" (2002, 1.9).If we are going to place more reliance on the PPS adjustments, then their distributional salience needs to be addressed. The economic and financial crisis has made this even more important.

29. The targeted population is defined as the number of persons who are at risk of poverty and social exclusion according to three indicators: the standard EU "at-risk-of-poverty" indicator (discussed in this chapter); an indicator of "severe material deprivation" (a variation on the EU indicator of deprivation discussed in this chapter, in which the deprivation threshold has been raised from three to four out of the same nine items); and a measure of very low household work intensity. See Eurostat Web site for exact definitions and national figures: http://epp.eurostat.ec.europa.eu/portal/page/portal/europe_2020_indicators/headline_indicators.

References

Atkinson, Tony, Bea Cantillon, Eric Marlier, and Brian Nolan. 2002. *Social Indicators: The EU and Social Inclusion.* Oxford: Oxford University Press.

Barroso, José Manuel 2010. "Foreword." In *Income and Living Conditions in Europe.* Edited by Anthony B. Atkinson and Eric Marlier, 3. Luxembourg: OPOCE (Publications Office of the European Union).

Deaton, Angus 2002. "Data for Monitoring the Poverty MDG." Research Program in Development Studies, Princeton University, Princeton.

Dewilde, Caroline 2009. "A Life-Course Perspective on Social Exclusion and Poverty." In *The Life Course Reader: Individuals and Societies across Time.* Edited by W. R. Heinz, A. Weymann, and J. Huinink, 252–269. Frankfurt: Campus Verlag.

Dickes, Paul, Alessio Fusco, and Eric Marlier. 2010. "Structure of National Perceptions of Social Needs across EU Countries." *Social Indicators Research* 95 (1): 143–167.

Erikson, Robert 1974. "Welfare as a Planning Goal." *Acta Sociologica* 17: 273–288.

EU Council of Ministers. 1975. "Council Decision of 22 July 1975 Concerning a Program of Pilot Schemes and Studies to Combat Poverty," 75/458/EEC, OJEC, L 199, Brussels.

———. 2009a. *Joint Employment Report 2008/2009*. Luxembourg: Office for Official Publications of the European Communities. http://ec.europa.eu/social/main. jsp?catId=101&langId=en.

———. 2009b. Joint Report on Social Protection and Social Inclusion 2009. (Together with supporting document and country profiles.) Luxembourg: Office for Official Publications of the European Communities. http://ec.europa.eu/ social/main.jsp?catId=757&langId=en.

European Commission. 1992. "Towards a Europe of Solidarity: Intensifying the Fight against Social Exclusion, Fostering Integration." Communication from the Commission, COM(92)542, Brussels.

———. 2009a. *Indicators for Monitoring the Employment Guidelines Including Indicators for Additional Employment Analysis. 2009 Compendium*. Luxembourg: Office for Official Publications of the European Communities. http://ec.europa. eu/social/main.jsp?catId=101&langId=en.

———. 2009b. *Portfolio of Indicators for the Monitoring of the European Strategy for Social Protection and Social Inclusion. 2009 Update*. Luxembourg: Office for Official Publications of the European Communities. http://ec.europa.eu/social/ main.jsp?catId=756&langId=en.

Guio, Anne-Catherine. 2009. *What Can Be Learned from Deprivation Indicators in Europe?* Luxembourg: Eurostat. http://epp.eurostat.ec.europa.eu/cache/ITY_ OFFPUB/KS-RA-09-007/EN/KS-RA-09-007-EN.PDF.

Hagenaars, Aldi, Klaas de Vos, and Asghar Zaidi. 1994. *Poverty Statistics in the Late 1980s*. Luxembourg: Eurostat.

Jehoel-Gijsbers, Gerda, and Cok Vrooman. 2008. *Social Exclusion of the Elderly; a Comparative Study in EU Member States*. Brussels: Centre for European Policy Studies.

Lenoir, René. 1974. *Les exclus*. Paris: Seuil.

Marlier, Eric. 2008. "Commonly Agreed Social Indicators in the EU: Purpose, Specificities and Gaps." Paper presented at the EQUALSOC Berlin Conference, INCDIS Thematic Session, Berlin, April 10, 2008.

Marlier, Eric, and A. B. Atkinson. 2010. "Indicators of Poverty and Social Exclusion in a Global Context." *Journal of Policy Analysis and Management* 29: 285–304.

Marlier, Eric, A. B. Atkinson, Bea Cantillon, and Brian Nolan. 2007. *The EU and Social Inclusion. Facing the Challenges*. Bristol: The Policy Press.

Marlier, Eric, and David Natali, eds., with Rudi Van Dam. 2010. *Europe 2020: Towards a More Social EU?* Brussels: P.I.E. Peter Lang.

Nolan, Brian, and Christopher T. Whelan. 1996. *Resources, Deprivation and Poverty*. Oxford: Oxford University Press.

———. 2010. "Using Non-Monetary Deprivation Indicators to Analyze Poverty and Social Exclusion: Lessons from Europe?" *Journal of Policy Analysis and Management* 29: 305–325.

O'Higgins, Michael, and Stephen Jenkins. 1990. "Poverty in Europe: Estimates for 1975, 1980 and 1985, Analysing Poverty in the European Community." Special edition, *Eurostat News* 1.

Room, Graham, ed. 1995. *Beyond the Threshold*. Bristol: The Policy Press.

Sen, Amartya. 1985. "Well-Being, Agency and Freedom: the Dewey Lectures 1984."
    Journal of Philosophy 82: 169–221.
————. 1992. *Inequality Reexamined*. Cambridge, MA: Harvard University Press.
Silver, Hilary. 1995. "Reconceptualizing Social Disadvantage: Three Paradigms of
    Social Exclusion." In *Social Exclusion: Rhetoric, Reality, Responses*. Edited by Gerry
    Rodgers, Charles Gore, and José Figueiredo. Geneva: ILO.
Social Protection Committee. 2001. Report on Indicators in the Field of Poverty and
    Social Exclusion. Brussels: Social Protection Committee.
Walker, Robert. 1995. "The Dynamics of Poverty and Social Exclusion." In *Beyond the
Threshold*. Edited by Graham Room, pages 102–128. Bristol: The Policy Press.

Table 15.A.1 LIST OF EU COUNTRIES WITH THEIR OFFICIAL ABBREVIATIONS

Old Member States		New Member States	
AT	Austria		2004 enlargement
BE	Belgium	CY	Cyprus
DK	Denmark	CZ	Czech Republic
FI	Finland	EE	Estonia
FR	France	HU	Hungary
DE	Germany	LV	Latvia
EL	Greece	LT	Lithuania
IE	Ireland	MT	Malta
IT	Italy	PL	Poland
LU	Luxembourg	SK	Slovakia
NL	The Netherlands	SI	Slovenia
PT	Portugal		
ES	Spain		2007 enlargement
SE	Sweden	BG	Bulgaria
UK	United Kingdom	RO	Romania

NOTE: Various European Union averages are presented in this chapter. In these averages, countries are weighted by their population sizes:
• EU-15 averages are weighted averages limited to the 15 old member states;
• NMS-10 (New Member States 10) are weighted averages limited to the 10 new member states that joined the EU in 2004;
• EU-25 averages are weighted averages covering all 27 EU member states except Bulgaria and Romania; and
• EU-27 averages are weighted averages covering all 27 EU member states.

DATA SOURCES, DATA COLLECTION YEAR, INCOME
REFERENCE YEAR, AND INCOME CONCEPT

Figures discussed in this chapter come from the EU Statistics on Income and Living Conditions (EU-SILC) and the EU Labor Force Surveys (LFS). For detailed information on these sources, see Eurostat Web site: http://epp.eurostat.ec.europa.eu/portal/page/portal/eurostat/home.

The most recent EU-SILC data available when finalizing this chapter (in December 2009) were those collected in 2007. Therefore, with a view to ensuring consistency between the two sources, both EU-SILC and LFS data analyzed in this chapter are from 2007 except for very few national results (all exceptions are clearly indicated).

It is important to stress that in EU-SILC, *income data* generally refer to the total annual income of households (c.g., earnings, social benefits, income from capital) in the year prior to the survey as this is generally considered the best *proxy* for the current total annual household income. The sole exceptions are the United Kingdom (total annual household income calculated on the basis of current income) and Ireland (calculation on the basis of a moving income reference period covering part of the year of the interview and part of the year prior to the survey). It is important to keep in mind that the definition of income used for all income-based indicators that have been commonly agreed by the EU for monitoring the social OMC excludes nonmonetary income components such as imputed rents, the value of goods produced for own consumption and noncash employee income. It is also important to mention that in order to reflect differences in household size and composition, all commonly agreed income-based indicators for the social OMC are computed on the basis of income per "equivalent adult" or "equivalized income." In other words, the total household income (which includes earnings from work, income from investment and property, and all social benefits received in cash) is divided by its equivalent size using the so-called *modified OECD equivalence scale*. This scale assigns a value of 1 to the first adult in the household, 0.5 to each other adult, and 0.3 to each child below the age of 14 years. The resulting figure is attributed to each member of the household, whether adult or children. The equivalent size of a household that consists of two adults and two children below the age of 14 years is therefore: $1.0 + 0.5 + (2 \times 0.3) = 2.1$.

Most data analyzed were downloaded from the Eurostat Web page dedicated to the indicators for the social inclusion strand of the social OMC (date of download: December 15, 2009): http://epp.eurostat.ec.europa.eu/portal/page/portal/employment_social_policy_equality/omc_social_inclusion_and_social_protection/social_inclusion_strand.

For the indicator on "unmet need for care," the source is the Eurostat Web site related to public health statistics. Calculations are based on the statistic "people with unmet needs for medical examination" and, in line with the EU definition, combines the three following reasons: "waiting list," "too expensive," and "too far to travel": http://epp.eurostat.ec.europa.eu/portal/page/portal/health/public_health/data_public_health/database.

For the indicator on "employment gap of immigrants," the data source is European Commission (2009a).

Finally, some calculations not (yet) available from the Eurostat Web site were kindly carried out by the EU-SILC team at Eurostat. This is the case for the mean number of "lacked" items (EU indicator on material deprivation) among the income-poor and non-income-poor population as well as for the two EU indicators on housing (housing costs burden and overcrowding). At the time of calculation, Bulgarian data were not yet available for the mean number of "lacked" items among the income-poor and non-income-poor population (Figure 15.6c). We are very grateful to Eurostat for providing us with these calculations.

16

Using Nonmonetary Deprivation Indicators to Analyze European Poverty and Social Exclusion

BRIAN NOLAN AND CHRISTOPHER T. WHELAN ■

INTRODUCTION

Research and monitoring of poverty in rich countries relies primarily on household income to capture living standards and distinguish the poor. Significant efforts have been made to broaden the measure of financial resources and capture the dynamics of income over time. At the same time, there is increasing interest in using nonmonetary information to improve the measurement and understanding of poverty. Such nonmonetary indicators are increasingly used in individual European countries, as well as at the European Union (EU) level, with the suite of indicators employed to monitor the EU's social inclusion process recently expanded to include a summary deprivation measure (see Atkinson et al. 2002; Marlier et al. 2012, Chapter 15).[1] One may see this as reflecting distinct but interrelated concerns about relying solely on income. This chapter focuses first on the rationales underpinning the use of measures of material deprivation and at the variety of ways they are employed in research and monitoring poverty. We look at some key patterns revealed by deprivation indicators across the EU, and then we discuss the implications for capturing poverty and its multidimensionality. Finally, we highlight some important conclusions and challenges in the further development and use of such measures.

USING NONMONETARY DEPRIVATION INDICATORS TO STUDY POVERTY AND SOCIAL EXCLUSION

Most research on poverty in European countries takes as a point of departure that people are in poverty when "their resources are so seriously below those commanded by the average individual or family that they are, in effect, excluded from ordinary living patterns, customs and activities"—the influential formulation by the sociologist Peter Townsend (1979, p. 31). The European Council adopted a similar definition in the mid-1980s, referring to "persons whose resources (material, cultural and social) are so limited as to exclude them from the minimum acceptable way of life in the Member State in which they live," which underpins the EU social inclusion process.

So poverty from this starting- point is about the inability to participate, attributable to inadequate resources.[2] Most quantitative research then employs income to distinguish the poor, with a great deal of research and debate on how best to establish a poverty threshold. In parallel, though, relying purely on income for this purpose has also been questioned. This originated first of all from the perspective that low income could be used to identify the poor, but did not tell us all we needed to know about what it was like to be poor, and how people arrived at and coped with that situation. This is exemplified by Townsend's pioneering use of nonmonetary indicators to derive and validate an income poverty threshold and to bring out graphically what it meant to be poor in Britain in terms of deprivation.

Even though Townsend's derivation of an income poverty threshold was hotly debated, as deprivation indicators started to become more widely available they were used to underpin a more radical critique of reliance on income: low income fails in practice to identify those unable to participate in their societies due to lack of resources. This argument was put forward most emphatically by Ringen (1988), who asserted that income was both an indirect and unreliable measure of the underlying concept of poverty. In a similar vein, Mack and Lansley (1985) used deprivation indicators directly to identify those experiencing exclusion in Britain, and a number of subsequent British studies (Gordon et al. 2000; Pantazis, Gordon, and Levitas 2006) have done so with a more extensive set of indicators. By contrast, studies for Ireland (Callan, Nolan, and Whelan 1993; Nolan and Whelan 1996), identified the *consistently poor*—those having both low incomes and reporting deprivation in terms of specific basic items—as meeting both elements of the underlying concept. A similar approach has been applied in some other countries (e.g., Forster 2005), and the United Kingdom is including a combined measure of low income and material deprivation in monitoring progress toward its target of eradicating child poverty by 2020. Bradshaw and Finch (2003) have looked at those reporting not only low income and deprivation, but also a subjectively bad financial situation, terming it *core poverty*. Nonmonetary indicators of deprivation have by now been used in various ways in measuring poverty in many European countries, for example, Muffels and Dirven (1998) with Dutch data, Hallerod (1995) for Sweden, Kangas and Ritakallio (1998) for Finland, Bohnke and Delhey (1999) for Germany, and Tsakloglou and Panopoulou (1998) for Greece.[3]

Rather than (or as well as) the more accurate identification of the poor, a further argument for the use of nonmonetary indicators is that they can help to capture the multidimensionality of poverty and social exclusion. The widespread adoption of the terminology of social exclusion/inclusion in Europe reflects inter alia the concern that focusing simply on income misses an important part of the picture. Social exclusion may involve not only poverty as low income/financial resources, but also educational disadvantage, poor health and access to health services, inadequate housing, and exclusion in the labor market. Reflecting such concerns, a multidimensional approach to capturing exclusion is being adopted in many of the EU member states and other developed countries (as well as in measuring progress in alleviating poverty in developing countries, notably by the Millennium Development Goals). This can reflect the view that conceptually social exclusion is distinct from and broader than poverty, or that the underlying notion of poverty that evokes social concern is itself (and always has been) intrinsically multidimensional and about "more than money" (e.g., see Nolan and Whelan 2007; Burchardt, Le Grand, and Piachaud 2002).[4] In either case, a variety of nonmonetary indicators come into play in seeking to capture such multidimensionality.

So, in sum, nonmonetary indicators are now being used in a variety of ways in European countries and at the EU level in the belief that they can bring out what it means to be poor, help to do a better job than income on its own in identifying the poor, and directly capture the multifaceted nature of poverty and exclusion. There is no consensus about how best to employ them, and the underlying rationale(s) may often be implicit rather than explicit, but the volume of research employing material deprivation indicators and the interest in it within policy circles is certainly growing. We now proceed to illustrate the types of indicators that are commonly used, concentrating on those employed in comparative European research and monitoring.

NONMONETARY DEPRIVATION INDICATORS AND INDICES

The development of measures of material deprivation has been rather ad hoc, with different countries learning from each other while having their own preoccupations.[5] Comparative studies often have to rely on a limited set of items and also face problems of ensuring the relevance and comparability of those items from one country to another. Here, in seeking to illustrate the types of indicators commonly employed and bring out some important issues in how they are framed and interpreted, we focus on the European cross-country perspective. We do so using the European Community Household Panel Survey (ECHP) organized by Eurostat and carried out in most of the (then) EU member states from the mid-1990s to 2001 (see Eurostat 1996), and data now being collected under the EU Statistics on Income and Living Conditions (EU-SILC) framework, which replaced the ECHP (see Eurostat 2007). Each of these data sources has problems. The ECHP, being a panel survey following respondents over time, inevitably has attrition from one year to the next and this varies across types of households and across countries; furthermore, differential weighting and imputation procedures may also affect comparability (e.g., see Peracchi 2002). The EU-SILC, unlike the ECHP, is not a harmonized survey but rather a mechanism for obtaining prespecified variables from each country, with scope for variation in how they choose to collect it; this may also give rise to problems of reliability and comparability (e.g., see Hauser [2008] on the German EU-SILC). Nonetheless, these sources allow for analyses to be carried out across a wide range of countries with data that is much closer to being comparable than would usually be the case and serve to illustrate key points in relation to measures of material deprivation and their use.

The deprivation indicators included in the ECHP drew on previous national studies and cover a wide range of areas, from food and clothing to durables, social activities, and problems with housing.[6] The aim was to capture situations where the person was going without due to lack of financial resources, rather than because of other constraints or because they did not want the item, so in some cases the survey asked: "Indicate whether or not your household possesses [the item]. If you do not have [item], please indicate whether you a) would like to have it but cannot afford it, or

b) do not have it for other reasons, e.g. you don't want or need it." This was the format adopted for

- A car,
- A color television,
- A VCR
- A microwave
- A dishwasher, and
- A telephone.

For some other items, the format was: "There are some things many people cannot afford even if they would like them. Can I just check whether your household can afford these if you want them?"

- Keep your home adequately warm
- Pay for a week's annual holiday away from home
- Replace any worn-out furniture
- Buy new, rather than secondhand, clothes
- Eat meat, chicken, or fish every second day, if you wanted to
- Have friends or family for a drink or a meal at least once a month

For some other items, the question simply asked, "Does this dwelling have the following amenities":

- A bath or shower
- An indoor flushing toilet
- Hot running water

Finally, in relation to various problems, the question was "Do you have any of the following problems with your accommodation":

- Shortage of space
- Noise from neighbors or outside
- Too dark, not enough light
- Lack of adequate heating facilities
- Leaky roof
- Damp walls, floors, foundations, etc.
- Rot in window frames or floors
- Vandalism or crime in the area
- Pollution, grime or other environmental problems caused by traffic or industry

The individual nonmonetary indicators are of significant interest in themselves, but most often the aim is to combine them into some overall measure of deprivation, or sets of measures capturing different aspects or dimensions. The simplest approach is to assign a value of 1 for each item where the household reports enforced deprivation and 0 where it does not, and aggregate those scores into a summary index. To illustrate, Table 16.1 shows mean deprivation scores on such a summary index using the 24 items just listed for the 14 EU member states that participated in the ECHP

Table 16.1 MEAN DEPRIVATION SCORES AND RELATIVE INCOME POVERTY

	Mean Deprivation Score		Relative Income Poverty (%)		Mean Equivalized Income (PPP)	
	24 Items Index 1996	17 Items Index 2006	1996	2006	1996	2006
Austria	2.25	1.43	14	12	14,178	19,269
Belgium	2.26	1.82	15	15	14,384	17,962
Cyprus		2.90		16		18,840
Czech Republic		2.23		10		10,142
Germany	2.14	1.94	14	13	14,675	16,470
Denmark	1.62	1.31	10	12	14,220	17,156
Estonia		2.95		18		7,753
Spain	4.29	1.89	18	20	9,191	14,518
Finland	2.96	1.55	8	13	11,337	16,667
France	2.64	1.78	15	13	13,388	17,309
Greece	6.76	2.50	21	21	8,300	13,919
Hungary		3.20		12		7,975
Ireland	2.42	1.63	19	18	11,695	18,915
Iceland		1.21		10		21,169
Italy	3.42	2.02	20	20	10,490	15,937
Lithuania		3.95		20		6,419
Luxembourg	1.54	1.14	11	14	22,337	30,498
Latvia		4.70		23		6,576
Netherlands	1.96	1.51	12	10	12,910	18,812
Norway		0.96		11		22,357
Poland		3.72		19		6,817
Portugal	6.68	2.77	21	18	7,798	11,156
Sweden		0.97		12		15,893
Slovenia		2.10		12		13,735
Slovakia		2.90		11		7,686
United Kingdom	2.56	1.65	18	19	13,659	20,343
EU average	2.89	2.04	16.0	16.0	10,873	15,540

NOTE: PPP is purchasing power parity.

SOURCES: Eurostat, ECHP (1996) and Eurostat, EU-SILC 2006 (2007).

in 1996.[7] We see that the mean deprivation score ranges from 2 or below for countries like Denmark, the Netherlands, and Luxembourg up to nearly 7 for Portugal and Greece. While there is a strong relationship between average income per head in purchasing power parity terms–also shown in the table—and the average deprivation level, there are some differences in the rankings these produce. For example, Denmark has similar mean income but lower deprivation scores than Belgium, France, or Germany. Greece and Portugal have the lowest average income levels of the EU-15, but the gap between them and the other old member states in terms of deprivation level is very much greater.

It is then particularly interesting to look at similar results from EU-SILC, because this covers the enlarged EU (plus Iceland and Norway), which has a much wider span in terms of average income per capita. EU-SILC at present includes a more limited set of nonmonetary indicators, mostly drawn from the ECHP,[8] and Table 16.1 also shows mean levels on a summary deprivation index constructed using 17 indicators. We see that there is indeed now considerably more variation in mean deprivation levels. The range within the old EU-15 is from 1.3 to 1.5 in the case of Denmark, the Netherlands, and Luxembourg up to 2.5 to 2.8 in Greece and Portugal, but in Latvia, it reaches 4.7. Again this partly reflects differences in average income, but the gap in deprivation levels between, for example, Latvia and Lithuania is wider than that in average income.

So nonmonetary indicators, used in this fairly straightforward way, allow for a comparison of the extent of deprivation across countries that gives a very different picture to the relative income poverty rates that are widely used in comparative poverty research in Europe. These are also shown in Table 16.1 for comparison, using the 60 percent of median income threshold. We see that some countries with low relative income poverty rates have quite high mean deprivation levels (e.g., Hungary, Slovenia, and Slovakia), whereas others have high relative-income poverty rates but much lower mean deprivation levels (such as Ireland and the United Kingdom). These at-risk-of-poverty rates form a central component of the set of common indicators adopted to monitor progress in the EU's social inclusion strategy (see Atkinson et al. 2002; Marlier et al. 2007), but as shall be discussed it has recently been decided that these can be usefully complemented by measures of material deprivation. They also add to what we learn from comparisons of average income levels across countries. It is the combination of differences in average income levels and how those are distributed within countries that underpins variations in deprivation.

The use of nonmonetary deprivation indicators is not confined to such an "absolute" comparison, where doing without a particular item or activity is taken to represent the same level of deprivation irrespective of how many other people are in that situation. If instead one wishes to look at deprivation in relative terms and use the country as the frame of reference, one can weight items by prevalence in the country—so doing without something that almost everyone in the country has is given much more weight than something many others cannot afford. Alternatively, the views of the population about which represent "necessities" can serve as the basis for differentially weighting items.

Another important issue is whether the available indicators are employed in the form of simple summary indices of the type shown in Table 16.1 or used to distinguish different aspects or dimensions of deprivation. Both national and comparative studies have investigated how different items relate to each other and cluster into dimensions, most often via exploratory or confirmatory factor analysis. The results generally show that a better fit statistically is obtained when a number of different dimensions are distinguished, rather than treating all the indicators as if they related to a single underlying dimension. Once again, we can illustrate this with results from the ECHP and EU-SILC. Factor analysis suggests that with the items available in the ECHP a five-factor solution provides the best fit statistically, distinguishing:

- Basic lifestyle deprivation—being unable to afford items such as food and clothing, a yearly holiday, replacing worn-out furniture, and avoid arrears.
- Secondary lifestyle deprivation—not being able to afford items such as a car, a phone, a color television, a video, a microwave, and a dishwasher.
- Housing facilities—such as not having a bath or shower, an indoor flushing toilet, and hot and cold running water.
- Housing deterioration—having problems such as a leaking roof, dampness, and rotting in window frames and floors.
- Environmental problems—having problems such as noise, pollution, vandalism, and inadequate space and light.

This set of dimensions performs well across all the countries, which is substantively very interesting and also very convenient analytically, because it means that one can employ common dimensions in cross-country comparisons.

The more limited set of indicators available from the EU-SILC appears to allow only three dimensions to be distinguished[9]:

- *Consumption deprivation*—items relating to food, heat, a holiday, a car or a PC, and avoiding arrears on rent or utilities.
- *Household facilities*—such as bath or shower and indoor toilet, a telephone, a color TV, and a washing machine.
- *Neighborhood environment*—noise, pollution, crime, and violence.

Different dimensions of deprivation in the ECHP have been studied in, for example, Eurostat (2003), Whelan et al. (2001), and Guio (2005). Standard statistical tests of reliability for the scales provide reassurance about the extent to which the individual items are tapping the same underlying phenomenon.[10] Table 16.2 shows the mean levels for each participating country on summary indices for each of the five dimensions previously described. Interesting variation in the cross-country patterns across the dimensions can be seen, with much more differentiation in the consumption than the environment dimension, for example, and very low mean levels of deprivation in housing facilities except in Greece and Portugal. Various countries are below the EU-15 average for some dimensions and above it for others.

Table 16.3 shows the corresponding figures for the three dimensions distinguished in the EU-SILC. There is once again a striking contrast between the consumption dimension, which ranges from a mean level of 0.7 in Denmark up to 2.8 in Latvia, and the neighborhood/environment dimension, where there is much less variation across countries. With the expansion of the EU to include countries with a much wider range in terms of average income per head, relying entirely on relative poverty measures benchmarked against each country's median income has come to be seen as more problematic, and that is one reason the indicators employed to monitor the

Table 16.2 Mean Deprivation Scores by Dimension of Deprivation
across Countries, 1996

	Basic life-style Deprivation (7 items)	Secondary life-Style deprivation (5 items)	Housing Facilities (3 items)	Housing Deterioration (3 items)	Environ-mental Problems (5 items)
Austria	0.95	0.35	0.11	0.16	0.70
Belgium	0.85	0.24	0.10	0.25	0.81
Denmark	0.55	0.34	0.04	0.16	0.53
Germany	0.72	0.51	0.06	0.13	0.73
Spain	1.97	0.81	0.05	0.38	1.09
Finland	1.58	0.36	0.09	0.09	0.86
France	1.12	0.33	0.09	0.29	0.83
Greece	3.82	0.96	0.78	0.39	0.81
Ireland	1.01	0.56	0.13	0.22	0.52
Italy	1.71	0.38	0.07	0.16	1.10
Luxembourg	0.55	0.20	0.05	0.16	0.60
Netherlands	0.63	0.22	0.02	0.24	0.85
Portugal	2.79	1.46	0.45	0.84	1.13
United Kingdom	1.06	0.28	0.01	0.26	0.95
EU	1.24	0.48	0.09	0.24	0.88

SOURCE: Eurostat, ECHP (1996).

EU's social inclusion process have recently been expanded to include a summary deprivation measure employing items relating to consumption and housing facilities (see Marlier et al. 2012, Chapter 15).

Such cross-country comparisons add to what can be learned from income-based poverty measures and mean income comparisons (see Table 16.1),[11] but the indicators also serve other valuable purposes. In-depth analysis focusing on the factors associated with different types of deprivation and how these vary across countries has the potential to uncover important features of the causal processes underpinning them. For example, deprivation in current consumption has been found to be strongly linked to income, whereas poor housing facilities, housing deterioration, and neighborhood environmental problems display a very weak relationship even with persistent low income (e.g., see Layte et al. 2001; Whelan, Layte, and Maitre 2003). Factors such as age, household composition, urban/rural location, and tenure status have been found to play an important role in predicting housing and neighborhood-related dimensions, and this is clearly critical in thinking about how policy in those domains needs to respond.[12]

Table 16.3 MEAN DEPRIVATION SCORES BY DIMENSION OF DEPRIVATION
ACROSS COUNTRIES, 2006

	Consumption (7 items)	Housing facilities (5 items)	Neighborhood environment (3 items)
Austria	0.8	0.0	0.4
Belgium	0.9	0.1	0.6
Cyprus	1.7	0.1	0.7
Czech Republic	1.4	0.1	0.5
Germany	1.1	0.0	0.7
Denmark	0.7	0.0	0.4
Estonia	1.5	0.5	0.6
Spain	1.0	0.0	0.6
Finland	0.9	0.1	0.5
France	1.0	0.1	0.5
Greece	1.6	0.1	0.5
Hungary	2.2	0.2	0.4
Ireland	1.0	0.0	0.4
Iceland	0.8	0.0	0.2
Italy	1.1	0.0	0.6
Lithuania	2.5	0.7	0.4
Luxembourg	0.4	0.0	0.5
Latvia	2.8	0.6	0.8
Netherlands	0.6	0.0	0.6
Norway	0.6	0.0	0.3
Poland	2.5	0.3	0.4
Portugal	1.6	0.2	0.6
Sweden	0.5	0.0	0.3
Slovenia	1.2	0.1	0.5
Slovakia	2.2	0.1	0.5
United Kingdom	0.8	0.0	0.6
EU	1.2	0.1	0.6

SOURCE: Eurostat, EU-SILC (2006).

Looking at how the different dimensions of deprivation relate to one another is a valuable complement to examining them individually. The correlation between dimensions is often quite low—for the "consumption" and "household facilities" dimensions in EU-SILC, for example, it is only 0.3. It is not surprising, then, that both national and cross-country studies suggest that the numbers experiencing high levels of deprivation across a number of dimensions together are often quite modest. Figure 16.1 provides an illustration with the five dimensions distinguished in the ECHP. Only in Portugal and Greece does the number reporting deprivation on all five dimensions rise appreciably above 0, and elsewhere, the percentage reporting deprivation on four or more dimensions is also low. The "cumulatively deprived" are however clearly of particular interest from a policy perspective, having distinctive needs and in all likelihood requiring specially designed forms of intervention.

Finally, information on material deprivation may help us to more reliably identify those who are experiencing poverty rather than having low incomes alone, as we elaborate in the next section.

DEPRIVATION AND LOW INCOME

The relationship between deprivation measures and household income is clearly of central importance in thinking about how nonmonetary indicators are best interpreted and used. To look at this relationship, we use the income measure employed in the at-risk-of-poverty indicator in the EU's social inclusion portfolio (as presented in Table 16.1). The income recipient unit is the household, and household income is adjusted to take differences in size and composition into account by dividing by an equivalence scale assigning the first adult in the household a value of 1, each additional adult a value of 0.5, and each child a value of 0.3. The accounting period for income is the previous calendar year. When different dimensions of deprivation are distinguished, the relationship with income is consistently stronger for some dimensions than others. With ECHP data and the five dimensions described

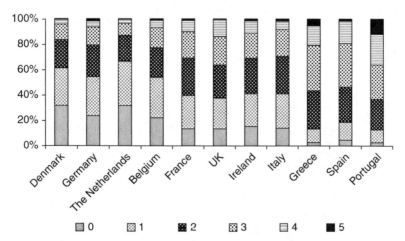

Figure 16.1 Percentage of Persons Lacking at Least One Item for Five Deprivation.
SOURCE: Eurostat, ECHP(1994).

earlier, for example, basic and secondary deprivation are a good deal more strongly correlated with income than housing conditions and facilities, with the local environmental dimension having the lowest correlation (e.g., see Whelan, Layte, and Maître 2003). The relationship between basic deprivation and income is also stronger in the less affluent countries than in those with higher average income per head. When countries are categorized in terms of welfare regime, those with the highest levels of income and more generous welfare state arrangements tend to display the weakest degree of association between current income and relative deprivation. But even at its highest, selecting the types of indicators/aspects of deprivation that are most strongly associated with income and the countries where this is most pronounced, the correlation between income and deprivation does not exceed -0.5.

In assessing the extent of overlap between poverty measured in terms of low income versus deprivation, it is of particular interest to focus on the dimensions that are most strongly related to income, so Table 16.4, using EU-SILC data, shows the percentage of those below the 60 percent of median income poverty threshold who also have high deprivation scores (of 3 or more) on an index of "consumption deprivation." We see that this ranges from about 28 percent to 50 percent. The mismatch between income and deprivation is by no means confined to households with little or no income, although it is particularly pronounced for them: a significant proportion of households with incomes between say 40 percent and 60 percent of the median do not report high levels of deprivation (compared with others in the country in question). Conversely, a substantial proportion of those reporting high deprivation are not below conventional income poverty thresholds (though they may not be far above). This is despite the widespread use of questions about deprivation that seek to focus the respondent's mind on things they have to do without because they cannot afford them. Panel surveys allow the relationship between income and deprivation over time to be studied, and analysis of data from the ECHP shows that over a three-year window about 45–55 percent of the persistently income poor had (relatively) high deprivation levels in each year, whereas about another one-fifth had high levels in some but not all the years. Mean levels of income and deprivation over a number of years are more highly correlated than in a cross-section (Whelan and Maitre 2008; Berthoud, Bryan, and Bardasi 2004).

The factors that seem to underpin this limited degree of overlap between low income and deprivation merit careful consideration. A household's standard of living depends on its command over resources and its needs, and neither would be adequately reflected in current (equivalized) income even if it were measured with perfect accuracy.[13] Savings add to the capacity to consume, as does past investment in consumer durables, whereas servicing accumulated debt reduces it: owner-occupied housing and noncash income in the form of goods and services provided by the state also compose major resources for many households (see OECD 2008, Chapter 9). Current income is an imperfect indicator of long-term or permanent income. The choice of equivalence scale may affect which households are below the income threshold (e.g., see Buhman et al. 1988; Aaberge and Melby 1998) and thus the overlap with material deprivation. Needs differ across households in ways that conventional equivalence scales will not capture, notably with respect to health and disability (see Zaidi and Burchardt 2005). Household surveys also find it particularly difficult to adequately capture income from self-employment, from home

Table 16.4 PERCENTAGE OF THOSE BELOW 60 PERCENT MEDIAN
WITH CONSUMPTION DEPRIVATION SCORE OF 3+, 2006

	Percentage
Austria	33.3
Belgium	44.8
Cyprus	32.2
Czech Republic	38.7
Germany	33.3
Denmark	34.7
Spain	33.0
Greece	43.2
Estonia	45.2
Finland	40.6
France	38.6
Hungary	41.3
Ireland	47.8
Italy	45.9
Latvia	41.7
Lithuania	46.8
Luxembourg	40.2
Netherlands	27.8
Poland	43.4
Portugal	41.2
Sweden	31.7
Slovakia	32.1
Slovenia	37.3
United Kingdom	47.0

SOURCE: Eurostat, EU-SILC (2006).

production, from capital, and from the imputed rent attributable to homeowners. Mismeasurement in a panel context leads to underestimation of the persistence of both income poverty and severe deprivation (Breen and Mosio 2004; Whelan and Maitre 2006). There may also be selective attrition of the deprived (Berthoud, Bryan, and Bardasi 2004). Nonresponse on survey questions about deprivation does not generally appear to be a major problem, though, unlike income (on which, see, e.g., Frick and Grabka 2007). Although it may be difficult to link short-term deprivation dynamics to specific events or influences, there is ample evidence that both income and deprivation are strongly influenced by factors affecting the longer term

accumulation and erosion of resources (including labor market experience, education, and social class). Having controlled for persistently low income, individual and
household characteristics such as education, labor market experience and social
class, marital status and household structure remain significant in explaining deprivation levels (Whelan, Layte, and Maitre 2002).

Some households on low income may be able to avoid severe deprivation by, for
example, drawing on assets, borrowing, and receiving support from extended family.
Furthermore, some people may be exceptionally good managers of limited resources.
However, some persistently low income households may also not be reporting their
actual deprivation levels accurately, having become habituated to doing without, or
having different expectations from the majority (Halleröd 2006; McKay 2004;
Dominy and Kempson 2006). Conversely, households in the top half of the income
distribution but reporting substantial deprivation may be particularly poor managers
of their income, have gotten heavily into debt, or simply having different priorities in
allocating their spending relative to the norm. Deprivation conceptually relates to
being denied the opportunity to have or do something. The difficulty is in empirically
identifying the consequences of a constrained opportunity set as opposed to differences in preferences/tastes. As we will argue, this means that using deprivation indicators to measure poverty, one may wish to exclude high-income households
reporting that they cannot afford things that many lower income households have.

It is reasonable to conclude that measured income and material deprivation each
contain valuable information about the situation of households, reflecting their
resources and needs and how these have evolved. This conclusion is underpinned
when one looks at how income and deprivation levels relate to people's overall subjective evaluations of their own situation.[14] A widely used measure of self-assessed
economic strain, included in the ECHP and EU-SILC, is based on the following
question: "Thinking now of your household's total income, from all sources and from
all household members, would you say that your household is able to make ends
meet?" Respondents are offered responses ranging from "with great difficulty" to
"very easily." Levels of self-assessed economic strain are generally found to be considerably higher for those above the deprivation threshold than for those in income
poverty. Table 16.5 compares the percentage reporting great or some difficulty among
those below the 60 percent relative income line with those above the deprivation
threshold that distinguishes the same proportion of the sample but with the highest
deprivation scores (Whelan et al. 2001). In every country, levels of self-assessed economic strain are considerably higher for those above the deprivation threshold than
for those in income poverty.[15]

The Implications for Using Deprivation Indicators in
Measuring Poverty and Exclusion

We now focus on the implications for how best to employ deprivation indicators in
measuring, tracking, and understanding poverty and exclusion. The conceptual and
measurement problems in relying on income alone to identify the poor suggest that
incorporating deprivation into the process could have significant potential. Where
income is genuinely low but this is unusual for the household and it has savings to
run down, for example, or where income has been misreported as low, nonmonetary

Table 16.5 PERCENTAGE EXPERIENCING ECONOMIC STRAIN AMONG THOSE FALLING BELOW THE 60 PERCENT MEDIAN INCOME LINE AND ABOVE THE CORRESPONDING DEPRIVATION THRESHOLD

	Below 60 percent income line	Above corresponding deprivation threshold
Germany	16.4	32.3
Denmark	22.5	55.4
Netherlands	40.8	65.5
Belgium	28.0	47.1
France	42.3	61.0
United Kingdom	43.1	61.8
Ireland	53.8	69.6
Italy	44.5	59.6
Greece	78.1	91.5
Spain	62.3	74.5
Portugal	57.0	71.5

SOURCE: Eurostat, ECHP (1996).

indicators might correctly suggest a higher standard of living than income. Where the household benefits from noncash support from the state, this should enable them to attain a higher standard of living, again reflected in lower levels of deprivation, ceteris paribus. Where a household faces particular needs that act as a drain on income, due to disability, for example, then deprivation levels should be higher than for others on the same income.

This does not mean that income can be ignored, focusing simply on deprivation. We have seen that some middle- and even high-income households report deprivation with conventional measures. Though this seems to be telling us something important about those households, it does not seem a reliable basis for concluding that they are poor. Given two relevant pieces of information about a household—income and deprivation—each with limitations from both conceptual and measurement perspectives, incorporating both into the measurement process is one way to seek to improve reliability. A relatively straightforward way of doing so is to focus on those who have both a low (relative) income and experience high (relative) levels of deprivation. This approach was developed and applied in Ireland in the early 1990s to distinguish those who are "consistently poor" and was subsequently adopted as the official measure of poverty for use in the Irish government's National Anti-Poverty Strategy. It excluded many of those reporting low income from self-employment, and highlighted inter alia the relatively disadvantaged situation of families with children in "working poor" households, with a considerable influence on the development of policy.

Such an approach has also been applied in some other countries (notably Austria) and in making comparisons across EU countries (e.g., Förster 2005). It is illustrated with ECHP data in Table 16.6, showing for each country the percentage both below the 60 percent relative income threshold and above a deprivation threshold that cuts off the same proportion of the sample. The rank ordering of countries remains similar to relative income lines, but because the degree of overlap between income and deprivation is greater in countries with higher income poverty rates, the disparities are sharper. This approach has also received some attention in EU circles and may be considered for incorporation into the suite of common indicators at some point in the future.

The usefulness of this approach in capturing change over time can also be illustrated by the Irish experience. The consistent poverty measure declined markedly over the period from the mid-1990s when economic growth reached spectacular heights;[16] whereas, poverty measures based on purely relative income thresholds, on the other hand, were stable or even rising over this period (e.g., see Layte et al. 2001).

Finally, using nonmonetary indicators to distinguish different dimensions of deprivation opens up two complementary and valuable forms of analysis. First, in-depth analyses focusing on the factors associated with each specific type of deprivation helps tease out the causal processes underlying them and frame the appropriate policy response. Second, as already noted, looking at the extent to which the same people are affected by multiple forms of deprivation helps in capturing the multidimensionality of poverty and exclusion and the extent of cumulative disadvantage. Statistical methods such as latent class analysis (Whelan and Maitre 2005; Nolan and Whelan, 2007; Dewilde, 2004), structural equations modeling (Tomlinson, Walker, and Williams 2008); and item response theory (Capellari and Jenkins 2007) have

Table 16.6 PERCENTAGE BELOW 60 PERCENT INCOME LINE AND ABOVE THE DEPRIVATION THRESHOLD COMPARED WITH PERCENTAGE BELOW LINE

	Percentage Below 60 Percent Income Line and Above Deprivation Threshold	Percentage Below 60 Percent Income Line
Germany	4.9	14
Denmark	1.5	10
Netherlands	4.7	12
Belgium	5.6	15
France	6.2	15
United Kingdom	8.9	18
Ireland	9.2	19
Italy	9.3	20
Greece	9.4	21
Spain	7.9	18
Portugal	10.0	21
Average	7.1	16.6

SOURCE: Eurostat, ECHP (1996).

been applied in this context, and this is likely to be a fruitful area for future development (Thorbecke 2007). However, there will continue to be a tension between the power of sophisticated methods in summarizing the range of indicators available and the transparency required for policy makers and public debate.

CONCLUSIONS

Nonmonetary indicators of deprivation are now widely used in studying poverty in Europe. This reflects the recognition that income, though central, has serious limitations in identifying the poor, as well as the desire to capture multidimensional aspects of poverty and exclusion. Material deprivation indicators now complement income-based poverty measures in the EU's portfolio of social inclusion indicators and in official monitoring of poverty in a range of countries. They are being used to capture different dimensions of deprivation and also to measure who is multiply deprived across them. This allows for new insights in making comparisons across countries, in tracking changes over time, and in framing policies to respond to the needs of different groups. Although serious methodological and measurement issues remain to be addressed, much has been learned to date from the development of material deprivation indicators and their use is likely to increase in the future.

ACKNOWLEDGMENTS

The authors thank the editor Ken Couch and participants at the Joint OECD/ University of Maryland International Conference Measuring Poverty, Income Inequality, and Social Exclusion: Lessons from Europe, Paris, March 2009, for their most helpful comments. Funding from the Irish Research Council for the Humanities and Social Sciences is gratefully acknowledged.

Notes

1. Various measures of material hardship have also been employed in studying poverty in the United States, for example, Mayer and Jencks (1989) and Mayer (1993), and studies exploring how they might best be used there include Bauman (1998, 1999, 2003); our focus here though is on the European experience.
2. This is echoed in the definition put forward by an influential expert panel in the United States as insufficient resources for basic living needs, defined appropriately for the United States today (Citro and Michael 1995).
3. Boarini and Mira d'Ercole (2006) provide a review of the literature on material deprivation in OECD countries, as does OECD (2009).
4. Swedish welfare research has employed such a multidimensional approach since the 1960s, using individuals' command over resources in terms of family and social relations, material living conditions, health, education, working conditions, political life, leisure time activities, and housing conditions, to capture their "level of living."

5. The focus here, as in the literature being discussed, is on measures obtained at micro-level for individuals and households, rather than aggregate-level indicators for the country.

6. In all, the ECHP contained data on about 40 variables that could potentially serve as nonmonetary indicators of deprivation (e.g., see Eurostat 2000). These include some purely subjective indicators—such as how difficult it is to make ends meet—that we employ herein.

7. Not all these countries participated in 1994 and 1995, so this represents the first observation for the maximum number of countries; Sweden did not participate in the ECHP.

8. The basis on which these were selected is not entirely clear, but they include items in the ECHP that were widely employed in comparative studies. A special module included in EU-SILC in 2009 investigates a broader set of indicators to inform selection of items for the future.

9. See also Guio and Engsted-Maquet (2007). A variety of national studies have also investigated dimensionality using similar statistical methods (e.g., see Saunders and Adelman 2006), and these again bring out that the dimensions distinguished will depend on the range of items available.

10. Standard statistical tests suggest that the first two dimensions in EU-SILC are reasonably reliable but the environmental dimension may require some additional items (Whelan, Nolan, and Maitre 2008).

11. In a similar vein, Boarini and Mira d'Ercole (2006) present a range of comparative data for different OECD countries on the percentage of households unable to satisfy basic needs and basic leisure activities, lacking various consumer durables, in poor housing conditions, and so on.

12. For other national and comparative studies of the characteristics associated with different types of deprivation, see, for example, Tsaklogou and Papadopoulos (2002); Lollivier and Verger (1997); and Gordon et al. (2000).

13. See the discussions in, for example, Atkinson et al. (2002) and Mayer (1993).

14. See Van den Bosch (2001) for an in-depth discussion of subjective assessments of income adequacy.

15. Using panel data on income over time helps to explain differences in economic strain, but deprivation levels remain significant determinants (Whelan, Layte, and Maitre 2004).

16. It is worth noting that in the switch from the ECHP to EU-SILC as applied in Ireland, some changes in the way the questions are worded, framed, and located in the questionnaire may also have affected the level of deprivation reported.

References

Aaberge, Rolf, and Ingrid Melby. 1998. "The Sensitivity of Income Inequality to Choice of Equivalence Scales," *Review of Income and Wealth* 44 (4): 565–569.

Atkinson, Anthony B., Bea Cantillon, Eric Marlier, and Brian Nolan. 2002. *Social Indicators: The EU and Social Inclusion*. Oxford: Oxford University Press.

Bauman, Kurt. 1998. "Direct Measures of Poverty as Indicators of Economic Need: Evidence from the Survey of Income and Program Participation." Population Division Technical Working Paper 30, US Census Bureau, Washington, DC.

———. 1999. *Extended Measures of Well-Being: Meeting Basic Needs.* Current Population Reports P. 70–67. Washington, DC: US Census Bureau.

———. 2003. *Extended Measures of Well-Being: Living Conditions in the United States.* Current Population Reports P. 70–87. Washington, DC: US Census Bureau.

Berthoud, Richard, Mark Bryan, and Elena Bardasi. 2004. *The Dynamics of Deprivation: The Relationship between Income and Material Deprivation over Time.* Research Report Number 219. London: Department for Work and Pensions.

Bohnke, Petra, and Jan Delhey. 1999. *Poverty in a Multidimensional Perspective: Great Britain and Germany in Comparison.* FS III 99–413. Berlin: WZB.

Boarini, Romini, and Marco Mira d'Ercole. 2006. "Measures of Material Deprivation in OECD Countries." OECD Social Employment and Migration Working Papers37. Organization for Economic Co-operation and Development, Paris.

Bradshaw, Jonathan, and Naomi Finch. 2003. "Overlaps in Dimensions of Poverty." *Journal of Social Policy* 32: 513–525.

Breen, Richard, and Pasi Moiso. 2004. "Overestimated Poverty Mobility: Poverty Dynamics Corrected for Measurement Error." *Journal of Economic Inequality* 2: 171–191.

Buhmann, Brigitte, Lee Rainwater, Gunther Schmauss, and Tim Smeeding. 1988. "Equivalence Scales, Well-Being, Inequality, and Poverty: Sensitivity Estimates across Ten Countries Using the Luxembourg Income Study (LIS) Database." *Review of Income and Wealth* 34: 115–142.

Burchardt, Tania, Julian Le Grand, and David Piachaud. 2002. "Degrees of Exclusion: Developing a Dynamic, Multidimensional Measure." In *Understanding Social Exclusion.* Edited by J. Hills, J. Le Grand, and D. Piachaud, 30–43. Oxford: Oxford University Press.

Callan, Tim, Brian Nolan, and Christopher T. Whelan. 1993. "Resources, Deprivation and the Measurement of Poverty." *Journal of Social Policy* 22: 141–172.

Cappellari, Lorenzo, and Stephen P. Jenkins. 2007. "Summarising Multiple Deprivation Indicators." In *Poverty and Inequality: New Directions.* Edited by J. Micklewright and S. P. Jenkins, 166–184. Oxford: Oxford University Press.

Citro, Constance F., and Robert Michael. 1995. *Measuring Poverty: a New Approach.* Washington, DC: National Academy Press.

Dewilde, Caroline. 2004. "The Multidimensional Measurement of Poverty in Belgium and Britain: A Categorical Approach." *Social Indicators Research* 68: 331–369.

Dominy, Nicola, and Elaine Kempson. 2006. *Understanding Older People's Experiences of Material Deprivation.* Research Report 363. London: Department of Work and Pensions.

Eurostat. 1996. *European Community Household Panel: Methods Volume 1.* Luxembourg: Office for Official Publications of the European Communities.

———. 2000. *European Social Statistics: Income Poverty and Social Exclusion (1st Report).* Luxembourg: Office for Official Publications of the European Communities.

———. 2003. *European Social Statistics: Income Poverty and Social Exclusion (2nd Report).* Luxembourg: Office for Official Publications of the European Communities.

———. 2007. *Comparative EU Statistics on Income and Living Conditions: Issues and Challenges.* Proceedings of the EU-SILC conference, Helsinki, November 6–8, 2006. Luxembourg: Office for Official Publications of the European Communities.

Förster, Michael 2005. "The European Union Social Space Revisited: Comparing Poverty in the Enlarged European Union." *Journal of Comparative Policy Analysis* 7: 29–48.

Frick, Joachim, and Markus Grabka. 2007. *Item Non-Response and Imputation of Annual Labor Income in Panel Surveys from a Cross-National Perspective.* IZA Discussion Paper 3043. Bonn: IZA.

Gordon, David, Linda Adelman, Karen Ashworth, Jonathan Bradshaw, Ruth Levitas, Sue Middleton, Christina Pantazis, et al. 2000. *Poverty and Social Exclusion in Britain.* York: Joseph Rowntree Foundation.

Guio, Anne-Catherine. 2005. *Material Deprivation in the EU.* Eurostat, Statistics in Focus 21/2005. Luxembourg: Office for Official Publications of the European Communities.

Guio, Anne-Catherine, and Isabelle Engsted-Maquet. 2007. "Non-Income Dimension in EU-SILC: Material Deprivation and Poor Housing." In *Comparative EU Statistics on Income and Living Conditions: Issues and Challenges, Proceedings of the EU-SILC Conference (Helsinki, 6–8 November 2006).* Edited by Eurostat, 193–228. Luxembourg: Office for Official Publications of the European Communities.

Hallerod, Bjorn. 1995. "The Truly Poor: Direct and Indirect Measurement of Consensual Poverty in Sweden." *European Journal of Social Policy* 5: 111–129.

———. 2006. "Sour Grapes: Relative Deprivation, Adaptive Preferences and the Measurement of Poverty." *Journal of Social Policy* 35: 371–390.

Hauser, Richard. 2008. *Problems of the German Contribution to EU-SILC—A Research Perspective, Comparing EU-SILC, Microcensus and SOEP.* SOEP Papers on Multidisciplinary Panel Data Research86. Berlin: DIW Berlin. http://ideas.repec.org/p/diw/diwsop/diw_sp86.html.

Kangas, Olli, and Velli-Matti Ritakallio. 1998. "Different Methods—Different Results? Approaches to Multidimensional Poverty." iIn *Empirical Poverty Research in a Comparative Perspective.* Edited by H. -J. Andress, 167–203. Aldershot: Ashgate.

———. 2001. "Explaining Deprivation in the European Union." *Acta Sociologica* 44: 105–122.

Lollivier, Stéfan, and Daniel Verger. 1997. "Pauvreté d. existence, monétaire ou subjective sont distinctes." *Economie et Statistique* 308–310: 113–142.

Mack, Joanna, and Stewart Lansley. 1985. *Poor Britain.* London: Allen and Unwin.

Marlier, Eric, Bea Cantillon, Brian Nolan, Karel Van den Bosch, and Tim Van Rie. (2012). "Developing and Learning from EU Measures of Social Inclusion." In *Counting the Poor: New Thinking about European Poverty Measures and Lessons for the United States.* Edited by Douglas J. Besharov and Kenneth A. Couch, 297–342. New York: Oxford University Press.

Mayer, Susan. 1993. "Living Conditions among the Poor in Four Rich Countries." *Journal of Population Economics* 6: 261–286.

Mayer, Susan, and Christopher Jencks. 1989. "Poverty and the Distribution of Material Hardship." *Journal of Human Resources* 24: 88–114.

McKay, Stephen. 2004. "Poverty of Preference: What Do Consensual Deprivation Indicators Really Measure?" *Fiscal Studies* 25: 201–224.

Muffels, Ruud, and Henk Dirven. 1998. "Long-Term Income and Deprivation-Based Poverty among the Elderly." In *Empirical Poverty Research in a Comparative Perspective.* Edited by H. -J. Andress, 229–256. Aldershot: Ashgate.

Nolan, Brian, and Christopher T. Whelan. 1996. *Resources, Deprivation and Poverty.* Oxford: Oxford University Press.

———. 2007. "On the Multidimensionality of Poverty and Social Exclusion." In *Poverty and Inequality: New Directions.* Edited by J. Micklewright and S. P. Jenkins, 146–165. Oxford: Oxford University Press.

OECD. 2009. *Growing Unequal? Income Distribution and Poverty in OECD Countries.* Paris: Organization for Economic Co-operation and Development.

Pantazis, Christina, David Gordon, and Ruth Levitas, eds. 2006. *Poverty and Social Exclusion in Britain: The Millennium Survey.* Bristol: Policy Press.

Peracchi, Franco. 2002. "The European Community Household Panel: A Review." *Empirical Economics* 27: 63–90.

Ringen, Stein. 1988. "Direct and Indirect Measures of Poverty." *Journal of Social Policy* 17: 351–366.

Saunders, Peter, and Laura Adelman. 2006. "Income Poverty, Deprivation and Exclusion: A Comparative Study of Australia and Britain." *Journal of Social Policy* 35: 559–584.

Thorbecke, Erik. 2007. "Multidimensional Poverty: Conceptual and Measurement Issues." In *The Many Dimensions of Poverty.* Edited by N. Kakawani and J. Silber, pages. Basingstoke: Palgrave Macmillan.

Tomlinson, Mark, Alan Walker, and G. Williams. 2008. "Measuring Poverty in Britain as a Multi-Dimensional Concept, 1991 to 2003." *Journal of Social Policy* 37: 597–620.

Townsend, Peter. 1979. *Poverty in the United Kingdom.* Harmondsworth: Penguin.

Tsakloglou, Peter, and Giota Panopoulou. 1998. "Who Are the Poor in Greece? Analysing Poverty under Alternative Concepts of Resources and Equivalence Scales." *Journal of European Social Policy* 8: 229–252

Tsakloglou, Panos, and Fotis Papadopoulos. 2002. "Aggregate Level and Determining Factors of Social Exclusion in Twelve European Countries." *Journal of European Social Policy* 12: 211–225.

Van den Bosch, Karel 2001. *Identifying the Poor: Using Subjective and Consensual Measures.* Aldershot: Ashgate.

Whelan, Christopher T., and Betrand Maître. 2005. "Vulnerability and Multiple Deprivation Perspectives on Economic Exclusion in Europe: A Latent Class Analysis." *European Societies* 7: 423–450.

———. 2006. "Comparing Poverty and Deprivation Dynamics: Issues of Reliability and Validity." *Journal of Economic Inequality* 4: 303–323.

———. 2008. "Social Class and Risk: A Comparative Analysis of the Dynamics of Economic Vulnerability." *British Journal of Sociology* 60: 637–659.

Whelan, Christopher T., Richard Layte, and Bertrand Maître. 2002. "Multiple Deprivation and Persistent Poverty in the European Union." *Journal of European Social Policy* 12: 91–105.

———. 2003. "Persistent Income Poverty and Deprivation in the European Union." *Journal of Social Policy* 32: 1–18.

———. 2004. "Understanding the Mismatch between Income Poverty and Deprivation: A Dynamic Comparative Analysis." *European Sociological Review* 20: 287–302.

Whelan, Christopher T., Richard Layte, Bertrand Maître, and Brian Nolan. 2001. "Income, Deprivation and Economic Strain: An Analysis of the European Community Household Panel." *European Sociological Review* 17: 357–372.

Whelan, Christopher T., Brian Nolan, and Bertrand Maître. 2008. "Measuring Material Deprivation in the Enlarged EU." Working Paper 249, Economic and Social Research Institute, Dublin.

Zaidi, Asghar and Tania Burchardt. 2005. "Comparing Incomes When Needs Differ: Equivalisation for the Extra Costs of Disability in the UK." *Review of Income and Wealth* 51: 89–114.

17

Poverty Redefined as Low Consumption and Low Wealth, Not Just Low Income

Psychological Consequences in Australia and Germany

BRUCE HEADEY, PETER KRAUSE, AND GERT G. WAGNER ■

In this chapter, we suggest that measures of financial poverty should be based on individuals having low consumption and low wealth, as well as low income. Having set out a case for doing this, we provide revised estimates of poverty based on all three dimensions of economic well-being in Australia. Then, using this extended measure of financial poverty, we reassess links between poverty and a range of subjective/psychological outcomes relating to life satisfaction, perceived standard of living, personal relationships, and health. The analysis indicates that poverty, measured in this more comprehensive manner, has worse effects, a wider range of effects, and perhaps more complicated effects than most recent research has admitted.

After completing the initial analysis for Australia, we check for robustness of our estimates by implementing a similar measure of financial poverty in Germany requiring individuals to have both low income and low wealth to be considered poor. Using this revised measure for Germany, we largely confirm the initial findings for Australia. Despite the inability to also look at those with low consumption levels in Germany, we nonetheless find that the relationship of financial poverty as measured in Germany is more strongly related to adverse perceptions of subjective/psychological outcomes in the areas of life satisfaction, perceived standard of living, and personal relationships than in Australia. Financial poverty, as measured here, appears to only result in clearly worse outcomes in Australia than in Germany in the dimension of health. Thus, the robustness check within the German data confirms the initial findings.

Most research has found that income in general, and income poverty in particular, has statistically significant but only small effects on life satisfaction and some other aspects of well-being (Easterlin 1974, 1995; Headey and Wearing, 1989, 1992; Diener et al. 1999; Argyle 2001; Frijters, Haisken-DeNew, and Shields 2004; Clark, Frijters, and Shields 2008). However, a recent paper by Stevenson and Wolfers (2008) seriously challenges this finding. The explanation provided for the usual finding is that,

in Western countries with welfare state programs, income mainly impacts life satisfaction through its effects on social status (Easterlin 1974, 1995). That is, people with
higher incomes than others in the same society feel slightly more satisfied with life,
but only because they enjoy higher status. The Easterlin paradox is that, even if
everyone's income increased by the same amount—even if it was a large amount—
no-one would be more satisfied because status positions would be unchanged.

Social workers, welfare agencies, and others who work directly with low-income
people have frequently expressed skepticism regarding research that might be taken
to imply that the detrimental psychological effects of poverty mainly relate to feel-
ings of low status (Townsend 1979). They have often reported evidence collected
from poor people about the humiliations of living in poverty, including degradation
related to not being able to keep up a "mainstream" lifestyle and appearing to others
as poor (Townsend 1979; Mack and Lansley 1985).

However, from a research standpoint, it ought to be conceded that most of this
published research rests on measures of poverty that, from a theoretical point of
view, are quite seriously flawed. The measures deal with *relative income poverty*,
typically defined as an equivalized income below 50 or 60 percent of the national
median. No account is taken of other dimensions of economic well-being. Further,
the measures used are often cross-sectional. They only deal with the level of current
income or the total over the last year. Plainly, medium- and long-term poverty should
be of greater humanitarian and policy concern than shorter episodes. This latter concern has been addressed in panel studies, starting with the Michigan Panel Study of
Income Dynamics, which invariably find that most poverty is short-term, although
people who have suffered spells of poverty in the past are at risk of recurrence
(Duncan 1984); Bane and Ellwood 1986; Stevens 1994).

It is not clear that income-based measures adequately capture what economists
and others usually say they mean by *poverty*. At a conceptual level, *poverty* is usually
defined as *involuntary low consumption*. Low consumption *is* a low material standard
of living. As Stein Ringen (1987) has observed, low income is only an indirect or
proxy measure for low consumption. At best, income is a measure of the potential
standard of living or command over resources. Ringen (1987) has shown that in
some countries, there is only a moderate overlap between those who, at one moment
in time, have low incomes and those who have low consumption.

The economist's concept of *permanent income* implies that individuals and households try to smooth consumption over a lifetime (Friedman 1957). During periods
of low income (e.g., during student years or in their twenties), individuals may be
able to borrow to improve their consumption. They may also receive subsidies in
cash or in kind from parents and other relatives. Later in life, imputed rental income
due to housing equity may boost *real income* above *nominal income*.

The reasons for taking account of net worth in measures of poverty are also quite
compelling. If a family has a high or even moderate level of assets, it makes little
sense to describe it as poor, even if its current income is low. This can be a substantively important point because, in some countries, there are many people who are
moderately asset-rich but also income-poor. In Australia, the Bureau of Statistics
reports that households in the lowest decile of income are, on average, in the middle
quintile of net worth. Many of those with low current incomes are older people who
own their dwellings outright (ABS 2005), and this places them higher up the distribution of wealth holdings. Clearly, households with substantial assets, such as a

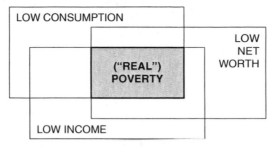

Figure 17.1 Redefining Financial Poverty: Intersection of Low Income, Low Consumption, and Low Net Worth.

home with no mortgage, may be able to ride out a period of low income without a big fall in consumption. Obviously, this is easier if the assets are liquid, rather than in the form of property or other nonfinancial assets. (Later in the chapter, we use two alternative measures, one of which is restricted to liquid assets). It may be noted that some recent research has suggested that in several countries, including the two considered here, wealth has as much if not more impact on life satisfaction than income (Headey, Muffels, and Wooden 2008).

The multidimensional (income, wealth, and consumption) concept of financial poverty that we prefer can readily be illustrated in a diagram. As Figure 17.1 indicates, "real" financial poverty might be viewed as the overlap or intersection of low income, low consumption, and low net worth. (Operational measures—or specific poverty lines—for low income, consumption, and net worth are proposed later in the chapter). It might reasonably be argued that the flip side of this conceptualization is that households that are close to or below poverty lines using measures of just one or two of these dimensions of economic well-being might be at risk of future poverty. This is an empirical issue as well as a conceptual one. In a previous paper, the first author showed that households which, in a given year, have low net worth, are in the bottom half of the income distribution and consume more than their current income, have about a 10 percent chance of becoming poor in year $t + 1$ (Headey 2008).

The arithmetic relationship between household income, consumption, and net worth should be borne in mind.

$$HH\ Consumption\ =\ HH\ Disposable\ income - HH\ Change\ in\ net\ worth$$

In any given year, a household's material standard of living or consumption is going to depend on its disposable income minus its change in net worth (assets minus debts). If it wants to spend more than it earns, it runs down wealth/savings, or borrows. If it earns more than it spends, it foregoes consumption and its wealth increases. The definition of consumption here includes the market value of consumption goods, plus imputed rental values for durables (e.g., housing; see following discussion). Household disposable income includes government benefits and is net of taxes. Capital gains or losses, whether realised or unrealised, are included in income. Net worth comprises all assets (both financial and nonfinancial) minus all debts.

The previous equation might be taken to imply that, in making survey-based measures of financial poverty, we could rely on consumption measures alone, or alternatively measure any two of the three concepts and calculate results for the third.

In practice, this would not be sensible because, as economists and government statistical offices are well aware, there is considerable error in survey measures of wealth, income, and consumption. So in practical terms it makes sense to "triangulate" and directly measure all three concepts.

The most serious practical problems hindering implementation of the concept of financial poverty preferred here has been the perceived inability to measure household expenditures and consumption in a standard survey format. It is generally believed that the only valid approach is to get respondents to fill in a shopping diary for at least a week, as is done in government household expenditure surveys. This time-consuming approach is out of the question for panel surveys like Household, Income, and Labour Dynamics in Australia (HILDA) for Australia and the Socio-Economic Panel (SOEP) for Germany, which are essential if we want to measure long-run or permanent income, as theory requires. But the effort to measure consumption in a panel survey does not have to be abandoned due to the large time and survey costs associated with obtaining expenditure information by the method of weekly diaries. Building on Canadian work (Browning, Crossley, and Weber 2003), the HILDA team has developed a page of expenditure questions that appear to give reasonable estimates of over 50 percent of total household expenditure. This methodological issue and others are addressed in the next section regarding data used in the analysis.

METHODS

The Australian HILDA Panel Survey

The HILDA Survey is commissioned by the Australian Government and conducted by the Melbourne Institute of Applied Economic and Social Research at the University of Melbourne. It is a national household panel survey with a focus on issues relating to families, income, employment, and well-being. Described in more detail in Watson and Wooden (2004), the survey began in 2001 with a national probability sample of households occupying private dwellings. Interviews are conducted annually with all household members aged 15 and over. The initial household response rate was 66 percent, with 13,969 individuals completing interviews. By 2006, the sample size was 12,905. As is the case in most national panel surveys, sample representativeness is maintained not just by reinterviewing sample members who stay in the same household, but also by following "split-offs" (that is, individuals who leave to form separate households) and adding members of their new households. So, for example, young people who leave home to get married remain in the sample, and their new partners are added.

Measuring Consumption

As noted earlier, the general view has been that to ask expenditure questions in a standard survey format would yield invalid data because, without the assistance of a diary, respondents would be unable to remember how much they spent on many goods and services. However, recent work in Canada has shown that, in fact, some items of expenditures are more validly reported in standard surveys than a diary, in part because respondents tell us how much they "usually" spend on items, which is exactly what we want to know for the purpose of analyses that investigate individual or household relationships between consumption, other measures of well-being, and social and economic outcomes more generally (Browning, Crossley, and Weber 2003).[1] A defect of diaries for these purposes is that they record expenditures in a specific time period (usually a week or two), which may or may not be typical for an individual respondent or household. Consequently, individual- or household-level correlation and regression analyses cannot sensibly be undertaken, although aggregate national estimates for each variable should be correct.[2]

Further, the Canadian researchers showed that total household expenditures can be accurately extrapolated from the validly reported items.[3] The official Canadian statistical agency, Statistics Canada, now regularly uses standard survey methods to collect expenditure data.[4] It should be noted, however, that their instrument appears too long for inclusion in panel surveys like HILDA and SOEP.

For the HILDA panel, the data managers have developed a page of questions that appear to provide valid measurement of a wide range of household expenditures, but not all. The approach is to divide expenditures into weekly, monthly, and annual items. It seems natural or at least sensible for some items (e.g., groceries, public transport, and taxis) to ask how much is spent in "a typical week." For other items (e.g., motor vehicle fuel and telephone calls), the HILDA survey questions relate to how much is spent in "a typical month," and for a third set (e.g., holidays, costs of education) the question relates to the whole year.

In the 2005 survey, all the consumption goods on which households spend at least a moderate amount of money were included: groceries, meals eaten out, alcohol, cigarettes and tobacco, public transport and taxis, motor fuel, car repairs, telephone costs, utilities (gas, electricity, other heating fuels), home maintenance, health insurance, education, clothing and footwear, health care, holidays, hobbies, and child care. The only consumer durable that was included was housing, both mortgages and rents. Other durables were omitted in 2005, but then were attempted in the 2006 and 2007 surveys.

Benchmarking HILDA Consumption Data for 2005

The obvious way to assess measurement validity is to make an adjustment for inflation and benchmark results against the latest official survey for which published data are available, namely the Australian Bureau of Statistics (ABS) Household Expenditure Survey (HES) for 2003–2004.[5] In benchmarking, we mainly rely on comparisons between mean expenditures reported in HES and in HILDA. The standard deviations reported in the HES are in many cases much higher than in HILDA precisely because, for some items, HES did not ask about "usual" expenditures but recorded expenditures in a survey/diary week. Inevitably, this led to inclusion of some expenditures that were unusually high or low for the households concerned, thereby inflating standard deviations.

It transpires that HILDA appears to have recorded accurate measurement (to within about plus or minus 10 percent) of items comprising 53.4 percent of total household expenditure on goods and services.[6,7] The validly measured items were the first 12 on the list in the previous subsection, starting with groceries, plus housing and rent (see Appendix Table 17.A.1). The items for which HILDA estimates proved inaccurate were the last five on the list, starting with clothing and footwear.

In regard to the validly measured items, the total expenditure figure in HILDA differs by only 3.8 percent in real terms from the HES total for the same items, after adjusting for inflation.[8] A key point is that the putatively validly measured items correlate 0.76 with total household expenditure.[9] Further, and relevant to the measurement of poverty, the same correlation was found for low-income households. Finally, it may be noted that, within the HES data set, a regression equation that uses just those items that appear to be well-measured in a survey format, plus standard demographics, accounts for 78.3 percent of the variance in total household expenditure.[10]

On the basis of the benchmarking evidence, it appears reasonable to regard the sum of expenditures on the well-measured HILDA consumption items as a valid proxy for total household expenditures. We can then proceed to calculate measures of consumption poverty. In this chapter, expenditure estimates are treated as equivalent to consumption, except in the case of owner-occupier housing.[11] Here the consumption benefit has been equated to a rental value set at 4 percent of the current value of the house if sold today (as estimated by HILDA survey respondents).[12]

Further in regard to measurement issues, it should be noted that over 80 percent of households provided information about their expenditures for all items included in the 2005 and 2006 HILDA surveys. Imputed values for total consumption (but not individual items) were added for the remaining individuals who had some missing data.[13] The Pearson correlation coefficient between household consumption measured in 2005 and 2006 was 0.80. This is a higher correlation than was found for disposable income (0.69), indicating consumption smoothing. Also, as permanent income theory would predict, consumption was also more equally distributed than income. For example, the Gini coefficient of household consumption in 2005 was about 20 percent lower than the Gini for income.

Measures of Income and Wealth in HILDA

The validity of the measures of income and wealth collected in HILDA have been assessed in previous publications and will only be briefly summarized here (Watson and Wooden 2004; Headey, Marks and Wooden 2005). HILDA collects annual data on all main sources of labor income, asset income, private transfers, and government benefits. Income taxes, the Medicare Levy, and Family Tax Benefits are imputed by the survey data managers. The HILDA totals for gross incomes (income from all sources, including government) and disposable incomes match up well with ABS sources.

HILDA measured wealth—assets and debts—in 2002 and then again in 2006. Most household- and individual-level surveys seriously underestimate wealth, when matched up against aggregate data sources. However, when the HILDA data are benchmarked against ABS and Reserve Bank of Australia sources, it appears that underestimation is only moderate. Average (mean) financial and nonfinancial assets in HILDA are both over 90 percent of the appropriate benchmark, and debts are over 80 percent (Headey, Marks, and Wooden 2005).[14]

Operational Definitions of Financial Poverty—50 Percent and 60 Percent of Median

In Australia, poverty lines based on 50 percent of median income are still generally used, whereas in the European Union (EU), a 60 percent line is preferred.[15] In line with the view that poverty should be measured as a combination of persistent low income, low income, and low liquid assets, we regard an individual as persistently poor if he/she has an equivalized income below either (1) 50 percent of national median equivalized income and 50 percent of median equivalized consumption or (2) 60 percent of median income and consumption. Additionally, a person is only defined as poor if he/she is also poor in terms of net worth or liquid assets (see definitions that follow).

How best to measure low wealth or low net worth (assets minus debts) for present purposes? One simple practical approach is just to exclude any individual/household with substantial net worth from being defined as poor. Here we say that any household with a net worth of $200,000 or more is automatically excluded from poverty. A second approach has been developed by Caner and Wolff (2004). They have proposed several measures of what they term *asset poverty*. Their basic idea is that a household is *asset-poor* if it lacks enough wealth to survive for three months in an emergency (caused by, say, ill health or an unexpectedly large bill) with an income above a designated income poverty line. They propose several alternative measures: the one used here (in addition to the net worth measure) relates to the availability of liquid/financial assets valued at three times the income poverty line, thereby enabling them to stay out of poverty for three months in emergency. In other words, Caner and Wolff exclude nonfinancial assets such as housing, businesses, and farms that cannot easily be cashed in to cope with an emergency.

For comparison with the *poor*, we also define two other groups. A *middle group* was designated whose equivalized incomes and consumption were above income and consumption poverty lines but not in the top quintiles of these distributions, and who were also not poor in terms of low net worth, but not in the top quintile of net worth either. The *well-off* will be defined as those who had an equivalized income, equivalized consumption, and a level of net worth that placed them in the top quintile of these three distributions.

MEASURES OF LIFE SATISFACTION AND WELL-BEING

Now, we turn to a discussion of the measures of life satisfaction and well-being. Life satisfaction was measured on a single item 0–10 scale, where 0 meant "completely dissatisfied" and 10 meant "completely satisfied." This measure is widely used in national and international social and economic surveys, including household panels such as HILDA, and is regarded as adequately reliable and valid for many purposes (Diener et al. 1999). However, it is clearly less reliable and valid than well-constructed multi-item scales (Headey and Wearing 1989, 1992).

We also consider the impact of poverty on several other measures relating to well-being and stress. Satisfaction with "your financial situation" and "your relationship with your partner" were measured on the same 0–10 scale and were included in batteries of questions assessing satisfaction with a wide range of different aspects of life. General health and mental health were assessed by the SF-36 Health Scale, a well-regarded survey instrument designed to provide self-assessed health measures that is designed for completion by the general public (or patients) rather than health professionals (Ware, Snow, and Kosinski 2000). General health and mental health are recorded on standardised 0–100 scales, where a high score means "good" health.

For presentation in tables, all the well-being measures have been transformed to run from 0 to 100. This allows results to be interpreted as quasi-percentiles.[16] This arithmetic transformation does not in any way distort comparisons between groups and avoids the confusion sometimes caused by giving results based on a variety of scales that have differing (and arbitrary) lengths.

RESULTS

Estimates of Financial Poverty in 2005–2007 Based on Wealth and Consumption, As Well As Income

In Table 17.1 results are first given for poverty lines based solely on low income.[17] This is the conventional approach. Next, we observe lower poverty rates given by consumption measures. Then, we see how big a difference it makes to estimated rates when income and consumption are combined to provide income + consumption poverty lines. Finally, measures of net worth (or asset poverty) are added to give multidimensional income + consumption + wealth lines.

It can be seen that in Australia the choice of whether to define and measure poverty in terms of just income, or both income and consumption, makes a huge difference regarding how many people (and, as we shall see, which groups of people)

Table 17.1 AUSTRALIA: MEASURES OF FINANCIAL POVERTY IN 2007 BASED ON INCOME, CONSUMPTION, INCOME + CONSUMPTION, INCOME + CONSUMPTION + NET WORTH (LIQUID ASSETS)

	<50 percent of Median Poverty Line (%)	<60 Percent of Median Poverty Line (%)
Income poor	13.7	19.9
Consumption poor	9.9	15.9
Income poor + consumption poor	3.6	7.2
Income poor + consumption poor + net worth poor[a]	3.2	6.3
Income poor + consumption poor + liquid asset poor[a]	2.5	4.9

[a]Two alternative measures of low wealth are given in the last two rows of the table.

SOURCE: HILDA (2007).

are designated as poor. Inclusion of low wealth (whether taking account of all assets, or just liquid assets) at the last step has a small impact on the cross-sectional results. Fundamentally, the reason why inclusion of consumption has such a large effect is that consumption is about 20 percent more equally distributed than income. It is also only moderately highly correlated with income, the Pearson correlation in 2006 being 0.52.[18] It is also clear from Table 17.1 that choice of the poverty line (50 or 60 percent of median) has a large impact on the estimated poverty rate.

Income + consumption poverty lines give much lower estimates of poverty than income lines alone. Many households appear to engage in consumption smoothing, maintaining their standard of living during temporary periods of low income. Adding in net worth or liquid asset poverty then reduces estimated poverty rates a little more.

Next we show how the new multidimensional measures could be used to provide revised estimates of the persistence of financial poverty. As noted earlier, poverty persistence is of much greater normative and policy significance than short-term poverty, or poverty at one moment in time. However, with only three years of data for the new measures, the evidence is purely illustrative; plainly a three-year measure cannot sensibly be described as indexing *persistent* poverty. Using each of the alternative measures, Table 17.2 shows how many Australians were not poor in any year in 2005–2007, how many were poor in just one of these years, how many were poor for two (any two) of the three years, and how many were poor for three years running. Results for the rest of the chapter are only shown for the 60 percent of median poverty line.

Clearly, three-year poverty persistence is estimated to be a great deal lower if income-based measures are replaced by more comprehensive measures, such as the ones used here, that also incorporate consumption or consumption plus net worth. The results in Table 17.2 also provide further evidence of consumption smoothing. If the 60 percent income-based poverty line is used, three-year poverty is estimated at 10.6 percent, whereas if income, consumption, and net worth are all included, the rate is 2.6 percent (2.2 percent if liquid asset poverty is used instead of low net worth).

In summary, if the logic behind including these revised measures of poverty is accepted as sound, it also has to be accepted that existing income-based measures are seriously in error. The results they give are much too high. Saying this does not in any way diminish the importance of financial poverty as a public policy issue. The key aim is to define and measure poverty more accurately in order to provide improved evidence for public policy intervention.

Who is Income Poor But Not Consumption Poor—and Vice Versa?

Given that the groups diverge, it is valuable to ask the following question: "Who is income poor but not consumption poor—and vice versa?" Three hypotheses may be suggested about the characteristics of the first group. First, we might expect that many would be homeowners who have completely or nearly paid off their mortgage and so are living more or less rent-free.[19] Second, we might expect that some young people with high levels of human capital but a low current income would take a chance on consuming more than they earn because they consider that they can afford

Table 17.2 AUSTRALIA: THREE-YEAR PERSISTENCE OF FINANCIAL POVERTY IN 2005–2007 BASED ON 60 PERCENT OF MEDIAN POVERTY LINES: INCOME POVERTY CONSUMPTION POVERTY, INCOME + CONSUMPTION POVERTY, INCOME + CONSUMPTION + NET WORTH (LIQUID ASSETS)

N times Poor in 2005–2007	Income Poor 60 Percent Line (%)	Consumption Poor 60 Percent Line (%)	Income and Consumption Poor 60 Percent line (%)	Income, Consumption, and Net Worth Poor 60 Percent Line (%)[a]	Income, Consumption, and Liquid Asset Poor 60 Percent Line (%)[a]
Never poor	69.8	75.5	87.4	88.8	92.3
1 year poor	12.6	9.9	6.4	5.3	3.1
2 years poor	7.1	6.8	3.5	3.3	2.4
All 3 years poor	10.6	7.8	2.7	2.6	2.2
	(100.0)	(100.0)	(100.0)	(100.0)	(100.0)

[a] Two alternative measures of low wealth are given in the last two columns of the table.

SOURCE: HILDA (2007).

to take on debt. Third, and overlappping with the second group, we might expect to find some young people consuming more than they earn due to gifts from parents and relatives.[20]

All three hypotheses receive some confirmation. The largest set of people who lack income but whose consumption levels appear adequate are those who own their homes outright. Many are older people who have retired. For example, the estimated rate of poverty in 2007 for households headed by people aged 65 and over falls from 24.6 percent if the 60 percent of median income-based poverty line is used, down to 7.3 percent if a parallel measure combining income, consumption, and net worth is used.

Younger well-educated people also have a fairly high rate of income poverty. As noted previously, they may be borrowing to consume, or perhaps living partly off a parental subsidy.[21] Their decisions to spend more than they earn may be quite rational in so far as they have high earnings expectations down the track. Single women are particularly likely to have higher levels of consumption than earnings and may perhaps receive some subsidies from partners and boyfriends, in addition to borrowings and possible parental subsidies. In general, households headed by individuals or couples of prime working age (25–54 years) are less likely than households headed by younger or older people to be income poor but still have adequate levels of consumption.

It proved harder to identify specific groups who are consumption poor but not income poor. However, renters who have relatively low incomes and pay a high proportion of what they do earn in rent are one such group.[22]

Life Satisfaction, Personal Relationships, and Other Outcomes Related to Health and Well-being

In Table 17.3, we turn to our examination of the relationship to self-assessments of life satisfaction relative to the poverty measures developed in the chapter thus far. The data used in the analysis are drawn from 2007 and, as previously mentioned, only poverty measures based on 60 percent of median income and consumption lines (together with wealth measures) are used in the calculations.

As would be expected, the measures of life satisfaction are systematically ordered with less-well-off groups consistently reporting lower levels than for those contained in the middle and well-off categories. The gaps in the levels across the three categories are substantial (not merely statistically significant) for most of these measures. Furthermore, the gaps found using our revised multidimensional measures of poverty are for all variables greater than if a purely income-based measure had been used (see Appendix Table 17.B.1).[23] The most eye-catching finding is the difference in percentages of people who are partnered. Only 39 percent of prime age poor people—and only 35 percent of the women—were partnered, compared with 66 percent in the middle group and 75 percent in the well-off group. It appears that to be poor is to be unable to get or keep a partner. However in some cases—especially single mothers—individuals would have become poor as a consequence of their partnership splitting up, rather than being unable to get a partner because of poverty.

The other substantial differences between the three groups relate to satisfaction with "your financial situation," to general health, and to mental health. The first finding may appear self-evident, but notice that the financial satisfaction of poor men is

Table 17.3 AUSTRALIA: COMPARING THE POOR (LOW INCOME +
LOW CONSUMPTION + LOW NET WORTH) WITH MIDDLE AND WELL-OFF
GROUPS—LINKAGES TO LIFE SATISFACTION, FINANCIAL SATISFACTION,
PERSONAL RELATIONSHIPS, AND HEALTH, 2007

	Poverty: Low Income, Consumption, and Net Worth (%)[a]			Middle Income, Consumption, and Net Worth (%)			High Income, Consumption, and Net Worth (%)		
	All	Men	Women	All	Men	Women	All	Men	Women
Life satisfaction (0–100)	75	74	76	79	79	79	82	81	83
Financial satisfaction (0–100)	53	51	54	67	67	67	79	78	79
Partnered (%)	39	44	35	66	68	65	75	75	76
Partner satisfaction (0–100)	78	82	76	82	84	80	83	85	81
General health (0–100)	56	57	56	69	69	69	74	74	74
Mental health (0–100)	66	65	66	75	77	74	79	81	77

NOTE: Population weighted results.
[a]Low income and low consumption are defined as <60 percent of equivalized median income and equivalized median consumption. Low net worth is <$200,000.
SOURCE: HILDA (2007).

lower than that of poor women, probably reflecting the fact that prime age men feel particularly humiliated by not earning a good living. The health differences between the well-off and the poor may appear striking to a layperson, although no surprise to public health researchers or medical practitioners. Again, some reverse causation is certain to be at work. In other words, not only is it the case that poverty damages physical and mental health, but also poor health can be one cause of poverty.

Much recent research in economics has focused exclusively on the relationship between income and life satisfaction, which is treated as the main outcome of interest. In one sense, this may lead to misleading conclusions, or conclusions that are too sweeping. Even with the revised measure of poverty used here, we find quite small differences between the persistently poor, middle, and well-off groups. The gap between the poor and the well-off for the total population is 7 points on the 0–100 scale. Further, in multivariate analysis, the gap falls to just 2 percent (see the following); this is statistically significant at the 0.001 level, but substantively minor.

However, the main conclusions to be drawn from the evidence in Table 17.3 relate not to life satisfaction but to other more substantial differences in well-being between the three groups. These differences are surely not just due to status. We return to this issue in the Discussion section.

Multivariate results for the same six outcomes

Plainly, some of the results given in Table 17.3 could be spurious due to omitted variables correlated with both poverty and the outcome variables. Table 17.4 gives multivariate results for the same six outcomes, with "controls" consisting of a range of variables generally associated with subjective outcomes: gender, age, partner status, number of children in the household, years of education, unemployment status (1–0),

Table 17.4 AUSTRALIA: FINANCIAL POVERTY—LINKAGES TO LIFE SATISFACTION, FINANCIAL SATISFACTION, PERSONAL RELATIONSHIPS, AND HEALTH 2007: OLS AND PROBIT

	Life Satisfaction (0–100)	Financial Satisfaction (0–100)	Partner Status (1–0)	Partner Satisfaction (0–100)	Health (0–100)	Mental Health (0–100)
Poverty: low income, consumpton, and net worth	−1.92***	−11.53***	−0.25***	−3.08*	−5.36***	−4.24***
Female	0.70***	0.53	−0.07***	−2.31***	0.21	−2.50***
Age	0.47***	−0.68***	0.05***	−0.59***	−0.11	−0.09
Age²/10	0.06***	0.09***	0.00***	0.07***	0.00	0.02***
Partnered	4.06***	6.33***	—	—	0.65	2.63***
No. children	−0.25	−1.25***	0.14***	−1.12***	0.59**	0.06
Years of education	−0.22**	0.95***	0.01***	−0.02	0.52***	0.15
Unemployed	−2.70**	15.14***	−0.19***	−5.43***	1.65	−2.50*
Disability	−4.82***	−5.69***	−0.05***	−1.45**	−19.83***	−8.79***
Foreign (NESB)	−1.79***	−1.22	−0.02	−0.71	−1.01	−1.79***
Neuroticism	−2.37***	−2.43	0.01*	−3.00***	−3.98***	−5.41***
Extroversion	1.43***	0.48*	0.02***	0.79***	1.69***	1.85***
Adjusted R^2 (%)	11.7	14.3	17.5[a]	5.7	28.8	22.9
N	9,935	9,934	9,937	6,778	9,112	9,211

NOTE: *** significant at 0.001; ** significant at 0.01; * significant at 0.05.
[a]Pseudo R^2.
NESB means born in a non-English-speaking country.
SOURCE: HILDA (2007).

disability status (1–0), being born in a non-English speaking country, and the personality traits of neuroticism and extroversion (Costa and McCrae 1991). The poverty measure used here is again the low income (60 percent line) + low consumption (60 percent line) + low net worth index for 2007, and results in Table 17.4 come from ordinary least squares (OLS) regressions, with the exception of the outcome "partner status" for which a marginal effects probit regression was appropriate.

It is clear that, net of controls, four of these six outcomes are strongly associated with poverty. (Again, though, it should be noted that two-way, rather than just one-way causation is certain to be involved). A poor person's chances of finding and keeping a partner are 25 percent less than a nonpoor person's chances are. Poor people rate 11.5 percent (quasi percentiles) lower than others on "satisfaction with your financial situation," 5.4 percent lower on the SF-36 General Health Scale, and 4.2 percent lower on the SF-36 Mental Health Scale. On the other hand, the satisfaction levels of the poor with "your relationship with your partner" were only about 3 percent lower than for the nonpoor, and life satisfaction was only about 2 percent lower.

PSYCHOLGICAL CONSEQUENCES OF FINANCIAL POVERTY IN CROSS-NATIONAL PERSPECTIVE

To test the cross-national robustness of results regarding the subjective consequences of poverty, we also used data from the SOEP. The SOEP is a multidisciplinary representative longitudinal study in Germany starting in 1984, in which direct annual interviews are carried out with all individuals of respondent age (16 years and older) who live together in the same household (Wagner, Frick, and Schupp 2007). The SOEP includes annual measures of household income, earnings, satisfaction, labor market participation, education, and sociodemographic characteristics of individuals and the household.[24] Wealth was surveyed as a special module in 2002 (and repeated in 2007). In 2005, the SOEP added special topical modules on personality concepts.[25] Further measures of health[26] have also been added and they are included for the 2005 population as well.

In this chapter, empirical analyses of the SOEP are mostly restricted to the cross-sectional population of wave 22 (2005), which contains more than 22,000 individual respondents living in about 12,000 households. The longitudinal character of the survey has been used to include health and wealth measures from previous waves and for a long-term measure of poverty. Wealth was measured as a special module in 2002—net worth has been imputed for the same households in 2005.[27]

For Germany, using the same measure, we find a slightly lower income poverty rate than for Australia: in 2005, 17.2 percent of the total population and 15.5 percent of the adult respondent population were living below the EU's 60 percent of median income poverty line (Table 17.5). The long-term poor comprised 10.3 percent of respondents (long-term poverty is measured according to the procedure for the EU-Laeken indicators as being relative-income-poor in the current year *and* poor for at least two of three previous years; see Atkinson et al. [2002], Marlier et al. [2007]; Krause and Ritz [2006]).

One-quarter of the population in Germany in 2005 lived in households with an equivalent net worth of less than 3 months of the relevant poverty line. Taking income poverty and low assets together, the population at risk declines to

Table 17.5 GERMANY: INCIDENCE OF MULTIDIMENSIONAL FINANCIAL
POVERTY, 2005

2005	Total Population			Respondents (age 17+ years)		
	Poor		Nonweighted	Poor		Nonweighted
	(%)	(N)	(1.000)	(%)	(N)	(1.000)
Type of poverty						
Poor (60%-med)	17.2	2.996	14.044	15.5	2.205	10.525
Long-term poor	11.7	1.591	8.048	10.3	1.206	6.126
Low wealth	26.9	5.352	19.734	25.8	4.033	15.728
Poor and low wealth	7.9	1.400	5.827	7.1	990	4.340
Long-term poor and low wealth	6.2	903	4.070	5.6	667	3.129

NOTE: Poor—less than 60 percent of median equivalent income (revised OECD scale); long-term poor—relative-income-poor in current year and in at least 2 of the three previous years; low wealth—net worth (from 2002), equivalized <3 months of equivalized household net income at current poverty line.

SOURCE: SOEP (2005).

7.1 percent—and further to 5.6 percent, if the long-term measure is used. That is, 5.6 percent of all respondents were living in Germany in 2005 in long-term poverty (according to the EU-Laeken indicators) with little net worth to fall back on in order to keep them for at least 3 months above the income poverty threshold. Given that lack of consumption is not yet taken into account, this rate appears quite similar to the corresponding value in Australia (see Tables 17.1 and 17.2).

To test the robustness of results relating to the subjective consequences of poverty, we now compare results for Australia (Table 17.3) with similar although not identical calculations for Germany (Table 17.6). In the case of Australia, we were able to simultaneously consider the case of low income, low assets, and also low consumption. For Germany, data on consumption are unavailable, so instead, we employ a measure that simultaneously considers both low income and low wealth. Although it would have been desirable to incorporate all three measures in the Germany analysis, we nonetheless anticipate finding similar patterns in the data. Moreover, this points toward standard problems regarding data availability in performing comparative empirical studies across multiple countries.

Despite the somewhat less inclusive measure of poverty based on the German SOEP data, for satisfaction with life, financial satisfaction, and satisfaction with living standards (which refers to the subjective aspects of consumption), the subjective levels for the most financially deprived are lower than in Australia (life satisfaction 58 compared to 75 in Australia; financial satisfaction 39 compared to 53 in Australia). Also, the gaps between poor, middle, and well-off groups appear greater in the German than in the Australian data. As in the Australian data, the differences between the poor and the well-off in subjective well-being are greater for the revised measure of multidimensional poverty compared to income-based differences (see Appendix Tables 17.B.1 and 17.B.2).

The differences in those who are partnered show the same pattern in both countries—under 50 percent of those in multidimensional financial poverty are living in

Table 17.6 Germany: Comparing the Poor (Low Income + Long Term Poor + Low Net Worth) with Middle and Well-Off Groups: Linkages to life Satisfaction, Financial Satisfaction, Personal Relationships, and Health, 2005

	Poverty: low Long-term Income and Low Net Worth (%)[a]			Middle Income and Net Worth (%)			High Income and Net Worth (%)		
	All	Men	Women	All	Men	Women	All	Men	Women
Life satisfaction (0–100)	58	56	60	69	69	69	74	74	73
Financial satisfaction (0–100)	39	35	41	63	62	63	74	73	74
Partnered (%)	49	50	46	76	82	71	81	82	80
Living standard satisfaction (0–100)	55	53	56	71	70	71	78	76	79
General health (factor loading)	29	27	30	30	30	31	32	34	31
Mental health (factor loading)	28	26	29	32	31	32	32	34	31

NOTE: Population weighted results. SOEP.
[a]Low income is defined as <60 percent of equivalized median income. Low net worth is (equivalized) assets less than 3months of equivalent household-net incomes at poverty line.

SOURCE: SOEP (2005).

Germany in partner households (partnered themselves or living in a household of partnered male and female heads)—compared to more than 80 percent in the well-off group.

The large differences in health found in the Australian data between poor and the other groups considered were not replicated for Germany. The operationalization of the constructs for physical and mental health are somewhat different across the two countries, so we cannot yet be sure that health conditions really differ. However, given the high-quality German health care system, the results could well be valid.

We additionally conducted duplicative multivariate analyses for the German data, using OLS and probit regressions (Table 17.7) with sets of control variables corresponding to those used in the Australian data (Table 17.4). The results from the German data again point toward the robustness of the previous results. Low satisfaction with household incomes and partner status are very strongly associated with poverty. Net of controls, the German data mostly show larger negative impacts associated with multidimensional poverty than were found in Australia, although the general patterns are similar. Financial satisfaction of the poor in Germany is 15 percent lower than for the nonpoor (12 percent lower in Australia). The chances of a poor person being partnered are 29 percent lower in Germany compared to the nonpoor (25 percent lower in Australia). In Germany, even life satisfaction is quite clearly lower for the

Table 17.7 Germany: Multidimensional Financial Poverty: Linkages to Life Satisfaction, Financial Satisfaction, Personal Relationships, and Health, 2005: OLS and Probit

	Life Satisfaction (0–100)	Financial Satisfaction (0–100)	Partner Status (1–0)	Health (Factor Loading)	Mental Health (Factor Loading)
Poverty: low long-term income and low net worth	–5.19***	–15.24***	0.29***	–2.49**	–2.66**
Female	1.75***	1.65***	–0.10***	–0.77	–0.79
Age	–0.32***	–0.38***	0.02***	0.16*	0.33***
Age^2/10	0.03***	0.05***	–0.00***	–0.03***	–0.03***
Partnered	3.26***	6.30***	—	–1.97***	–0.39
No. children	0.17	–0.79***	0.16***	1.06***	0.41
Years of education	0.28***	0.69***	–0.01***	0.33***	–0.01**
Disability	–7.30***	–5.70***	–0.01	—	—
Unemployed	–13.22***	–20.01***	–0.10***	0.30	0.45
Neuroticism	–4.48***	–2.84***	0.02***	–1.00***	–2.45***
Extroversion	1.62***	0.83***	–0.00	0.22	0.84***
Cons	71.28***	56.86***	—	30,0***	23.6***
Adjusted R^2 (%)	15.5	16.2	10.3	2.5	1.3
N	15,619	15,372	(15,643)	15,722	15,722

NOTE: Pseudo R^2. *** significant at 0.001; ** significant at 0.01; * significant at 0.05.

SOURCE: SOEP (2005).

poor than for the nonpoor; 5 percent lower compared with 2 percent lower in Australia. Finally, unemployment seems to have a greater negative impact on subjective well-being in Germany. The life satisfaction of the unemployed is 13.2 percent lower than the rest of the population, compared to 2.7 percent lower in Australia.

As mentioned before, it should be borne in mind that, with most of these linkages, some reverse causation might be at work. So further panel regression models are necessary to clarify the different paths of causation. One example where one might wonder if reverse causation is at play is in trying to determine whether poverty prevents individuals from finding a partner and causes separations, or whether not having a partner increases the risk of falling into poverty. Despite these issues regarding causation, the evidence presented in the chapter through the cross-national comparisons presented provide rather strong support for the inference that poverty—and especially multidimensional financial poverty—has strong negative psychological consequences.

DISCUSSION

The analysis of the extended poverty measures for Australia, which incorporates both assets and consumption, and Germany, which incorporates assets, indicates that these wider measures of financial poverty have strong associations with a wide range of well-being outcomes. Recent research linking wealth and income to well-being has focused heavily on "life satisfaction" as the outcome of interest (Veenhoven 2003; Clark, Frijters, and Shields 2008; Headey, Muffels, and Wooden 2008; Stevenson and Wolfers 2008). The evidence in this chapter suggests that other outcomes are affected more seriously. The evidence also indicates that it is incorrect to claim that income levels and poverty only relate to well-being via their impact on a person's social status. Not having a partner and having low levels of physical and mental health are plainly not just matters of status. They are seriously detrimental in themselves and may perhaps be regarded as links in the chain leading from poverty to low life satisfaction.

Our proposed multidimensional measures of financial poverty lead to much lower estimates of poverty in the population than standard income-based measures (see Appendix 17.B for results using standard measures). It also appears to be true that the commonly reported result that poverty, measured by income alone, has quite modest relationships with subjective outcomes is partly a consequence of misclassification of poor and nonpoor people. Once we measure poverty more sharply, its impact is seen to be considerably greater.

Notes

1. The authors showed that in Canada one can account for about 79 percent of the cross-sectional variance total household nondurable expenditures with a regression equation that includes standard demographics plus questions eliciting spending on four items: food eaten at home; food eaten out; telephone costs; and gas, electricity, and water.
2. Given a national representative sample and a representative time slice.
3. It is far from certain, however, that a *longitudinal series of estimates* of total expenditure could be validly obtained in this way. In other words, a few items may or may not provide an adequate basis for estimating annual *changes* in expenditure. Clearly, the prime purpose of HILDA is to provide longitudinal estimates.
4. The ABS HES ask for some items to be recorded in a "shopping diary" and uses a survey recall method for other more "lumpy" items.
5. Only the 2005 HILDA data are used for benchmarking. The 2006 and 2007 data are further removed in time from the 2003–2004 HES benchmark data.
6. We allowed ourselves a bit of leeway over 10 percent where there was good reason to believe that the HILDA estimates might be reasonably satisfactory. In particular, in view of large housing price increases in recent years, we accepted that HILDA's high estimate of housing consumption might well be valid.
7. Total household goods and services expenditure recorded in HES 2003–2004 was $893 per week. This figure includes payments of mortgage interest but not principal. In HILDA, the question about mortgage payments made no

distinction between interest and principal. So, for comparison with HILDA, one must add to $893 a sum of $36, which was the mean weekly amount of principal repayments in 2003–2004. HILDA appears validly to measure items that in HES amount to 53.4 percent of $929 ($893 + $36).

8. Given good economic growth, one would expect a real increase of about this amount between the midpoint of the HES in January 2004 and September–October 2005 when the HILDA survey was conducted.

9. This correlation was supplied by ABS, based on the HES for 2003–2004.

10. See Browning, Crossley, and Weber (2003, 557) for a similar result in Canada.

11. This seems realistic, given the list of items accurately measured. Clearly it would not be realistic if more consumer durables, in addition to housing, were included.

12. Four percent of current sale value is a fairly standard rule of thumb for the rent that a dwelling would be likely to attract. Clearly, actual rental values in specific suburbs can differ quite widely from this guideline.

13. The imputation was done by the author, using the SPSS MVA (missing values analysis) program. The imputation is likely to be revised in future years, when it is expected that the HILDA statistical team will undertake a longitudinal imputation of the kind already done for individual and household incomes and wealth.

14. For reasons explained in Headey, Warren, and Wooden (2007), we use an ABS benchmark for financial assets and an Reserve Bank of Australia benchmark for non assets and specifically housing.

15. Strictly speaking, the EU refers to households below the 60 percent line as being "at risk of poverty." However, the line is conventionally referred to as the EU's measure of relative income poverty (European Commission and Eurostat 2000).

16. Of course, they are not true percentages. One cannot say, for example, that someone who scores 80 on the 0–100 scale is twice as satisfied or healthy as someone who scores 40.

17. Strictly speaking, the dates of the wealth, consumption, and income poverty measures are not the same. The wealth and consumption measures apply to the dates on which the survey was conducted (September–October 2007). The income measures relate to financial year 2006–2007.

18. It also quite important to realise that household consumption is more highly related to net worth (correlation in 2006 = 0.62).

19. Note that, in this chapter, the value of their homes is included in our measure of net worth. An alternative approach (see Frick and Grabka [2012, Chapter 6]) is to include an estimate of imputed rent in a revised measure of income.

20. In principle, gifts should be recorded as income in HILDA, but survey research experience suggests substantial underrecording.

21. As noted earlier, parental subsidies should be recorded in surveys as interhousehold transfers but are, in practice, often omitted as a source of income.

22. It is not really clear why. In some cases, they may be saving a lot; for example, to buy a house.

23. However, contrary to expectation, it is not the case that people who had already been poor for 2 or 3 years in 2007 reported lower scores on most of these measures than people who were 1-year poor. The opposite is true. It appears that,

from a subjective standpoint, the shock of becoming poor has a larger effect than persistent poverty. This accords with much research on the impact of life events on life satisfaction, where it is found that the impact of most events is greatest at first and then tends to diminish rapidly.

24. Partnership has been included as a household variable—"being partnered or living in a household where the heads are living in partnership."

25. The personality inventory used here is based on empirical work indicating that personality differences between individuals can be attributed to five basic traits (McCrae andCosta 1987): openness to experience, extroversion, conscientiousness, agreeableness, and neuroticism. To apply this concept within the SOEP representative survey, a short version of items has been used with at least three items per dimension to get robust results (Gerlitz and Schupp 2005). In fact, the five factor structure was replicated and tests of reliability and validity confirmed the use of this concept within the SOEP representative survey.

26. Physical and mental health derived from the SF-12 concept (Ware, Kosinski, and Keller 1998).

27. For new households joining the sample after 2002, this value is missing.

28. The HES total for the items was $929, being $893 for what HES terms "total goods and services expenditure," plus $36 for mortgage principal repayments. The HES separates out mortgage interest and mortgage principal and does not include the latter in total goods and services expenditure. By contrast, the HILDA mortgage repayment question made no distinction between interest and principal payments.

References

Argyle, Michael 2001. *The Psychology of Happiness.* 2nd ed. London: Methuen.

Atkinson, Antony B., Bea Cantillon, Eric Marlier, Brian Nolan. 2002. Social *Indicators:* The EU and Social Inclusion. Oxford: Oxford University Press.

ABS. 2005. *Household Expenditure Survey 2003–2004.* Canberra: Australian Bureau of Statistics.

Bane, Mary J., and David T. Ellwood. 1986. "Slipping into and out of Poverty: The Dynamics of Spells." *Journal of Human Resources* 21: 1–23.

Browning, Martin, Thomas F. Crossley, and Guglielmo Weber. 2003. "Asking Consumption Questions in General Purpose Surveys." *Economic Journal* 113: 540–567.

Caner, Asena, and Edward N. Wolff. 2004. "Asset Poverty in the United States, 1984–99: Evidence from the Panel Study of Income Dynamics." *Review of Income and Wealth* 50: 493–518.

Clark, Andrew E., Paul Frijters, and Michael Shields. 2008. "Relative Income, Happiness and Utility: An Explanation of the Easterlin Paradox and Other Puzzles." *Journal of Economic Literature* 46: 95–144.

Costa, Paul T., and Robert R. McCrae. 1991. *NEO PI-R.* Odessa, FL: PAR.

Diener, Ed, Eunkook M. Suh, Richard E. Lucas, and Heidi L. Smith. 1999. "Subjective Well-Being: Three Decades of Progress." *Psychological Bulletin* 125: 276–302.

Duncan, Greg J. *Years of Poverty, Years of Plenty.* Ann Arbor: ISR, University of Michigan.

Easterlin, Richard. A. 1974. "Does Economic Growth Improve The Human Lot? Some Empirical Evidence." In *Nations and Households in Economic Growth: Essays in Honour of Moses Abramowitz.* Edited by P. A. David and M. W. Reder, 89–125. New York: Academic Press.

———. 1995. "Will Raising the Incomes of All Increase the Happiness of All?" *Journal of Economic Behavior and Organization* 27: 35–47.

European Commission and Eurostat. 2000. *European Social Statistics, Income, Poverty and Social Exclusion.* Luxembourg: Office for Official Publications of the European Communities.

Frick, Joachim R., and Markus M. Grabka. 2012. "Accounting for Imputed and Capital Income Flows." In *Counting the Poor: New Thinking about European Poverty Measures and Lessons for the United States.* Edited by Douglas J. Besharov and Kenneth A. Couch, 117–142. New York: Oxford University Press.

Friedman, Milton. 1957. *A Theory of the Consumption Function.* Princeton: Princeton University Press.

Frijters, Paul, John P. Haisken-DeNew, and Michael A. Shields. 2004. "Money Does Matter! Evidence from Increasing Real Incomes and Life Satisfaction in East Germany Following Reunification." *American Economic Review* 94: 730–741.

Gerlitz, Jean-Yves, and Jürgen Schupp. 2005. *Zur Erhebung der Big-Five-basierten Persönlichkeitsmerkmale im SOEP.* Research Notes 2005 (4). Berlin: DIW Berlin.

Headey, Bruce W. 2008. "Poverty Is Low Consumption and Low Wealth, Not Just Low Income." *Social Indicators Research* 89: 23–39.

Headey, Bruce W., Gary Marks, and Mark Wooden. 2005. "The Structure and Distribution of Household Wealth in Australia." *Australian Economic Review* 38: 159–175.

Headey, Bruce W., Ruud Muffels, and Mark Wooden. 2008. "Money Does Not Buy Happiness–or Does It? A Reassessment Based on the Combined Effects of Wealth, Income and Consumption." *Social Indicators Research* 87: 65–82.

Headey, Bruce, Diana Warren, and Mark Wooden. (2007). *The Structure and Distribution of Household Wealth in Australia: Cohort Differences and Retirement Issues.* Canberra: Department of Family and Community Services and Indigenous Affairs (FACSIA).

Headey, Bruce W., and Alexander J. Wearing. 1989. "Personality, Life Events and Subjective Well-Being: Toward a Dynamic Equilibrium Model." *Journal of Personality and Social Psychology* 57: 731–739.

———. 1992. *Understanding Happiness: A Theory of Subjective Well-Being.* Melbourne: Longman Cheshire.

Krause, Peter, and Daniel Ritz. 2006. "EU-Indikatoren zur sozialen Inklusion in Deutschland." *Vierteljahreshefte zur Wirtschaftsforschung* 75 (1): 152–173.

Mack, Joanna, and Stewart Lansley. 1985. *Poor Britain.* London: Allen and Unwin.

Marlier, Eric, Antony B. Atkinson, Bea Cantillon, and Brian Nolan. 2007. *The EU and Social Inclusion. Facing the Challenges.* Bristol: The Policy Press / University of Bristol.

McCrae, Robert R., and Paul T. Costa. 1987. "Validation of the Five-Factor Model of Personality across Instruments and Observers." *Journal of Personality and Social Psychology* 52 (1): 81–90.

Ringen, Stein. 1987. *The Possibility of Politics.* Oxford: Clarendon Press.

Stevens, Ann H. 1994. "The Dynamics of Poverty Spells: Updating Bane and Ellwood." *American Economic Review (Papers and Proceedings)* 84 (5): 34–37.

Stevenson, Betsey, and Justin Wolfers. 2008. *Economic Growth and Subjective Well-Being: Reassessing the Easterlin Paradox.* Brookings Papers on Economic Activity, Spring. Washington, DC: Brookings Institute

Townsend, Peter. 1979. *Poverty in the United Kingdom.* Harmondsworth: Penguin.

Veenhoven, Ruut. 2003. *World Database of Happiness.* Rotterdam: Erasmus University.

Wagner, Gerd G., Joachim R. Frick, and Juergen Schupp. 2007. "The German Socio-Economic Panel Study (SOEP)–Scope, Evolution and Enhancements." *Schmollers Jahrbuch* 127 (1), 139–169.

Ware, John E., Mark Kosinski, and Susan D. Keller. 1998. *SF-12®: How to Score the SF-12® Physical and Mental Health Summary Scales.* 3rd ed. Lincoln, RI: QualityMetric Incorporated.

Ware, John E., Kristin K. Snow, and Mark Kosinski. 2000. *The SF-36 Health Survey: Manual and Interpretation Guide.* Lincoln, RI: QualityMetric Incorporated.

Watson, Nicole, and Mark Wooden. 2004. "Assessing the Quality of the HILDA Survey Wave 2 Data." HILDA Technical Paper (May), HILDA, Melbourne.

BENCHMARKING: HOUSEHOLD EXPENDITURE ITEMS
MEASURED VALIDLY IN HILDA 2005 COMPARED
WITH HES 2003–2004

This appendix benchmarks HILDA results for 2005 against the HES for 2003–2004. Weekly expenditures are shown. The HILDA figures have been deflated by 4.7 percent to allow for the increase in consumer price index between January 2004 (midpoint of the HES data collection) and September 2005 (midpoint of the HILDA data collection). Only items that appear to be reasonably accurately measured in HILDA are shown. A margin of plus or minus 10 percent between HILDA and HES was considered reasonably satisfactory, subject to a few small additional deviations explained herein. In general, one would expect the HILDA figures to be a few percent higher than the HES figures, because real disposable per capita (and hence per household) incomes increased in the 21 months between the two data collections. In fact, this is what we do find.

Using a band of plus or minus 10 percent, the well-measured items amount to 53.4 percent of total household expenditure on goods and services as reported in HES. Within HES[28], these items correlated 0.76 with total expenditure. Also within HES, a regression equation using these items plus standard demographics accounted for 78.3 percent of the variance in total expenditure. (See Table 17A.1)

Table 17.A.1 HOUSEHOLD WEEKLY EXPENDITURES

	HES 2003–2004	HILDA 2005[a]
Groceries[b]	$131	$142
Alcohol	$23	$22
Tobacco	$12	$13
Public transport and taxis	$7	$7
Meals eaten out	$42	$41
Motor fuel	$33	$34
Car maintenance	$14	$15
Telephone	$27	$26

(*Continued*)

Table 17.A.1 HOUSEHOLD WEEKLY EXPENDITURES (*CONT'D*)

	HES 2003–2004	HILDA 2005[a]
Home fuel	$23	$22
Home maintenance	$21	$19
Health insurance	$17	$15
Education	$18	$16
Mortgage payments[c]	$82	$92
Rent[d]	$46	$51
Total	$496	$515

NOTE: Items that did not benchmark satisfactorily, but which we attempted to measure in HILDA (2005) were clothing and footwear, holidays, recreation, health care, and child care.

[a]HILDA figures deflated by 4.7 percent for consumer price index.

[b]The HILDA question, which was made more precise in 2006, is related specifically to food, cleaning products, pet food, and personal care products.

[c]The difference between HES and HILDA is a little over 10 percent. Given the big increase in house prices in recent years, this difference seems acceptable. Note that households are included even if they pay no mortgage.

[d]The difference between HES and HILDA is a little over 10 percent. Given the increase in rents in recent years, this difference seems acceptable. Note that households are included even if they pay no rent.

COMPARING THE PSYCHOLOGICAL CONSEQUENCES OF INCOME-BASED POVERTY WITH POVERTY DEFINED AS LOW INCOME + LOW CONSUMPTION + LOW WEALTH

This appendix is included to enable comparisons to be made between the psychological consequences of poverty measured in the standard income-based way with the consequences as assessed by a measure based on income + consumption + wealth.

It is plain that differences between the poor, on the one hand, and middle and well-off groups, on the other, are much larger if account is taken of all three dimensions of economic well-being. (See Tables 17.B.1 and 17.B.2.)

Table 17.B.1 Australia: Comparing the Income Poor with Middle Income and Well–Off Groups—Linkages to Life Satisfaction, Financial Satisfaction, Personal Relationships, and Health, 2007

	Income Poor: Below 60 Percent of Median (%)			Middle Income: Not Poor and Not in Top Quintile (%)			High Income: Top Quintile (%)		
	All	Men	Women	All	Men	Women	All	Men	Women
Life satisfaction (0–100)	77	76	77	79	78	79	79	79	81
Financial satisfaction (0–100)	60	57	61	65	65	66	73	73	74
Partnered (%)	51	57	46	62	61	62	69	66	72
Partner satisfaction (0–100)	82	85	80	81	82	80	82	83	81
General health (0–100)	59	58	60	69	70	69	74	73	74
Mental health (0–100)	69	70	69	75	76	74	77	78	76

NOTE: Population-weighted results.
SOURCE: HILDA (2007).

Table 17.B.2 GERMANY: COMPARING THE INCOME POOR WITH MIDDLE INCOME
AND WELL-OFF GROUPS—LINKAGES TO LIFE SATISFACTION, FINANCIAL
SATISFACTION, PERSONAL RELATIONSHIPS, AND HEALTH, 2005

	Income Poor: Below 60 Percent of Median (%)			Middle Income: Not Poor and Not in Top Quintile (%)			High Income: Top Quintile (%)		
	All	Men	Women	All	Men	Women	All	Men	Women
Life satisfaction (0–100)	62	58	64	68	68	68	74	73	74
Financial satisfaction (0–100)	45	39	48	60	59	60	73	72	74
Partnered (%)	54	58	52	71	77	67	79	80	78
Living standard satisfaction (0–100)	59	56	61	68	68	69	77	76	79
General health (factor loading)	28	27	28	30	30	30	32	34	31
Mental health	27	27	27	31	31	30	32	33	31

NOTE: Population-weighted results.

SOURCE: SOEP (2005).

18

Anomalies in European Measures of Poverty and Social Exclusion

NEIL GILBERT ■

The conventional view of poverty in the European Union (EU) countries is based on a relative measure that defines all those with incomes below 60 percent of the median as poor. In the United States, poverty is defined according to an absolute measure— the federal poverty line computed by the Census Bureau—which was $22,350 for a family of four in 2011 (somewhat higher in Alaska and Hawaii). In tallying up national rates of poverty, both the absolute and relative measures are adjusted for family size.

Although these income-based measures generate social indicators that are concrete, plausible, and convenient to use, they fail to convey the experiential quality of poverty as a condition of life—living hungry, cold, unable to meet normal social expectations, and in dread of what the future holds. They also overlook the possession of other resources and sources of support that can alleviate the conditions of poverty. Several of the papers presented at the Joint OECD/University of Maryland International Conference on Measuring Poverty, Income Inequality, and Social Exclusion: Lessons from Europe aim to overcome these omissions by assessing levels of material deprivation and including measures of consumption and wealth in addition to income.

MATERIAL DEPRIVATION AND INCOME-BASED POVERTY

Expressing the Europeans' concerns about the inadequacies of the conventional approach to estimating poverty, Marlier et al. (2012, Chapter 15), explore the multidimensional nature of poverty by casting it within the framework of a broader concept of social inclusion. The authors review and analyze what is identified as a "commonly agreed upon portfolio" of indicators of social inclusion, which contends with some of the limitations of a narrower income-based measure of poverty.[1] The portfolio consists of a number of primary and secondary indicators, including the conventional European measure of 60 percent of median income along with several other measures involving unemployment, employment gap of immigrants, education, health care, and material deprivation.

The strength of these indicators is that they indeed convey a broader, more detailed account of the experiential circumstances associated with poverty—unemployment, lack of education, unmet medical needs, deficient shelter, and material deprivation, along with relatively low income. According to the authors, one of the main objectives of the indicators is to "facilitate comparison of actual performance achieved by EU countries" through their social policies. My assessment of these indicators is framed by four questions:

1. How much does the index of material deprivation add to our understanding of poverty beyond the knowledge gained from an income-based measure?
2. How reliable is the material deprivation index as a comparative measure of poverty/exclusion?
3. How applicable are multidimensional measures of poverty for comparative analysis and policy decision making?
4. To what extent do the alternative nonmonetary measures facilitate comparisons of performance that produce greater transparency than an income-based poverty measure?

Let me start with the issue of the knowledge added by the material deprivation index. This indicator examines nine aspects of material living conditions by asking respondents whether they can afford the following: (1) a washing machine; (2) a personal car; (3) a color television; (4) a telephone; (5) a one-week annual holiday away from home; (6) to face unexpected expenses; (7) to pay for arrears (rent, utilities, etc.); (8) a meal with meat, chicken, or fish every second day; and (9) to keep a home adequately warm. Because the items in this index begin with the question "Can you afford?", they must have a cash value in the respondents' minds. To what extent does the material deprivation index provide a deeper understanding of poverty than that gleaned from a standard monetary indicator?

The chapter reports a weak positive correlation ($r = 30$) between the risks of poverty (defined as the percentage of people living below 60 percent of the national equivalized median income) and levels of material deprivation (defined as the percentage of people deprived of at least three items) in the EU countries. This indicates that although the relationship is in the expected positive direction, the monetary indicator of the risk of poverty or relatively low income explains only 9 percent of the variance in material deprivation. Without looking too closely, one conclusion that might be drawn from this finding is that the nonmonetary indicator of deprivation captures a significant, perhaps alternative, dimension of poverty/exclusion beyond that represented by a monetary indicator.

However, a very different conclusion emerges when one examines the relationship between material deprivation (as previously defined) and the income thresholds used to define poverty in the EU countries. The results here show a strong negative relationship of $r = -0.831$ ($p < 0.001$). The poverty thresholds explain about 70 percent of the variance in the levels of material deprivation among countries. Simply put, the lower a country's median income, the higher the percentage of people living there that are materially deprived. This is hardly surprising. These findings highlight an essential problem in using the relative definition of poverty in comparative analysis—it fails to deliver an accurate representation of the differences in the material well-being of citizens in countries with a wide range of median incomes.

A question still remains as to what extent the 30 percent of variance in levels of material deprivation among the EU countries that is not explained by the different poverty thresholds represents a meaningful nonmonetary dimension of poverty/exclusion, which is captured by the index, and how much is due just to measurement error in response to the index. This brings us to the second issue concerning the reliability of the deprivation index. Because the potential costs of most of the items in this index vary dramatically, it is difficult to interpret exactly what individual responses mean. For example, the question can you "afford an unexpected expense" might include everything from the cost of replacing a broken window pane to a new roof. (The answer might reflect the respondents' optimism contemplating costs of the unexpected more than anything else.) One week's annual holiday away from home can involve everything from camping in the forest to a luxury cruise in the Mediterranean. A color television can range in price from less than $100 to more than $5,000. There are no stable values associated with each item and, although a car tends to be more expensive than a telephone, there is no ordinal ranking of affordability among all of the items. The open-ended definitions of these items raises questions about the face validity and reliability of this composite indicator. When two respondents can imagine that the same question means different things, what exactly does the index measure? If the questions were posed as, for example, "Can you afford a TV that costs $100," how much might the 30 percent of unexplained variance decline?

The questionable reliability of these items for use in cross-sectional analysis is compounded by the fact that the material deprivation index does not lend itself well to longitudinal analysis. Over time, the costs of items will vary. Several of the items in this index are likely to become more affordable as costs are driven down by innovations and new methods of production—which changes the meaning of lack of affordability. In 1971, for example, only 43 percent of all households in the United States had color televisions, whereas 30 years later over 97 percent of *poor* households owned color televisions (Cox and Alm 1995). Research indicates that over time many products shift in the public's perception from luxuries to necessities (PEW Research Center 2006).

The third issue concerns how multidimensional measures inform comparative analysis and policy making, particularly when discrepancies arise between the commonly agreed upon indicators, such as risk of poverty and deprivation. For example, the risk of poverty in Hungary, Slovakia, the Czech Republic, and Slovenia is lower than in most other EU countries that have much higher median incomes (such as Finland, France, Germany, Ireland, Luxembourg, and the United Kingdom). While having lower risks of poverty than many of the Western European countries, however, these four Eastern European countries have higher levels of material deprivation, measured as the percentage of the population that could not afford at least three of the nine items in the material deprivation index. Findings that show that a fair proportion of the EU countries have lower levels (or risks) of poverty, yet higher levels of material deprivation than many other countries, present policy makers with a confusing discourse on the relation between poverty and material deprivation—as these terms are commonly understood.

The implications for policy making remain puzzling, despite efforts to elaborate and refine the material deprivation index. Drawing on the EU Statistics on Income and Living Conditions data, for example, Nolan and Whelan (2010) analyze an expanded version of the nine-item index discussed above, which includes a selection of 17 items of material deprivation as shown in Table 18.1. These items are incorporated into two composite measures for each country: a mean household deprivation index score and a measure of the percentage of three-item deprivation among those below 60 percent of the median income.

The mean household deprivation score is developed by assigning each item the value of 1, adding the number of items identified by each household, and calculating the mean. Composite scores of this sort always involve value judgments. Giving each item an equal weight is not so much an expression of neutrality as a judgment of value, which implies that the inability to afford a personal computer is an equivalent degree of deprivation to the lack of an indoor toilet, and each of these is equivalent to having noisy neighbors (which is unlikely to occur in Geneva, where there is an ordinance against making excessive noise, particularly between 21:00 and 7:00).

The second composite scores show the percentage of households that have both incomes below 60 percent of the median and are deprived for at least three of the six consumption deprivation items (see Table 18.1). Here again, there arises an apparent

Table 18.1 SELECTION OF ITEMS INCLUDED IN EU-SILC USED AS INDICATORS OF MATERIAL DEPRIVATION

Afford to pay unexpected required expenses[a]

Weeks holiday away from home[ab]

Meals with meat, chicken, fish (or vegetarian) [ab]

Can afford a personal computer[b]

Arrears relating to mortgage payments, rent, utility bills, hire purchase[ab]

Inability to keep home adequately warm[ab]

Household can afford to have a car[ab]

Bath or shower in dwelling

Indoor toilet

Can afford a telephone[a]

Can afford a color television[a]

Can afford a washing machine[a]

Pollution, grime, or other environmental problems in the area

Noise from neighbors or noise from the street

Crime, violence, or vandalism in the area

Rooms too dark, light problems

Leaking roof, damp walls/ceilings/floors/foundations, rot in doors, window frames

[a] Items in the Marlier et al. (2012, Chapter 15) nine-item deprivation index. [b] Items in the "consumption deprivation" index.
SILC is Statistics on Income and Living Conditions.
SOURCE: Nolan and Whelan (2010).

discrepancy between where different countries rank on this indicator and the customary understanding of the association between low income and deprivation. Slovakia, Slovenia, and the Czech Republic, for example, have a lower percentage of households that are both below 60 percent of their median incomes and are deprived for at least three of the six items in the consumption deprivation index than Luxembourg, Finland, and Belgium. At almost 37,000 purchasing power standard (PPS) units, the poverty threshold in Luxembourg represents a level of income three to four times higher than in the Eastern European countries.[2] According to this finding, a higher percentage of households with incomes up to 37,000 PPS in one country experience three or more consumption deprivations (such as inability to afford food, heat, and a holiday) than households with incomes up 8,400 PPS in another country. From a policy perspective, if a financial transfer is to be made to reduce poverty/social exclusion, should it go to Luxembourg before Slovakia?

But really, how can it be that those below 60 percent of Luxembourg's median income have a higher percent of material deprivation than the poor in Slovakia? The authors offer several possible explanations, which essentially boil down to measurement error in both income and deprivation.

Beyond problems of measurement and interpretation, the nonincome based multidimensional indicators of poverty/exclusion suffer from a lack of transparency. The issue here is not so much that the different measures yield different, sometime curious, results, but who decides which items are commonly agreed upon and on what basis? In operationalizing indicators of social exclusion, are there systematic criteria that might help policy makers and the public understand why certain indicators are included and others excluded? For example, the broad portfolio of commonly agreed upon indicators includes a measure of the employment gap of immigrants but excludes a gender employment gap or a sexual orientation employment gap. The portfolio includes a measure of unemployment but not one of employment security or security about one's life situation in retirement. Measures of access to health care do not address the issue of quality of care. One could easily imagine adding a considerable number of items to the 17-item material deprivation index, from ability to afford microwaves and compact disk players, to children's access to a garden, outdoor playing fields, and public transportation. At the same time, one might ask how material deprivation of respondents in Scandinavian and Mediterranean countries can be compared by the question about their ability to afford "keeping a home adequately warm."

To the extent that multidimensional measures convey a detailed account of different experiential circumstances associated with poverty, they are useful in helping to expand the purview of social research and to highlight areas of social life that may be suitable for improvement. Efforts to formulate these measures stimulate thinking about the phenomena of poverty and social exclusion, generating new insights and different ways of counting social needs—helping to build new knowledge about different aspects of poverty. Indeed this approach is a valuable academic/intellectual pursuit in seeking to enumerate the empirical essence of social inclusion or even the good life.

However, I have serious questions about the extent to which they provide guidance to inform social policy by offering a more valid, reliable, and transparent depiction of poverty than a direct measure of income. Most citizens and policy makers can envision what it means when they hear a statement to the effect that 20 percent of households are poor or excluded from participation in normal social life because they have only X dollars to live on after taxes. Although they may agree or disagree as to whether

X dollars is the right amount, it is more difficult to formulate any judgment on a statement to the effect that 20 percent of households are socially excluded because they have an average deprivation score of 3 or more on 17 items ranging from being able to afford a phone to not having much choice but to live in a noisy environment.

CONSUMPTION, WEALTH, AND LIFE SATISFACTION

Nonmonetary indicators seek to address the inadequacies of conventional income-based measures by defining poverty as a multidimensional problem. This approach enlarges the analytic frame on poverty and social exclusion beyond low income to encompass material deprivation, lack of education, unemployment, and other problems, which transmits an expansive progressive agenda for social policy. In contrast, an alternative line of analysis confronts the limits of monetary measures by expanding the financial account to include more than income and then examining nonmonetary considerations in terms of the psychological consequences of poverty under the broader financial definition. Concentrating on this financial approach, Headey, Krause, and Wagner (2012, Chapter 17) measure poverty in Australia and Germany according to household income, wealth, and consumption (including imputed rent calculated at 4 percent of the estimated market value of the house). The rates of financial poverty are estimated for three groups: those who are poor in terms of income (having income below 50 percent of the national equivalized median); in terms of consumption (below 50 percent of the median equivalized consumption); and the "asset poor" (lacking wealth to survive for three months in an emergency with an income above 50 percent of the national median). In light of these measures, the analysis illustrates the extent to which the rates of financial poverty decline when the definition shifts from only those who are income poor to those who remain poor after taking into account income, consumption, and assets. The authors then examine the psychological consequences of being poor according to this definition.

The findings reveal that when consumption and wealth measures are included, the level of financial poverty sharply declines. In Australia, where the poverty line is usually set at 50 percent of the median income, the poverty rate in 2007 decreased from 13.7 percent to 2.5 percent (at the 60 percent of median income, the rates decreases from 19.9 percent to 4.9 percent) under the expanded financial definition. The rate of persistent poverty, defined as those under 60 percent of the median income for three years, declines from 10.6 percent using the conventional measure of income to 2.2 percent when consumption and wealth are included. The data show a similar decline in Germany (from 17.2 percent to 7.9 percent in 2005), though the 60 percent of median income poverty rate does not fall as low as in Australia, in part because the German measures included income and wealth, but not consumption.

Based on these findings, Headey, Krause, and Wagner (2012, Chapter 17) argue that the existing income-based measures are seriously in error, yielding poverty results that are much too high. If the definition of poverty as being simultaneously income-poor, consumption-poor, and asset-poor were commonly accepted, it would surely have profound implications, at least in Australia; with only 2.5 percent of the population falling beneath the established poverty line, the problem is virtually solved.

In an effort to probe the experiential quality of poverty, the psychological consequences of being poor according to the broad financial definition are analyzed, using self-assessed ratings of satisfaction with one's life, financial situation, relationship with a partner, general health, and mental health. The most striking finding here is that the impact of poverty on life satisfaction, while statistically significant, is substantively inconsequential. The difference in life satisfaction between the people in the middle income category and the poor is 4 points on a scale of 0–100. When other factors that might impact life satisfaction, such as being partnered, number of children, unemployment, disability, neuroticism, and age are controlled for, the impact of poverty is only a 2 point difference on the 0–100 point scale of life satisfaction. The entire model including money, health, family, youth, work, and mental health accounted for only 11.7 percent of the variance in life satisfaction. In Germany, the data showed that after controlling for a wide range of demographic, health, personality, and interpersonal characteristics, being poor increased the proportion of explained variance in life satisfaction by only 1.2 percent.

Other findings revealed that being poor had a strong association with several specific measures of well-being, such as living without a partner, health, mental health, and financial satisfaction. It is well-known, however, that correlation is not the same as causality. Where poverty and the indicators of well-being are concerned, cause and effect are difficult to untangle, except for the finding that poor people are 11.6 percent less satisfied with their financial situation than the nonpoor, which does not generate a great deal of insight. Regarding the other measures of well-being, having a low income may affect one's chances of finding a partner, particularly if the reason for being poor is related to factors such as mental illness and disability; although being poor may lead to the deterioration of one's health and mental health, it is equally the case that being physically disabled or mentally ill may have a strong influence on becoming poor.

One might read the main results of this study and their implications as somewhat different from those of studies based on multidimensional nonincome measures of poverty. That is, the data here show that the rates of income-related poverty as defined by many public agencies fall to very low levels when measured by empirical indicators of financial resources that are more comprehensive than the conventional measure of income. Among the relatively low percentage of households that are poor by this measure, an even lower percentage stay that way for three years. And although, as might be expected, people who are financially poor are less satisfied with their financial situation than the nonpoor are, there is almost no substantive difference between the poor and nonpoor regarding their general satisfaction with life.

If one agrees with this interpretation, then in the cases studied empirically, there is not a great deal of traction to advance poverty as a pressing social issue on the public agenda. Those seeking to advance progressive policies designed to improve social life need to reframe the issue, which perhaps lends strategic justification to the lack of transparency associated with the multidimensional nonincome measures of poverty and social inclusion.

LESSONS FOR THE UNITED STATES

If poverty research is to focus on developing multidimensional measures, such as material deprivation indices that go beyond monetary calculations, there are trade-offs worth considering. The multidimensional approach offers the benefits of greater detail about a range of poverty-related problems, along with a wider frame of investigation that might generate new insights and lend impetus to a progressive policy agenda. These benefits must be weighed against the issues raised concerning reliability, face validity, and transparency for building knowledge and policy making. In the current stage of development, multidimensional measures of poverty face serious analytical challenges, which cast doubt on their utility as rigorous scientific indicators for comparative analysis.

When standard income-based calculations of poverty are refined to include consumption and assets, the rates of poverty are much lower than those reported in the official measures. Analyses of consumption and assets are fertile areas for research that can sharpen the focus of monetary-based measures, which are easily grasped by policy makers and the public. If consumption and assets are included among financial resources in official calculations of poverty, however, one would anticipate an outpouring of recommendations to recalibrate official poverty lines in Europe and the United States, according to the total package of household financial resources.

Notes

1. These indicators were developed and agreed upon by the EU Social Protection Committee Indicators Sub-Group.
2. PPS units are euros adjusted for purchasing power parity.

References

Cox, Michael W., and Richard Alm. 1995. *By Our Own Bootstraps: Economic Opportunity and the Dynamics of Income Distribution*. Federal Reserve Bank of Dallas Annual Report 22. Dallas: Federal Reserve Bank.

Headey, Bruce, Peter Krause, and Gert G. Wagner. 2012. "Poverty Redefined as Low Consumption and Low Wealth, Not Just Low Income: Psychological Consequences in Australia and Germany." In *Counting the Poor: New Thinking about European Poverty Measures and Lessons for the United States*. Edited by Douglas J. Besharov and Kenneth A. Couch, 363–388. New York: Oxford University Press.

Marlier, Eric, Bea Cantillon, Brian Nolan, Karel Van den Bosch, and Tim Van Rie. 2012. "Developing and Learning from EU Measures of Social Inclusion." In *Counting the Poor: New Thinking about European Poverty Measures and Lessons for the United States*. Edited by Douglas J. Besharov and Kenneth A. Couch, 297–342. New York: Oxford University Press.

Nolan, Brian, and Christopher Whelan. 2010. "Using Non-Monetary Deprivation Indicators To Analyze Poverty and Social Exclusion: Lessons from Europe?" *Journal of Policy Analysis and Management* 29: 305–325.

Pew Research Center. 2006. "Luxury or Necessity? Things We Can't Live Without: The List Has Grown in the Past Decade." Pew Research Center, Washington, DC. http://pewresearch.org/pubs/323/luxury-or-necessity.

PART SIX

Conclusion

19

New Comparative Measures of Income, Material Deprivation, and Well-Being

TIMOTHY M. SMEEDING ∎

Most societies, rich and poor, seek to measure progress in reducing poverty and need, as indicated by material deprivation or social exclusion. The yardsticks used to assess progress and policy impact mainly include income-based poverty, but broader measures of poverty based on consumption, wealth, and material depriva- tion are also now coming into use. Both Europeans and Americans also have a strong interest in reducing income inequality: It is reported as a "serious problem" by two- thirds of survey respondents in the United States and over 90 percent of respondents in Europe (Förster and Mira d'Ercole 2012, Chapter 2). However, although both agree that income inequality is a social ill, there is far less consensus on how to attack the problem.

Income inequality rose in most rich nations in the Organization for Economic Co-operation and Development (OECD) over the 1990–2005 period, but by consid- ering both tails of the income distribution, we see that most of the rise in inequality was generated by increases at the top of the distribution or by the ratio of the 90th percentile income to the median income, and not by changes at the bottom or by the ratio of the 10th percentile to the median (Förster and Mira d'Ercole 2012, Chapter 2; Salverda, Nolan, and Smeeding 2009). Many analysts look at the Gini coefficient and see rising inequality if the Gini increases.[1] They are technically correct. But a change in a single parameter coefficient like the Gini does not show which part of the distribution changed, and different changes have different policy implications. If the rich pull away from the middle class, the policy implications are likely to be very dif- ferent than if the poor fall farther behind the middle class.

ABSOLUTE VERSUS RELATIVE MEASURES

At the Joint OECD/University of Maryland Conference on Measuring Poverty, Income Inequality, and Social Exclusion: Lessons from Europe, the major debate, as expected, was about poverty measurement in absolute (fixed line with respect to income changes) versus relative (fully changing with income) terms. Although this topic has been debated before (e.g., Notten and de Neubourg 2007; Smeeding 2006), it was especially prominent at this meeting. The absolute-poverty-line backers argued that there should be a widely agreed upon poverty market basket that is held constant, except for consumer price index changes, and, therefore, is fixed in real terms. In economic terms, the absolute poverty line has an income elasticity of 0. The relative-poverty cadre argued that poverty lines ought to rise (or fall) fully with the median household income, and, therefore, the relative line has an income elasticity of 1. The choice of the measure depends on one's philosophy of poverty measurement. There is also a middle ground whereby one could "anchor" the relative poverty line in a given year and measure progress in reducing absolute poverty since that time by comparing contemporary income to price changes in that older median line, as well as measuring fully relative poverty as defined herein. The United Kingdom now follows such an approach (UK Department of Work and Pensions 2008). Using such an anchored measure, almost all rich nations made progress against poverty between 1990 and 2000, though that progress has been halted or reversed since 2002 (Smeeding 2006).

Many American academics favor the absolute approach on which the official US statistics are measured, while most Europeans believe in a fully relative approach, with the European Union (EU) formally agreeing in the mid-1990s to measure poverty and social exclusion by incomes less than 60 percent of the annual median income. Progress against poverty by such an exacting and high relative standard has been slow in Europe and elsewhere. It is interesting that, in the new world of global economic recession, we might actually find that relative poverty decreases (depending on how the median household fares), while absolute poverty increases in 2008 and 2009 (due to falling real incomes across the entire distribution).

UPDATING THE US POVERTY MEASURE

Efforts to revise the US absolute poverty measure require resolving many thorny issues, as seen in Johnson (2009). In employing different measures of poverty, European and developing nations have addressed many of the same issues and their experience can enrich our own thinking. In Europe as well as the developing world, the income elasticity of the poverty line, while not 1, is clearly not 0 either. Indeed, a paper by Ravallion and Chen (2009) compares the "official" national poverty lines in 116 countries (700 observations) with real incomes over the period from 1981 to 2006. They find that their data are consistent with an income elasticity of the poverty line of about 0.65, not far from the classic US estimate of 0.75 (Fisher 1996; Kilpatrick 1973). The US poverty line was fully half of median income in 1963, but had fallen to 27 percent of the median by 2006 (Blank 2008; Smeeding 2006). An acceptable middle ground outcome for the United States, and possibly for Europe as well, might be to have a poverty line that is higher than the current absolute poverty line developed in the 1960s and which also rises in real terms over time in response to increases in the general standard of living and the rising cost of a basket of goods and services—as recommended by the report of the National Academy of Sciences (Citro and Michael 1995). Although the poverty line would increase from the current line, the change would not be directly tied to income changes, but rather to a basket of goods and services deemed necessary for a minimally adequate living standard. In any case, the poverty standard would rise with real incomes (Johnson 2009). How great the resulting elasticity might be is hotly debated in American policy circles. But it is clear that the elasticity is indeed above 0. Not only should the poverty measure rise with national income, but also the new market basket ought to reflect the costs of going to work and other necessities, as proposed by both the National Academy of Sciences (Citro and Michael 1995) and Blank and Greenberg (2008).

Poverty measures require two components: a measure of economic need, as discussed previously, and a comparable measure of resources (like income) to meet those needs. The resource measure also was the subject of much comment at the conference. The resource measure employed by the rest of the rich world is annual disposable household income, which subtracts direct taxes and adds in the cash value of refundable tax credits (like the Earned Income Tax Credit, EITC), near-cash benefits like Supplementary Nutritional Assistance Program (historically known as the Food Stamp Program), and housing allowances. These are the income definition guidelines for inequality and poverty measurement set by almost all major statistical offices in the Canberra Report (Canberra Group 2001) and now used by the OECD and by the EU. Additional comments on this revised poverty measure can be found in Johnson (2009), but a change in the US income or resource definition to something like this definition is also clearly called for.

If we are to chart progress in fighting poverty, including the effects of recent changes in the safety net, the poverty line measure and the income measure used to evaluate antipoverty effects need to be changed. Indeed, the recent US federal stimulus package that was enacted as part of the American Recovery and Reinvestment Act contains about $175 billion in direct aid to individuals, including $20 billion in additional Supplementary Nutritional Assistance Program funding, $40 billion for expanded unemployment insurance benefits, and $70 billion in refundable tax credits, including the EITC. Only the expanded unemployment benefits would be counted as fighting poverty by the official US statistics. The rest are outside the bounds of the current poverty measure. In my own state of Wisconsin, the combined effects of the new EITC, the state EITC, and the refundable tax credits now exceed $8,000 at the maximum for a family with two children and earnings of $15,000 (Riemer 2009). This represents a very large impact for a policy explicitly designed and targeted to enhance incomes and remove families with children from poverty, and yet we do not count it using the current poverty measure.

MEASUREMENT AND CONCEPTUAL ISSUES

Förster and Mira d'Ercole (2012, Chapter 2), Tóth and Medgyesi (2009), Maquet and Stanton (2012, Chapter 3), and Ravallion and Chen (2009) presented papers at the conference that covered the span of nations from the rich OECD to the entire EU-27 to 119 less-rich countries. As far as I know, such a common discussion based on various sets of harmonized data could not be done and was not done before this historic session. Thirty years ago, the evidence base for cross-national analyses of poverty and inequality was empty. In the mid-1980s the Luxembourg Income Study (LIS) became available and now offers over 40 nations' cross-sectional income and asset data in rich countries, as well as in Latin America and Asia. These efforts were closely followed by the creation of comparative Cross-National "Equivalent" panel income data files for up to 5 countries in the early 1990s, and then followed in 1994 by the EU's first cross-national coordinated panel income survey, the European Community Household Panel, for 12 nations. The European Community Household Panel was superseded more recently by the 2005 EU Statistics on Income and Living Conditions (SILC) for 27 EU nations plus a few additional neighboring countries. The EU-SILC has become the EU reference source for income, poverty, and social exclusion, though it is unavailable for direct analysis by non-EU-sponsored researchers at this time. The main contribution of the EU-SILC was to provide data on the 12 newest EU member states (as well as the older 15) in comparable terms. Further transparency in its measures (sampling, response rates, imputation procedures) and its open use by those outside the EU would further add to the growing armada of income and well-being data available to researchers worldwide. At the heart of a large part of the monetary comparisons of well-being is the development of more complete and accurate indices for purchasing power parity that can be used to measure "real incomes" across increasingly diverse nations. For more on the perils of using purchasing power parities with microdata, see Bradbury and Jäntti (2001).

In the mid-1990s, the OECD began work on secondary analyses of national data sets using the 2001 Canberra Report as a guide. This work culminated in the 2008 report *Growing Unequal,* which is already in its third printing. At the same time that the OECD and LIS were proceeding, the World Bank was compiling secondary data sets on inequality for a large range of nations, though not without some critique (Atkinson and Brandolini 2001). This work and related efforts at the World Bank produced the "PovcalNet" meso-data set, which has been widely used by the bank for analyses of poverty in the developing world. Soon the new Luxembourg Middle-Income Countries Study project will fill in and add context by uniting the richest 30-plus nations already in LIS with the next 20 to 25 richest "middle-income" countries, including Brazil, China, India, many "Asian tiger" countries, and South Africa.

The four papers mentioned above each argue for the importance of developing indicators that are responsive to policy changes. It is clear that in societies with as wide a disparity in real income measures as the new EU has—with the median in the richest countries six times that of the poorest, according to Tóth and Medgyesi (2009)—that measures in addition to income alone are needed to chart progress against poverty and deprivation. Indeed, Maquet and Stanton (2012, Chapter 3) show a completely inverse relationship between the relative poverty line (60 percent of median income in each nation) and material deprivation as measured by the EU index. Hence, rich countries with greater inequality and larger spreads between the median and the 60 percent poverty line were high-poverty but low-material deprivation nations; and the poorer countries had in general more compressed distributions and, therefore, lower relative poverty, but higher material deprivation.

The notion of what constitutes material deprivation or social exclusion is also debated (see also Gilbert 2009). Issues related to need versus choice are at the heart of the debate. Whereas everyone agrees that not having enough money to pay the mortgage or rent, buy food, or pay for heating are good measures of deprivation, some other measures are more open to debate. The *Breadline Britain* survey and report (Gordon and Pantazis 1997) makes a very nice distinction between those who "don't want" something and those who "can't afford" it, versus those that just "don't have" it. The "can't afford" notion is clearly preferable for deprivation measurement and for social exclusion.

However, choice will always remain at the heart of the differences. For example, Americans work more hours per year than workers in any rich country, with the major difference being weeks worked per year (Alesina, Glaser, and Sacerdote 2005). Most Europeans enjoy a minimum of four weeks a year in paid vacation and count anyone without a minimum amount of paid vacation as socially excluded. It is doubtful that an American measure of exclusion would include such an element. Similarly, before the current housing slump, Americans were spending an increasingly larger fraction of their incomes on housing than they had in past decades. To some, this is a matter of need. Indeed, the British tradition until recently was to measure poverty "after housing costs." From this perspective, there is a limit on how much one can spend on housing, and, therefore, those above the limit are somehow materially deprived. But as Blank (2004) argues, most Americans are now living in larger and better quality houses with more features than ever before. In the American case, high housing outlays are, for the most part, a choice (though not always a good one, as we have recently seen), not a sign of deprivation. In the end, I would agree with Brian Nolan and Chris Whelan (2010) that both income poverty *and* material deprivation provide useful insights on the human condition. But I would also take care about how we measure deprivation.

NEW MEASURES OF WELL-BEING

In rich nations, poverty is not measured by consumption for several reasons. First and foremost is the difficulty in measuring consumption over an appropriate period. Second, most consumption data is collected for the purpose of providing weights for measuring the consumer price index, not for measuring consumption per se. Moreover, consumption or expenditure surveys have small samples—7,000 in the US Consumer Expenditure Survey (CEX) in recent years—and many nations only do them periodically, such as every five years. Finally, whereas income data is also secondarily (and for the most part poorly) collected along with consumption data in most nations' CEX files, there has been little or no attempt to make a household balance sheet with allocations of income to consumption or changes in debts or assets. In the United States, the last CEX to do so was conducted in 1960 to 1961.

In the European Community, consumption was briefly considered for poverty measurement (Hagenaars, De Vos, and Zaidi, 1995), but then quickly abandoned due to survey size, periodicity, and difficulty of harmonization across the EU-12 at that time. Instead, the EU began the European Community Household Panel and used income from that survey for their first official low income or poverty measures, now followed by the SILC, as previously mentioned. The United Kingdom's *Family Expenditure Survey* was used to measure income poverty and expenditures, but not expenditure poverty, for several decades. It was replaced in the 1990s by the *New Income Survey* in order to improve income measurement. This survey is the basis for the official UK poverty estimates. Consumption-based poverty measurement is not widely practiced in any rich nation. However, in the poorest nations, most analysts prefer to measure consumption instead of income.

In middle- and low-income countries, therefore, the case is very different, yet still problematic. Peter Lanjouw (2012, Chapter 13) argues that in a developing or middle-income country like Brazil, consumption is a better measure of well-being than income, though he admits that consumption is difficult to measure. Most middle- and lower-income countries collect both consumption (and expenditure) data and income data, along with remittances (private transfers) and public direct taxes and transfers. These countries also collect a great deal of information about production for own consumption or barter, especially in rural areas.

If we stick to the Haig-Simons income definition (consumption plus [or minus] change in net worth equals income), then capacity to consume and consumption are likely not that different when it comes to measurement practice. The new Luxembourg Middle-Income Country Study is facing the trade-offs between income and consumption measures head on. Income is preferred in cities and places where wages and salaries are most prevalent and where cash and near-cash social insurance benefits and income transfers are beginning to be provided. But in rural areas, where "self-employment" (production for own consumption) is the largest source of income, consumption may be a preferable measure of well-being.

The spread between income and consumption in rural versus urban areas is very high in nations like Brazil, China, and India. Therefore, measuring poverty by comparing consumption or income with one "national" poverty line may produce very disparate results, mainly reflecting the wide differences in living standards in rural versus urban places. In such situations, one might also use regional or local area poverty lines and incomes to more accurately measure poverty and deprivation (see Gao et al. 2008).

Assets, debts, financial stress, imputed rent (IR) on owner-occupied homes, and imputed capital income (CI) are much more likely to become a part of rich nations' measures of well-being and poverty than are comparable consumption data. Indeed, the Canberra Report (Canberra Group 2001, 62–69) template, which currently guides income distribution statistics in many nations, has called for the addition of IR and CI, including capital gains or losses, as well as better income measures for middle-income countries and inclusion of in-kind income. The Canberra Report focused mainly on income measurement and did not cover the use of wealth or asset data separately from the flows that come from these stocks. In the future, we ought to consider such approaches.

Using German data, Frick and Grabka's conference paper (2012, Chapter 6) finds that CI and IR have become increasingly important sources of economic inequality over the last two decades. Net IR (including adjustments for the cost of owning) tends to exert a dampening effect on inequality and relative poverty, very much driven by the increasing share of outright ownership among the middle class and especially among the elderly. In Germany, they find a much stronger role of imputed CI in increasing overall inequality as CI flows occur mainly to the income rich, especially among the nonelderly. The items in their measure of CI are limited, and the imputation procedure is less well-developed than is the IR estimate. In fact, due to a recent project of the EU, in which conference authors were participants, we have good and comparable measures of IR for at least five major OECD nations (Frick and Grabka 2003), and we also have less well-developed measures for additional OECD nations (Marin and Zaidi 2007). But until additional measures of CI flows are available for a number of countries, one must think hard about how to include a better measure of capital income in our poverty and income distribution data.

Brandolini, Magri, and Smeeding (2010) take a different tack and instead of only turning wealth stocks into CI flows, they consider the role of stocks of wealth alone. They compute measures of income net worth (by which wealth stocks are turned into flows for a number of countries), but they also introduce a relatively new concept of wealth poverty. They also tell us how assets and debts might improve or complement income-based measures of disadvantage. Poverty is generally defined as income (or sometimes expenditure) insufficiency, but the economic condition of a household also depends on its real and financial asset holdings, as well as on the possibility to access the credit market and forestall unexpected debts they might face. Using various indicators of household net worth, they explore asset poverty and compare its intersection with income poverty. They develop new measures of financial stress and vulnerability (inability to pay rent, loans, credit card debts, mortgages) that complement the material deprivation measures presented by others. These measures are based on the new 10-nation cross-national asset data from the Luxembourg Wealth Study and on SILC. In the end, Brandolini and colleagues present a convincing case on how access to credit, debt, and net worth might complement existing measures of income poverty, especially among the elderly, homeowners, and debtors. The United States ought to make better use of such data in its deprivation and well-being measures.

In 2001, the Canberra Report set the stage for greater comparability among income distribution and poverty statistics for rich nations. As Förster and Mira d'Ercole (2012, Chapter 2) attest, almost all OECD nations use the definition of disposable income after tax and benefits (including near-cash transfers). More controversial are attempts to measure well-being using health and education subsidies as income measures (Garfinkel, Rainwater, and Smeeding 2006). Now eight years later, we are moving beyond this definition, into the areas where the Canberra Report mentions future development, while also utilizing new data on asset position and financial stress. These are great beginnings, and even though all need additional study and estimation, the field of economic and social well-being measurement is moving forward at a rapid clip.

CROSS-NATIONAL LEARNING IN POLICY AS WELL AS MEASUREMENT

One of the great advantages of cross-national analyses of social policy, such as those underway with the Association for Public Policy and Management and coordinated by Doug Besharov, is the fact that many major social policy, redistribution, and poverty issues are almost universal. Many papers at the conference discussed the anti-poverty effectiveness of policy, but few connected the dots across the nations. Income support in old age, avoiding child poverty, the tax transfer treatment of lone parents, subsidizing education, and the employability of young males and older manual workers with poor job skills are important policy issues in all rich nations. Indeed, different countries' approaches to these problems offer natural experiments in which one can compare the effectiveness, costs, and equity of different policy responses. But one also finds that there are no "magic bullets" that solve any one of these problems to everyone's satisfaction. Every country needs to find its own set of programs and policies that fit its institutions, history, culture, and values.

However, many solutions appeal to a broad range of nations and the potential for cross-national learning about effective antipoverty programs is vast—and the learning goes both ways. For example, an American contribution is the EITC, a program that encourages market work and makes work pay more than the prevailing wage for low earners. Various versions of the EITC are copied in many rich nations at present. Child allowances and refundable tax credits are now being adopted more readily by Americans, whereas they have been part and parcel of rich OECD nations' income packages for decades. And various experiments with need-based aid to mostly lone parents, using carrots—like the EITC and child care subsidies—and sticks—like work requirements in Temporary Assistance for Needy Families —are now a large part of the comparative landscape. Americans in turn are learning from the developing world about conditional cash transfers like *Oportunidades* in Mexico and *Bolsa Familia* in Brazil, whereby support is given in return for behaviors related to work effort and parenting (maintaining child health and keeping children in school). The programs clearly reduce poverty and also increase access to health care and education. Indeed, the mayor of New York City has embarked on just such a policy experiment, which is now being evaluated by MDRC. Support in old age via a minimum social retirement benefit and the use of "active labor market policies" for reskilling the structurally unemployed are also being compared across nations. It appears that both the measurement of and solutions to the poverty problem are progressing in large part as a result of cross-national policy exchanges as well as by developing comparable cross-national measures of well-being.

CONCLUSION

More than most, I have been part of these issues since we began the LIS in 1983. The LIS represents a major step forward in the cross-national dialogue about measuring income, poverty, and well-being—a dialogue that was not even a glimmer in my eye 28 years ago. As the Joint OECD/University of Maryland conference demonstrated, there is now a strong groundwork for cross-national comparisons, including learning about measuring well-being and its distribution, about comparable poverty measurement, about poverty outcomes, and about the effectiveness of efforts designed to reduce poverty. This is a solid achievement and a credit to Association for Public Policy and Management's leadership in comparative cross-national social policy research.

Note

1. The Gini coefficient is the most popular single parameter measure of the inequality in a country's income distribution.

References

Alesina, Alberto, Edward Glaeser, and Bruce Sacerdote. 2005. "Why Do Americans Work So Hard?" *Public Policy Research* 12: 148–157.

Atkinson, Anthony B., and Andrea Brandolini. 2001. "Promises and Pitfalls in the Use of Secondary Data-Sets: Income Inequality in OECD Countries as a Case Study." *Journal of Economic Literature* 39: 771–800.

Blank, Rebecca M. 2004. "Comments for Seminar on Revisiting the U.S. Poverty Rate." Paper presented to the American Enterprise Institute, Washington, DC, September 1, 2004.

———. 2008. "How to Improve Poverty Measurement in the United States." *Journal of Policy Analysis and Management* 27 (2): 233–254.

Blank, Rebecca M., and Mark H. Greenberg. 2008. *Improving the Measurement of Poverty*. Hamilton Project Discussion Paper 2008–17. Washington, DC: Brookings Institution. http://www.brookings.edu/~/media/Files/rc/papers/2008/12_poverty_measurement_blank/12_poverty_measurement_blank.pdf.

Bradbury, Bruce, and Markus Jäntti. 2001. "Child Poverty across the Industrialized World: Evidence from the Luxembourg Income Study." In *Child Wellbeing, Child Poverty, and Child Policy in Modern Nations*. Edited by Koen Vleminckx and Timothy Smeeding, 11–32. Bristol, UK: Policy Press.

Brandolini, Andrea, Silvia Magri, and Timothy Smeeding. 2010. "Asset-Based Measurement of Poverty." *Journal of Policy Analysis and Management* 29: 267–284.

Canberra Group. 2001. *Expert Group on Household Income Statistics: Final Report and Recommendations*. Ottawa: Statistics Canada.

Citro, Constance F., and Robert T. Michael. 1995. *Measuring Poverty: A New Approach*. Washington, DC: National Academy Press.

Fisher, Gordon M. 1996. "Some Popular Beliefs about the U.S. Poverty Line as Reflected in Inquiries from the Public." *Sociologist (Newsletter of the District of Columbia Sociological Society)* 30 (2): 6.

Förster, Michael F., and Marco Mira d'Ercole. 2012. "The OECD Approach to Measuring Income Distribution and Poverty." In *Counting the Poor: New Thinking about European Poverty Measures and Lessons for the United States*. Edited by Douglas J. Besharov and Kenneth A. Couch, 25–58. New York: Oxford University Press.

Frick, Joachim R., and Markus M. Grabka. 2003. "Imputed Rent and Income Inequality: A Decomposition Analysis for the U.K., West Germany, and the USA." *Review of Income and Wealth* 49 (4): 513–537.

———. 2012. "Accounting for Imputed and Capital Income Flows." In *Counting the Poor: New Thinking about European Poverty Measures and Lessons for the United States*. Edited by Douglas J. Besharov and Kenneth A. Couch, 117–142. New York: Oxford University Press.

Gao, Qin, P. Saunders, Timothy Smeeding, and Coady Wing. 2008. "Elder Poverty in an Ageing World: Conditions of Social Vulnerability and Low Income for Women in Rich and Middle-Income Nations." Luxembourg Income Study Working Paper Series 497, Luxembourg. http://www.lisproject.org/publications/liswps/497.pdf.

Garfinkel, Irwin, Lee Rainwater, and Timothy M. Smeeding. 2006. "A Reexamination of Welfare State and Inequality in Rich Nations: How In-Kind Transfers and Indirect Taxes Change the Story." *Journal of Policy Analysis and Management* 25 (4): 855–919.

Gilbert, Neil 2009. "European Measures of Poverty and 'Social Exclusion': Material Deprivation, Consumption, and Life Satisfaction." *Journal of Policy Analysis and Management* 28: 738–744.

Gordon, David , and Christina Pantazis. 1997. *Breadline Britain in the 1990s*. London: Ashgate.

Hagenaars, Aldi J. M., Klaas de Vos and Ashgar Zaidi. 1994. "Patterns of Poverty in Europe." *Focus* 17 (2). Institute for Research on Poverty, University of Wisconsin–Madison. http://www.irp.wisc.edu/publications/focus/textver/17.2.a/measuring_poverty.txt.

Johnson, David 2009. "Impressionistic Realism: The Europeans Focus the U.S. on Measurement." *Journal of Policy Analysis and Management* 28: 725–731.

Kilpatrick, Robert W. 1973. "The Income Elasticity of the Poverty Line." *Review of Economics and Statistics* 55: 327–332.

Lanjouw, Peter. 2012. "Consumption-Based Measures in Developing Nations: Lessons from Brazil." In *Counting the Poor: New Thinking about European Poverty Measures and Lessons for the United States.* Edited by Douglas J. Besharov and Kenneth A. Couch, 273–290. New York: Oxford University Press.

Maquet, Isabelle, and David Stanton. 2012. "Income Indicators for the EU's Social Inclusion Strategy." In *Counting the Poor: New Thinking about European Poverty Measures and Lessons for the United States.* Edited by Douglas J. Besharov and Kenneth A. Couch, 59–78. New York: Oxford University Press.

Marin, Bernd and Ashgar Zaidi. 2007. *Mainstreaming Ageing: Indicators to Monitor Sustainable Progress and Policies.* London: Ashgate.

Nolan, Brian and Christopher Whelan. 2010. "Using Non-Monetary Deprivation Indicators To Analyze Poverty and Social Exclusion: Lessons from Europe?" *Journal of Policy Analysis and Management* 29: 305–325.

Notten, Geranda and Christopher de Neubourg 2007. *Relative or Absolute Poverty in the US and EU? The Battle of the Rates.* MPRA Paper 5313. Munich: University Library of Munich.

OECD. 2008. *Growing Unequal? Income Distribution and Poverty in OECD Countries.* Paris: Organization for Economic Co-operation and Development

Ravallion, Martin and Shaohua Chen. 2009. "Weakly Relative Poverty." Paper presented at Measuring Poverty, Income Inequality and Social Exclusion: Lessons from Europe, Paris, March 16–17, 2009. http://umdcipe.org/conferences/oecdumd/conf_papers/index.shtml.

Reimer, David 2009. *Packaging Policies To Reduce Poverty.* Milwaukee, WI: Community Advocates Public Policy Institute.

Salverda, Wiemer, Brian Nolan, and Timothy M. Smeeding, eds. 2009. *Oxford Handbook of Economic Inequality.* Oxford: Oxford University Press.

Smeeding, Timothy M. 2006. "Poor People in Rich Nations: The United States in Comparative Perspective." *Journal of Economic Perspectives* 20 (1): 69–90.

Tóth, István, and Márton Medgyesi. 2009. "Income Distribution in New (and Old) EU Member States." Paper presented at Measuring Poverty, Income Inequality and Social Exclusion: Lessons from Europe, Paris, March 16–17, 2009. http://umdcipe.org/conferences/oecdumd/conf_papers/Papers/oecd_toth_medgyesi_v090507.pdf.

UK Department of Work and Pensions. 2008. *Households below Average Income, Annual Report 2008.* London: UK Department of Work and Pensions.